MW00824859

The Cycle of Excellence

The Cycle of Excellence

Using Deliberate Practice to Improve Supervision and Training

Edited By
Tony Rousmaniere
Rodney K. Goodyear
Scott D. Miller
Bruce E. Wampold

This edition first published copyright 2017
© 2017 John Wiley & Sons, Ltd.

All rights reserved. No part of this publication may be reproduced, stored in a retrieval system, or transmitted, in any form or by any means, electronic, mechanical, photocopying, recording or otherwise, except as permitted by law. Advice on how to obtain permission to reuse material from this title is available at http://www.wiley.com/go/permissions.

The right of Tony Rousmaniere, Rodney K. Goodyear, Scott D. Miller, and Bruce E. Wampold to be identified as the authors of the editorial material in this work has been asserted in accordance with law.

Registered Offices
John Wiley & Sons, Inc., 111 River Street, Hoboken, NJ 07030, USA
John Wiley & Sons Ltd, The Atrium, Southern Gate, Chichester, West Sussex, PO19 8SQ, UK

Editorial Office
The Atrium, Southern Gate, Chichester, West Sussex, PO19 8SQ, UK

For details of our global editorial offices, customer services, and more information about Wiley products visit us at www .wiley.com.

Wiley also publishes its books in a variety of electronic formats and by print-on-demand. Some content that appears in standard print versions of this book may not be available in other formats.

Limit of Liability/Disclaimer of Warranty

While the publisher and author have used their best efforts in preparing this book, they make no representations or warranties with respect to the accuracy or completeness of the contents of this book and specifically disclaim any implied warranties of merchantability or fitness for a particular purpose. It is sold on the understanding that the publisher is not engaged in rendering professional services and neither the publisher nor the authors shall be liable for damages arising herefrom. If professional advice or other expert assistance is required, the services of a competent professional should be sought.

Library of Congress Cataloging-in-Publication Data

Names: Rousmaniere, Tony, editor. | Goodyear, Rodney K., editor. | Miller,
    Scott D., editor. | Wampold, Bruce E., 1948- editor.
Title: The Cycle of Excellence : Using Deliberate Practice to Improve
    Supervision and Training / [edited by] Tony Rousmaniere, Rodney K.
    Goodyear, Scott D. Miller, Bruce E. Wampold.
Description: Chichester, UK ; Hoboken, NJ : John Wiley & Sons, 2017. |
    Includes index.
Identifiers: LCCN 2017015214 (print) | LCCN 2016055347 (ebook) | ISBN
    9781119165569 (Paperback) | ISBN 9781119165583 (Adobe PDF) | ISBN 9781119165576 (ePub)
Subjects: LCSH: Career development. | Supervision of employees.
Classification: LCC HF5549.5.C35 S86 2017 (ebook) | LCC HF5549.5.C35 (print)
    | DDC 616.89/14023—dc23
LC record available at https://lccn.loc.gov/2017015214

Cover Design: Wiley
Cover Image: © eugenesergeev/Gettyimages

Set in 11/13 WarnockPro by SPi Global, Chennai, India

10 9 8 7 6 5 4 3 2 1

Dedicated to therapists who strive to improve their results

Contents

About the Editors

Tony Rousmaniere, PsyD, is a psychologist in private practice in Seattle and a member of the clinical faculty at the University of Washington in Seattle, where he also maintains a private practice. He is the author of *Deliberate Practice for Psychotherapists: A Guide to Improving Clinical Effectiveness* and coeditor of *Using Technology for Clinical Supervision: A Practical Handbook* (American Counseling Association Press, 2015). Dr. Rousmaniere provides clinical training and supervision to therapists around the world, with an emphasis on using deliberate practice to improve the effectiveness of clinical skill development.

Rodney K. Goodyear, PhD, received his doctorate at the University of Illinois at Urbana-Champaign. He is a professor at the University of Redlands in Redlands, California as well as emeritus professor of counseling psychology at the University of Southern California, and was the 2015 president of the Society for the Advancement of Psychotherapy. A major theme of his scholarship has been supervision and training of counselors and psychologists. Dr. Goodyear's book with Janine Bernard—*Fundamentals of Clinical Supervision* (Pearson, 2014)—is in its fifth edition and is arguably the most-used supervision book in the world; he was a member of the American Psychological Association's task group that developed the APA's supervision guidelines; and he received the APA's 2015 award for Distinguished Lifetime Contributions to Education and Training.

Scott D. Miller, PhD, is the founder of the International Center for Clinical Excellence, an international consortium of clinicians, researchers, and educators dedicated to promoting excellence in behavioral health services. Dr. Miller conducts workshops and training in the United States and elsewhere, helping hundreds of agencies and organizations, both public and private, to achieve superior results. He also is one of a handful of invited faculty whose work, thinking, and research are featured at the prestigious Evolution of Psychotherapy Conference. His humorous and engaging presentation style and command of the research literature consistently inspire practitioners, administrators, and policy makers to make effective changes in service delivery.

Bruce E. Wampold, PhD, is professor emeritus of counseling psychology at the University of Wisconsin–Madison, director of the Research Institute at Modum Bad Psychiatric Center in Vikersund, Norway, and chief scientist of Theravue, an electronic platform for therapist consultation and improvement. He is a fellow of the American Psychological Association (Divisions 12, 17, 29, 45) and is board certified in counseling psychology by the American Board of Professional Psychology. He is the author of over 200 books, chapters, and articles related to counseling, psychotherapy, statistics, and research methods and is the recipient of the 2007 Distinguished Professional Contributions to Applied Research Award from the American Psychological Association and the Distinguished Research Career Award from the Society for Psychotherapy Research.

Currently Dr. Wampold's work involves understanding counseling and psychotherapy from empirical, historical, and anthropological perspectives. His pursuit of evidence on psychotherapy has led to the application and development of sophisticated statistical methods to understand the complexities of the field. He has contributed to various areas related to psychotherapy, including the relative efficacy of various approaches, therapist effects, the therapeutic alliance, placebo effects in medicine and in psychotherapy, trajectories of change, multicultural competence, and expertise in psychotherapy. His analysis of empirical evidence, which led to the development of a contextual model from which to understand the benefits of counseling and psychotherapy, is found in *The Great Psychotherapy Debate: The Evidence for How Psychotherapy Works* (with Z. Imel, Routledge, 2015).

List of Contributors

Robbie Babins-Wagner, PhD, RSW, is the chief executive officer of Calgary Counselling Centre and an adjunct professor and sessional instructor with the Faculty of Social Work, University of Calgary, Calgary, Alberta, Canada. Her research interests focus on domestic abuse and psychotherapy outcomes in community-based, nonprofit mental health services. Robbie is a sought-after conference presenter, locally, provincially, nationally, and internationally.

Nicholas Bach, MA, is a clinical psychology student at Spalding University in Louisville, Kentucky. He has worked clinically in a private practice, public schools, a residential treatment facility, and a college counseling center. His research focuses on psychotherapy outcome, romantic relationships, religion and spirituality, and military active-duty personnel and veterans.

Matt Barnard, MA Cantab, is the head of the Child Outcomes Research Consortium (CORC). Before joining CORC, Matt was head of evaluation at the NSPCC, where he led one of the largest-ever programs of evaluation and learning in the children's sector.

Stephanie Winkeljohn Black, PhD, is an assistant professor of psychology in the Department of Psychology and Social Sciences at Penn State Harrisburg, Pennsylvania. Her area of research focuses on religious and spiritual behaviors and mental health across diverse groups and on trainees' cultural competency as it relates to religious and spiritual identities.

Jenny Bloxham, MA, is the communications and influencing manager at the Child Outcomes Research Consortium in London. She has a wealth of experience working for children's education and health charities in both the United Kingdom and elsewhere, including Save the Children, the International Catholic Migration Commission, and the UN Refugee Agency. Jenny holds an undergraduate degree in modern European studies and a master's in communications, new media, governance, and democracy.

Norah A. Chapman, PhD, is an assistant professor at Spading University in Louisville, Kentucky. Her primary research interests are in evaluating components of psychotherapy process and outcome, both in person and via telepsychology, to develop evidence-based practices that increase access to and the quality of mental health care among underserved populations.

Daryl Chow, PhD, is a senior associate and certified trainer with the International Center for Clinical Excellence, where he conducts research on deliberate practice and professional development for psychotherapists. He is currently based in Western Australia, working with a group of vibrant private practitioners (Specialist Psychological Outreach Team [SPOT]) located in Fremantle, WA. He is a coeditor of and contributing author to the book *The Write to Recovery: Personal Stories & Lessons About Recovery from Mental Health Concerns* and is coauthor of *Reach: Pushing Your Clinical Performance to the Next Level* with Scott Miller, PhD (forthcoming).

Kate Dalzell, MA, is practice lead at the Child Outcomes Research Consortium (CORC) and head of innovation and dissemination at the Anna Freud National Centre for Children and Families, both located in London. Kate has worked in service development in local authority and health contexts for over 10 years, in particular in applying data-driven approaches to embed a focus on outcomes and in supporting cross-sector collaboration to address local needs.

Marc J. Diener, PhD, is an associate professor in the clinical psychology doctoral program at Long Island University Post, and he maintains a part-time independent practice. His program of research examines personality assessment as well as psychotherapy process and outcome. His publications have focused on attachment, psychotherapy technique, psychotherapy outcome, supervision, application of meta-analytic methodology, and self-report and performance-based measures of personality.

Joanna M. Drinane, MEd, is a doctoral candidate in counseling psychology at the University of Denver, Colorado. Her areas of interest include psychotherapy process and outcome research. More specifically, she studies therapist effects, multicultural orientation, mental health disparities, and the ways in which culture influences the therapeutic relationship.

Simon B. Goldberg, BA, is a doctoral candidate in counseling psychology at the University of Wisconsin–Madison and a psychology intern at the Veterans Affairs Puget Sound, Seattle Division. His research program is focused on common and specific factors at play in psychological interventions. He has a particular emphasis on mindfulness-based interventions and quantitative research methods.

Mark J. Hilsenroth, PhD, is a professor of psychology at the Derner Institute of Advanced Psychological Studies at Adelphi University in Garden City, New York, and the primary investigator of the Adelphi University Psychotherapy Project. His areas of professional interest include personality assessment, training/supervision, psychotherapy process and treatment outcomes. In addition, he is currently editor of the American Psychological Association Division 29 journal *Psychotherapy,* and he maintains a part-time clinical practice.

Mark A. Hubble, PhD, grew up near Baltimore, Maryland, bodysurfing the cold waters of the Atlantic. Currently he works as a psychologist and national consultant. An accomplished writer and editor, Mark has published numerous articles and is coauthor of *The Heart and Soul of Change, Escape from Babel, Psychotherapy with "Impossible" Cases,* and *The Handbook of Solution-Focused Brief Therapy.*

Jenna Jacob, MSc, is the research lead for the Child Outcomes Research Consortium (CORC). Her particular research interests are in personalized care and outcomes for children and families, which includes goal setting and tracking as part of shared decision making.

Emma Karwatzki, D.Clin.Psy., is a clinical psychologist working in Hertfordshire, UK. She has worked as a clinician and supervisor in child mental health services for over 10 years and trains clinical psychologists.

Duncan Law, D.Clin.Psy., is a consultant clinical psychologist at the Anna Freud National Centre for Children and Families in London and director of MindMonkey Associates (www.mindmonkeyassociates.com). In addition, he is an honorary senior lecturer at University College London and a founder member of the Child Outcomes Research Consortium (CORC) in London.

Kate Martin, MA, is founder and director of Common Room Consulting Ltd, a consultancy led by lived experience, which connects the views and expertise of children, young people, researchers, and practitioners to promote collaborative practice across disability, health, and mental health.

William C. McGaghie, PhD, is professor of medical education and professor of preventive medicine at the Northwestern University Feinberg School of Medicine in Chicago. His area of research interest focuses on the use of medical simulation coupled with deliberate practice and mastery learning to produce translational medical education outcomes.

John McLeod, PhD, holds positions at the University of Oslo, Norway, and the Institute for Integrative Counselling and Psychotherapy, Dublin. He has extensive experience as a counselor, supervisor, trainer, and researcher. His many publications include these books: *Personal and Professional Development for Counsellors, Psychotherapists and Mental Health Practitioners,* published by Open University Press, and *Using Research in Counselling and Psychotherapy,* published by Sage.

Donald Meichenbaum, PhD, is distinguished professor emeritus, University of Waterloo, Ontario, Canada, and is currently research director of the Melissa Institute for Violence Prevention in Miami, FL (www.melissainstitute.com). He is one of the founders of cognitive behavioral therapy, and he specializes in trauma and resilience. (Please see www.roadmap-toresilience.org.)

Greg J. Neimeyer, PhD, is professor emeritus at the University of Florida, Gainesville, where he has served as a faculty member, director of training, and graduate coordinator. With over 200 publications in the areas of counseling and professional development, he has been recognized by the American Psychological Association with its Award for Outstanding Research in Career and Personality Psychology.

Jesse J. Owen, PhD, is an associate professor and chair of the Counseling Psychology Department at the University of Denver in Colorado. He is also a licensed psychologist and has a private practice in Denver. His research and practice interest includes psychotherapy process and outcome with a specific emphasis on multicultural processes and therapist expertise.

Benjamin Ritchie, MSc, is the lead of Child Outcomes Research Consortium (CORC) Informatics, which supports CORC's member services and central team in processing and managing large data sets. He has particular experience in the fields of data handling and information governance. His current work with partnerships of organizations in the health, education, and social care sectors aims to link data sources in order to allow service-user outcomes to be considered from different perspectives.

Jennifer M. Taylor, PhD, is an assistant professor of counseling psychology and counseling at the University of Utah in Salt Lake City. Her research interests include professional competence, continuing education, lifelong learning, continuing professional development, and mentoring. She serves as the chair of the Continuing Education Committee for the American Psychological Association and is the coeditor of *Continuing Professional Development and Lifelong Learning: Issues, Impacts, and Outcomes* (Nova Science, 2012).

Isabelle Whelan, MA, is a research editor with 10 years' experience working in research communication and international development.

Miranda Wolpert, D.Clin.Psy., is founder and director of the Child Outcomes Research Consortium (CORC), the UK's leading membership organization that collects and uses evidence to improve the mental health and well-being of children and young people, and professor of evidence-based practice and research at University College London. She is committed to understanding how best to support and evaluate effective service delivery to promote resilience and meet children's and young people's mental health needs.

Part I

The Cycle of Excellence

1

Introduction

Tony Rousmaniere, Rodney K. Goodyear, Scott D. Miller, and Bruce E. Wampold

> *An ounce of practice is worth more than tons of preaching.*
>
> —Mahatma Gandhi

Over the past century, dramatic improvements in performance have been experienced in sports, medicine, science, and the arts. This is true, for example, in every Olympic sport (e.g., Lippi, Banfi, Favaloro, Rittweger, & Maffulli, 2008). College athletes in running, swimming, and diving perform better than gold medal winners from the early Olympic Games (Ericsson, 2006). In medicine, the number of diseases that can be treated effectively has steadily increased, while mortality from medical complications has decreased (Centers for Disease Control, 2012; Friedman & Forst, 2007). In mathematics, calculus that previously required decades to learn is now taught in a year of high school (Ericsson, 2006). In the arts, modern professional musicians routinely achieve or exceed technical skill that previously was attainable only by unique masters like Mozart (Lehmann & Ericsson, 1998).

Unfortunately, the same cannot be said of mental health treatment. Although the number and variety of psychotherapy models have grown rapidly, the actual effectiveness of psychotherapy has not experienced the dramatic improvements seen in the fields described (Miller, Hubble, Chow, & Seidel, 2013). For example, in modern clinical trials, cognitive behavioral therapy appears to be less effective than was demonstrated in the original trials from the 1970s (Johnsen & Friborg, 2015). That we have remained on this performance plateau is clearly not due to a lack of desire for improvement—virtually all mental health clinicians want to be more effective. So what have we been missing? How can we get better at helping our clients? In this book, we outline procedures that lead to increasing the effectiveness of psychotherapy.

The Cycle of Excellence: Using Deliberate Practice to Improve Supervision and Training,
First Edition. Edited by Tony Rousmaniere, Rodney K. Goodyear, Scott D. Miller, and Bruce E. Wampold.
© 2017 John Wiley & Sons, Ltd. Published 2017 by John Wiley & Sons, Ltd.

The Overall Effectiveness of Psychotherapy

First, let's step back to examine the big picture concerning the effectiveness of psychotherapists. Good news: The consistent finding across decades of research is that, as a field, we successfully help our clients. Studies examining the effectiveness of clinicians working across the field, from community mental health centers, to university counseling centers, to independent practice, show that, on average, mental health clinicians produce significant positive change for their clients (Lambert, 2013; Wampold & Imel, 2015). The average psychologically distressed person who receives psychotherapy will be better off than 80% of the distressed people who do not (Hubble, Duncan, & Miller, 1999; Wampold & Imel, 2015). Dozens of studies show that the effects of psychotherapy and counseling are at least as large as the effects of psychotropic medications and that psychotherapy and counseling are less expensive, have fewer troubling side effects, and last longer (Forand, DeRubeis, & Amsterdam, 2013; Gotzsche, Young, & Crace, 2015).

Opportunity for Improvement

Although the big picture is positive, there is room for improvement. For example, in clinical trials, only 60% of clients achieve clinical "recovery," and between 5% and 10% actually deteriorate during treatment (Lambert, 2013). The percentage of clients who terminate care prematurely falls between 20% and 60%, depending on how "prematurely" is defined (Swift, Greenberg, Whipple, & Kominiak, 2012), and these rates have remained largely unchanged for the past five decades.

Furthermore, there is considerable between-clinician variability in effectiveness. Whereas the most effective therapists average 50% better client outcomes and 50% fewer dropouts than therapists in general (Miller et al., 2013), these "super shrinks" (Miller, Hubble, & Duncan, 2007) are counterbalanced by those therapists who produce, on average, no change or may even cause most of their clients to deteriorate (Baldwin & Imel, 2013; Kraus, Castonguay, Boswell, Nordberg, & Hayes, 2011; Wampold & Brown, 2005). So there is clear room for many therapists to demonstrably increase their effectiveness.

How, then, can clinicians become more effective? Some may assume that the best way to get better at something is simply to do it a lot. A significant body of research documents that musicians, chess players, and athletes, in the correct circumstances, improve with time and experience (at least up to the point of competency; Ericsson & Pool, 2016). However, psychotherapy is a field in which practitioners' proficiency does not automatically increase with experience (Tracey, Wampold, Goodyear, & Lichtenberg, 2015; Tracey, Wampold, Lichtenberg, & Goodyear, 2014). Two large studies have shown that "time in the saddle" itself does not automatically improve therapist effectiveness (Goldberg, Rousmaniere et al., 2016; Owen, Wampold, Rousmaniere, Kopta, & Miller, 2016). One of these studies, based on the outcomes of 173 therapists over a period of time up to 18 years, found considerable variance in the outcomes achieved by the therapists over time. Although some of the therapists were able to continually improve, client outcomes on average tended to decrease slightly as the therapists gained more experience (Goldberg, Rousmaniere et al., 2016). Another study examined the change in outcomes of 114 trainees over an average of 45 months. As in the Goldberg, Rousmaniere et al. (2016) study, in the Owen et al. (2016) study, there was considerable variance in the outcomes achieved by trainees over time. Although trainees, on average, demonstrated small-size growth in outcomes over time, this growth was moderated by client severity, and some trainees demonstrated worse outcomes over time, leading the authors to observe that "trainees appear to have various trajectories in their ability to foster positive client outcomes over time, and at times not a positive trajectory" (p. 21).

Current Strategies for Improving Effectiveness

What accounts for the failure to improve? Answering that question requires first looking at the four most widely used methods for improving therapist effectiveness: supervision, continuing education (CE), the dissemination of evidence-based treatments, and outcome feedback systems.

Supervision provides trainees with important professional preparation. For example, supervision has been shown to provide basic helping skills, improve trainees' feelings about themselves as therapists and understanding about being a therapist, and enhance trainees' ability to create and maintain stronger therapeutic alliances, the component of therapy most associated with positive outcomes (e.g., Hill et al., 2015; Hilsenroth, Kivlighan, & Slavin-Mulford, 2015; Wampold & Imel, 2015). However, evidence concerning the impact of supervision—as it has been practiced—on improving client outcomes is mixed at best (Bernard & Goodyear, 2014; Rousmaniere, Swift, Babins-Wagner, Whipple, & Berzins, 2016). Indeed, prominent supervision scholars (e.g., Beutler & Howard, 2003; Ladany, 2007) have questioned the extent to which supervision improves clinical outcomes. Summarizing the research in this area, Watkins (2011) reported, "[W]e do not seem to be any more able now, as opposed to 30 years ago, to say that supervision leads to better outcomes for clients" (p. 252).

Continuing education (CE) ("further education" in the United Kingdom) is a second method for improving, or at least maintaining, therapist effectiveness. Many jurisdictions require CE to maintain licensure, certification, or registration necessary for practice. CE is commonly delivered via a passive-learning format, such as lecture or video (perhaps with some discussion). This format may be effective at imparting knowledge about particular topics (laws, ethics, new treatments, etc.), but typically it includes little interactive practice or corrective feedback for participants and thus has questionable impact on actual skill development. Research from CE in medicine has demonstrated that passive-learning formats have "little or no beneficial effect in changing physician practice" (Bloom, 2005, p. 380). Summarizing concerns about the limits of CE, Neimeyer and Taylor (2010) reported, "A central concern follows from the field's failure to produce reliable evidence that CE translates into discernibly superior psychotherapy or outcomes, which serves as the cornerstone of the warrant underlying CE and its related commitment to the welfare of the consumer" (p. 668).

A third prominent method for improving therapist effectiveness that has gained considerable momentum over the past half century is the dissemination of evidence-based treatments (EBTs, also called empirically supported treatments or psychological treatments with research support). Using EBTs to improve the quality of mental health care is based on a two-step process: (a) clinical trials are used to determine which specific therapy models are effective for treating specific psychiatric disorders, and (b) these models are disseminated by training therapists to be competent in the EBTs. Over the years, hundreds of EBTs have been tested in clinical trials for an ever-increasing range of disorders, and the results of these trials commonly show EBTs to be more effective than no treatment. However, there is a paucity of evidence that becoming competent in EBTs improves the effectiveness of individual therapists in actual practice (Laska, Gurman, & Wampold, 2014). For example, Branson, Shafran, and Myles (2015) found no relationship between cognitive behavioral therapy competence and patient outcome. In fact, large studies frequently show that clinicians in general practice achieve the same outcomes as those deemed competent in clinical trials (Wampold & Imel, 2015). In a meta-analysis of clinical trials comparing an EBT to a treatment-as-usual condition, Wampold et al. (2011) showed that when treatment as usual involved legitimate psychotherapy, the outcomes of treatment as usual and EBT were not statistically different. Notably, clinical trials often show more variability in outcomes among clinicians than between treatments, suggesting that more attention is needed to skill acquisition by individual clinicians (based on their personal clients' outcome data) across all treatment models (Baldwin & Imel, 2013; Miller et al., 2007; Wampold & Imel, 2015). In summary, competence in evidence-based treatment models does not appear to be itself sufficient for improving the effectiveness of psychotherapy by individual clinicians in actual practice.

A fourth method for improving therapist effectiveness that has been increasingly adopted over the past two decades is feedback systems, also called practice-based evidence, in which clinicians monitor their clients' progress by examining outcome data session to session. Feedback systems have been shown to improve the quality of psychotherapy, in part by identifying and preventing failing cases (Lambert & Shimokawa, 2011). In fact, two feedback systems—the Partners for Change Outcome Management System (PCMOS, 2013) and OQ-Analyst—have such a powerful impact on client outcome that they are now considered an "evidence-based practice" by the Substance Abuse and Mental Health Services Administration. However, feedback systems have not been shown to lead to the development of clinical expertise for individual therapists (Miller et al., 2013; Tracey et al., 2014). That is, although therapists who receive feedback about particular clients can alter the treatment for those particular clients, receiving the feedback does not appear to reliably generalize to other cases or improve therapists' overall clinical skills.

Each of these methods for professional improvement has clear value. However, despite the attention that has been given to strengthening supervision and training (American Psychological Association, 2015), CE (Wise et al., 2010), the dissemination of empirically based treatments (McHugh & Barlow, 2010), and routine clinical feedback (Lambert, 2010), overall psychotherapy outcomes have not improved over the past 40 years (Miller et al., 2013). Simply put, our field has lacked a successful model for therapist skill advancement. So, we return to our question: How can clinicians become more effective? To help answer this question, let's look beyond our field and see what we can learn from others.

The Science of Expertise

During the past two decades, a growing body of research has examined the methods professionals use to attain expertise (e.g., Ericsson, 1996, 2009). The *science of expertise* has been concerned with identifying how professionals across a wide range of fields—from musicians, to chess players, to athletes, to surgeons—move from average to superior performance. The findings confirm results cited earlier regarding the development of expertise in psychotherapy: Simply accumulating work experience does not itself lead to expert performance (Ericsson, 2006). Rather, researchers have identified a universal set of processes that accounts for the development of expertise as well as a step-by-step process that can be followed to improve performance within a particular discipline (Ericsson, Charness, Feltovich, & Hoffman, 2006).

The Cycle of Excellence

Informed by findings reported by researchers (Ericsson, 1996, 2009; Ericsson, Charness, Feltovich, & Hoffman, 2006; Ericsson, Krampe, & Tesch-Romer, 1993) and writers (Colvin, 2008; Coyle, 2009; Shenk, 2010; Syed, 2010) on the subject of expertise, Miller et al. (2007) identified three components critical for superior performance. Working in tandem to create a "cycle of excellence," these components include:

1. Determining a baseline level of effectiveness, including strengths and skills that need improvement;
2. Obtaining systematic, ongoing, formal feedback; and
3. Engaging in deliberate practice. (See Figure 1.1.)

A brief description of each step follows.

In order to improve, it is essential to know how well one fares in a given practice domain, including strengths and skills that need improvement. Top performers, research shows, are constantly comparing what they do to their own "personal best," the performance of others, and existing standards or baselines (Ericsson, 2006). As reviewed, in the realm of

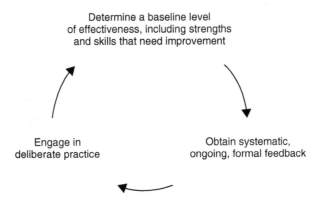

Determine a baseline level
of effectiveness, including strengths
and skills that need improvement

Engage in
deliberate practice

Obtain systematic,
ongoing, formal feedback

Figure 1.1 Cycle of Excellence.

psychotherapy, numerous well-established outcome measurement systems are available to clinicians for assessing their baseline (Miller et al., 2013). Each of these systems provides therapists with real-time comparisons of their results with national and international norms (Lambert, 2010; Miller, Duncan, Sorrell, & Brown, 2005). Specific clinical strengths and skills that need improvement can be identified by supervisors, trainers, or peers, depending on the developmental level of the therapist.

The second element in the Cycle of Excellence is obtaining formal, ongoing feedback. Feedback comes from two sources: (a) empirical outcome measures and (b) coaches and teachers—in psychotherapy, these often are referred to as supervisors—whose job it is to identify the skills that need to be developed and provide specific suggestions and training experiences specifically designed to enhance the individual's performance. High-level performers, it turns out, both seek out and have more access to such mentoring from recognized experts (Hunt, 2006). As discussed earlier, research has shown that ongoing feedback from supervisors can improve trainees' clinical skills, such as the ability to build a strong therapeutic working alliance (e.g., Hill et al., 2015; Hilsenroth, Ackerman, Clemence, Strassle, & Handler, 2015).

Although feedback is necessary for improvement, it is not itself sufficient. Creating a Cycle of Excellence requires an additional essential step: engaging in deliberate practice (Ericsson, 2006). Briefly, this type of practice is focused, systematic, and carried out over extended periods of time. Generally, it involves identifying where one's performance falls short, seeking guidance from recognized experts, setting aside time for reflecting on feedback received, and then developing, rehearsing, executing, and evaluating a plan for improvement (Ericsson, 1996, 2006; Ericsson et al., 1993). Deliberate practice involves a tight focus on repetitively practicing specific skills until they become routine. Because it requires sustained concentration and continuous corrective feedback outside the trainee's comfort zone, deliberate practice typically is not enjoyable or immediately rewarding (Coughlan, Williams, McRobert, & Ford, 2013; Ericsson & Pool, 2016). Deliberate practice intentionally causes a manageable level of strain to stimulate growth and adaptation: "[E]lite performers search continuously for optimal training activities, with the most effective duration and intensity, that will appropriately strain the targeted physiological system to induce further adaptation without causing overuse and injury" (Ericsson, 2006, p. 12). For these reasons, deliberate practice is distinctly different from the two activities most common for therapists: routine performance and passive learning, as illustrated in Table 1.1.

How Much Practice Is Enough?

Elite performers across many different domains, including professional musicians, athletes, and chess players, devote hours to deliberate practice every day, often including weekends (Ericsson, 1996, 2006; Ericsson et al., 1993). Researchers have found that achieving expert performance does not just take a few years of training but rather requires much more effort—thousands of hours of deliberate practice, often requiring 10 to 30 years of sustained effort and focus (Ericsson, 2006). Furthermore, research indicates that continued deliberate practice throughout the career span is required for maintenance of expert performance (Ericsson, 2006).

Table 1.1 Comparison of routine performance, passive learning, and deliberate practice.

Activity	Definition	Examples	Goal	Characteristics
Routine performance	Simply performing work as usual	Providing therapy	To earn an income by providing a service	Often feels enjoyable and immediately rewarding
Passive learning	Learning without a practice and feedback component	Attending lectures Reading about psychotherapy models	To build general knowledge about models, theories, and skills	May be enjoyable and feel immediately rewarding
Deliberate practice	Repetitively practicing specific skills with continuous corrective feedback	Reviewing videos of therapy sessions with expert providing feedback Repeatedly role-playing solutions to mistakes made in videotaped sessions	To address knowledge deficits specific to therapist; works exactly at therapist's performance threshold; makes specific skills routine and automatic by moving performance into procedural memory	Feels challenging and hard; not inherently enjoyable or immediately rewarding

The concept of the "10,000-hour" or "10-year rule" was brought to popular awareness by the book *Outliers* (Gladwell, 2008), referring to the amount of time necessary to become an expert in a field. (Research actually has found that the number of hours required for mastery varies by field; Ericsson & Pool, 2016.) However, a common misconception is that thousands of hours of *routine work experience* lead to expert performance. In contrast, researchers have found something much more challenging: Thousands of hours of *deliberate practice*, on top of hours spent in routine work performance, usually are required for expert performance.

Could the same process apply to mental health professionals? Chow, Miller, Seidel, Kane, and Andrews (2015) recently examined this question by surveying a group of therapists about the amount of time and effort they dedicated to deliberate practice. Their findings are strikingly similar to what expertise researchers discovered about other fields: Highly effective therapists devoted 4.5 times more hours to activities specifically designed to improve their effectiveness than less effective therapists (Chow et al., 2015). Figure 1.2 compares the findings about therapists from Chow et al. (2015) with the findings from a similar study about violinists (Ericsson et al., 1993).

Unfortunately, to date, professional training programs have encouraged deliberate practice to a very limited extent, despite the recognition that training should be "sequential, cumulative and graded in complexity" (Commission on Accreditation, 2013, p. 7). Opportunities to engage in deliberate practice become even fewer once clinicians complete their training. For most therapists, a serious focus on skill acquisition ends at the beginning of their career, right after graduate school. As seen in Figure 1.3, performance of the typical therapist does not improve through the professional career (i.e., after professional training), a result supported by longitudinal study of therapist outcomes (Goldberg, Rousmaniere

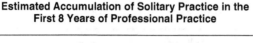

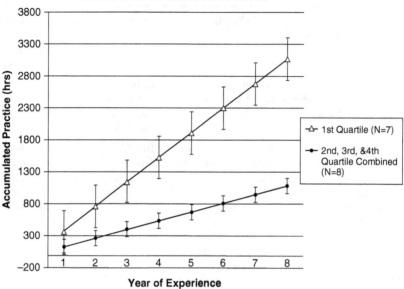

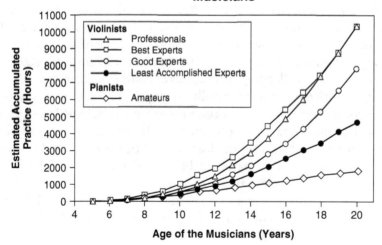

Figure 1.2 Comparing the relationship between the hours of deliberate practice and improved performance for therapists and violinists.
Sources: Chow et al. (2015, p. 342) and Ericsson et al. (1993, p. 379).

et al., 2016). It appears that students in graduate training acquire skills (e.g., Hill et al., 2015) and improve their outcomes over the course of training, although the improvement in outcomes may be quite gradual and not consistent (Owen et al., 2016). It is worth noting that even for domains where expertise is clearly visible (e.g., musicians, athletes, chess players),

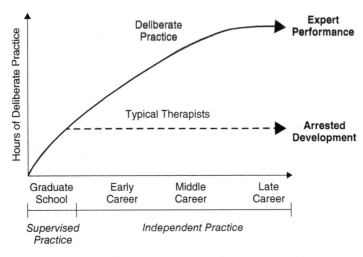

Figure 1.3 Improved performance via deliberate practice.

few achieve a level recognized as expert. Many of us are passably good musicians (we might sing or play guitar at gatherings or religious services), but we are clearly not in an elite group. Those who are elite, regardless of natural talent, have engaged in deliberate practice.

Bringing the Science of Expertise to Psychotherapy

Our goal for this book is to bring the science of expertise to the field of mental health. We do this by proposing a model for using the Cycle of Excellence throughout therapists' careers, from supervised training to independent practice.

Stage 1: Deliberate Practice in Supervised Training

The first major stage of clinicians' careers is intensive formal training, with the goal of achieving professional competency. Trainees in this stage work under supervision. Supervision, one of the four methods of development discussed earlier, is a relationship in which a more senior clinician monitors and guides a trainee's work in order both to facilitate trainee development and to ensure quality of client care (American Psychological Association, 2015; Bernard & Goodyear, 2014). Supervision provides a strong yet flexible relationship in which a seasoned expert can identify errors and the skills necessary for improvement, on a case-by-case basis. Supervisors can provide the essential ingredients for deliberate practice (McMahan, 2014) by:

1. Explaining and demonstrating models for effective practice (e.g., cognitive behavioral therapy or psychodynamic psychotherapy);
2. Determining each therapist's zone of proximal development (i.e., their exact threshold of understanding and opportunity for improvement);
3. Providing corrective feedback and guidance in style that is congruent and accessible to the learner;

4. Offering emotional encouragement to boost the learner's morale and buffer against the emotional challenges inherent in deliberate practice (Duckworth, Kirby, Tsukayama, Berstein, & Ericsson, 2011); and

5. Teaching trainees how to work appropriately within various professional domains (clinical, legal, administrative, etc.).

During their first few years of graduate school, trainees are not only learning their craft but also being socialized into the culture of their field. Supervision is the perfect opportunity to instill the habits and attitudes necessary for a "culture of expertise" that will help clinicians use deliberate practice throughout their careers.

Stage 2: Deliberate Practice in Independent Practice

After clinicians complete their formal training and become licensed, they move into the second (and final) major stage of their career: independent practice. At this point, they become responsible for their own learning, which generally can be of several types (Lichtenberg & Goodyear, 2012): incidental learning (i.e., spontaneous, unplanned learning that might occur through, e.g., reviewing a manuscript or hearing a radio interview with an expert); CE experiences; and intentional, self-directed learning. Deliberate practice concerns that third type of learning and has the goals of maintaining competency and gradually developing mastery of the craft. The mechanisms to support deliberate practice are varied in this stage, and include:

• advanced training with experts,
• skill assessment and case consultation with experts or peers, and
• solo study (e.g., watching videotapes of one's own work).

Table 1.2 describes the different goals, settings, areas of focus, and methods of deliberate practice for each career stage.

Table 1.2 Deliberate practice goals, settings, areas, and methods across the career span.

	Deliberate Practice			
	Goals	**Settings**	**Areas of Focus**	**Methods**
Career Stage 1: Supervised Training	Achieve professional competency	Under supervision	Attain competency in all basic skills	Videotape review, clinical role-plays, assigned homework, etc.
Career Stage 2: Independent Practice	Assess skills, maintain competency, develop expertise, leading to mastery of craft	In consultation with experts, peers, and solo study	Develop advanced skills in areas of specialty. Address specific deficiencies	Videotape review with experts, peers, and by oneself. Advanced training with experts, self-study, etc.

Sources of Motivation to Engage in Deliberate Practice

Students enter training programs in the mental health professions with excitement. They are highly motivated to seek and capitalize on learning opportunities. But as Stoltenberg and McNeill (2010) have discussed, students' motivation fluctuates across time. It is our impression that most clinicians remain intellectually curious throughout their professional lives but, once they attain basic competence, the curiosity is manifest more in diffuse ways than in focused ways. As discussed, deliberate practice is hard work, and learners typically find it both challenging and inherently unpleasant (Duckworth et al., 2011; Ericsson, 2006).

Researchers have identified a subset of very high-achieving therapists who do engage in deliberate practice (Miller et al., 2007, 2013). They demonstrate grit, which is "perseverance and passion for long-term goals" (Duckworth, Peterson, Matthews, & Kelly, 2007, p. 1087) and have "the capacity to stay committed to a challenging, far-off, but 'sweet' goal" (Duckworth et al., 2011, p. 174). Indeed, Duckworth et al. (2011) found that level of grit predicted the extent to which spelling bee competitors engaged in deliberate practice and, in turn, how they performed. Given the challenges of sustaining internal motivation to engage in the deliberate practice necessary to develop expertise, both institutional support and effective mechanisms of accountability are essential to encouraging it (Goodyear, 2015). This is especially true for licensed clinicians who can be tempted to "coast" instead of engaging in ongoing deliberate practice. Recent research at a community mental health center in Canada has shown that agency-wide support for deliberate practice, led by senior management, can improve client outcomes (Goldberg, Babins-Wagner et al., 2016). In this book, we describe evidence-based methods that treatment centers can use to support clinicians' engagement in the Cycle of Excellence.

About This Book

The goals of this book are to provide clinicians and clinical supervisors with (a) the theory of deliberate practice and the Cycle of Excellence, (b) a new model to integrate deliberate practice into clinical training and independent practice, and (c) case examples of how deliberate practice is being used across a range of psychotherapy settings. This book is organized into four parts.

Part I: The Cycle of Excellence reviews the science of clinical outcomes, expertise, and supervision and proposes a new model for integrating deliberate practice into clinical practice at every stage of a career, from supervised training to independent practice.

Part II: Tracking Performance focuses on an essential ingredient of deliberate practice: empirically tracking therapist effectiveness. In the field of mental health, this means measuring client outcome, which has the full richness and complexity of the human experience. The chapters in this part describe accessible methods supervisors and clinicians can use to track client outcomes at the case, therapist, and agency levels, using both quantitative and qualitative methods.

Part III: Applications for Integrating Deliberate Practice into Supervision explores innovative programs for using deliberate practice to enhance psychotherapy training across a broad spectrum of areas, including psychodynamic psychotherapy, cognitive behavioral therapy, agency-level improvement, and CE. This part also includes a chapter that describes how deliberate practice has been integrated into medical education, presented as a model and learning opportunity for the field of mental health.

Part IV: Recommendations concludes the volume by pulling together the previous chapters and proposing steps that can be taken to contribute to the mission of improving psychotherapeutic expertise.

Questions from John Norcross, PhD

For each chapter in this volume, we editors have posed several questions to the authors that a critical reader might ask. Answers by the chapter authors appear at the end of each chapter. For those chapters in which one or two of us were authors, others of our team took the role of asking challenging questions.

Because the four of us all were authors of this chapter, we reached outside the team and asked John Norcross, a prominent psychotherapy researcher and trainer, to pose the questions to us. In his characteristic way, he asked questions that were both insightful and rigorous.

Question #1. There is yet but a single research study attesting to the effectiveness of deliberate practice among psychotherapists in routine care. You review the research literature on the value of deliberate practice among other professionals, but those professions are notable for working by themselves and with inanimate objects (e.g., chess pieces, musical instruments), without the reciprocal influence of a client/patient. How do you respond to those who argue that you are recommending a practice (and writing an entire book) well beyond the supportive research evidence with psychotherapists?

Answer from Editors: We wholeheartedly agree with this question's underlying implication that clinical supervision and training methods should be subject to rigorous empirical testing. Indeed, we are arguing for a stance of empirical skepticism toward the effectiveness of *all* methods of clinical training, old and new. Too many of the field's current supervision practices are in wide use because they have been handed down via tradition rather than having been intentionally adopted on the basis of the research evidence (e.g., Ellis & Ladany, 1997).

In this volume, we are proposing that clinical supervision, training, and CE be reformed along the *principles* of deliberate practice. This marks a significant departure from the current approaches to clinical supervision and training. For example, we propose (a) to evaluate clinical supervision and training by the impact on client outcomes (rather than adherence and competence in a treatment model); (b) to emphasize active learning methods, such as repetitive behavioral rehearsal of clinical skills via role-plays with corrective feedback (rather than discussions about psychotherapy theory); and (c) that clinicians receive personal performance feedback continuously throughout their career (rather than stopping when they are licensed).

The question of whether these principles that have been shown to improve performance across a range of fields apply as well to the practice of psychotherapy is valid. Psychotherapy *is* a unique pursuit by virtue of its interpersonal context and demands. When we cite evidence from other fields such as music, athletics, or medicine, our goal is to focus on the learning processes rather than any implied similarities between psychotherapy and the functions of those other fields, to make the case that the principles of deliberate practice improve skill acquisition apply across a wide variety of fields and tasks. (For example, Zen Buddhism and other spiritual traditions have relied on deliberate practice for millennia.) Each of these fields is unique, and each has developed its own specific methods of deliberate practice to specifically address its particular pedagogic challenges.

All these fields rely on a human being having learned a particular skill or set of skills. The large body of research that forms the science of expertise identifies principles that improve the effectiveness of human skill acquisition, and we argue this research applies to psychotherapy, including the development of necessary interpersonal skills (e.g., Anderson, McClintock, Himawan, Song, & Patterson, 2015; see Chapter 3).

In short, our primary concern is with new principles of supervision and training. The methods we suggest for implementing these principles are largely drawn from the research evidence (directly or as extrapolations). The next task for our field, though, is for researchers and clinicians to develop new methods of supervision and training, based on these principles, and then subject them to rigorous empirical testing and evaluation in both clinical labs and actual practice.

Question #2. Your "cycle of excellence" bears strong resemblance to other, well-established models of active learning, such as that by David Kolb. What distinguishes your cycle from those of others, and what specific research support does your model enjoy?

Answer from Editors: This is an excellent question. And because others likely will wonder about it as well, we welcome the chance to address it. At the heart of the Cycle of Excellence model is the assumption that people learn from observing and critiquing their work. This same assumption has informed training since at least the time of Dewey (1938). In fact, other prominent models, such as those of Kolb (e.g., Kolb & Fry, 1975) and Schön (1988), owe a huge intellectual debt to Dewey's observations on the role of experience.

But the Cycle of Excellence differs from these models in at least two fundamental ways. The first of these concerns the essential role that a coach or supervisor has in providing feedback and direct instruction. This is in contrast with discovery learning, which so often is assumed to be common to models such as that of Kolb or Schön. Whereas discovery learning has an intuitive appeal, Kirschner, Sweller, and Clark (2006) offered a scathing critique of its effectiveness.

The second fundamental difference is in the role that intentional practice is assumed to play in skill development. Those models stress the cognitive processes that lead to new understandings about therapists' work and how they then might modify what they do. The models do not, though, focus on the hard work of really practicing and consolidating skills that lead to effective psychotherapy practice.

What we are proposing is that the Cycle of Excellence and deliberate practice emphasize maximizing opportunities for behavioral rehearsal and continuous corrective feedback. The goal is to give trainees ample opportunity to experiment with specific skills, so they can fail and get correction many times before trying the skills with real clients. This can be accomplished through the use of role-plays and other behavioral training drills in supervision. To illustrate, our model aims to be more like how one learns to drive (behavioral rehearsal with continuous corrective feedback), while traditional supervision is more like how one learns philosophy (discussing theory). These two models are not mutually exclusive; trainees, of course, need to learn psychotherapy theory. Rather, we are suggesting that behavioral rehearsal with continuous corrective feedback be given a stronger emphasis within the supervision hour than it has been given previously.

Question #3. Many researchers have indeed questioned the value-added benefit of clinical supervision on client outcomes. At the same time, the supervision research and supervision guidelines have converged on a series of best practices, which certainly contain the recommendations for supervision advanced in your chapter. Can you explain how your recommendations (e.g., demonstrate effective practice, provide corrective feedback, offer emotional encouragement) differ from those generic best practices?

Answer from Editors: The supervision "best practices" that various professions have developed (e.g., American Psychological Association, 2014; Association for Counselor Education and Supervision, 2011) represent the wisdom of supervision experts and stand as expected supervision competencies. It is inevitable, then, that we would incorporate them in our model as minimal expectations for effective supervisory practice. To illustrate: All of the available supervision guidelines stress the importance of supervisors directly observing their supervisees' work with clients in contrast to the current dominant practice of relying on supervisees' self-reports of their work. Directly observing supervisees' work is imperative in our model, which assumes that expertise development is only as effective as the feedback available to guide it. But our model is not limited to that type of feedback and requires, for example, the use of information from routine outcome monitoring. In this way, our model goes beyond expected best practices.

This question also implicitly raises the important distinction between competence and expertise. Competence, as either a supervisor or a psychotherapist, is about performing work in an expected way. When professionals are held accountable for competence, they are responsible for what Lerner and Tetlock (2003) describe as *process accountability* (see also Goodyear, 2015): To what extent is this person executing a skill set as expected, regardless of the obtained outcomes?

But in our model, expertise development is assessed in terms of client outcomes. Therapists and supervisors are held to outcome accountability (Lerner & Tetlock, 2003): To what extent is this person achieving intended outcomes, regardless of how she or he performed? Both forms of accountability are important, although we give outcome accountability the greater weight: Process should not overshadow outcome. This is especially true as one does not predict the other (see, e.g., Webb, DeRubeis, & Barber, 2010).

This book is concerned primarily with ways that psychotherapists can move from competence to expertise. Although we give it less emphasis in the book, we assume as well that supervisors would commit to a similar process of development and that the measure of their evolving expertise would be client outcomes, just as it is with therapists.

Question #4: Figure 2.3 in Chapter 2 shows huge growth in performance among "experts" using deliberate practice. Is this figure based on an actual study, in which the experts achieved twice the performance/client outcomes of "typical therapists"? Or perhaps the figure just represents a conceptual promise?

Answer from Editors: As the growing research on implementation science makes clear, *all* research offers a "conceptual promise." There is no guarantee of results. Differences in contexts, clients, management, and providers make any simple transfer and application of research findings to real-world clinical settings challenging in the best of circumstances. More, as evidenced by the study reported in Figure 2.3, deliberate practice is hard work, the gains are slow in coming and not immediately rewarding. A further threat is that practitioners with average results already consider themselves as effective as the best while devoting significantly less time to efforts aimed at improving their outcomes. At the same time, this same graph, together with findings from other studies cited, shows that the most effective therapists engage in significantly more deliberate practice than their more average counterparts. Indeed, with clients of therapists in the top quartile achieving outcomes more than *twice* the size of those in the bottom (Wampold & Brown, 2005), deliberate practice serves to benefit both clinicians and recipients of mental health services.

In sum, the promise of deliberate practice depicted in Figure 2.3 is indeed real. However, its realization depends on two critical factors: (a) continuous effort and (b) long-term commitment. Although a number of studies are in the works, knowledge regarding the application of deliberate practice to improving performance as a psychotherapist is still very much in its infancy. Evidence regarding what is required for helping practitioners sustain the commitment necessary to realize the gains is, for all points and purposes, unavailable. Until a time in the future, practitioners and the field will be reliant on studies from other domains (e.g., sport, music, medicine, computer programming, teaching).

References

Anderson, T., McClintock, A. S., Himawan, L., Song, X., & Patterson, C. L. (2015). A prospective study of therapist facilitative interpersonal skills as a predictor of treatment outcome. *Journal of Consulting and Clinical Psychology, 84*(1), 57–66. doi:10.1037/ccp0000060

American Psychological Association. (2014). *Guidelines for clinical supervision in health service psychology.* Retrieved from http://apa.org/about/policy/guidelines-supervision.pdf

Association for Counselor Education and Supervision. (2011). *Best practices in clinical supervision.* Retrieved from https://goo.gl/3n5qp2

Baldwin, S. A., & Imel, Z. E. (2013). Therapist effects: Findings and methods. In M. J. Lambert (Ed.), *Bergin and Garfield's handbook of psychotherapy and behavior change* (6th ed., pp. 258–297). Hoboken, NJ: Wiley.

Bernard, J. M., & Goodyear, R. K. (2014). *Fundamentals of clinical supervision* (5th ed.). Boston, MA: Merrill.

Beutler, L. E., & Howard, M. (2003). Training in psychotherapy: Why supervision does not work. *Clinical Psychologist, 56*(4), 12–16.

Bloom, B. S. (2005). Effects of continuing medical education on improving physician clinical care and patient health: A review of systematic reviews. *International Journal of Technology Assessment in Health Care, 21*(3), 380–385. doi:10.1017/S026646230505049X

Branson, A., Shafran, R., & Myles, P. (2015). Investigating the relationship between competence and patient outcome with CBT highlights. *Behaviour Research and Therapy, 68*, 19–26. doi:10.1016/j.brat.2015.03.002

Centers for Disease Control and Prevention. (2012). *Death rate from complications of medical and surgical care among adults aged ≥ 45 years, by age group—United States, 1999–2009.* Retrieved from http://goo.gl/fpElbC

Chow, D., Miller, S.D., Seidel, J., Kane, R., & Andrews, B. (2015). The role of deliberate practice in the development of highly effective psychotherapists. *Psychotherapy, 52*(3), 337–345.

Colvin, G. (2008). *Talent is overrated: What really separates world-class performers from everybody else.* New York, NY: Penguin.

Commission on Accreditation. (2013). *Guidelines and principles for accreditation of programs in professional psychology.* Washington, DC: American Psychological Association.

Coughlan, E. K., Williams, A. M., McRobert, A. P., & Ford, P. R. (2014). How experts practice: A novel test of deliberate practice theory. *Journal of Experimental Psychology. Learning, Memory, and Cognition, 40*(2), 449–58. doi:10.1037/a0034302

Coyle, D. (2009). *The talent code: Greatness isn't born. It's grown. Here's how.* New York, NY: Bantam Dell.

Dewey, J. (1938). *Experience and education.* New York, NY: Collier Books

Duckworth, A. L., Kirby, T. A., Tsukayama, E., Berstein, H., & Ericsson, K. A. (2011). Deliberate practice spells success: Why grittier competitors triumph at the National Spelling Bee. *Social Psychological and Personality Science, 2*(2), 174–181. doi:10.1177/1948550610385872

Duckworth, A. L., Peterson, C., Matthews, M. D., & Kelly, D. R. (2007). Grit: Perseverance and passion for long-term goals. *Journal of Personality and Social Psychology, 92*(6), 1087–1101. doi:10.1037/0022-3514.92.6.1087

Ellis, M. V., & Ladany, N. (1997). Inferences concerning supervisees and clients in clinical supervision: An integrative review. In C. E. Watkins (Ed.), *Handbook of psychotherapy supervision* (pp. 447–507). New York, NY: Wiley.

Ericsson, K. A. (1996). The acquisition of expert performance: An introduction to some of the issues. In K. A. Ericsson (Ed.), *The road to excellence: The acquisition of expert performance in the arts and sciences, sports, and games* (pp. 1–50). Mahwah, NJ: Erlbaum.

Ericsson, K. A. (2006). The influence of experience and deliberate practice on the development of superior expert performance. In K. A. Ericsson, N. Charness, P. J. Feltovich,

& R. R. Hoffman (Eds.), *The Cambridge handbook of expertise and expert performance* (pp. 683–703). Cambridge, UK: Cambridge University Press.

Ericsson, K. A. (2009). Enhancing the development of professional performance: Implications from the study of deliberate practice. In *Development of professional expertise: Toward measurement of expert performance and design of optimal learning environments* (pp. 405–431). New York, NY: Cambridge University Press.

Ericsson, K. A., Charness, N., Feltovich, P. J., & Hoffman, R. R. (2006). *The Cambridge handbook of expertise and expert performance*. Cambridge, UK: Cambridge University Press.

Ericsson, K. A., Krampe, R. T., & Tesch-Romer, C. (1993). The role of deliberate practice in the acquisition of expert performance. *Psychological Review, 100*, 363–406.

Ericsson, K. A., & Pool, R. (2016). *Peak: Secrets from the new science of expertise*. New York, NY: Houghton Mifflin Harcourt.

Forand, N. R., DeRubeis, R. J., & Amsterdam, J. D. (2013). Combining medication and psychotherapy in the treatment of major mental disorders. In M. J. Lambert (Ed.), *Bergin and Garfield's handbook of psychotherapy and behavior change* (pp. 735 – 774). Hoboken, NJ: Wiley.

Friedman, L. S., & Forst, L. (2007). The impact of OSHA recordkeeping regulation changes on occupational injury and illness trends in the US: A time-series analysis. *Occupational and Environmental Medicine, 64*(7), 454–460.

Gladwell, M. (2008). *Outliers*. New York, NY: Little, Brown.

Goldberg, S., Babins-Wagner, R., Rousmaniere, T. G., Berzins, S., Hoyt, W. T., Whipple, J. L., . . . Wampold, B. E. (2016). Creating a climate for therapist improvement: A case study of an agency focused on outcomes and deliberate practice. *Psychotherapy, 53*, 367–375.

Goldberg, S., Rousmaniere, T. G., Miller, S. D., Whipple, J., Nielsen, S. L.., Hoyt, W. T. & Wampold, B. E. (2016). Do psychotherapists improve with time and experience? A longitudinal analysis of outcomes in a clinical setting. *Journal of Counseling Psychology, 63*, 1–11.

Goodyear, R. (2015, November). Using accountability mechanisms more intentionally: A framework and its implications for training professional psychologists. *American Psychologist, 70*(8), 736–743. doi:10.1037/a0039828

Gøtzsche, P. C., Young, A. H., & Crace, J. (2015). Does long term use of psychiatric drugs cause more harm than good? *British Medical Journal, 350*, h2435. doi:10.1136/bmj.h2435

Hill, C. E., Baumann, E., Shafran, N., Gupta, S., Morrison, A., Rojas, A.E.P., . . . Gelso, C. J. (2015). Is training effective? A study of counseling psychology doctoral trainees in a psychodynamic/interpersonal training clinic. *Journal of Counseling Psychology, 62*, 184–201.

Hilsenroth, M. J., Ackerman, S. J., Clemence, A. J., Strassle, C. G., & Handler, L. (2002). Effects of structured clinician training on patient and therapist perspectives of alliance early in psychotherapy. *Psychotherapy: Theory, Research, Practice, Training, 39*(4), 309–323. doi:10.1037/0033-3204.39.4.309

Hilsenroth, M. J., Kivlighan, D. M., & Slavin-Mulford, J. (2015). Structured supervision of graduate clinicians in psychodynamic psychotherapy: Alliance and technique. *Journal of Counseling Psychology*. Advance online publication. doi:10.1037/cou0000058

Hubble, M. A., Duncan, B. L., & Miller, S. D. (1999). *The heart and soul of change: What works in therapy*. Washington, DC: American Psychological Association.

Hunt, E. (2006). Expertise, talent, and social encouragement. In K. A. Ericsson, N. Charness, P. J. Feltovich, & R. R. Hoffman (Eds.), *The Cambridge handbook of expertise and expert performance* (pp. 31–38). Cambridge, UK: Cambridge University Press.

Johnsen, T. J., & Friborg, O. (2015). The effects of cognitive behavioral therapy as an anti-depressive treatment is falling: A meta-analysis. *Psychological Bulletin.* Advance online publication. 10.1037/bul0000015

Kirschner, P. A., Sweller, J., & Clark, R. E. (2006). Why minimal guidance during instruction does not work: An analysis of the failure of constructivist, discovery, problem-based, experiential, and inquiry-based teaching. *Educational Psychologist, 41*(2), 75–86.

Kolb. D. A., & Fry, R. (1975). Toward an applied theory of experiential learning. In C. Cooper (Ed.), *Theories of group process* (pp. 125–149). London, UK: Wiley.

Kraus, D. R., Castonguay, L., Boswell, J. F., Nordberg, S. S., & Hayes, J. A. (2011). Therapist effectiveness: Implications for accountability and patient care. *Psychotherapy Research, 21*(3), 267–276.

Ladany, N. (2007). Does psychotherapy training matter? Maybe not. *Psychotherapy: Theory, Research, Practice, Training, 44*(4), 392–396. doi:10.1037/0033-3204.44.4.392

Lambert, M. J. (2010). Yes, it is time for clinicians to routinely monitor treatment outcome. In B. L. Duncan, S. D. Miller, B. E. Wampold, & M. A. Hubble (Eds.), *The heart and soul of change: Delivering what works in therapy* (pp. 239–266). Washington, DC: American Psychological Association.

Lambert, M. J. (2013). The efficacy and effectiveness of psychotherapy. In M. J. Lambert (Ed.), *Bergin and Garfield's handbook of psychotherapy and behavior change* (pp. 169–218). Hoboken, NJ: Wiley.

Lambert, M. J., & Shimokawa, K. (2011). Collecting client feedback. *Psychotherapy: Theory, Research, Practice, Training, 48*, 72–79.

Laska, K. M., Gurman, A. S., & Wampold, B. E. (2014). Expanding the lens of evidence-based practice in psychotherapy: A common factors perspective. *Psychotherapy, 51*, 467–481. doi: 10.1037/a0034332

Lehmann, A. C., & Ericsson, K. A. (1998). The historical development of domains of expertise: Performance standards and innovations in music. In A. Steptoe (Ed.), *Genius and the mind* (pp. 67–94). Oxford, UK: Oxford University Press.

Lerner, J., & Tetlock, P. E. (2003). The impact of accountability on cognitive bias: Bridging individual, interpersonal, and institutional approaches to judgment and choice. In S. Schneider & J. Shanteau (Eds.), *Emerging perspectives in judgment and decision-making* (pp. 431–457). New York, NY: Cambridge University Press.

Lichtenberg, J. W., & Goodyear, R. K. (2012). Informal learning, incidental learning, and deliberate continuing education: Preparing psychologists to be effective lifelong learners. In G. J. Neimeyer & J. M. Taylor (Eds.), *Continuing education: Types, roles, and societal impacts* (pp. 71–80). Hauppauge, NY: Nova Science.

Lippi, G., Banfi, G., Favaloro, E. J., Rittweger, J., & Maffulli, N. (2008). Updates on improvement of human athletic performance: Focus on world records in athletics. *British Medical Bulletin, 87*(1), 7–15. Retrieved from http://bmb.oxfordjournals.org/content/87/1/7.long

McHugh, R. K., & Barlow, D. H. (2010). The dissemination and implementation of evidence-based psychological treatments: A review of current efforts. *American Psychologist, 65*(2), 73–84. doi:10.1037/a0018121

McMahan, E. H. (2014). Supervision: A nonelusive component of deliberate practice toward expertise. *American Psychologist, 69,* 711–712. doi:/10.1037/a0037832

Miller, S. D., Duncan, B. L., & Hubble, M. A. (2004). Beyond integration: The triumph of outcome over process in clinical practice. *Psychotherapy in Australia, 10,* 2–19.

Miller, S. D., Duncan, B. L., Sorrell, R., & Brown, J. (2005). The Partners for Change Outcome System. *Journal of Clinical Psychology: In Session, 61,* 199–208.

Miller, S. D., Hubble, M. A, Chow, D. L., & Seidel, J. A. (2013). The outcome of psychotherapy: Yesterday, today, and tomorrow. *Psychotherapy, 50*(1), 88–97. doi:10.1037/a0031097

Miller, S. D., Hubble, M. A., and Duncan, B. L. (2007). Supershrinks: Learning from the field's most effective practitioners. *Psychotherapy Networker, 31,* 26–35, 56.

Neimeyer, G. J., & Taylor, J. M. (2010). Continuing education in psychology. In J. C. Norcross, G. R. VandenBos, & D. K. Freedheim (Eds.), *History of psychotherapy: Continuity and change* (pp. 663–671). Washington, DC: American Psychological Association.

Neimeyer, G. J., Taylor, J. M., & Wear, D. M. (2009). Continuing education in psychology: Outcomes, evaluations, and mandates. *Professional Psychology: Research and Practice, 40*(6), 617–624.

Owen, J., Wampold, B. E., Rousmaniere, T. G., Kopta, M., & Miller., S. (2016). As good as it gets? Therapy outcomes of trainees over time. *Journal of Counseling Psychology, 63,* 12–19.

PCOMS. (2013). *Partners for Change Outcome Management System: International Center for Clinical Excellence.* Retrieved from http://legacy.nreppadmin.net/ViewIntervention.aspx?id=249

Rousmaniere, T. G., Swift, J. K., Babins-Wagner, R., Whipple, J. L., & Berzins, S. (2016). Supervisor variance in psychotherapy outcome in routine practice. *Psychotherapy Research, 26*(2), 196–205.

Schön, D. (1988). *Educating the reflective practitioner.* San Francisco, CA: Jossey-Bass.

Shenk, D. (2010). *The genius in all of us: Why everything you've been told about genetics, talent, and IQ is wrong.* New York, NY: Random House.

Stoltenberg, C. D., & McNeill, B. W. (2010). *IDM supervision: An integrative developmental model for supervising counselors and therapists* (3rd ed.). New York, NY: Routledge.

Swift, J. K., Greenberg, R. P., Whipple, J. L., & Kominiak, N. (2012). Practice recommendations for reducing premature termination in therapy. *Professional Psychology: Research and Practice, 43*(4), 379–387. doi:10.1037/a0028291

Syed, M. (2010). *Bounce: Mozart, Federer, Picasso, Beckham, and the Science of Success.* New York, NY: HarperCollins.

Tracey, T.J.G., Wampold, B. E., Goodyear, R. K., & Lichtenberg, J. W. (2015). Improving expertise in psychotherapy. *Psychotherapy Bulletin, 50*(1), 7–13.

Tracey, T.J.G., Wampold, B. E., Lichtenberg, J. W., & Goodyear, R. K. (2014). Expertise in psychotherapy: An elusive goal? *American Psychologist, 69,* 218–229.

Wampold, B. E., & Brown, J. (2005). Estimating variability in outcomes attributable to therapists: A naturalistic study of outcomes in managed care. *Journal of Consulting and Clinical Psychology, 73*(5), 920.

Wampold, B. E., Budge, S. L., Laska, K. M., del Re, A. C., Baardseth, T. P., Fluckiger, C., . . . Gunn, W. (2011). Evidence-based treatments for depression and anxiety versus treatment-as-usual: A meta-analysis of direct comparisons. *Clinical Psychology Review, 31*(8), 1304–1312. Retrieved from http://doi.org/10.1016/j.cpr.2011.07.012

Wampold, B. E., & Imel, Z. (2015). *The great psychotherapy debate: The evidence for what makes psychotherapy work.* New York, NY: Routledge.

Watkins, D. (2011). Does psychotherapy supervision contribute to patient outcomes? Considering thirty years of research. *Clinical Supervisor, 30,* 235–256. doi:10.1080/07325223.2011.619417

Webb, C. A., DeRubeis, R. J., & Barber, J. P. (2010). Therapist adherence/competence and treatment outcome: A meta-analytic review. *Journal of Consulting and Clinical Psychology, 78*(2), 200–211.

Wise, E. H., Sturm, C. A., Nutt, R. L., Rodolfa, E., Schaffer, J. B., & Webb, C. (2010). Life-long learning for psychologists: Current status and a vision for the future. *Professional Psychology: Research and Practice, 41*(4), 288–297.

2

Professional Development

From Oxymoron to Reality
Scott D. Miller, Mark A. Hubble, and Daryl Chow

Nothing is so fatiguing as the eternal hanging on of an uncompleted task.
—William James

Psychotherapy works (Miller, Hubble, Chow, & Seidel, 2013). Across a large and diverse number of approaches and populations, the average treated person is better off than 80% of those receiving no treatment (Wampold & Imel, 2015). Not only is the overall efficacy firmly established, but so is its effectiveness in real-world clinical settings (American Psychological Association, 2012; Duncan, Miller, Wampold, & Hubble, 2010; Wampold, 2001). On average, more practicing clinicians achieve outcomes commensurate with results obtained in tightly controlled, randomized clinical trials (Barkham et al., 2006; Minami, Serlin, Wampold, Kircher, & Brown, 2008). Fifty years after Eysenck (1952) claimed that psychological treatments did nothing to facilitate recovery and actually hindered change, the scientific basis of psychological treatments is unassailable (Miller et al., 2013).

As encouraging as these general results are, other data provide the profession with little reason to be sanguine. For example, for close to four decades, the outcome of psychotherapy has remained flat. In their comprehensive review of the literature, Wampold and Imel (2015) noted, "From the various meta-analyses conducted over the years, the aggregate effect size related to absolute efficacy is remarkably consistent" (p. 94). Efforts to improve outcome by creating a psychological formulary—specific treatments for specific disorders—have done nothing to alter this fact. Indeed, studies in which one treatment is directly compared with another reveal few, if any, differences (Duncan et al., 2010; Hubble, Duncan, & Miller, 1999). Not surprisingly, neither clinicians' competence in conducting specific types of therapy nor their adherence to evidence-based protocols has been "found to be related to patient outcome and indeed . . . estimates of their effects [are] very close to zero" (Webb, DeRubeis, & Barber, 2010, p. 207).

Equally discouraging, additional findings show that the results obtained by individual clinicians are far from uniform (Crits-Christophe & Mintz, 1991; Garfield, 1997; Luborsky, McLellan, Woody, O'Brien, & Auerbach, 1985; Miller, Duncan, Sorrell, & Brown, 200; Okiishi,

The Cycle of Excellence: Using Deliberate Practice to Improve Supervision and Training,
First Edition. Edited by Tony Rousmaniere, Rodney K. Goodyear, Scott D. Miller, and Bruce E. Wampold.
© 2017 John Wiley & Sons, Ltd. Published 2017 by John Wiley & Sons, Ltd.

Lambert, Egget, & Vermeersch, 2003). Simply put, some therapists are more (or less) helpful than others (Miller, Hubble, & Duncan, 2007). Moreover, instead of improving with experience, the effectiveness of the average practitioner plateaus early on and slowly deteriorates (Miller & Hubble, 2011). To illustrate, in the largest study of its kind, Goldberg, Rousmaniere, and colleagues (2016) documented an erosion in performance in a sample of 170 therapists working with more than 6,500 clients, tracked over a 5-year period. This decline was unrelated to initial client severity, number of sessions, early termination, caseload size, or various therapist factors (e.g., age, years of experience, theoretical orientation).

What does reliably improve is therapists' confidence in their abilities (Miller et al., 2007). Studies show that the least effective believe they are as good as the most effective and that average clinicians overestimate their outcomes on the order of 65% (Chow, 2014; Hiatt & Hargrave, 1995; Walfish, McAlister, O'Donnell, & Lambert, 2012). Ironically, it is as if practitioners have taken the advice of famed French psychiatrist Coué who, more than 100 years ago, instructed his patients to tell themselves repeatedly, morning and evening, "Every day, in every way, I'm getting better and better" (Clement, 1994).

Whatever outcome research shows, clearly therapists want to develop professionally. A large, 20-year, multinational investigation of 11,000 clinicians, conducted by researchers Orlinsky and Rønnestad together with members of the Society for Psychotherapy Research, confirms this deeply held desire (Orlinksy & Rønnestad, 2005; Rønnestad & Orlinsky, 2005). This same research revealed that improving clinicians' skills, deepening their understanding of therapeutic process, and overcoming past limitations are key to sustaining morale, reducing burnout, and maintaining enthusiasm for clinical work (Miller & Hubble, 2015). With respect to professional development, then, it is not a matter of a therapist's will; it is a matter of *way*.

Clinicians invest a great deal of time, energy, and money in professional growth. They undergo personal therapy, receive ongoing postgraduate supervision, and attend continuing education (CE) events (Rønnestad & Orlinsky, 2005). Nevertheless, one searches in vain for any evidence that such efforts help therapists accomplish their goal.

Taking each in order, although nearly 80% of practitioners cite a personal therapy as key to becoming a better therapist—second only to supervision (Orlinksy & Rønnestad, 2005)— the findings are at best "mixed and inconclusive" (Malikiosi-Loizos, 2013, p. 43; Geller, Norcross, & Orlinksy, 2005). Supervision fares no better. After reviewing a century of the literature and research on the practice, Watkins (2011) concluded, "We do not seem any more able to say now (as opposed to 30 years ago) that psychotherapy supervision contributes to patient outcome" (p. 235). More recently, Rousmaniere, Swift, Babins-Wagner, Whipple, and Berzins (2016) examined the impact of supervision on outcomes using hierarchical linear modeling (clients nested within therapists and therapists nested within supervisor). Data were gathered for more than 5 years on 23 supervisors working in a real-world setting. Supervision was not found to be a significant contributor to client outcome. Neither did the supervisors' experience level, profession (social work versus psychology), or qualifications predict differences between supervisors in client outcomes.

Finally, with regard to CE, although clinicians report being satisfied and believing these kinds of experiences lead to more effective and ethical practice, no proof of knowledge acquisition or growing clinical competency exists. In truth, although continuing education is mandated by licensing and regulatory bodies worldwide, any connection between the quality and outcome of professional services and participation in CE has yet to be established (Neimeyer, Taylor, & Wear, 2009).

The question naturally arises: Where can a clinician go for instruction and guidance about becoming more effective? As seen, the field's traditions and methods have rendered "professional development" an oxymoron. Fortunately, research outside the field provides direction for making the growth clinicians seek a reality. These findings, drawn from the study of expertise, are less concerned with the particulars of a given performance domain than with how mastery of any human endeavor is achieved (Colvin, 2008; Ericsson, 2009; Ericsson, Charness, Feltovich, & Hoffman, 2006).

Learning from Experts

> Few if any of the people around you are truly great at what they do . . . . Why—exactly why—aren't they?
>
> —*Geoff Colvin (2008)*

In 1993, researchers Ericsson, Krampe, and Tesch-Romer published the results of a groundbreaking study on the acquisition of expert performance. "The search for stable heritable characteristics that could predict or at least account for the superior performance of eminent individuals has been surprisingly unsuccessful," they observed (p. 365). "Neither," they continued, is "the maximal level of performance . . . in a given domain . . . attained automatically as a function of experience" (p. 366). In sum, expertise is not inherited nor does it directly follow from mere time spent in a given field or profession. Instead, top performers are made, a result of their "life-long . . . *deliberate* effort to improve" (p. 400, emphasis added).

Using violinists as the subjects for study, Ericsson and colleagues (1993) found that the best worked harder and smarter at improving their craft than the less capable players. Specifically, those at the top spent significantly more time—three times as much—than those at the bottom engaged in solitary activities specifically designed to better their performance. The best were more dedicated in every way. They devoted less time to leisure and more time to music-related activities. Additionally, they knew when they were slacking off, unlike the other subjects in the study who tended to underestimate time spent in recreation and relaxation.

Since the publication of this initial research, similar results have been found in sports, chess, business, computer programming, teaching, medicine, and surgery (Charness, Tuffiash, Krampe, Reingold, & Vasyukova, 2005; Duckworth, Kirby, Tsukayama, Berstein, & Ericsson, 2011; Ericsson et al., 1993; Keith & Ericsson, 2007; Krampe & Ericsson, 1996; Starkes, Deakin, Allard, Hodges, & Hayes, 1996). Ericsson et al. (1993) introduced the term *deliberate practice* (DP) to refer to the universal process associated with the development and maintenance of expertise across a variety of pursuits.

As the name implies, DP is purposeful and cognitively demanding, going beyond the execution of skills associated with routine work. The key attribute of DP is to "seek out challenges that go beyond their current level of reliable achievement—ideally in a safe and optimal learning context that allows immediate feedback and gradual refinement by repetition" (Ericsson, 2009, p. 425). The process, as Ericsson et al. (1993) defined it, involves regular engagement in a set of tasks "rated high on relevance for performance, high on effort, and comparatively low on inherent enjoyment" (p. 373).

With regard to the specific nature of the activities, the deliberate practice framework contains four key elements:

1. A focused and systematic effort to improve performance pursued over an extended period
2. Involvement of and guidance from a coach/teacher/mentor
3. Immediate, ongoing feedback
4. Successive refinement and repetition via solo practice outside of performance (see Figure 2.1; Ericsson et al., 1993; Ericsson & Charness, 1994; Ericsson & Lehmann, 1996)

According to Ericsson (2006), the notion that superior performance required at least "10,000 hours" of practice—popularized in Malcolm Gladwell's book *Outliers* (2008)—is but a rough estimate.

Expert performance is believed to be mediated by "complex integrated systems of representations for the planning, analysis, execution, and monitoring of performance" (Ericsson, 2006, p. 698)—a mental map also called "domain-specific" knowledge (Ericsson & Staszewski, 1989). Bearing this in mind, engagement in DP is transformational. In pushing performers beyond their current abilities, DP gradually changes the physiologic and cognitive structures mediating performance (Ericsson, 1996, 2004). The data further suggest that the best purposefully and continuously work at acquiring higher levels of control over what they do (Ericsson, Nandagopal, & Roring, 2009). In the study of chess players, for example, improvements in performance have been found to follow an individual's development of more complex and selective mental representations of the game. In short, the best players approach the board

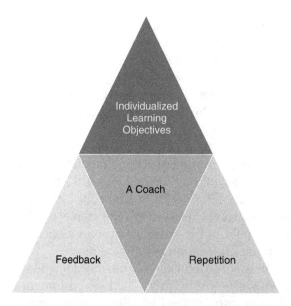

Figure 2.1 Four primary components of deliberate practice framework.

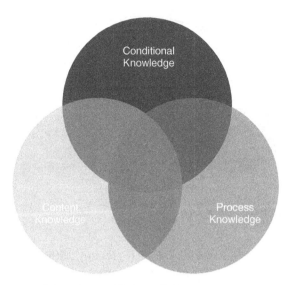

Figure 2.2 Three components of domain-specific knowledge.

very differently from novice players. Having developed higher-order units, or "chunks," for conceiving, understanding, and organizing their actions, chess masters store and retrieve relevant information with greater ease, speed, and effect (Feltovich, Prietula, & Ericsson, 2006).

Domain-specific knowledge can be further understood and elaborated as being comprised of three interacting components. (See Figure 2.2.) The first, *content knowledge*, is the body of understandings comprising a particular field or performance domain. In fencing, for example, a riposte is defined as a quick return thrust following an opponent's parry. Such information is customarily conveyed in books, instructional media, and classrooms. If content knowledge is about the "what," *process* is the "how." Recognizing and describing a riposte is not the same as being able to execute the move. Finally, *conditional knowledge* involves knowing the right or opportune moment to apply "what" one knows "how" to do. By engaging in DP, performers are continuously pushing themselves to expand and refine the three types of knowledge with the goal of achieving a higher level of functioning.

In any given realm or field, no single activity, if practiced by all, invariably leads to expertise (Ericsson et al., 1993). What works for one will not necessarily work for another. For DP to be effective, it must be highly individualized, targeting personal objectives that lie just beyond an individual's current level of proficiency.

Successful DP also includes a continuous and conscious effort on the part of performers to monitor what they do. Specific attention is directed toward identifying errors and then taking steps to reduce those errors during their next round of DP (Ericsson, 1996, 2006). Top-performing stand-up comedians provide an excellent example of this "error-centric" approach (Coyle, 2008). Average comedians focus on telling jokes. In contrast, headliners are not invested in any particular gag or routine. Their purpose is to entertain. To that end, they watch, observe, and listen to the audience, using audience reactions to rework, change, and nuance their material until it elicits what they are there to evoke, laughter.

Although some performers reach a plateau and disengage from deliberate practice, evidence suggests the best purposefully work to counteract *automaticity* so as to acquire

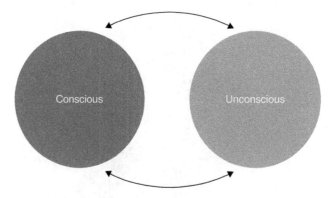

Figure 2.3 Cycle of overcoming automaticity.

higher levels of control over their performance (Ericsson, 2009). Through ongoing, deliberate reflection, superior performers consciously synthesize their knowledge and skills, ultimately enabling them to perform a particular task more efficiently and effectively (Feltovich et al., 2006). The cycle of making conscious what is unconscious and of making unconscious what is conscious is vital not only for the acquisition of superior performance but also for skill maintenance (see Figure 2.3; Ericsson et al., 2009; Krampe & Ericsson, 1996).

Although it may seem self-evident, what is practiced must lead to the acquisition of knowledge or skills causally related to a better outcome. As a case in point, consider the practice of astrology. Someone interested in interpreting the movements and positions of celestial objects for the purpose of divination could use and apply the principles of DP. Indeed, much has been written by scholars of the "esoteric arts" on the importance of practice (cf. Edmundson, 2004). In time, mastery of the extensive and complex knowledge base associated with this endeavor would result (Garner, 2010). Despite the effort expended and the confidence felt, however, one would be no better at predicting the future than anyone else.

Finally, DP requires a supportive social context—a frequently invisible, interlocking network of people, places, resources, and circumstances. Miller and Hubble (2011) termed this social scaffolding the "culture of excellence." DP is hard work. As Ericsson (1993) observed, "Unlike play, [it] is not inherently motivating; and unlike work, it does not lead to immediate social and monetary rewards . . . . . and [actually] generates costs" (p. 386). Not surprisingly, without strong, consistent validation, encouragement, and sponsorship (e.g., financial backing), top performance remains out of reach for all but a few.

Application of Deliberate Practice in Psychotherapy

> To practice isn't to declare that I am bad. To practice is to declare that I can be better.
> —*Dan Heath (2012)*

It is important to note that clinical practice and deliberate practice are not one and the same. Although necessary, clinical practice is insufficient for developing and refining the skills associated with superior performance. Clinical practice is an "output"—the result of efforts to be helpful. Deliberate practice, in contrast, is an "input" aimed at improving skills. The returns are often not immediate, and rarely monetarily rewarding, but nonetheless they improve the quality of a practitioner's clinical work.

In 2015, Chow and associates published the first study on the impact of deliberate practice on therapist development. The research examined the relationship between outcome and a variety of practitioner variables, including demographics, work practices, participation in professional development activities, beliefs regarding learning and growth as a therapist, and personal appraisals of therapeutic effectiveness. As in previous studies, gender, qualifications, professional discipline, years of experience, time spent conducting therapy, and clinician self-assessment of effectiveness were not related to outcome (Anderson, Ogles, Patterson, Lambert, & Vermeersch, 2009; Malouff, 2012; Walfish, McAlister, O'Donnell, & Lambert, 2012; Wampold & Brown, 2005). Consistent with findings reported in the expert performance literature, the amount of time therapists spent in activities intended to improve their ability was a significant predictor.

The cumulative impact deliberate practice exerted on clinician effectiveness can be seen in Figure 2.4. In the first 8 years of their professional work, the top quartile of practitioners spent, on average, nearly 2.8 times more time engaged in deliberate practice than those in the bottom three.

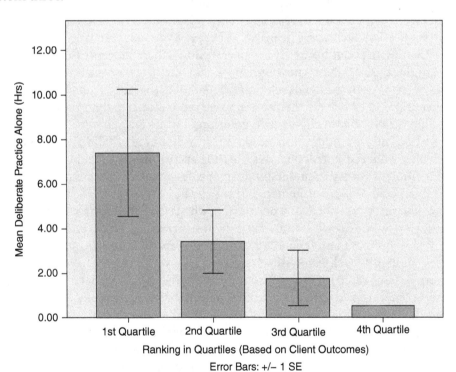

Figure 2.4 Therapists grouped in quartiles based on their adjusted client outcomes as a function of estimated time spent on "deliberate practice alone" per typical workweek.
Note. SE = standard error of mean; 4th quartile consists of only one therapist. Therefore, no error bar was included.

Chow et al.'s (2015) study further examined what therapists actually do when they engage in deliberate practice. Informed by prior research on expertise, the investigators designed a survey assessing the type of activities study subjects pursued, the amount of time spent in each, the perceived relevance to skill improvement, and the cognitive effort required to complete them (Chow & Miller, 2012). Consistent with the results reported by Ericsson et al. (1993) in their investigation of violinists, Chow and colleagues (2015) found that no one activity reliably produced better outcomes. In point of fact, what needs to be practiced will vary from one person to the next depending on where the individual "starts" and whatever is instrumental in either impeding or improving his or her specific performance.

Miller et al. (2007) identified three steps for constructing an individualized professional development plan. Working in tandem to create a "cycle of excellence," they include: (a) determining a baseline level of effectiveness; (b) obtaining systematic, ongoing, formal feedback; and (c) repeatedly engaging in activities specifically designed to refine and improve performance. Together, the steps integrate Ericsson's work with very recent innovations in psychotherapy outcome research that, when implemented, enable practitioners to achieve real gains in their effectiveness. Each step is discussed in turn.

Step 1: Determining a Baseline Level of Effectiveness

Improving performance and growing as a therapist begin with determining one's current level of effectiveness. It stands to reason. If one calls for directions to a particular destination, the first question likely to be heard is "Where are you *now*?" In truth, most practitioners have no hard data about how they are performing—their success rates (Boswell, Kraus, Miller, & Lambert, 2013). Not knowing where they are, they have no reference point for charting a course of professional development. As noted, therapists' personal appraisals are grossly inaccurate. They believe themselves to be more effective than they are, chronically underestimate the number of clients who deteriorate while in their care, and think they are improving when they are not (Chow et al., 2015; Miller et al., 2007; Walfish et al., 2012). More, such bias is not self-correcting, despite time and experience. Taking all these findings into consideration, it is easy to understand why professional development has remained so elusive (Hannan et al., 2005; Kahneman, 2011; Kruger, 1999).

Across a wide variety of endeavors, performers who rise to the top are constantly comparing what they do with existing standards or norms (Ericsson, 2006). Fortunately, owing to advances in measurement and technology, psychotherapists can do the same. Over the last two decades, numerous, well-established scales for assessing outcome have become available (cf. Corcoran & Fischer, 2013; Froyd & Lambert, 1989; Ogles, Lambert, & Masters, 1996). Additionally, computerized systems exist that automate calculations of individual clinician effect sizes, thus facilitating comparisons with national and international norms (cf. Lambert, 2012; PCOMS, 2013). Any of these tools or systems can be used to establish a personal benchmark against which efforts aimed at improving can be assessed.

Two systems—the Partners for Change Outcome Management System (PCOMS) and the Outcome Questionnaire Psychotherapy Quality Management System (OQ-Analyst)—have been reviewed independently and listed on the National Registry of Evidence-based Programs and Practices of the Substance Abuse and Mental Health Services Administration (2012). The registry identifies mental health and substance abuse interventions that have met national criteria for evidence of positive outcomes and readiness for implementation. Both systems were purposely designed to be used across treatment modalities, diagnoses, and professional discipline. They are simple, require little time to administer and score, and yield valid and reliable measures of client progress. PCOMS includes a scale for assessing the quality of the therapeutic relationship, a robust predictor of client engagement and outcome (Norcross, 2010; Orlinsky, Rønnestad, & Willutzki, 2004; Wampold & Imel, 2015). OQ-Analyst provides additional information about the alliance, patient motivation, social supports, and negative life events.

Lead versus Lag Measures

Although the measurement of outcomes is essential for determining one's effectiveness level, it is not enough to aid in professional development or improved performance. Indeed, focusing exclusively on outcomes cannot lead to better results as doing so does not inform the performer about *how* or *what* to improve. On this score, distinguishing between lead and lag measures is helpful (McChesney, Covey, & Huling, 2012). Briefly, *lag measures* are defined as penultimate or distal outcomes; in psychotherapy, for example, the ideal lag measure is improved client outcomes. *Lead measures* are those that predict, lead to, or impact lag measures. Using the simple example of losing weight, the lag outcome is pounds lost. Caloric intake and time spent exercising, both items within the performer's control, would be considered lead measures.

To aid in the identification of lead measures most likely to aid in individual practitioner development, Chow and Miller (2015) developed the Taxonomy of Deliberate Practice Activities Worksheets (TDPA).[1] Using the worksheets, clinicians and their supervisors routinely rate key aspects of the supervisee's work. The TDPA isolates multiple aspects of practice that are known to exert a high degree of influence on the lag measure of therapy: client outcomes. As the clinician progresses, developing mastery in a particular therapeutic domain, the target of deliberate practice efforts can shift.

Step 2: Feedback

The second step in fostering professional development is obtaining systematic, ongoing feedback. Therapists need to know when they are on the right track and be given direction when they are not. Lambert et al. (2001) were the first to document what happens when therapists are provided with ongoing feedback about the effectiveness of their work. In their study, alerting therapists to cases most at risk of failure resulted in better outcomes and reduced rates of dropout and deterioration.

Since that pioneering work, research on feedback has continued and accelerated. Positive findings have been reported in outpatient and inpatient settings, counseling and university training centers, individual and group therapies, and specialized treatment programs (Anker, Duncan, & Sparks, 2009; Berking, Orth, & Lutz, 2006; Bickman, Kelley, Breda, Andrade, & Riemer, 2011; Brodey et al., 2005; Byrne, Hooke, Newnham, & Page, 2012; Crits-Cristoph et al., 2012; De Jong et al., 2014; Hansson, Rundberg, Österling, Öjehagen, & Berglund, 2013; Harmon et al., 2007; Hawkins, Lambert, Vermeersch, Slade, & Tuttle, 2004;

---

1 To request a copy of the taxonomy, contact daryl@darylchow.com.

Murphy, Rashleigh, & Timulak, 2012; Probst et al., 2013; Probst, Lambert, Dahlbender, Loew, & Tritt, 2014; Reese, Norsworthy, & Rowlands, 2009; Reese, Toland, Slone, & Norsworthy, 2010; Reese, Usher et al., 2009; Schuman, Slone, Reese, & Duncan, 2015; Simon, Lambert, Harris, Busath, & Vazquez, 2012; Simon et al., 2013; Slade, Lambert, Harmon, Smart, & Bailey, 2008; Sorrell, 2007). To date, five meta-analyses demonstrate the consistently favorable impact of providing progress feedback to therapists: Lambert et al. (2003); Knaup, Koesters, Schoefer, and Puschner (2009); Shimokawa, Lambert, and Smart (2010); Lambert and Shimokawa (2011); and Davidson, Perry, and Bell (2015).

Consistent with studies on expert performance in other professions, research specific to psychotherapy underscores the importance of the availability, frequency, and immediacy of whatever feedback is provided. Without access to a formal system for assessing progress, therapists fail to predict or identify deterioration in their clients (Hannan et al., 2005; Hatfield, McCullough, Frantz, & Krieger, 2010). Making outcome data available to both clients and therapists enhances outcome (Hawkins et al., 2004). Pertaining to immediacy, Slade and colleagues (2008) found that feedback delivered at the time of service had a considerably larger impact than when delayed by 2 weeks. Even the mere anticipation of more immediate feedback, as opposed to delayed results, improves performance (Kettle & Haubl, 2010).

At present, both of the systems approved by the Substance Abuse and Mental Health Services Administration, PCOMS and OQ-Analyst, meet the requirements for the type and quality of feedback most likely to impact the course of treatment. The measures are administered when service is delivered. Client scores are immediately plotted against empirically established norms for progress and made available to the client and therapist. (See Figure 2.5.) If needed, treatment can be altered in real time whenever deviations from the expected trajectory are found.

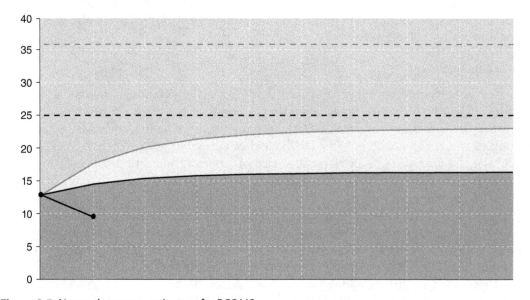

Figure 2.5 Normed progress trajectory for PCOMS.
Note. Client scores for two sessions are plotted as a thick black line against a normed trajectory. Scores falling in the light gray zone are predictive of eventual success; in the dark gray, an indeterminate result; and in the black, a negative or null outcome.

Clinical Supervision

Few supervisors use outcome monitoring as a tool (Swift et al., 2015). Working without information about the progress of a supervisee's clients is like the coach of a football team working without knowledge of the scoreboard. Worthen and Lambert (2007) suggested that to maximize improvement in those clients who are not responding to treatment, both therapists and supervisors need to monitor progress. To date, only one study has examined the use of such monitoring in supervision (Reese, Usher et al., 2009). Doing so resulted in statistically significant benefits in terms of client outcomes.

As the Goldberg, Rousmaniere et al. (2016) study cited earlier makes clear, receiving feedback about performance does not necessarily mean one is learning (Bjork & Bjork, 2011; see Figure 2.6). At the same time, learning may not necessarily result in improved performance in the short term. Thus, while systematic, session-by-session feedback about client progress is vital, feedback about how one is developing is also critical to success. The former may be called performance feedback (PF); the latter, learning feedback (LF).

As the name implies, PF is focused on outcomes as assessed by the lead and lag measures discussed earlier. LF, by contrast, refers to individualized performance objectives, the achievement of which can be assessed by the gradual acquisition of a well-defined skill set identified by the performer in collaboration with a supervisor/coach. For LF to be effective, the coach/supervisor focuses on the objective at hand, avoids criticizing the learner, and breaks the feedback provided into portions that are manageable and enable clinicians to reach beyond their current comfort zones (Shute, 2008). A basketball player, for example, receives immediate PF when shooting the ball. It either goes in the basket or does not. To improve, LF must take place. Before and after the game, the coach reviews video recordings and works with the player to identify small errors and develop specific skills. Similarly, a psychotherapist receives immediate PF about the quality of the relationship when a standardized alliance measure is administered at the end of a session. By reviewing audio or video recordings with a supervisor, therapists have the opportunity to receive LF about their performance.

Step 3: Successive Refinement

The accumulation of experience does not necessarily translate into increased expertise. Indeed, clinical experience is not and has never been a predictor of good outcomes (Beutler et al., 2004; Chow et al., 2015; Wampold & Brown, 2005). Similarly, as powerful an effect as

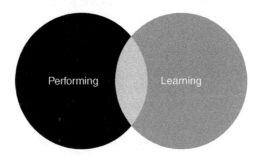

Figure 2.6 Differentiation between performance and learning.

measurement and feedback have on outcome, they are not enough to ensure professional development. Together, they function much like a global positioning system. Measurement pinpoints an operator's location and indicates progress toward the desired location. Feedback alerts drivers when they are off track, providing directions for resuming progress and even suggesting alternate routes. What the global positioning system does *not* do, however, is improve overall navigational skills or knowledge of the territory (Miller et al., 2007; Miller & Hubble, 2011).

More than a decade ago, Lambert pointed out practitioners did not improve in their ability to detect when cases were off track or at risk for dropout or deterioration, despite measuring and receiving feedback about their outcomes on a daily basis for 3 years (Miller, Duncan, & Hubble, 2004). De Jong, van Sluis, Nugter, Heiser, and Spinhoven (2012) later confirmed these findings. Clearly, to learn from the information that measurement and feedback provide, the third step of "successive refinement" is necessary. Going beyond mere "course correction," it entails setting aside time for self-reflection, identification of errors or deficiencies in one's performance, obtaining guidance, and then developing, rehearsing, executing, and continuously evaluating a plan for improvement, based on PT and LF.

With regard to specifics, individual therapists can use the data generated by whatever measures they employ to identify opportunities for professional development. Indeed, computerized outcome management systems provide an unprecedented wealth of data for profiling a particular practitioner's strengths and weaknesses. Therapists can, for example, examine their dropout, no-show, and deterioration rates. They can also determine whether these rates and their overall effectiveness vary depending on the presenting problem or client population.

Of the steps discussed thus far, step 3 is the most labor-intensive. Disciplined concentration and focus are required as performers push themselves to the limits of their abilities. Without planning ahead and dedicating time to the process—whether reflecting on and planning for a challenging case, reviewing a recording of a recent session, or becoming acquainted with a new area of clinical practice—the path of least resistance will be followed (Newport, 2016).

One fundamental element known to be highly predictive of therapeutic success is a clinician's ability to establish a working alliance (Norcross, 2010; Wampold & Imel, 2015). In the largest meta-analysis to date, involving 190 studies and more than 14,000 cases, Horvath, Del Re, Flückiger, and Symonds (2011) showed the alliance accounted for 8% of outcome variance. As noted in the discussion of the three components of domain-specific knowledge, knowing "what" is important—*content* knowledge—does not necessarily result into knowing "how"—*process* knowledge. (See Figure 2.2.) For example, despite awareness of the key role the alliance plays in a course of treatment, major differences obtain in therapists' ability to form and sustain helpful relationships (Baldwin, Wampold, & Imel, 2007). There is more. Research by Anderson and colleagues (2009) found that differences among therapists in the depth of their *conditional* knowledge—the "when" to do "what" one knows "how" to do—explained this variability. In that study, the more effective the clinicians, the more they were able to interact empathically and collaboratively when faced with a broader and more diverse group of clients and presenting complaints. Additionally, their interactions were much less likely to create interpersonal distance. More recently, Anderson, Crowley, Himanwan, Holmberg, and Uhlin (2015) found that therapists who scored higher in these relational skills obtained higher client-rated alliance scores than their colleagues from the outset of treatment.

Investigators have established that "healing involvement"—a practitioner's experience of an empathic, engaging, flexible, and constructive interpersonal interaction—tops therapists' aspirations (Orlinsky & Rønnestad, 2005). However, evidence suggests that therapists' self-perceived healing involvement is inversely related to their outcomes (Chow, 2014). That is, therapists who rate themselves higher on healing involvement tend to perform more poorly than their peers. Moreover, neither training nor time spent doing therapy has proven effective in enhancing clinician abilities in this area (Anderson et al., 2009, 2015; Horvath, 2001). A recent study by Chow, Lu, Owen, and Miller (2015) is an exception.

Chow et al. (2015) applied the three steps of deliberate practice to enhancing empathic attunement, a critical component of the therapeutic relationship. Empathy is not only one of the most consistent predictors of psychotherapy outcome; it is among the largest, having an effect size exceeding .6 (Wampold & Imel, 2015). In this study, participants watched a video depicting a difficult moment in a therapy session. The subjects were given a brief description of the client and instructed to respond as if the person were seated in front of them. The baseline performance of each subject was established by rating their responses to the video on a standardized scale of relational abilities (subscales of the Facilitative Interpersonal Skills; Anderson, Patterson, & Weis, 2007). In a second trial, no feedback was provided, but participants were given time and instructed to self-reflect in an attempt to improve their responses. In the third and fourth trials, participants watched the same video, followed by individualized LF derived from their scores. Again, LF was provided and time set aside for therapists to reflect on how they might improve their responses. In a fifth, and final trial, a new video was introduced involving a different client and presenting problem. Once more, participants responded and were rated, this time to determine whether any learning had generalized to the new scenario.

As illustrated in Figure 2.7, the provision of immediate, individualized LF, with time to reflect and plan for improvement, enhanced the subjects' ability to respond warmly, empathically, and collaboratively. More, these gains generalized to the new vignette.

Making Professional Development a Reality

> If we don't change direction, we'll end up where we're going.
> —*Professor Irwin Corey*

When it comes to professional development, two facts are apparent. The first, to the credit of practicing psychotherapists worldwide, is that they want to get better at what they do. This is not only a shared goal; it is a core value. The second is that the traditions and practices informing and comprising professional development do not work. When it comes to improving outcomes, the time, money, and effort expended—even mandated by licensing

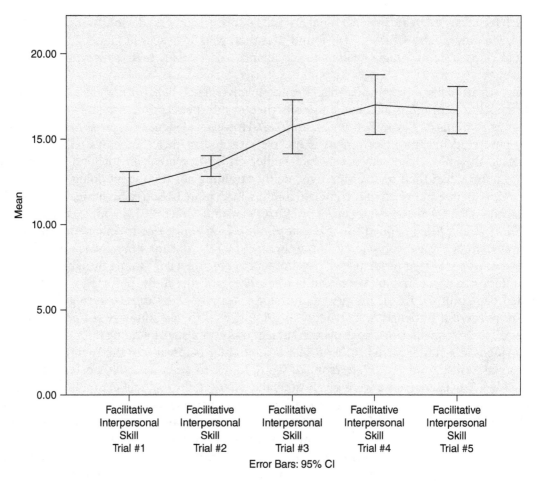

Figure 2.7 Mean scores based on subscales of the Facilitative Interpersonal Skills ratings across the five trials in difficult conversations in therapy.
Note. CI = confidence interval.

and certification bodies—are largely wasted. The overall effectiveness of psychotherapy has remained stagnant, and the results of individual clinicians do not improve with time, training, and experience.

Research from the field of expertise and expert performance provides an evidence-based alternative for making professional development a reality. Although its application to the field of psychotherapy is in its infancy, research to date is quite promising. Studies by Chow and colleagues (2015), for example, established the role deliberate practice plays in the development of highly effective therapists and its potential usefulness in fostering improvement in core therapeutic skills among individual practitioners. To date, one study has documented the results of consciously and planfully implementing the three steps of the "cycle of excellence" (Goldberg Babbins-Wagner et al., 2016). Specifically, routine outcome monitoring, combined with systematic feedback and deliberate practice, incrementally improved the outcomes of individual therapists and overall agency results. Notably, therapists continued improving every year over 7 years, highlighting the potentially large cumulative effect of small changes accrued over time (Ericsson et al., 1993; Imel, Sheng, Baldwin, & Atkins, 2015). The study further highlights the importance of establishing a social context—including policies, procedures, administrative approval, and funding—supportive of a culture of excellence (Ferlie & Shortell, 2001; Miller & Hubble, 2011). In the chapters that follow, the promise and possibilities of deliberate practice are presented and explored.

Questions from the Editors

Question #1. You mention that no one specific training activity reliably produces better outcomes and that what works for one therapist may not work for another. What advice do you have for therapists who want to experiment with deliberate practice and discover which training activities help them most?

Answer from Authors: One of the biggest challenges of deliberate practice (DP) is sustaining it. Therefore, a framework to aid experimentation and leveraging on key activities are important pillars to support such efforts. We use the acronym *ARPS* to stand for *a*utomated structure, *r*eference point, *p*layful experimentations, and *s*upport (Chow, in press).

1. Automated Structure
   - Block out 1 hour a week for deliberate practice. Avoid bingeing, and stick to a time limit.
   - Plan on how you will spend your time for the week ahead (e.g., reflection, reviewing segments of a therapy recording).
   - Set up automated reminders for DP on your digital devices.
   - Set up a simple system to audio-video/audio-record your sessions. Make sure to obtain consent from clients. Explain that the aim of the recordings is to improve your work with clients. Do not record when clients express discomfort. Automate this decision making with recording as a default mode.
2. Reference Point
   - Keep one eye on your outcome data (individual cases and aggregated performance indices) and the other eye on systematically monitoring your learning objectives. The TDPA can greatly assist in tracking your professional development based on defined learning objectives that you have specified with the help of a clinical supervisor/coach. With continuous use of the TDPA, key learning objectives are likely to change and evolve.
   - At the end of each workweek, utilize a note-taking app (e.g., simplenote.com or evernote.com) to jot down your weekly learnings. Borrowing from Twitter's philosophy of constraint, limit yourself to 140 words. Just ask yourself: Based on my week's worth of clinical engagement, what is the one thing that stands out, that WE want to remember?
   - As mentioned in the chapter, we highly encourage recording your sessions. As you start out in your DP efforts, pick a session that stands out as representative of you at your best. Analyze the session and tease out what makes it stand out. Then get your supervisor/coach to review it, and elicit feedback from him or her.

3. Playful Experimentation
   - Watch a 5- to 10-minute segment of your therapy recording. Pause and consider how you might carry on the session more constructively.
   - Highly effective therapists report being more surprised by clients' feedback than their average cohorts (Chow, 2014). Seek to be disconfirmed by your clients' feedback rather than to be confirmed. Without looking at client scores, fill out the alliance measure at the same time as your client. Compare and contrast the ratings. Ask what surprises you about how your client scored the alliance.
4. Support
   - Seek out a supervisor/coach who is willing to do three key things:
     1. He or she must be willing to analyze your therapy recording segments rather than just talk about the sessions.
     2. He or she incorporates the outcome and alliance information into the discussion.
     3. Your supervisor/coach should not only discuss cases with you; rather, he or she should help you develop key learning objectives to guide your professional development.
   - Form a small community of practitioners as dedicated as you are to reaching for excellence. When no one is available locally, reach out globally. The technology available today can help to facilitate these connections.

Question #2. Please describe an example of a therapist who has used deliberate practice and the Cycle of Excellence to improve their clinical effectiveness.

Answer from Authors: Using the ARPS framework mentioned in the last question, here's an example of a therapist working in a mental health institution who employs the key principles of DP.

1. Automated Structure

   Jean, who is trained as a psychologist with 8 years of experience, sets aside two batches of periods for DP in her Google calendar (set to repeat). Once a week is devoted to solitary deliberate practice (e.g., reviewing of cases that are at risk of poor outcomes, watching 5- to10-minute segments of such cases, and inquiry learning on specific content that she lacks knowledge in when needed).

   The other period is set aside for fortnightly supervision. Jean brings in the at-risk cases for discussion. She brings into the supervision session outcomes and alliance information, along with the video recording segments.

   Jean uses her laptop as a straightforward video-recording system. She learns from experience and discussion with her colleagues that opting out of recording is due more to the therapist's discomfort than to the client's.

2. Reference Point

   Jean routinely reviews her outcomes on her outcome management system, coupled with the TDPA that she has established with her supervisor, which reminds her of her key learning objective at that point in time.

   She also writes down her weekly learnings on Fridays in her iPhone Notes app, indicating the date for each "therapy learning." By the end of a year, she will have approximately 40 to 45 individualized learnings that she can review and reflect on.

3. Playful Experimentation

During her weekly DP, Jean watches a 10-minute segment of her therapy recording that is not going well. She pauses it and reflects on how she can better engage the client. She writes out longhand how she will deal with this situation differently.

During her clinical practice, she would score the Session Rating Scale, attempting to predict how the client would rate it. Jean would then compare and contrast, and use any discrepancy to guide her questions in eliciting feedback.

4. Support

Jean has the support of her supervisor. Unfortunately, she is rather a lone voice in her efforts in DP. Her supervisor is not on staff at her agency. Jean struggles to form a small community of practitioners for support and is now seeking connections outside of her workplace.

Question #3. You mention that deliberate practice is "hard work" that takes time, energy, and money, three resources that therapists at all career stages may have in limited supply. What advice do you have for busy therapists who want to try to fit deliberate practice into their schedule?

Answer from Authors: The key is not to try to "fit" in deliberate practice. Build it into the workweek (see "1. Automated Structure" in our response to Question #1). Protect it like sacred ground.

Let's face it: We are all busy. If we leave it to our ongoing week-by-week decision making, we will not have the time to do something that is not immediately rewarding. What is more, it is cognitively taxing always trying to fit in time for hard work. We would rather attend to what is knocking on doors right now.

References

American Psychological Association. (2012, August 9). *Resolution on the recognition of psychotherapy effectiveness. American Psychological Association.* Retrieved from http://www.apa.org/about/policy/resolution-psychotherapy.aspx

Anderson, T., Crowley, M.E.J., Himawan, L., Holmberg, J. K., & Uhlin, B. D. (2015, September). Therapist facilitative interpersonal skills and training status: A randomized clinical trial on alliance and outcome. *Psychotherapy Research, 26,* 511–519. doi:10.1080/10503307.2015.1049671

Anderson, T., Ogles, B. M., Patterson, C. L., Lambert, M. J., & Vermeersch, D. A. (2009). Therapist effects: Facilitative interpersonal skills as a predictor of therapist success. *Journal of Clinical Psychology, 65*(7), 755–768. doi:10.1002/jclp.20583

Anderson, T., Patterson, C. L., & Weis, A. (2007). *Facilitative interpersonal skills performance analysis rating method.* Unpublished coding manual. Department of Psychology, Ohio University, Athens, OH.

Anker, M. G., Duncan, B. L., & Sparks, J. A. (2009). Using client feedback to improve couple therapy outcomes: A randomized clinical trial in a naturalistic setting. *Journal of Consulting & Clinical Psychology, 77*(4), 693–704.

Baldwin, S. A., Wampold, B. E., & Imel, Z. E. (2007). Untangling the alliance–outcome correlation: Exploring the relative importance of therapist and patient variability in the alliance. *Journal of Consulting & Clinical Psychology, 75*(6), 842–852. doi:10.1037/0022-006X.75.6.842

Barkham, M., Connell, J., Stiles, W. B., Miles, J. N., Margison, F., Evans, C., & Mellor-Clark, J. (2006). Dose–effect relations and responsive regulation of treatment duration: The good enough level. *Journal of Consulting and Clinical Psychology, 74*(1), 160–167.

Berking, M., Orth, U., & Lutz, W. (2006). Wie effektiv sind systematische rückmeldungen des therapieverlaufs an den therapeuten? Eine empirische studie in einem stationär-verhaltenstherapeutischen setting. *Zeitschrift für Klinische Psychologie und Psychotherapie, 35*, 21–29.

Beutler, L. E., Malik, M., Alimohamed, S., Harwood, T. M., Talebi, H., Noble, S., & Wong, E. (2004). Therapist variables. In M. J. Lambert (Ed.), *Bergin and Garfield's handbook of psychotherapy and behavior change* (5th ed., pp. 227–306). Hoboken, NJ: Wiley.

Bickman, L., Kelley, S. D., Breda, C., Andrade, A.R.D., & Riemer, M. (2011). Effects of routine feedback to clinicians on mental health outcomes of youths: Results of a randomized trial. *Psychiatric Services, 62*(12), 1423–1429. doi:10.1176/appi.ps.002052011

Bjork, E. L., & Bjork, R. A. (2011). Making things hard on yourself, but in a good way: Creating desirable difficulties to enhance learning. In M. A. Gemsbacher, R. W. Pew, L. M. Hough, & J. R. Pomerantz (Eds.), *Psychology and the real world: Essays illustrating fundamental contributions to society* (pp. 56–64). New York, NY: Worth.

Boswell, J. F., Kraus, D. R., Miller, S. D., & Lambert, M. J. (2013). Implementing routine outcome monitoring in clinical practice: Benefits, challenges, and solutions. *Psychotherapy Research, 25*(1), 6–19. doi:10.1080/10503307.2013.817696

Brodey, B. B., Cuffel, B., McCulloch, J., Tani, S., Maruish, M., Brodey, I., & Unutzer, J. (2005). The acceptability and effectiveness of patient-reported assessments and feedback in a managed behavioral healthcare setting. *American Journal of Managed Care, 11*(12), 774–780.

Byrne, S. L., Hooke, G. R., Newnham, E. A., & Page, A. C. (2012). The effects of progress monitoring on subsequent readmission to psychiatric care: A six-month follow-up. *Journal of Affective Disorders, 137*(1–3), 113–116. doi:10.1016/j.jad.2011.12.005

Charness, N., Tuffiash, M., Krampe, R., Reingold, E., & Vasyukova, E. (2005). The role of deliberate practice in chess expertise. *Applied Cognitive Psychology, 19*(2), 151–165. doi: http://doi.org/10.1002/acp.1106

Chow, D. (2014). *The study of supershrinks: Development and deliberate practices of highly effective psychotherapists* (Doctoral dissertation). Curtin University, Australia. Retrieved from http://www.academia.edu/9355521/The_Study_of_Supershrinks_Development_and_Deliberate_Practices_of_Highly_Effective_Psychotherapists_PhD_Dissertation_

Chow, D. (in press). The practice and the practical: Pushing your clinical effectiveness to the next level. In D. Prescott, C. Maeschalck, & S. D. Miller (Eds.), *Reaching for excellence: Feedback-informed treatment in practice*. Washington, DC: American Psychological Association.

Chow, D., Lu, S., Owen, J., & Miller, S. D. (2015). *Difficult conversations in therapy (DCT): Can psychotherapists learn in an environment of immediate feedback with simulated client video vignettes*. Manuscript in preparation.

Chow, D., & Miller, S. D. (2012). *Retrospective analysis of psychotherapists' involvement in deliberate practice (RAPIDPractice)*. Unpublished manuscript.

Chow, D., & Miller, S. (2015). *Taxonomy of deliberate practice*. Chicago, IL: ICCE.

Chow, D., Miller, S. D., Seidel, J. A., Kane, R. T., Thornton, J., & Andrews, W. P. (2015). The role of deliberate practice in the development of highly effective psychotherapists. *Psychotherapy, 52*(3), 337–345. doi:http://doi.org/10.1037/pst0000015

Clement, P. W. (1994). Quantitative evaluation of 26 years of private practice. *Professional Psychology: Research and Practice, 25*(2), 173–176. doi:http://doi.org/10.1037/0735-7028.25.2.173

Colvin, G. (2008). *Talent is overrated: What really separates world-class performers from everybody else*. London, UK: Nicholas Brealey.

Corcoran, K., & Fischer, J. (2013). *Measures for clinical practice and research: A sourcebook* (5th ed.). Oxford, UK: Oxford University Press.

Coyle, D. (2008). *Talent code*. New York, NY: Bantam Books.

Crits-Christoph, P., & Mintz, J. (1991). Implications of therapist effects for the design and analysis of comparative studies of psychotherapies. *Journal of Consulting and Clinical Psychology, 59*, 20–26.

Crits-Christoph, P., Ring-Kurtz, S., Hamilton, J. L., Lambert, M. J., Gallop, R., McClure, B., . . . Rotrosen, J. (2012). A preliminary study of the effects of individual patient-level feedback in outpatient substance abuse treatment programs. *Journal of Substance Abuse Treatment, 42*(3), 301–309. doi:http://doi.org/10.1016/j.jsat.2011.09.003

Davidson, K., Perry, A., & Bell, L. (2015). Would continuous feedback of patient's clinical outcomes to practitioners improve NHS psychological therapy services? Critical analysis and assessment of quality of existing studies. *Psychology and Psychotherapy: Theory, Research and Practice, 88*(1), 21–37. doi:10.1111/papt.12032

De Jong, K., Timman, R., Hakkaart-Van Roijen, L., Vermeulen, P., Kooiman, K., Passchier, J., & Busschbach, J. V. (2014). The effect of outcome monitoring feedback to clinicians and patients in short and long-term psychotherapy: A randomized controlled trial. *Psychotherapy Research, 24*(6), 629–639. doi:10.1080/10503307.2013.871079

De Jong, K., van Sluis, P., Nugter, M. A., Heiser, W. J., & Spinhoven, P. (2012). Understanding the differential impact of outcome monitoring: Therapist variables that moderate feedback effects in a randomized clinical trial. *Psychotherapy Research, 22*(4), 464–474. doi:10.1080/1 0503307.2012.673023

Duckworth, A. L., Kirby, T. A., Tsukayama, E., Berstein, H., & Ericsson, K. (2011). Deliberate practice spells success: Why grittier competitors triumph at the National Spelling Bee. *Social Psychological and Personality Science, 2*(2), 174–181. doi:http://doi.org/10.1177/1948550610385872

Duncan, B. L., Miller, S. D., Wampold, B. E., & Hubble, M. A. (Eds.). (2010). *The heart and soul of change: Delivering what works in therapy* (2nd ed.). Washington, DC: American Psychological Association.

Edmundson, G. (2004). *The ostrich factor: A practice guide for magicians*. Denton, TX: Author.

Ericsson, A. K. (1996). The acquisition of expert performance: An introduction to some of the issues. In K. A. Ericsson (Ed.), *The road to excellence: The acquisition of expert performance in the arts and sciences, sports, and games* (pp. 1–50). Mahwah, NJ: Erlbaum.

Ericsson, K. A. (2004). Deliberate practice and the acquisition and maintenance of expert performance in medicine and related domains. *Academic Medicine, 79*(10 Suppl.), 988–994. doi:10.1111/j.1553-2712.2008.00227.x

Ericsson, K. A. (2006). The influence of experience and deliberate practice on the development of superior expert performance. In K. A. Ericsson, N. Charness, P. J. Feltovich, & R. R. Hoffman (Eds.), *The Cambridge handbook of expertise and expert performance* (pp. 683–703). Cambridge, UK: Cambridge University Press.

Ericsson, K. A. (Ed.) (2009). *Development of professional expertise: Toward measurement of expert performance and design of optimal learning environments.* New York, NY: Cambridge University Press.

Ericsson, K. A., & Charness, N. (1994). Expert performance: Its structure and acquisition. *American Psychologist, 49*(8), 725–747.

Ericsson, K. A., Charness, N., Feltovich, P. J., & Hoffman, R. R. (Eds.). (2006). *The Cambridge handbook of expertise and expert performance.* Cambridge, UK: Cambridge University Press.

Ericsson, K. A., Krampe, R. T., & Tesch-Romer, C. (1993). The role of deliberate practice in the acquisition of expert performance. *Psychological Review, 100*(3), 363–406.

Ericsson, K. A., & Lehmann, A. C. (1996). Expert and exceptional performance: Evidence of maximal adaptation to task constraints. *Annual Review of Psychology, 47*(1), 273–305. doi:10.1146/annurev.psych.47.1.273

Ericsson, K. A., Nandagopal, K., & Roring, R. W. (2009). Toward a science of exceptional achievement: Attaining superior performance through deliberate practice. In W. C. Bushell, E. L. Olivio, & N. D. Theise (Eds.), *Longevity, regeneration, and optimal health: Integrating Eastern and Western perspectives (Annals of the New York Academy of Sciences)* (pp. 199–217). Hoboken, NJ: Wiley-Blackwell.

Ericsson, K. A., & Staszewski, J. J. (1989). Skilled memory and expertise: Mechanisms of exceptional performance. In D. Klahr & K. Kotovsky (Eds.), *Complex information processing: The impact of Herbert A. Simon* (pp. 235–267). Hillsdale, NJ: Erlbaum.

Eysenck, H. J. (1952). The effects of psychotherapy: An evaluation. *Journal of Consulting Psychology, 16,* 319–324. doi:10.1037/h0063633

Feltovich, P. J., Prietula, M. J., & Ericsson, K. (2006). Studies of expertise from psychological perspectives. In K. A. Ericsson, N. Charness, P. J. Feltovich, & R. R. Hoffman (Eds.), *The Cambridge handbook of expertise and expert performance* (pp. 41–67). Cambridge, UK: Cambridge University Press.

Ferlie, E. B., & Shortell, S. M. (2001). Improving the quality of health care in the United Kingdom and the United States: A framework for change. *Milbank Quarterly, 79*(2), 281–315.

Froyd, J., & Lambert, M. (1989, May). *A 5-year survey of outcome measures in psychotherapy research.* Paper presented at the Western Psychological Association Conference, Reno, NV.

Galdwell, M. (2008). *Outliers: The story of success.* New York, NY: Little, Brown.

Garfield, S. L. (1997). The therapist as a neglected variable in psychotherapy research. *Clinical Psychology: Science & Practice, 4*(1), 40–43.

Garner, C. (2010). *Readings: From the client's point of view.* Auckland, NZ: Brookfield Press.

Geller, J. D., Norcross, J. C., & Orlinsky, D. E. (Eds.). (2005). *The psychotherapist's own psychotherapy: Patient and clinician perspectives.* Oxford, UK: Oxford University Press.

Goldberg, S. B., Babins-Wagner, R., Rousmaniere, T. G., Berzins, S., Hoyt, W. T., Whipple, J. L., . . . Wampold, B. E. (2016). Creating a climate for therapist improvement: A case study of an agency focused on outcomes and deliberate practice. *Psychotherapy, 53,* 367–375.

Goldberg, S. B., Rousmaniere, T., Miller, S. D., Whipple, J., Nielsen, S. L., Hoyt, W. T., & Wampold, B. E. (2016). Do psychotherapists improve with time and experience? A longitudinal analysis of outcomes in a clinical setting. *Journal of Counseling Psychology, 63,* 1–11.

Hannan, C., Lambert, M. J., Harmon, C., Nielsen, S. L., Smart, D. W., Shimokawa, K., & Sutton, S. W. (2005). A lab test and algorithms for identifying clients at risk for treatment failure. *Journal of Clinical Psychology, 61*(2), 155–163. doi:10.1002/jclp.20108

Hansson, H., Rundberg, J., Österling, A., Öjehagen, A., & Berglund, M. (2013). Intervention with feedback using Outcome Questionnaire 45 (OQ-45) in a Swedish psychiatric outpatient population: A randomized controlled trial. *Nordic Journal of Psychiatry, 67*(4), 274–281. doi:10.3109/08039488.2012.736534

Harmon, S., Lambert, M. J., Smart, D. M., Hawkins, E., Nielsen, S. L., Slade, K., & Lutz, W. (2007). Enhancing outcome for potential treatment failures: Therapist–client feedback and clinical support tools. *Psychotherapy Research, 17*(4), 379–392. doi:http://doi.org/10.1080/10503300600702331

Hatfield, D., McCullough, L., Frantz, S.H.B., & Krieger, K. (2010). Do we know when our clients get worse? An investigation of therapists' ability to detect negative client change. *Clinical Psychology & Psychotherapy, 17*(1), 25–32. doi:10.1002/cpp.656

Hawkins, E. J., Lambert, M. J., Vermeersch, D. A., Slade, K. L., & Tuttle, K. C. (2004). The therapeutic effects of providing patient progress information to therapists and patients. *Psychotherapy Research, 14*(3), 308–327. doi:10.1093/ptr/kph027

Heath, D. (2012). Foreword. In D. Lemov, E. Woolway, & K. Yezzi, *Practice perfect: 42 ways of getting better at getting better.* San Francisco, CA: Jossey-Bass.

Hiatt, D., & Hargrave, G. (1995). The characteristics of highly effective therapists in managed behavioral providers networks. *Behavioral Healthcare Tomorrow, 4,* 19–22.

Horvath, A. O. (2001). The alliance. *Psychotherapy: Theory, Research, Practice, Training, 38*(4), 365–372. doi:http://doi.org/10.1037/0033-3204.38.4.365

Horvath, A. O., Del Re, A., Flückiger, C., & Symonds, D. (2011). Alliance in individual psychotherapy. *Psychotherapy: Theory, Research, Practice, Training, 48*(1), 9–16. doi:10.1037/a0022186

Hubble, M. A., Duncan, B. L., & Miller, S. D. (1999). *The heart and soul of change: What works in therapy* (pp. xxiv, 462). Washington, DC: American Psychological Association.

Imel, Z. E., Sheng, E., Baldwin, S. A., & Atkins, D. C. (2015). Removing very low-performing therapists: A simulation of performance-based retention in psychotherapy. *Psychotherapy, 52*(3), 329–336. doi:http://doi.org/10.1037/pst0000023

Kahneman, D. (2011). *Thinking, fast and slow.* New York, NY: Farrar, Straus and Giroux.

Keith, N., & Ericsson, K. (2007). A deliberate practice account of typing proficiency in everyday typists. *Journal of Experimental Psychology: Applied, 13*(3), 135–145. doi:http://doi.org/10.1037/1076-898X.13.3.135

Kettle, K. L., & Haubl, G. (2010). Motivation by anticipation: Expecting rapid feedback enhances performance. *Psychological Science, 21*(4), 545–547. doi:10.1177/09567976103 63541

Knaup, C., Koesters, M., Schoefer, D., Becker, T., & Puschner, B. (2009). Effect of feedback of treatment outcome in specialist mental healthcare: meta-analysis. *British Journal of Psychiatry, 195*(1), 15–22. doi:10.1192/bjp.bp.108.053967

Krampe, R., & Ericsson, K. (1996). Maintaining excellence: Deliberate practice and elite performance in young and older pianists. *Journal of Experimental Psychology: General, 125*(4), 331–359.

Kruger, J. (1999). Lake Wobegon be gone! The "below-average effect" and the egocentric nature of comparative ability judgments. *Journal of Personality and Social Psychology, 77*(2), 221–232. doi:http://doi.org/10.1037/0022-3514.77.2.221

Lambert, M. J. (2012). Helping clinicians to use and learn from research-based systems: The OQ-Analyst. *Psychotherapy: Theory, Research, Practice, Training, 49*(2), 109–114.

Lambert, M. J., & Shimokawa, K. (2011). Collecting client feedback. *Psychotherapy: Theory, Research, Practice, Training, 48*(1), 72–79. doi:10.1037/a0022238

Lambert, M. J., Whipple, J. L., Hawkins, E. J., Vermeersch, D. A., Nielsen, S. L., & Smart, D. W. (2003). Is it time for clinicians to routinely track patient outcome? A meta-analysis. *Clinical Psychology: Science and Practice, 10*(3), 288–301. doi:http://doi.org/10.1093/clipsy/bpg025

Lambert, M. J., Whipple, J. L., Smart, D. W., Vermeersch, D. A., Nielsen, S. L., & Hawkins, E. J. (2001). The effects of providing therapists with feedback on patient progress during psychotherapy: Are outcomes enhanced? *Psychotherapy Research, 11*(1), 49–68. doi:10.1080/713663852

Luborsky, L., McClellan, A. T., Woody, G. E., O'Brien, C. P., & Auerbach, A. (1985). Therapist success and its determinants. *Archives of General Psychiatry, 42*(6), 602–611.

Malikiosi-Loizos, M. (2013). Personal therapy for future therapists: Reflections on a still debated issue. *European Journal of Counselling Psychology, 2*(1), 33–50. doi:10.5964/ejcop.v2i1.4

Malouff, J. (2012). The need for empirically supported psychology training standards. *Psychotherapy in Australia, 18*(3), 28–32. Retrieved from http://search.informit.com.au/documentSummary;dn=316992349249508;res=IELHEA

McChesney, C., Covey, S., & Huling, J. (2012). *The 4 disciplines of execution.* London, UK: Simon and Schuster.

Miller, S. D., Duncan, B. L., & Hubble, M. A. (2004). Beyond integration: The triumph of outcome over process in clinical practice. *Psychotherapy in Australia, 10*, 2–19.

Miller, S. D., Duncan, B. L., Sorrell, R., & Brown, G. S. (2005, February). The Partners for Change Outcome Management System. *Journal of Clinical Psychology, 61*(2), 199–208.

Miller, S. D., & Hubble, M. (2011). The road to mastery. *Psychotherapy Networker, 35*(3), 22–31.

Miller, S., & Hubble, M. (2015). Burnout reconsidered. *Psychotherapy Networker, 39*, 18–23, 42–43.

Miller, S. D., Hubble, M. A., Chow, D. L., & Seidel, J. A. (2013). The outcome of psychotherapy: Yesterday, today, and tomorrow. *Psychotherapy, 50*(1), 88–97. doi:10.1037/a0031097

Miller, S. D., Hubble, M. A., & Duncan, B. L. (2007). Supershrinks: What's the secret of their success? *Psychotherapy Networker, 31*(6), 27–35, 56. Retrieved from http://proquest.umi.

com.dbgw.lis.curtin.edu.au/pqdweb?did=1378057261&Fmt=7&clientId=22212&RQT=309&VName=PQD

Minami, T., Serlin, R., Wampold, B., Kircher, J., & Brown, G. (2008). Using clinical trials to benchmark effects produced in clinical practice. *Quality and Quantity, 42*(4), 513–525.

Murphy, K. P., Rashleigh, C. M., & Timulak, L. (2012). The relationship between progress feedback and therapeutic outcome in student counselling: A randomised control trial. *Counselling Psychology Quarterly, 25*(1), 1–18. doi:10.1080/09515070.2012.662349

Neimeyer, G. J., Taylor, J. M., & Wear, D. M. (2009). Continuing education in psychology: Outcomes, evaluations, and mandates. *Professional Psychology: Research and Practice, 40*(6), 617–624. doi:http://doi.org/10.1037/a0016655

Newport, C. (2016). *Deep work: Rules for focused success in a distracted world.* London, UK: Piatkus.

Norcross, J. C. (2010). The therapeutic relationship. In B. L. Duncan, S. D. Miller, B. E. Wampold, & M. A. Hubble (Eds.), *The heart and soul of change: Delivering what works in therapy* (pp. 113–142). Washington, DC: American Psychological Association.

Ogles, B. M., Lambert, M. J., & Masters, K. S. (1996). *Assessing outcome in clinical practice.* Boston, MA: Allyn and Bacon.

Okiishi, J. C., Lambert, M. J., Eggett, D., Nielsen, L., Dayton, D. D., & Vermeersch, D. A. (2006). An analysis of therapist treatment effects: Toward providing feedback to individual therapists on their clients' psychotherapy outcome. *Journal of Clinical Psychology, 62*(9), 1157–1172.

Okiishi, J. C., Lambert, M. J., Nielsen, S. L., & Ogles, B. M. (2003). Waiting for supershrink: An empirical analysis of therapist effects. *Clinical Psychology & Psychotherapy, 10*(6), 361–373. doi:http://doi.org/10.1002/cpp.383

Orlinsky, D. E., & Rønnestad, M. H. (2005). *How psychotherapists develop: A study of therapeutic work and professional growth.* Washington, DC: American Psychological Association.

Orlinsky, D. E., Rønnestad, M. H., & Willutzuki, U. (2004). Fifty years of psychotherapy process-outcome research: Continuity and change. In M. Lambert (Ed.), *Bergin and Garfield's handbook of psychotherapy and behavior change* (5th ed., pp. 307–389). Hoboken, NJ: Wiley.

PCOMS. (2013). *Partners for Change Outcome Management System: International Center for Clinical Excellence Version.* Retrieved from http://legacy.nreppadmin.net/ViewIntervention.aspx?id=249

Probst, T., Lambert, M. J., Dahlbender, R. W., Loew, T. H., & Tritt, K. (2014). Providing patient progress feedback and clinical support tools to therapists: Is the therapeutic process of patients on-track to recovery enhanced in psychosomatic in-patient therapy under the conditions of routine practice? *Journal of Psychosomatic Research, 76*(6), 477–484. doi: http://doi.org/10.1016/j.jpsychores.2014.03.010

Probst, T., Lambert, M. J., Loew, T. H., Dahlbender, R. W., Göllner, R., & Tritt, K. (2013). Feedback on patient progress and clinical support tools for therapists: Improved outcome for patients at risk of treatment failure in psychosomatic in-patient therapy under the conditions of routine practice. *Journal of Psychosomatic Research, 75*(3), 255–261. doi:http://doi.org/10.1016/j.jpsychores.2013.07.003

Reese, R. J., Norsworthy, L. A., & Rowlands, S. R. (2009). Does a continuous feedback system improve psychotherapy outcome? *Psychotherapy: Theory, Research, Practice, Training, 46*(4), 418–431. doi:http://doi.org/10.1037/a0017901

Reese, R. J., Toland, M. D., Slone, N. C., & Norsworthy, L. A. (2010). Effect of client feedback on couple psychotherapy outcomes. *Psychotherapy: Theory, Research, Practice, Training, 47*(4), 616–630. Retrieved from http://ovidsp.ovid.com/ovidweb.cgi?T=JS&CSC=Y&NEWS =N&PAGE=fulltext&D=ovftk&AN=00011673-201004740-00015

Reese, R. J., Usher, E. L., Bowman, D. C., Norsworthy, L. A., Halstead, J. L., Rowlands, S. R., & Chisholm, R. R. (2009). Using client feedback in psychotherapy training: An analysis of its influence on supervision and counselor self-efficacy. *Training and Education in Professional Psychology, 3*(3), 157–168. doi:http://doi.org/10.1037/a0015673

Rogers, C. R. (1939). *The clinical treatment of the problem child.* Boston, MA: Houghton Mifflin.

Rohrer, D., & Taylor, K. (2007). The shuffling of mathematics practice problems improves learning. *Instructional Science, 35,* 481–498.

Rønnestad, M., & Orlinsky, D. (2005). Therapeutic work and professional development: Main findings and practical implications of a long-term international study. *Psychotherapy Bulletin, 40,* 27–32.

Rousmaniere, T. G., Swift, J. K., Babins-Wagner, R., Whipple, J. L., & Berzins, S. (2016). Supervisor variance in psychotherapy outcome in routine practice. *Psychotherapy Research, 26*(2), 196–205. doi:10.1080/10503307.2014.963730

Schuman, D. L., Slone, N. C., Reese, R. J., & Duncan, B. (2015). Efficacy of client feedback in group psychotherapy with soldiers referred for substance abuse treatment. *Psychotherapy Research, 25*(4), 396–407. doi:10.1080/10503307.2014.900875

Shimokawa, K., Lambert, M. J., & Smart, D. W. (2010). Enhancing treatment outcome of patients at risk of treatment failure: Meta-a and mega-analytic review of a psychotherapy quality assurance system. *Journal of Consulting and Clinical Psychology, 78*(3), 298–311. doi:10.1037/a0019247

Shute, V. J. (2008). Focus on formative feedback. *Review of Educational Research, 78*(1), 153–189. doi:http://doi.org/10.3102/0034654307313795

Simon, W., Lambert, M. J., Busath, G., Vazquez, A., Berkeljon, A., Hyer, K., . . . Berrett, M. (2013). Effects of providing patient progress feedback and clinical support tools to psychotherapists in an inpatient eating disorders treatment program: A randomized controlled study. *Psychotherapy Research, 23*(3), 287–300. doi:10.1080/10503307.2013.787497

Simon, W., Lambert, M. J., Harris, M. W., Busath, G., & Vazquez, A. (2012). Providing patient progress information and clinical support tools to therapists: Effects on patients at risk of treatment failure. *Psychotherapy Research, 22*(6), 1–10. doi:10.1080/10503307.2012.698918

Slade, K., Lambert, M. J., Harmon, S. C., Smart, D. W., & Bailey, R. (2008). Improving psychotherapy outcome: The use of immediate electronic feedback and revised clinical support tools. *Clinical Psychology & Psychotherapy, 15*(5), 287–303. doi:10.1002/cpp.594

Sorrell, R. (2007). Application of an outcome-directed behavioral modification model for obesity on a telephonic/web-based platform. *Disease Management, 10,* S23–26.

Starkes, J. L., Deakin, J. M., Allard, F., Hodges, N., & Hayes, A. (1996). Deliberate practice in sports: What is it anyway? In K. A. Ericsson (Ed.), *The road to excellence: The acquisition of expert performance in the arts and sciences, sports, and games* (pp. 81–106). Mahwah, NJ: Erlbaum.

Substance Abuse and Mental Health Services Administration. (2012). *Partners for Change Outcome Management System (PCOMS): International Center for Clinical Excellence.* Retrieved from http://legacy.nreppadmin.net/ViewIntervention.aspx?id=249

Swift, J. K., Callahan, J., Rousmaniere, T., Whipple, J. L., Dexter, K., & Wrape, E. R. (2015). Using client outcome monitoring as a tool for supervision. *Psychotherapy, 52*(2), 180–184. doi:http://doi.org/10.1037/a0037659

Walfish, S., McAlister, B., O'Donnell, P., & Lambert, M. J. (2012). An investigation of self-assessment bias in mental health providers. *Psychological Reports, 110*(2), 639–644. doi:http://doi.org/10.2466/02.07.17.PR0.110.2.639-644

Wampold, B. E. (2001). *The great psychotherapy debate: Models, methods and findings.* Mahwah, NJ: Erlbaum.

Wampold, B. E., & Brown, G. S. (2005). Estimating variability in outcomes attributable to therapists: A naturalistic study of outcomes in managed care. *Journal of Consulting & Clinical Psychology, 73*(5), 914–923. doi:10.1037/0022-006X.73.5.914

Wampold, B. E., & Imel, Z. E. (2015). *The great psychotherapy debate: The evidence for what makes psychotherapy work* (2nd ed.). New York, NY: Routledge.

Watkins, C. E. (2011). Does psychotherapy supervision contribute to patient outcomes? Considering thirty years of research. *Clinical Supervisor, 30*(2), 235–256. doi:10.1080/07325223.2011.619417

Webb, C. A., DeRubeis, R. J., & Barber, J. P. (2010). Therapist adherence/competence and treatment outcome: A meta-analytic review. *Journal of Consulting and Clinical Psychology, 78*(2), 200–211. doi:http://doi.org/10.1037/a0018912

Worthen, V. E., & Lambert, M. J. (2007). Outcome oriented supervision: Advantages of adding systematic client tracking to supportive consultations. *Counselling & Psychotherapy Research, 7*(1), 48–53. doi:http://doi.org/10.1080/14733140601140873

3

What Should We Practice?

A Contextual Model for How Psychotherapy Works

Bruce E. Wampold

A basic tenet of deliberate practice is, of course, practice. But *what* should we practice? Clearly, we should practice those skills that lead to better outcomes. But what are these skills? Unfortunately, various theoretical perspectives emphasize particular therapeutic actions that are thought to produce therapeutic benefits. Even within a theoretical orientation, supervisors may emphasize some skills over others or focus idiosyncratically on an aspect of therapy that they think is important.

In every profession, practitioners need to develop and refine skills that lead to improved performance and eschew spending time on skills that are irrelevant to performance. In psychotherapy, this is problematic for one of several reasons (Tracey, Wampold, Lichtenberg, & Goodyear, 2014). First, the skills we discuss in our field are often therapy-specific—for example, a behavior therapist may be taught the skills necessary to conduct prolonged exposure for posttraumatic stress disorder (PTSD) while another therapist may learn what is involved in eye movement desensitization and reprocessing. The issue is that the specific ingredients have not been shown to be what makes these treatments effective—when the ingredients are removed from therapies, the treatments seem to remain as effective as they were with the ingredient (Ahn & Wampold, 2001; Bell, Marcus, & Goodlad, 2013). Furthermore, as discussed in this chapter, adherence to the treatment protocol does not result in better outcomes (Webb, DeRubeis, & Barber, 2010), and the rated competence with which the specific ingredients of the treatment are delivered is not related to outcome (Branson, Shafran, & Myles, 2015; Webb et al., 2010). Moreover, a related problem is that there is variability in the outcome of therapists within therapeutic orientations (Baldwin & Imel, 2013)—that is, some therapists delivering Treatment A consistently achieve better outcomes than other therapists delivering the very same treatment. This seems to be true in clinical trials as well as in practice and is unrelated to the degree to which the therapist adheres to the treatment protocol (Wampold & Imel, 2015). Ergo, how one delivers a treatment is important, and one must learn the skills that make various treatments effective—delivering a treatment that has been designated as "evidence based" clearly is not sufficient to deliver the treatment effectively.

What is needed is a model that explains how psychotherapy works—that is, a model that specifies the key components of effective practice that have been identified by research

The Cycle of Excellence: Using Deliberate Practice to Improve Supervision and Training,
First Edition. Edited by Tony Rousmaniere, Rodney K. Goodyear, Scott D. Miller, and Bruce E. Wampold.
© 2017 John Wiley & Sons, Ltd. Published 2017 by John Wiley & Sons, Ltd.

evidence. In this chapter, I present a model for psychotherapy that is based on evidence related to what is known about how psychotherapy works and what is known about effective therapists. This model, called the "Contextual Model," is a meta-model because it is not an alternative to specific treatment models, such as cognitive behavioral therapy or emotion-focused therapy, but rather is a model that explains how all psychotherapies produce their benefits. This model is based on social science theory and research evidence from randomized clinical trials of psychotherapy as well as psychotherapy process research (Wampold & Imel, 2015). This model indicates a set of specific skills that should be the focus of deliberate practice.

Contextual Model

The Contextual Model (Wampold & Budge, 2012; Wampold & Imel, 2015) is a meta-model of how psychotherapy works. Psychotherapy is a complex process that unfolds over time. Thus, it is difficult to stipulate what makes psychotherapy work, yet there is theory and compelling evidence that psychotherapy exerts its effects through multiple pathways. The Contextual Model is not a model of how a particular therapy works but rather is a model of how *all* psychotherapies work. Thus, this model serves the purpose of this volume sufficiently well in that it identifies the skills that therapists need to master to increase their effectiveness. The model certainly is not the only one that could be adopted (e.g., Frank & Frank, 1991; Orlinsky & Howard, 1986). And most certainly it is not absolutely true—that is, aspects of it will change as evidence accumulates, and at some point the model may be rejected in favor of another model. What is important to understand is that the Contextual Model is a coherent way to organize what is known currently about psychotherapy and identifies the skills that are necessary to practice psychotherapy effectively.

The Contextual Model is presented in Figure 3.1. The model contains three pathways through which flows the power of psychotherapy. Some treatments emphasize one pathway over another, but to be optimally effective, any psychotherapy must utilize all three pathways. In this chapter, various indicators of the quality of a therapy in each pathway are discussed. In the following section, therapist skills that are needed to enact each pathway effectively are discussed. However, before we discuss the three pathways, the therapist must develop an initial therapeutic bond.

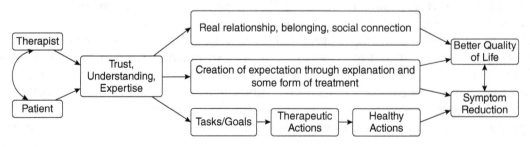

Figure 3.1 Contextual Model.

Initial Therapeutic Bond

Patients come to therapy with distress—they are having difficulties in life and are discouraged about finding solutions to their problems. They feel demoralized, in Jerome Frank's term (Frank & Frank, 1991). Patients also come to therapy with personalities, racial/ethnic backgrounds and identities, social networks (or lack of them), economic resources (or lack of them), occupation/vocation/work histories and situations, histories, and current life events (e.g., recent bereavement). Therapists also come to the initial meeting with personalities, racial/ethnic backgrounds and identities, histories, and current life events. It is a meeting of strangers, embedded in a professional context.

Patients are seeking immediate answers to some questions: Can this therapist understand me and my problems? Can I trust the therapist? Does the therapist have the capacity and expertise to help me? Ed Bordin (1979), who developed the concept of the therapeutic alliance as a pantheoretical concept, noted that the initial bond was necessary before therapeutic work began: "Some basic level of trust surely marks all varieties of therapeutic relationships, but when attention is directed toward the more protected recesses of inner experience, deeper bonds of trust and attachment are required and developed" (p. 254).

The formation of the initial bond is a combination of top-down and bottom-up processing. The top-down processing involves the belief that therapy will be effective and is based on what patients know about therapy, past experience, stories from friends or family members, and the like. Indeed, patients seem to experience significant benefit from the time they make the initial appointment to the time they present for the initial meeting with the therapist (Frank & Frank, 1991), as they are remoralized because they believe their involvement in the impending psychotherapy will be helpful. Expectations about the particular therapist may be present as well, because, for example, this therapist had been recommended by a friend who had benefited from therapy.

Humans are evolved to make quick judgments (within 100 ms) about the trustworthiness of another, based on facial features (Willis & Todorov, 2006). Of course, patients are also making judgments about psychotherapy from the context—for example, the warmth and efficiency of the clinic staff, the attractiveness and comfort of the waiting room, and the therapy room itself, including diplomas and pictures hung on the wall. It is clear that the initial interaction and patient engagement early in therapy are critical to the success of therapy, if for no other reason than that most patients who drop out of therapy prematurely do so after the first session; the second greatest number of patients drop out after the second session, and so on (Connell, Grant, & Mullin, 2006; Simon & Ludman, 2010).

Real Relationship

Patient and therapist have distinct roles in therapy—patients have a problem, complaint, or disorder that they want resolved, and therapists are the healers, providing something of value to patients, based on their training and experience. However, despite these roles, psychotherapy involves a deep and intimate interpersonal relationship between two human beings. This relationship can be described psychodynamically as the transference-free genuine relationship based on realistic perceptions (Gelso, 2009), where genuineness was defined by Gelso and Carter (1994) as "the ability and willingness to be what one truly is in the relationship—to be authentic, open and honest" and realistic perceptions as "those perceptions that are uncontained by transference distortions and other defenses . . . [the therapist and patient] see each other in an accurate, realistic way" (p. 297). In therapy, the real relationship involves a therapist who is warm, caring, and empathic with a contract that this relationship will continue regardless of the material discussed.[1]

The real relationship would appear to be fundamental to humanistic approaches, important for dynamic therapies, but generally not emphasized, or even ignored, by behavioral and cognitive therapies. However, there is a compelling case to be made that the real relationship is critical to the benefits of psychotherapy of all types. Humans evolved as social animals and attachment is fundamental to the survival of humans, as discussed by many prominent theorists (Baumeister, 2005; Bowlby, 1980; Cacioppo & Cacioppo, 2012; Lieberman, 2013; Wilson, 2012). Indeed, there is strong evidence that perceived loneliness places an individual at as great or greater risk for mortality than smoking, obesity, environmental pollutants, and lack of exercise (for the general population or those at risk of cardiac events) (Holt-Lunstad, Smith, Baker, Harris, & Stephenson, 2015; Holt-Lunstad, Smith, & Layton, 2010; Luo, Hawkley, Waite, & Cacioppo, 2012). Indeed, holding the hand of a beloved one, or even having a beloved person in the room, increases tolerance of pain, with the expected concomitant neural processes (Benedetti, 2011), suggesting that individuals in higher-quality relations benefit from greater regulatory effects on the neural system involved in negative emotions, e.g., the affective components of pain (Benedetti, 2011, p. 149).

The healing power of an empathic relationship should not be underestimated. The evidence is strong that an empathic, caring, and understanding relationship will be beneficial and will augment the effectiveness of treatments. The impact of empathy on healing in medicine has been discussed extensively (e.g., Decety & Fotopoulou, 2015). Consider a study of placebo effects on the symptoms, global improvement, adequate relief, and quality of life of patients with irritable bowel syndrome (Kaptchuk et al., 2008; Kelley et al., 2009). In this study, these patients were assigned to treatment as usual (TAU) by their physicians: TAU with a sham acupuncture (acupuncture in which the needles do not pierce the skin although patients believe they are receiving acupuncture) with limited interaction with the acupuncturist; and an augmented interaction in which patients received TAU and sham acupuncture, but the acupuncturist was warm, caring, and understanding. The results showed that the both placebo conditions were superior to TAU, but the augmented condition was significantly better than simple delivery of the sham acupuncture. That is, when the sham acupuncture involved a warm and caring practitioner, the benefits were greater, sometimes with effects twice as large. Research on the real relationship indicate that is it predictive of psychotherapy outcome (Gelso, 2014)

Some patients will benefit more from the real relationship than others. Those patients who present with attachment difficulties, insecure attachment styles, poor social support, impoverished social networks, chaotic interpersonal relations, and features of borderline personality disorder but find a relatively stable real relationship with their therapist will benefit more from the real relationship than patients with relatively supportive interpersonal relationships.

---

1 There are limitations to the continuity of therapy, as would be the case if there were a risk of danger to self or others, for example.

Creation of Expectation through Explanation and Treatment

Patients come to therapy with a maladaptive conception of their distress. These maladaptive explanations, sometimes called folk psychology, are culturally influenced and often are acquired from family, friends, and influential others as well as from the larger society (e.g., in advertisements for psychotropic medications). These explanations are not labeled maladaptive because they are unscientific, although surely many are, but because they fail to lead patients to find solutions to what is distressing (Budge & Wampold, 2015; Wampold, Imel, Bhati, & Johnson Jennings, 2006). An important aspect of healing practices, including Western medicine, is that patients are provided an explanation for their distress. Indeed, patients presenting to a physician would be quite disoriented if no explanation were provided—is the pain in my gut due to indigestion, an ulcer, or cancer? The explanation provides patients hope that there exists some treatment actions that will lead to improvement—in that way, therapists are substituting an adaptive explanation for a maladaptive explanation. Notice that we are not saying that the adaptive explanation is more scientific than the maladaptive one—what makes the explanation adaptive is that it allows for ameliorative actions. (See the next section.) Cognitive behavioral therapists, interpersonal therapists, emotion-focused therapists, eye movement desensitization and reprocessing, and dynamic therapists will offer their patients very different explanations of their distress and plans for getting better. What is critical is that patients accept the explanation and believe that it will lead, through the therapy process, to a reduction in distress. That is, patients believe that participating in and successfully completing the therapeutic tasks will be helpful in coping with their problems, which then further creates the expectation that patients have "control" over their problems. These expectations and beliefs are central to theories of how individuals change and behave, including theories involving mastery (Frank & Frank, 1991; Liberman, 1978), self-efficacy (Bandura, 1999), and response expectancies (Kirsch, 1985, 1999).

It is well known, scientifically as well as in our own experience, that expectations have a large effect on what is experienced. Compelling evidence for the power of expectations is found most profoundly in the placebo literature. Although there are several theories of how placebos produce effects, expectations are central to understanding why placebos are so powerful (see Benedetti, 2014; Kirsch, 1985; Price, Finniss, & Benedetti, 2008). It is beyond the scope of this chapter to review the placebo research, but a few perspicuous results will be convincing of the power of expectations. Placebos have been studied extensively for pain, including chronic pain, medically induced acute pain (e.g., postsurgical pain and dental procedures), and experimentally induced pain (e.g, the cold pressor test) (see Benedetti, 2009, 2014; Price et al., 2008, for a comprehensive review). It is well established that taking a placebo analgesic with the expectation that the substance or procedure will reduce pain reduces the experience of pain. Furthermore, it is also well established that taking the placebo results in the release of endogenous opioids into the brain, indicating that the placebo effect is not simply a subjective response but is mediated by a physiological process. Moreover, in an "open–hidden" paradigm, giving a postsurgical patient a given dose of morphine administered surreptitiously (the hidden condition, e.g., by an intravenous infusion from a machine out of the patient's awareness) is less effective (that is, the patient reported more pain and requested more additional doses of analgesics) than when the patient is aware that the drug was being administered (open condition, e.g., a clinician indicated to the patient that the drug was being delivered). Moreover, giving dental patients a placebo in an open condition was equivalent to giving a patient 6 to 8 mg morphine in a hidden condition for molar extraction. As a final example from pain, postoperative pain patients after a course of opioid analgesics were randomly assigned to one of three conditions: (a) patients received no verbal instructions (a natural history condition); (b) patients were told they would receive either a placebo or the painkiller they had previously received, but they were all given only the placebo (the typical instruction given in double-blind placebo-controlled randomized trial to test the efficacy of drugs); or (c) patients were told they would receive the painkiller (deceptive condition). Patients in the double-blind condition subsequently requested less medication than those in the natural history condition, but patients who were told (deceptively) that they were receiving a painkiller requested even less medication subsequently. What is clear from these studies (and hundreds of other studies) is that patients' expectation of pain relief results in pain relief and that these expectations are created by what is said to patients—that is, in verbal interactions with healers.

Demonstrable placebo effects are not limited to pain. Patients with Parkinson's disease benefit from placebos in terms of both symptoms (motoric activity) and levels of dopamine in the brain (see Benedetti, 2014). Not surprisingly, patients with cardiac problems and diabetes have lower mortality rates if they adhere to protocols of beneficial drugs (i.e., take the medication as instructed), but patients who are more adherent to the placebos in these trials also have lower mortality than those who are not adherent (Simpson et al., 2006). Adherence to a protocol is a sign that patients believe the treatment will be effective. In this instance, adhering to the placebo protocol (i.e., ingesting nothing medically active) can reduce death. In another interesting study, female hotel room attendants were told that their everyday work was good exercise. Compared to hotel workers who were not provided any information, the informed workers reported that they got more exercise and they had better health indicators (lower weight, lower blood pressure, and less body fat), *even though they did not do more exercise* (Crum & Langer, 2007). Over 90% of the effect of antidepressants is due to the placebo effect (Kirsch, 2010). Patients in psychotherapy who attribute their therapeutic gains to their own efforts rather than to a medication they had taken, which was actually a placebo, were significantly less likely to relapse (Liberman, 1978; Powers, Smits, Whitley, Bystritsky, & Telch, 2008).

Simply creating expectations through providing patients an explanation for their distress and describing the treatment is not sufficient. Patients actually must enact the therapeutic rituals—the explanation that a pill will decrease pain must be accompanied by the taking of the pill. The explanation and the ritual work together, and patients must believe that therapeutic progress is a result of their own efforts, which provides a sense of their own control over their distress. There is evidence that humans evolved to heal in a social context, such as psychotherapy (Benedetti, 2011; Wampold & Imel, 2015). The importance of expectations in psychotherapy has been well established (Constantino, Arnkoff, Glass, Ametrano, & Smith, 2011).

Critical to the acceptance of the explanation and to the creation of expectations is the therapeutic alliance. The alliance is defined as a pantheoretical construct that reflects collaborative and purposeful work and is composed of three components: (a) the bond between therapist and patient, (b) agreement about the goals of therapy, and (c) agreement about the tasks of therapy (Bordin, 1979; Hatcher & Barends, 2006; Horvath, 2006; Horvath & Luborsky, 1993). The alliance is the most researched construct in psychotherapy process research. Nearly 200 studies have investigated the correlation of alliance with outcome and have found meta-analytically that there is a strong association of the alliance, measured early in psychotherapy, and the final outcome, across all forms of psychotherapy (Flückiger, Del Re, Wampold, Symonds, & Horvath, 2012; Horvath, Del Re, Flückiger, & Symonds, 2011).

Enacting Health-Promoting Actions

The power of therapeutic rituals is not limited to the expectations that are created. The third pathway indicates an indirect effect of the relationship on outcome. A collaborative working relationship involving agreement about the goals of therapy and the tasks needed to achieve those goals will lead to the likelihood that patients will engage in therapeutic tasks. Apart from the relationship, the actual tasks may well have therapeutic benefit.

An important point to keep in mind is that different treatments utilize very different therapeutic actions. Cognitive behavioral therapists ask patients to think more adaptively and to change maladaptive cognitive schemas; behavioral therapists have patients approach previously avoided situations or people; interpersonal therapists work to improve the quality of relationships; and dynamic therapists encourage the expression of avoided emotions. For many disorders, a variety of treatments, utilizing very different treatment actions, have been found to be effective (Wampold & Imel, 2015).

Of course, every approach to psychotherapy has a different explanatory system for disorders, as Laska, Gurman, and Wampold (2014) describe in reference to PTSD:

> Each [treatment] posits a specific mechanism of change based on a given scientific theory. For example, prolonged exposure (PE) for PTSD (Foa, Hembree, & Rothbaum, 2007) is conceptually derived from emotional processing theory (Foa & Kozak, 1986), and the specific ingredients of PE (viz., imaginal and in vivo exposure) (a) activate the "fear network," (b) whereby clients habituate to their fears, and thus, (c) extinguish the fear response. On the other hand, interpersonal therapy (IPT) for PTSD (Markowitz, Milrod, Bleiberg, & Marshall, 2009) is derived from interpersonal and attachment theory (Bowlby, 1973; Sullivan, 1953) and "focuses on current social and interpersonal functioning rather than exposure" (Bleiberg & Markowitz, 2005, p. 181). (p. 468)

Indeed, treatments used in research to control for specific effects have been found to be effective. These treatments, which intentionally omitted specific ingredients thought to be necessary to help patients with particular disorders, are as effective as evidence-based treatments for the disorder when they are delivered by therapists who believe they are effective, the rationale is convincing to the patients, and there are cogent and coherent treatment actions. Indeed, these "control" treatments are so effective that they are now listed as evidence-based treatments, including behavioral activation for depression, interpersonal therapy for depression, and present-centered therapy for PTSD (Wampold & Imel, 2015).

Lifestyle changes have large but underestimated effects on mental health (Walsh, 2011). Improved mood and well-being suggest to patients that the treatment is working and augment the belief that the therapeutic components are efficacious. Again, patients believe that their own hard work (i.e., engaging in the activities inherent in the treatment) is responsible for the benefits of therapy. What all effective treatments have in common is that patients are persuaded to do something that promotes health and well-being.

Characteristics and Actions of Effective Therapists

In 2004, Beutler and colleagues reviewed what was known about the characteristics and actions of effective therapists and concluded that not much was known in this regard. Fortunately, since then there has been a renewed interest in this topic as well as methodological advances that can identify the therapist contribution to psychotherapy process and outcome. The characteristics and actions of effective therapists that have been identified are briefly reviewed in the remainder of this chapter. Those characteristics and actions that are not related to producing the benefits of psychotherapy will be discussed as well. These characteristics and actions are summarized in Table 3.1. This discussion is informative about what therapists should deliberately practice.

Table 3.1 Effective therapists.

Characteristics and Actions of Effective Therapists	Characteristics and Actions *Not* Related to Outcome
Formation of alliance across a range of patients	Age
Facilitative interpersonal skills (as demonstrated in response to difficult patient)	Gender
Verbal fluency	Profession
Warmth and empathy	Self-reported social skills
Emotional expression	Responses to interview questions about clinical skills
Persuasiveness	Theoretical orientation
Hopefulness	Adherence to treatment protocol
Alliance-bond capacity (see alliance)	Rated competence delivering specific ingredients of treatment
Problem focus	
Delivery of a cogent treatment	
Professional self-doubt	
Deliberate practice	

Alliance

As discussed previously, the working alliance is a central construct in the contextual model. The alliance is a vehicle used to create expectations and is necessary for patients to enact the rituals of psychotherapy, which lead to the enactment of health-promoting actions. Moreover, the bond in the alliance is quite similar to the real relationship. That is to say, the alliance seems to be central to therapeutic change, an observation strongly supported by the research evidence.

As strong as the research is relative to alliance, it is not clear that it is the therapist's contribution to the alliance that is important. Some patients come to therapy with strong social support, secure attachment style, interpersonal skills, and motivation to change. Such patients will form a relatively strong alliance with most therapists and have relatively good outcomes. Thus, it might well be that it is the patient's contribution to the alliance that is important. However, just the opposite has been found. Baldwin, Wampold, and Imel (2007) disentangled the therapist's and the patient's contributions to the alliance and found that *only* the therapist's contribution to the alliance predicted outcome, a result confirmed meta-analytically (Del Re, Flückiger, Horvath, Symonds, & Wampold, 2012). It is what therapists offer patients in terms of forming the alliance that produces better outcomes. The conclusion from this research is unequivocal: *Effective therapists form strong alliances across a range of patients.*

Facilitative Interpersonal Skills

Anderson and colleagues (Anderson, McClintock, Himawan, Song, & Patterson, 2015; Anderson, Ogles, Patterson, Lambert, & Vermeersch, 2009) used an interesting method to identify the characteristics and actions of effective therapists. Instead of using material from therapy sessions or asking therapists to provide information, they presented a video of a challenging patient (i.e., a stimulus that was constant across therapists) to 25 therapists at a college counseling center, and the therapists recorded their responses to the patient at various instances. The responses were then coded for what the authors called facilitative interpersonal skills, which included verbal fluency, emotional expression, persuasiveness, hopefulness, warmth, empathy, alliance-bond capacity, and problem focus.

Facilitative interpersonal skill components are endemic to the contextual model. *Empathy* is critical to the real relationship but, as discussed earlier, augments the effect of expectations and increases the likelihood that patients will form a collaborative working relationship and engage in therapy. Many believe that most therapists are empathic most of the time, but there is variation between and within therapists in empathic responding, particularly in response to interpersonally aggressive and difficult patients.

Verbal fluency is critical for providing a believable, succinct, and adaptive explanation and a cogent rationale for the therapeutic actions. Psychotherapy is, above all else, talk therapy. That is, the delivery of psychotherapy is via verbal means and thus an effective therapist must be able to communicate clearly and succinctly. Of course, some therapies emphasize particular components that are expressed verbally, such as interpretations in dynamic therapy or psychoeducation in cognitive behavioral therapy.

Emotion is central to the success of therapy (e.g., Diener, Hilsenroth, & Weinberger, 2007). Again, some therapies are explicitly focused on emotion (e.g., emotion-focused therapy or affect phobia therapy), but emotion is central to all therapies, including cognitive and behavioral therapies (see, e.g., Thoma, & McKay, 2015). Effective therapists are able to *modulate and express emotion*. Often therapists need to activate avoided emotions, such as sadness or anger, and must be able to appropriately model and express these emotions for patients. In other instances, therapists will assist patients to reduce or inhibit emotions, such as fear, guilt, and shame. For example, a behavior therapist conducting a panic induction with an extremely fearful patient will have to express calmness, even if the therapist is anxious, as might likely be the case. And, of course, therapists need to mask some of their affective reactions to patients, such as the disgust one might feel toward a patient who does not bathe regularly or anger toward a patient who is insulting of the therapist's level of skill.

As discussed, a key component of the contextual model is that patients accept the explanation provided by therapists and believe that the treatment will be beneficial. Not surprisingly, Anderson and colleagues (2009) found that effective therapists are *persuasive*. Moreover, effective therapists make it clear that patients' progress toward achieving therapeutic goals is paramount—that is, the *focus of the therapeutic encounter is on the patient's problems and their solution*. And, of course, effective therapists communicate *hopefulness and optimism* that patients can reach therapeutic goals, even if particular patients have made many unsuccessful attempts, within and outside of therapy, to solve their problems, (e.g., patients who abuse substances and have failed repeatedly to maintain sobriety for significant periods of time).

Delivery of a Cogent Treatment

It is becoming increasingly clear that treatments without structure or a focus on the problems that motivated patients to seek help are less effective, particularly with focal symptoms, than are treatments than have a problem/solution focus (Wampold & Imel, 2015). Unstructured treatments emphasize the real relationship as the change agent but ignore expectations created by an explanation and a plan of action and eliciting health-promoting behavior change, the last two pathways of the contextual model. Effective therapists collaboratively develop a cogent treatment so that patients understand what needs to be enacted in order to achieve their goals in therapy.

Professional Self-Doubt and Deliberate Practice

In a series of studies, Nissen-Lie and colleagues (Nissen-Lie, Monsen, & Rønnestad, 2010; Nissen-Lie, Monsen, Ulleberg, & Rønnestad, 2013; Nissen-Lie et al., 2015) found that therapists' self-reported professional self-doubt predicted outcome—that is, therapists who had more doubt about their skill in helping patients (e.g, "lacking confidence that you might have a beneficial effect on a patient" and "unsure about how best to deal effectively with a patient") had better outcomes, particularly if they also had a positive sense of self.

Perhaps therapists who doubted their effectiveness also were motivated to improve. Chow et al. (2015) found that the amount of time therapists reported spending on improving targeted therapeutic skills outside of therapy predicted their outcomes with patients. This practice meets the definition of deliberate practice (Ericsson & Lehmann, 1996) and is the focus of this volume.

Characteristics and Actions of Therapists that Are Not Related to Outcome

It is informative to understand what characteristics and actions of therapists are not related to outcome, as spending time and effort in those domains would not lead to improved outcomes. Generally, it has been found that the age of the therapist, the gender of the therapist, and the profession of the therapist (e.g., psychology, psychiatry, social work, professional counseling) do not predict outcome (Wampold & Imel, 2015)—of course, these are not variables that can be modified through practice, and they are of little relevance to the topics discussed in this volume.

Anderson and colleagues (2009), in the study discussed earlier, used a challenge test to assess facilitative interpersonal skills. Schöttke, Flückiger, Goldberg, Eversmann, and Lange (2016) coded a discussion among trainees following a provoking video and found results similar to those of Anderson and colleagues. It appears that therapists display important skills in challenging situations. Interestingly, in these studies, self-reported social skills (Anderson et al., 2009) and responses in a structured interview designed to assess clinical skills (Schöttke et al., 2016) did *not* predict outcomes. These studies suggest that, when therapists make decisions about what skills to practice, therapist self-report of skills is not useful in identifying particular skills that need attention; rather, therapists must be observed in challenging interpersonal situations.

Consistent with the more general literature on theoretical orientation (Wampold & Imel, 2015), the studies examining characteristics and actions of effective therapists have found that theoretical orientation did not predict a therapist's outcomes (Anderson et al., 2009; Chow et al., 2015; Schöttke et al., 2016). It is important to note that therapist adherence to treatment protocols also does not predict outcome (Boswell et al., 2013; Webb et al., 2010). That is to say, those therapists who more closely follow a treatment protocol do not achieve better outcomes, and, indeed, flexibility in terms of adherence appears to be more important (Owen & Hilsenroth, 2014). How a treatment is delivered is more important than the particular treatment that is offered to patients.

It also appears that competence in delivering a particular treatment, as rated by experts in clinical trials, does not predict the outcomes of therapy (Boswell et al., 2013; Webb et al., 2010). This is a curious finding because one would think that experts' rating of competence must be related to how well therapists perform and to the outcomes achieved. The key to understanding this finding is to emphasize that such competence measures are sensitive to *competence in a particular therapy* and not to competence in many factors discussed in this chapter, including alliance building, empathy, hopefulness, and persuasiveness. Indeed, training therapists to be more competent in a particular therapy does not seem to improve their outcomes (Branson et al., 2015).

Conclusions

Deliberate practice leads to expertise, provided practitioners practice those skills necessary for exemplary performance. It is possible to improve therapy performance if therapists practice those skills that lead to better outcomes. In this chapter, an evidence-based meta-model for how psychotherapy works was presented as well as the therapist skills required by the model.

Questions from the Editors

Question #1. In the chapter, you speak of the importance of providing a cogent rationale for client difficulties and the treatment process. How can clinicians understand evidence that the particular approach contributes little if anything to overall outcome with your claim that they need to adhere to a treatment with a cogent rationale with allegiance and belief in that treatment?

Answer from Author: Yes, at first glance, there is a dilemma here: Why should a clinician have an allegiance to a particular type of therapy when the evidence is clear that which type of therapy is used does not make a difference? To escape this dilemma, substitute the following belief: As a therapist, I believe that giving Treatment A will benefit my clients. Of course, the therapist probably finds Treatment A to be appealing and consistent with his or her values, attitudes, assumptions about the world, and so on. But such a statement demands two corollaries. First, belief is not sufficient. The benefit to clients must be documented: That is, there must be evidence that the treatment works well as delivered by the therapist—and that is where routine outcome monitoring is important. Second, choice of the treatment approach should not be based solely on what the therapist finds appealing. Importantly, the treatment needs to be compatible with the expectations, attitudes, values, and worldview of the client—some clients will find some treatments more acceptable than others. So, therapists have to have a repertoire of treatments.

Question #2. Doesn't embracing a contextual view of psychotherapy as described in the chapter risk exclusion from the broader medicalized healthcare system? If not, why?

Answer from Author: Navigating the world of healthcare delivery systems in various venues is complicated business. Historically medicine has emphasized particular treatments for particular diseases or conditions. So, when psychotherapy is delivered within a medical context, there is a strong inclination to follow the same road and ask which psychological treatment is most effective for which particular disorder. Some venues have followed this course and mandated that clinicians use only particular evidence-based treatments. The answer is that psychotherapy is remarkably effective, as effective as and longer-lasting than medications for most mental disorders, and has fewer (or no) side effects; however, the specific ingredients of particular treatments are not what makes psychotherapy work, as I discussed in this chapter. We need to continue to document the effectiveness of psychotherapy at a macro level (i.e., via clinical trials and meta-analyses) and at at the micro level—each therapist, each agency, and each system must be accountable for the results of mental health services.

Question #3. Can you describe a few ways how graduate programs might integrate the contextual model into training of students?

Answer from Author: The model of expertise that we are discussing in this volume constitutes a dramatic shift of the standard practice. To accomplish change, we need to focus first on training of therapists. Here are my suggestions:

• Graduate students/psychotherapy trainees need to be selected according to their potential to be effective therapists. The current criteria (exams, interviews, grades, personal statements, and letters of recommendation) are poor predictors of therapy effectiveness; challenge tests, such as the one devised by Tim Anderson, provide evidence for future psychotherapy effectiveness.
• Trainees need to learn various treatment approaches (see my answer to question #2), but strict adherence to protocols is not the goal.
• Trainees need to improve the skills discussed in this chapter, using deliberate practice methods. An implication here is that supervisors and trainers need be skilled in using deliberate practice procedures with their trainees.
• In all clinical work, trainees should use routine outcome monitoring to assess psychotherapy effectiveness.
• Recommendations for internship and clinical positions should be supported by evidence of trainees effectiveness derived from routine outcome monitoring.

References

Ahn, H., & Wampold, B. E. (2001). A meta-analysis of component studies: Where is the evidence for the specificity of psychotherapy? *Journal of Counseling Psychology, 48*, 262–267.

Anderson, T., McClintock, A. S., Himawan, L., Song, X., & Patterson, C. L. (2015). A prospective study of therapist facilitative interpersonal skills as a predictor of treatment outcome. *Journal of Consulting and Clinical Psychology.* doi:10.1037/ccp0000060

Anderson, T., Ogles, B. M., Patterson, C. L., Lambert, M. J., & Vermeersch, D. A. (2009). Therapist effects: Facilitative interpersonal skills as a predictor of therapist success. *Journal of Clinical Psychology, 65*(7), 755–768. doi:10.1002/jclp.20583

Baldwin, S. A., & Imel, Z. E. (2013). Therapist effects: Finding and methods. In M. J. Lambert (Ed.), *Bergin and Garfield's handbook of psychotherapy and behavior change* (6th ed., pp. 258–297). Hoboken, NJ: Wiley.

Baldwin, S. A., Wampold, B. E., & Imel, Z. E. (2007). Untangling the alliance–outcome correlation: Exploring the relative importance of therapist and patient variability in the alliance. *Journal of Consulting and Clinical Psychology, 75*, 842–852.

Bandura, A. (1999). Self-efficacy: Toward a unifying theory of behavioral change. In R. F. Baumeister (Ed.), *The self in social psychology* (pp. 285–298). New York, NY: Psychology Press.

Baumeister, R. F. (2005). *The cultural animal: Human nature, meaning, and social life*. New York, NY: Oxford University Press.

Bell, E. C., Marcus, D. K., & Goodlad, J. K. (2013). Are the parts as good as the whole? A meta-analysis of component treatment studies. *Journal of Consulting and Clinical Psychology, 81*(4), 722–736. doi:10.1037/a0033004

Benedetti, F. (2009). *Placebo effects: Understanding the mechanisms in health and disease*. New York, NY: Oxford University Press.

Benedetti, F. (2011). *The patient's brain: The neuroscience behind the doctor–patient relationship*. New York, NY: Oxford University Press.

Benedetti, F. (2014). *Placebo effects: Understanding the mechanisms in health and disease* (2nd ed.). New York, NY: Oxford University Press.

Beutler, L. E., Malik, M., Alimohamed, S., Harwood, T. M., Talebi, H., Noble, S., & Wong, E. (2004). Therapist variables. In M. J. Lambert (Ed.), *Bergin and Garfield's handbook of psychotherapy and behavior change* (5th ed., pp. 227–306). Hoboken, NJ: Wiley.

Bordin, E. S. (1979). The generalizability of the psychoanalytic concept of the working alliance. *Psychotherapy: Theory, Research & Practice, 16*(3), 252–260. doi:10.1037/h0085885

Boswell, J. F., Gallagher, M. W., Sauer-Zavala, S. E., Bullis, J., Gorman, J. M., Shear, M. K., . . . Barlow, D. H. (2013). Patient characteristics and variability in adherence and competence in cognitive-behavioral therapy for panic disorder. *Journal of Consulting and Clinical Psychology, 81*(3), 443–454. doi:10.1037/a0031437

Bowlby, J. (1980). *Attachment and loss*. New York, NY: Basic Books.

Branson, A., Shafran, R., & Myles, P. (2015). Investigating the relationship between competence and patient outcome with CBT. *Behaviour Research and Therapy, 68*, 19–26. doi:10.1016/j.brat.2015.03.002

Budge, S. L., & Wampold, B. E. (2015). The relationship: How it works. In O.C.G. Gelo, A. Pritz, & B. Rieken (Eds.), *Psychotherapy research: Foundations, process, and outcome* (pp. 213–228). New York, NY: Springer-Verlag.

Cacioppo, S., & Cacioppo, J. T. (2012). Decoding the invisible forces of social connections. *Frontiers in Integrative Neuroscience, 6*. doi:10.3389/fnint.2012.00051

Chow, D. L., Miller, S. D., Seidel, J. A., Kane, R. T., Thornton, J. A., & Andrews, W. P. (2015). The role of deliberate practice in the development of highly effective psychotherapists. *Psychotherapy, 52*(3), 337–345. doi:10.1037/pst0000015

Connell, J., Grant, S., & Mullin, T. (2006). Client-initiated termination of therapy at NHS primary care counselling services. *Counselling & Psychotherapy Research, 6*(1), 60–67. doi:10.1080/14733140600581507

Constantino, M. J., Arnkoff, D. B., Glass, C. R., Ametrano, R. M., & Smith, J. Z. (2011). Expectations. *Journal of Clinical Psychology, 67*(2), 184–192. doi:10.1002/jclp.20754

Crum, A. J., & Langer, E. J. (2007). Mind-set matters: Exercise and the placebo effect. *Psychological Science, 18*(2), 165–171. doi:10.1111/j.1467-9280.2007.01867.x

Decety, J., & Fotopoulou, A. (2015). Why empathy has a beneficial impact on others in medicine: Unifying theories. *Frontiers in Behavioral Neuroscience, 8*. doi:10.3389/fnbeh.2014.00457

Del Re, A. C., Flückiger, C., Horvath, A. O., Symonds, D., & Wampold, B. E. (2012). Therapist effects in the therapeutic alliance–outcome relationship: A restricted-maximum likelihood meta-analysis. *Clinical Psychology Review, 32*(7), 642–649. doi:10.1016/j. cpr.2012.07.002

Diener, M. J., Hilsenroth, M. J., & Weinberger, J. (2007). Therapist affect focus and patient outcomes in psychodynamic psychotherapy: A meta-analysis. *American Journal of Psychiatry, 164*(6), 936–941. doi:http://doi.org/10.1176/appi.ajp.164.6.936

Ericsson, K. A., & Lehmann, A. C. (1996). Expert and exceptional performance: Evidence of maximal adaptation to task constraints. *Annual Review of Psychology, 47,* 273–305.

Flückiger, C., Del Re, A. C., Wampold, B. E., Symonds, D., & Horvath, A. O. (2012). How central is the alliance in psychotherapy? A multilevel longitudinal meta-analysis. *Journal of Counseling Psychology, 59*(1), 10–17. doi:10.1037/a0025749

Frank, J. D., & Frank, J. B. (1991). *Persuasion and healing: A comparative study of psychotherapy* (3rd ed.). Baltimore, MD: Johns Hopkins University Press.

Gelso, C. J. (2009). The real relationship in a postmodern world: Theoretical and empirical explorations. *Psychotherapy Research, 19*(3), 253–264. doi:10.1080/10503300802389242

Gelso, C. (2014). A tripartite model of the therapeutic relationship: Theory, research, and practice. *Psychotherapy Research, 24*(2), 117–131.

Gelso, C. J., & Carter, J. A. (1994). Components of the psychotherapy relationship: Their interaction and unfolding during treatment. *Journal of Counseling Psychology, 41*(3), 296–306. doi:10.1037/0022-0167.41.3.296

Hatcher, R. L., & Barends, A. W. (2006). How a return to theory could help alliance research. *Psychotherapy: Theory, Research, Practice, Training, 43*(3), 292–299. doi:10.1037/0033-3204.43.3.292

Holt-Lunstad, J., Smith, T. B., Baker, M., Harris, T., & Stephenson, D. (2015). Loneliness and social isolation as risk factors for mortality: A meta-analytic review. *Perspectives on Psychological Science, 10*(2), 227–237. doi:10.1177/1745691614568352

Holt-Lunstad, J., Smith, T. B., & Layton, J. B. (2010). Social relationships and mortality risk: A meta-analytic review. *PLoS Medicine, 7*(7), e1000316.

Horvath, A. O. (2006). The alliance in context: Accomplishments, challenges, and future directions. *Psychotherapy: Theory, Research, Practice, Training, 43*(3), 258–263. doi:10.1037/0033-3204.43.3.258

Horvath, A. O., Del Re, A. C., Flückiger, C., & Symonds, D. (2011). Alliance in individual psychotherapy. *Psychotherapy, 48*(1), 9–16. doi:10.1037/a0022186

Horvath, A. O., & Luborsky, L. (1993). The role of the therapeutic alliance in psychotherapy. *Journal of Consulting and Clinical Psychology, 61,* 561–573.

Kaptchuk, T. J., Kelley, J. M., Conboy, L. A., Davis, R. B., Kerr, C. E., Jacobson, E. E., . . . Lembo, A. J. (2008). Components of placebo effect: Randomised controlled trial in patients with irritable bowel syndrome. *British Medical Journal, 336*(7651), 999–1003. doi:10.1136/bmj.39524.439618.25

Kelley, J. M., Lembo, A. J., Ablon, J. S., Villanueva, J. J., Conboy, L. A., Levy, R., . . . Kaptchuk, T. J. (2009). Patient and practitioner influences on the placebo effect in irritable bowel syndrome. *Psychosomatic Medicine, 71*(7), 789–797. doi:10.1097/PSY.0b013e3181acee12

Kirsch, I. (1985). Response expectancy as a determinant of experience and behavior. *American Psychologist, 40,* 1189–1202.

Kirsch, I. (1999). *How expectancies shape experience.* Washington, DC: American Psychological Association.

Kirsch, I. (2010). *The emperor's new drugs: Exploding the antidepressant myth.* New York, NY: Basic Books.

Laska, K. M., Gurman, A. S., & Wampold, B. E. (2014). Expanding the lens of evidence-based practice in psychotherapy: A common factors perspective. *Psychotherapy, 51*(4), 467–481. doi: 10.1037/a0034332

Liberman, B. L. (1978). The role of mastery in psychotherapy: Maintenance of improvement and prescriptive change. In J. D. Frank, R. Hoehn-Saric, S. D. Imber, B. L. Liberman, & A. R. Stone (Eds.), *Effective ingredients of successful psychotherapy* (pp. 35–72). Baltimore, MD: Johns Hopkins University Press.

Lieberman, M. D. (2013). *Social: Why our brains are wired to connect.* New York, NY: Crown.

Luo, Y., Hawkley, L. C., Waite, L. J., & Cacioppo, J. T. (2012). Loneliness, health, and mortality in old age: A national longitudinal study. *Social Science & Medicine, 74*(6), 907–914. doi:10 .1016/j.socscimed.2011.11.028

Nissen-Lie, H. A., Monsen, J. T., & Rønnestad, M. H. (2010). Therapist predictors of early patient-rated working alliance: A multilevel approach. *Psychotherapy Research, 20*(6), 627–646. doi:10.1080/10503307.2010.497633

Nissen-Lie, H. A., Monsen, J. T., Ulleberg, P., & Rønnestad, M. H. (2013). Psychotherapists' self-reports of their interpersonal functioning and difficulties in practice as predictors of patient outcome. *Psychotherapy Research, 23*(1), 86–104. doi:10.1080/10503307.2012.735775

Nissen-Lie, H. A., Rønnestad, M. H., Høglend, P. A., Havik, O. E., Solbakken, O. A., Stiles, T. C., & Monsen, J. T. (2015). Love yourself as a person, doubt yourself as a therapist? *Clinical Psychology & Psychotherapy.* doi:10.1002/cpp.1977

Orlinsky, D. E., & Howard, K. I. (1986). Process and outcome in psychotherapy. In S. L. Garfield & A. E. Bergin (Eds.), *Handbook of psychotherapy and behavior change* (3rd ed., pp. 311–381). New York, NY: Wiley.

Owen, J., & Hilsenroth, M. J. (2014). Treatment adherence: The importance of therapist flexibility in relation to therapy outcomes. *Journal of Counseling Psychology, 61*(2), 280–288.

Powers, M. B., Smits, J.A.J., Whitley, D., Bystritsky, A., & Telch, M. J. (2008). The effect of attributional processes concerning medication taking on return of fear. *Journal of Consulting and Clinical Psychology, 76*(3), 478–490.

Price, D. P., Finniss, D. G., & Benedetti, F. (2008). A comprehensive review of the placebo effect: Recent advances and current thought. *Annual Review of Psychology, 59,* 565–590.

Schöttke, H., Flückiger, C., Goldberg, S. B., Eversmann, J., & Lange, J. (2016, January). Predicting psychotherapy outcome based on therapist interpersonal skills: A five-year longitudinal study of a therapist assessment protocol. *Psychotherapy Research.* 10.1080/10503307.2015.1125546

Simon, G. E., & Ludman, E. J. (2010). Predictors of early dropout from psychotherapy for depression in community practice. *Psychiatric Services, 61*(7), 684–689. doi:10.1176/appi. ps.61.7.684

Simpson, S. H., Eurich, D. T., Majumdar, S. R., Padwal, R. S., Tsuyuki, S. T., Varney, J., & Johnson, J. A. (2006, June). A meta-analysis of the association between adherence to drug therapy and mortality. *British Medical Journal.* doi:10.1136/bmj.38875.675486.55

Thoma, N. C., & McKay, D. (Eds.). (2015). *Working with emotion in cognitive-behavioral therapy: Techniques for clinical practice.* New York, NY: Guilford Press.

Tracey, T.J.G., Wampold, B. E., Lichtenberg, J. W., & Goodyear, R. K. (2014). Expertise in psychotherapy: An elusive goal? *American Psychologist, 69,* 218–229. doi:10.1037/a0035099

Walsh, R. (2011). Lifestyle and mental health. *American Psychologist, 66*(7), 579–592. doi:10.1037/a0021769

Wampold, B. E., & Budge, S. L. (2012). The 2011 Leona Tyler Award address: The relationship—and its relationship to the common and specific factors of psychotherapy. *Counseling Psychologist, 40*(4), 601–623. doi:10.1177/0011000011432709

Wampold, B. E., & Imel, Z. E. (2015). *The great psychotherapy debate: The research evidence for what works in psychotherapy* (2nd ed.). New York, NY: Routledge.

Wampold, B. E., Imel, Z. E., Bhati, K. S., & Johnson Jennings, M. D. (2006). Insight as a common factor. In L. G. Castonguay & C. E. Hill (Eds.), *Insight in psychotherapy* (pp. 119–139). Washington, DC: American Psychological Association.

Webb, C. A., DeRubeis, R. J., & Barber, J. P. (2010). Therapist adherence/competence and treatment outcome: A meta-analytic review. *Journal of Consulting and Clinical Psychology, 78*(2), 200–211. doi:10.1037/a0018912

Willis, J., & Todorov, A. (2006). First impressions: Making up your mind after a 100-ms exposure to a face. *Psychological Science, 17*(7), 592–598. doi:10.1111/j.1467-9280.2006.01750.x

Wilson, E. O. (2012). *The social conquest of earth.* New York, NY: Liveright.

4

Helping Therapists to Each Day Become a Little Better than They Were the Day Before

The Expertise-Development Model of Supervision and Consultation

Rodney K. Goodyear and Tony Rousmaniere

Effective supervision is essential to the development of psychotherapeutic expertise. Therapists already credit supervision as the single most important contributor to their professional development (Orlinsky & Rønnestad, 2005), and experienced therapists continue to seek supervision and consultation even when they are not required to do so (see Lichtenberg, Goodyear, Overland & Hutman, 2014). Our concern, though, is with *effective* supervision, and by that criterion, therapists apparently put too much faith in supervision as it is usually practiced. Supervisees report that a large proportion of their supervisors are either ineffective or harmful (Ellis et al., 2014) and by the measure of improved client outcomes, the success of supervision is yet to be convincingly established (Watkins, 2011).

The premise of this chapter is that supervision *can* effectively increase therapists' ability to achieve better client outcomes. Our purpose is to describe how. Because virtually all therapists eventually will supervise or consult (Rønnestad, Orlinsky, Parks & Davis, 1997), this chapter is for all therapists. Even therapists who will not immediately use this material to supervise or consult can profit by becoming more effective consumers of supervision. In a sample of British registered practitioner psychologists, for example, those who were supervising reported more frequent use of audio or video recordings of their work when in the role of supervisee (Nicholas & Goodyear, 2015); that is, they made greater use of what we describe in this chapter as best practices. We interpret this as indirect evidence that being educated in a supervision model may result in better supervision when in the role of supervisee.

We begin this chapter by examining the functions of both supervision and consultation and the roles each plays in facilitating a person's development as a psychotherapist as she or he moves first toward competence and then toward expertise. We then devote the remainder of the chapter to describing the Expertise-Development Model of supervision and consultation.

The Cycle of Excellence: Using Deliberate Practice to Improve Supervision and Training,
First Edition. Edited by Tony Rousmaniere, Rodney K. Goodyear, Scott D. Miller, and Bruce E. Wampold.
© 2017 John Wiley & Sons, Ltd. Published 2017 by John Wiley & Sons, Ltd.

Concepts and Context for the Expertise-Development Model

This section lays the groundwork for the sections that follow. We begin by differentiating between the similar functions of supervision and consultation. We then distinguish between competence and expertise as training goals and discuss the importance of both to the model we are presenting.

Distinctions between Supervision and Consultation

Both supervision and consultation have essential roles to play in the Expertise-Development Model. They are similar processes, to the extent that they often are confused with one another (e.g., what usually is called peer supervision actually is consultation). The key distinction is that supervisors typically work with trainees whereas consultants typically work with therapists who are credentialed for independent practice. These differences have several implications (Bernard & Goodyear, 2014; Goodyear, Falender, & Rousmaniere, in press):

- **Goals.** Supervisors are responsible for helping supervisees develop competence across the entire domain of practice and so usually are attending to a number of areas of growth. In contrast, consultants usually have more focused goals with their consultees. In our model, the focus is explicitly on becoming increasingly more effective as a psychotherapist.
- **Level of responsibility to clients and to the profession.** Because of their responsibilities for client well-being and to the profession, supervisors have evaluative and gatekeeping responsibilities that consultants do not. Those responsibilities result in a hierarchical relationship in which supervisors have greater power. As a result, supervisees are required to comply with supervisor directives whereas consultees, who are credentialed for independent practice, are free to decide what consultant suggestions to follow. The hierarchical nature of the relationship also contributes to supervisees withholding and distorting information during supervision (Ladany, Hill, Corbett & Nutt, 1996; Yourman & Farber, 1996). This presents a particular challenge, given the learning processes we describe in this chapter.
- **Level of choice in arranging the relationship.** Supervisees often have only very limited choice about who their supervisors are to be (Bernard & Goodyear, 2014). Consultees, though, typically are free to choose their consultants. This is another possible effect on relationship quality: Nicholas and Goodyear (2015) found that British practitioner psychologists who chose their supervisors reported a stronger working alliance with them than supervisees who were assigned their supervisors.
- **Stance with respect to theoretical orientation.** Supervisees often report having adopted their supervisor's theoretical perspective (Guest & Beutler, 1988). This is useful as it is important that supervisees develop mastery of some model during their competence development phase of learning. But once therapists have moved beyond competence to begin developing expertise, we expect that they will use a model or models that work for them, in the sense that they can use the model to effectively and efficiently help patients reach their goals.
- **Level of familiarity with cases.** Trainees, especially when at the practicum level, carry relatively few cases. Scrutiny of those cases remains relatively close, as the ratio of supervision hours to client contact hours can be as low as 1 to 5 (California Board of Behavioral

Sciences, 2016) or even 1 to 4 (Association of State and Provincial Psychology Boards, 2009), depending on profession and jurisdiction. In contrast, licensed professionals can have large caseloads and, when they do have consultation, it is likely to be weekly at best.

In short, supervision and consultation are forms of pedagogy (see Goodyear, 2014) that rely on the same teaching and learning processes. Their differences are in terms of the specificity of training goals, level of responsibility for clients, the teacher–learner relationship processes, and how cases are identified for attention. With respect to the last, supervisors have broader training goals and responsibility for client welfare and so monitor cases more closely; consultants do not have those responsibilities and are focused exclusively on assisting therapists to become more effective. For that reason, consultants should, with the consultee, select cases to review that are consistent with that goal.

Training Goals: Competence or Expertise Development?

Figure 4.1 visually depicts two perspectives on training goals and on how the effectiveness of training should be assessed. The first is a competence perspective for which supervision is more relevant; the second, an expertise-development perspective for which consultation is more relevant. Both are important for, as the figure depicts, competence sets the stage for

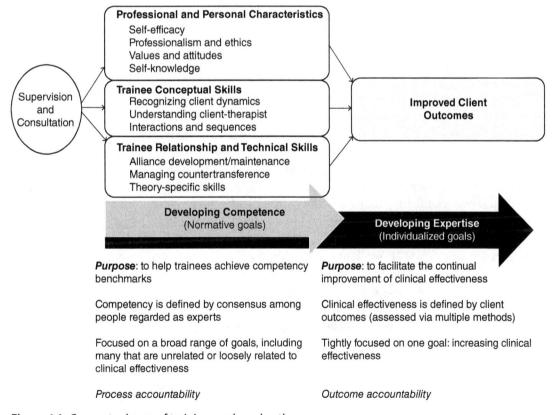

Figure 4.1 Conceptual map of training goals and pathways.

expertise development. Yet there are some who would assert that competence alone is a sufficient goal.

Competence Perspective

Carroll (2010) invoked the competence perspective when he noted:

> The acid test of how effective supervision is is simple: What are you (the supervisee) doing differently now that you were not doing before supervision? What have you learned from the past hour in supervision with me? What shifts have taken place in the supervisor room that have been transferred to your work? (p. 1)

In Figure 4.1, we employ Bernard's (1997) tripartite model to suggest that the supervisee changes to which Carroll alluded can occur with respect to supervisees' personal and professional characteristics, to their ability to conceptualize client and treatment dynamics, and to their ability to demonstrate particular relational and technical skills. These are broad domains of competence, and an increasingly robust supervision literature has established that supervision is successful in helping trainees achieve the goals nested within them (see Bernard & Goodyear, 2014; note that the research literature on consultation is much more limited and so we can infer mostly from the supervision literature).

Expertise-Development Perspective

Ellis and Ladany (1997) also invoked the metaphor of an acid test, but they proposed that this test be "the impact of clinical supervision on client outcome" (p. 485). This is much more rigorous than the tests of Carroll and of others who advocate a competence perspective (e.g., Fouad et al., 2009) propose. So far, the field has not convincingly established that supervisors routinely pass that test.

Although some studies have shown that supervision may improve clinical effectiveness (e.g., Bambling, King, Raue, Schweitzer, & Lambert, 2006; Callahan, Almstrom, Swift, Borja, & Heath, 2009; Reese et al., 2009), studies such as those of Rousmaniere, Swift, Babins-Wagner, Whipple, and Berzins (2016) throw those conclusions into question. Three literature reviews all have raised concerns about the impact of supervision on client outcomes (Freitas, 2002; Milne, Sheikh, Pattison, & Wilkinson, 2011; Watkins, 2011) and supervision scholars have voiced their own cautions. Ladany and Inman (2012) observed, for example, that "supervision may have an effect on client outcome; however, supervisors should recognize that the effect in many instances may be minimal" (p. 195). Beutler and Howard (2003) stated simply, "Supervision does not work" (p. 12). Watkins (2011) expressed this same perspective more diplomatically when he asserted, "We do not seem to be any more able now, as opposed to 30 years ago, to say that supervision leads to better outcomes for clients" (p. 252). The model we describe in this chapter responds to these concerns to suggest ways that supervisors or consultants can apply what we know *does* work in order to improve these impacts on client outcomes.

Developing Competence and Then Expertise

In Figure 4.1, we depict competence development as a necessary but insufficient step toward developing therapeutic expertise. It is necessary because competence builds the foundational skills on which further development can be based. It is insufficient, though, because attained competence does not appear to predict client outcome (Webb, DeRubeis, & Barber, 2010), which is the criterion by which expertise is best measured (Goodyear, Wampold, Tracey, & Lichtenberg, in press; Tracey, Wampold, Lichtenberg & Goodyear, 2014; Wampold, Lichtenberg, Goodyear & Tracey, in press).

As we noted earlier, supervisors focus on a broader range of training goals than do consultants, commensurate with the range of competencies that their supervisees are to attain. Panels of experts define competence and the associated training targets as normative, expected of all psychotherapists. Therapists are held to *process accountability* (Markman & Tetlock, 2000; see also Goodyear, 2015): being responsible for demonstrating particular target behaviors (e.g., fidelity to a particular treatment model) regardless of the impacts of those behaviors on clients.

But achieving clinical effectiveness means moving beyond competence to more reliably improve client outcomes. Learning objectives shift at this point from normative ones that others have declared to be desirable for all therapists to achieve (i.e., competence) to highly individualized goals informed by the learner's objectives and performance feedback. *Outcome accountability* (Goodyear, 2015) becomes especially salient. Outcome accountability concerns the extent to which the therapist is able to achieve intended client changes, independent of how the therapist might be performing expected tasks. Of course, the reasonable question in any discussion of accountability concerns "accountability to whom?" In this case, it ultimately is to the clients we serve.

Goodyear et al. (in press) used an example that not only illustrates a focus on outcome accountability but also highlights possible tensions between a focus on competence and a focus on performance: Emil Zatopek, a triple gold medalist at the 1952 Olympics,

> was not a graceful runner. With every step, his body rolled and heaved, his head lurched back and forth, and his tongue lolled out. . . . He was well aware of his less-than-perfect style, saying "I shall learn to have a better style once they start judging races according to their beauty. So long as it's a question of speed, then my attention will be directed to seeing how fast I can cover ground." (Sears, 2015, p. 196)

Judging the "beauty" of his performance would be to hold him to process accountability. This analogy of Zatopek's running to psychotherapy is imperfect because we *do* expect trainees to demonstrate expected forms of practice (i.e., competence), at least initially. In so doing, they are demonstrating performance beauty according to some standards. But in our model, adherence to expected forms of practice becomes less relevant as the therapist continues to develop beyond competence, toward expertise. The therapist at this point will be working with a supervisor in order to, as the title of this chapter suggests, become each day a little better as a therapist than she or he was the day before.

What therapists might become increasingly better at is suggested in the three broad domains of competence (therapist professional and personal characteristics, conceptual skills, relationship and technical skills) depicted in Figure 4.1. But Wampold (Chapter 3, this volume) makes clear that therapists should give particular emphasis to enhancing the strength and quality of their therapeutic alliances, their levels of empathic responding, and their ability to deliver a cogent rationale for treatment that will establish clients' expectations for change. Wampold also addresses the importance of the kind of relational responsiveness and flexibility captured in Anderson's measure of facilitative interpersonal skills (see, e.g., Anderson, Ogles, Patterson, Lambert, & Vermeersch, 2009).

The importance of developing these therapist qualities is underscored by the sometimes substantial effects that a client might have on therapist performance (Wampold & Imel, 2015). A therapist who has mastered the skills of a particular treatment model might look much more competent, for example, with a cooperative, engaged client than with one who is interpersonally aggressive and challenging. It is those therapist capabilities that Wampold addresses in Chapter 3 that help maximize therapeutic effectiveness across models and clients.

In summary, the Expertise-Development Model on which we focus in this chapter does not replace competency-focused supervision. In fact, it encompasses it, so certain aspects of the model have explicit application to supervisors who are helping trainees develop competence and certain aspects have explicit application for consultants helping therapists develop competence.

Expertise-Development Model of Supervision and Consultation

Deliberate practice (DP) is the central feature of the Cycle of Excellence. Miller, Hubble, and Chow (Chapter 2, this volume) describe DP as: (a) requiring focused, systematic, and ongoing efforts to improve performance; (b) receiving supervision or consultation for those efforts; (c) continually getting and using feedback (from supervisor or consultant; from supervisees and consultees); and (d) continual use of solo practice outside of performance to refine professional practice.

In this section, we focus particularly on the second element of the Miller et al. conception of DP and provide a model of supervision and consultation. Because it is based on the Cycle of Excellence (Chapter 1), this model draws from the large body of research on the science of expertise (e.g., Ericsson, 2006). But it also is informed by such other models as Bernard's discrimination model (1997), Miller's Feedback-Informed Supervision model (Maeschalck, Bargmann, Miller, & Bertolino, 2012), and the basic learning mechanisms used in teaching in the professions (Goodyear, 2015; McGaghie & Kristopaitis, 2015). This model is transtheoretical and therefore can be used by any supervisor or consultant, regardless of his or her approach to psychotherapy.

We focus primarily on one-on-one supervision or consultation. But readers should be able to discern ways in which the ideas and concepts apply to other supervision modalities, such as group or triadic supervision (see Goldberg, Dixon, & Wolf, 2012).

Essential Relationship-Maintenance Functions of the Supervisor or Consultant

Effective training can occur only to the extent to which supervisors and consultants have the trust and respect of those with whom they work. This affects, for example, how much supervisees are willing to disclose about their work and reactions to it (Ladany et al., 1996), how they receive feedback, and the extent to which they are willing to comply with directives and suggestions.

The literature (e.g., Bernard & Goodyear, 2014) suggests at least five relationship conditions that supervisors and consultants must meet. Given the length constraints available to us, our coverage of them is brief, despite their importance. They are essential to effective supervision. These conditions are that the supervisor or consultant will:

1. **Have obtained competence through formal training in both the provision of the services that are the focus of supervision or consultation *and* in the practice of supervision and consultation.** This competence not only affects what supervisors and consultants have the capacity to do but also establishes their credibility and trustworthiness, which is the basis for social influence (Heesacker, Petty, & Cacioppo, 1983) and which is undermined by perceptions that they are not providing adequate supervision (Ellis et al., 2014).

2. **Establish clear expectations about performance goals and about the responsibilities of each party in that relationship.** The supervisor–supervisee or consultant–consultee relationship should begin with a clear contract (preferably written) that addresses expectations and roles and is reviewed at the very first supervisor–supervisee or consultant–consultee meeting (American Psychological Association, 2015; Borders et al., 2014).

3. **Remain committed to resolving conflicts when they occur.** Even when supervisors and consultants take steps to reduce conflict with their supervisees and consultees (e.g., setting clear expectations), relationship strains still will occur. Whether and how those strains are resolved is important (Safran, Muran, & Proskurov, 2009). But because of the power differentials in supervision, the supervisee may be reluctant to raise issues of conflict, and the supervisor may be oblivious to them. It is important, then, that the supervisee or consultee have permission to express disappointment, frustration, concerns, or even anger toward the supervisor or consultant—and that these expressions be treated as nondefensively as possible. This means acknowledging mistakes (Grant, Schofield, & Crawford, 2012) and maintaining a stance of humility (Watkins, Hook, Ramaeker, & Ramos, 2016) and having the skills to resolve relationship strains (Safran, Muran, Stevens, & Rothman, 2008).

4. **Provide clear and ongoing feedback and evaluation.** This is key to ensuring learning, as we discuss later. But it also has relationship dimensions that supervisors often do not recognize. When Ladany, Lehrman-Waterman, Molinaro, and Wolgast (1999) asked supervisees to describe ethical violations they perceived their supervisors to have engaged in, the largest single category, accounting for a third of the reported instances, involved failures in providing appropriate and timely feedback and evaluation. More recently, Li et al. (2016) found that when supervisors and supervisees each were asked to rank the importance of 10 supervisor behaviors, supervisees gave their highest ranking to "feedback and correction." Supervisors, though, ranked this sixth.

5. **Demonstrate multicultural competence.** Given the many possible combinations of individual differences that occur by virtue of age, gender, race and ethnicity, culture, disability status, and so on, it is possible to argue that virtually all supervision is multicultural (Killian, 2001). An effective learning alliance depends on the ability of the supervisor or consultant to address these differences as they occur within the supervisory or consultation relationship and also as they occur within the therapist–client relationship.

The Expertise-Development Model's Teaching/Learning Processes

Researchers have documented the hard and sustained efforts elite performers make to achieve their levels of expertise (e.g., Ericsson, Krampe, & Tesch-Römer, 1993). The popular literature also provides inspiring anecdotes about individuals, including, for example, basketball standouts Larry Bird practicing 500 free throws per day while in high school (Katzeff, 2001) and Kobe Bryant's commitment to shooting 400 shots during each shooting practice throughout his career (Manfred, 2013). Our personal favorite is the story of the celebrated cellist Pablo Casals, who is reported to have "continued to practice 5 hours to 6 hours a day well into his 80s because as he once stated: 'I think I am making progress'" (Lee, 2016, p. 895).

But coaches were guiding these sometimes heroic efforts. Our concern in this chapter is with them and, particularly, with the teaching/learning processes those coaches, supervisors, and consultants use to help psychotherapists develop expertise. Deliberate practice needs to be "designed practice" (Ericsson, 2006) for which the coaches (and supervisors and consultants) are responsible. One exemplar is UCLA's legendary basketball coach John Wooden whose coaching offers two particular lessons for psychotherapy supervisors and consultants. The first was in how he designed practice:

> Coach Wooden is unabashedly an advocate of drill . . . . However, drill for Coach Wooden is a means to an end, not an end in itself. . . . "I tried to teach according to the whole-part method. I would show them the whole thing to begin with. Then I'm going to break it down into the parts and work on the individual parts and then eventually bring them together." (Gallimore & Tharp, 2004, pp. 132, 133)

The second was Wooden's instructional method during practice. Gallimore and Tharp (2004) describe an interaction sequence

> in which the Coach simultaneously scolds and then specifically reinstructs: "I have been telling some of you for three years not to wind up when you pass the ball: Pass from the chest!" Perhaps the example of greatest artistry is his use of modeling. His demonstrations are rarely longer than 3 seconds, but are of such clarity that they leave an image in memory much like a text-book sketch. . . . [During drills] Wooden will whistle-down play, demonstrate the correct way to perform an act (M+), and then imitate the incorrect way the player has just performed (M−). He then remodels the M+. This sequence . . . appears to be an extraordinarily effective way of providing both feedback and discrimination training. (p. 123)

In short, those who are developing expertise not only practice more, but are guided to practice in particular ways. In Chapter 1, we depicted the Cycle of Excellence as repeating series of steps in which the therapist will, in turn: (a) determine baseline levels of effectiveness, (b) obtain systematic and ongoing performance feedback, and (c) engage in deliberate practice. Our concern in this chapter is with the supervisory and consultative functions that facilitate those processes. In Figure 4.2, we depict the therapist's process at the center and, around the perimeter, depict the functions that the supervisor or consultant will enact to help the therapist engage in this process.

Coach Wooden broke basketball performance into its component parts, which is a strategy we discuss with respect to the expertise-development of psychotherapist. For purposes of presenting the instruction and learning aspects of our model, we similarly break the supervisor's or consultant's functions into discrete functions, as depicted in Figure 4.2. In so doing, we recognize that, in practice, these functions actually work together in interaction with one another. So, for example, a consultant and therapist might watch a video of that therapist's work while at the same time evaluating that work against their training goals and offering feedback and instruction as the video progresses. This is analogous to Coach Wooden's single interaction sequence of offering both feedback and instruction. But our treating each supervisory or consultative function as a separate part of a larger process allows us to give necessary, specific attention to each.

Function 1: Obtain Information about Therapist Performance

Deliberate practice focuses on tasks that are just outside the person's current levels of maximal performance (Ericsson, 2009). The supervisor's or consultant's first step, then, is to determine what those current levels are. To do this, the information comes from three

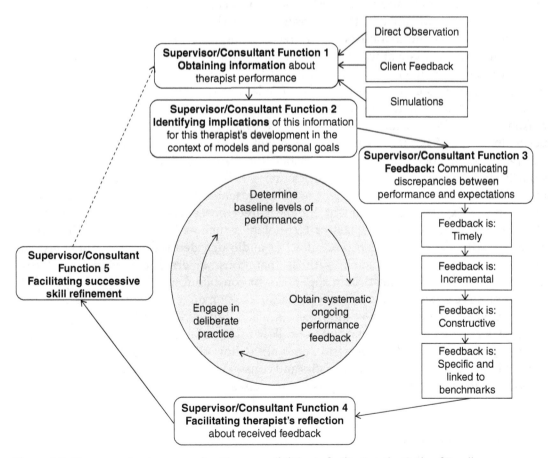

Figure 4.2 The supervisor's or consultant's responsibilities in facilitating the Cycle of Excellence.

sources: direct observation of the therapist's performance, information obtained from clients through routine outcome monitoring (ROM), and simulations of psychotherapy.

Direct Observation of Therapist's Performance

Supervisors and consultants rely heavily—and, too often, exclusively—on supervisees' and consultees' narrative accounts of their work with clients (Goodyear & Nelson, 1997; Hicks, 2009). Haggerty and Hilsenroth (2011) nicely underscored the challenges this poses:

> Suppose a loved one has to undergo surgery and you need to choose between two surgeons, one of whom has never been directly observed by an experienced surgeon while performing any surgery. He or she would perform the surgery and return to his or her attending physician and try to recall, sometimes incompletely or inaccurately, the intricate steps of the surgery they just performed. It is hard to imagine that anyone, given a choice, would prefer this over a professional who has been routinely observed in the practice of their craft. (p. 193)

Routine observation results in better training. Even when supervisees and consultees intend to provide a full and accurate verbal description of their work, their accounts will be limited by selective memory, by the constraints that verbal descriptions impose, and by the difficulties trainees and therapists have in recognizing which aspects of their interactions with clients are most salient to report. These limitations are compounded by the tendency for supervisees to deliberately withhold and distort information in supervision, mainly to manage the supervisor's impression of them (Ladany et al., 1996; Yourman & Farber, 1996). Even though practicing therapists who are seeking consultation for their work have less reason to withhold or distort information (i.e., they are not subject to the high-stakes evaluation that supervisees face), pride and other factors still can affect what they report.

Supervision practice guidelines (e.g., Association for Counselor Education and Supervision, 2011; American Psychological Association, 2014) are explicit in asserting the importance of direct observation of trainees, which is essential to supervisors and consultants who use the Expertise-Development Model. Direct observation can occur though live observation (through one-way glass or technologies such as http://www.isupelive.com/), cotherapy with the supervisee or consultee, or audio or video recordings. There also are internet-based technologies, such as those that Rousmaniere and Frederickson (2013) described, which enable a far-distant supervisor or consultant who has special expertise to directly observe sessions and even provide within-session directives to the therapist.

Each method of direct observation has its place. But audio—and, especially, video—recordings are especially important as they allow review of particular sequences and even microsequences, which live supervision does not (Chow et al., 2015; see also Chapter 8 in this volume). As we note later, supervisors and consultants also can assign therapists to use video recordings as part of their DP practice exercises.

Outcome Information Obtained from Clients

Information about week-to-week client functioning is also essential to the Expertise-Development Model. ROM systems that employ norm-referenced rating scales that clients complete after sessions have created important new opportunities for understanding psychotherapy impacts. The data they provide about both client functioning and client perceptions of the therapeutic alliance are invaluable for supervision and consultation (Reese et al., 2009; Swift et al., 2015).

In Chapter 5 of this volume, Chapman, Black, Drinane, Bach, and Owen describe the use of ROM data to improve client outcomes. Those data can help the therapist track the progress of individual clients and are especially valuable when they indicate that the client is not progressing as expected (Duncan & Reese, 2016). But ROM data also can provide information about how the therapist is performing with particular groups of clients, as shown in this example from Swift et al. (2015). In this case, the data in front of the supervisor and supervisee are a spreadsheet with progress information linked to various clients who are described by race and ethnicity as well as by diagnostic category.

> **Supervisor**   Looking at these results overall, what trends stand out to you?
>
> **Clinician**   I did notice that all three of my African American clients got better.
>
> **Supervisor**   Right. It might be worth reflecting on what worked with these clients, and helped them stick around for more sessions. Do you notice any other trends? What about presenting problems?
>
> **Clinician**   I seem to do better with anxiety and worse with depression.
>
> **Supervisor**   I noticed that too. It looks like two, possibly three, of your four clients with depression may have dropped out. Do you have any ideas about that?
>
> **Clinician**   Honestly, I never fully understood the treatment approach I was using. I felt like I was just reading out of the manual. The clients might have noticed that.
>
> **Supervisor**   Okay, so sounds like we will want to talk more about what was working with your African American clients and also review the treatment for depression that you have been learning. Looking at the spreadsheet, do you notice anything else? (Swift et al., 2015, p. 183)

As this example illustrates, ROM data do not provide guidance about what specific changes the therapist should enact or what skills need to be better developed. But those data do signal the need to look to other information that may provide the necessary help. This might include, for example:

- An especially close review of video recordings of sessions with that client (or, as in the example given, multiple clients of a particular type).
- Examining clients' perception of the alliance. Some ROM systems (e.g., Partners for Change Outcome Management System) readily provide that information to therapists. Miller, Hubble, and Chow (Chapter 2 in this volume) have usefully distinguished between *lag* ROM measures (i.e., trends in client functioning over sessions) and *lead* measures (i.e., measures of alliance). As the terms suggest, lag measures focus on performance that has occurred more distally in time; lead measures give more immediate data to inform therapist improvement.
- In addition, the therapist might obtain additional information from the client or clients using qualitative methods, as described by McCleod in Chapter 6 of this volume, or dialogues with the client, as Chapman et al. describe in Chapter 5.

Before ending this subsection, we would add that client dropout rates (Swift & Greenberg, 2015) are an important additional type of information to use. But because this information accrues over time, it is another type of lag measure; in fact, it has even greater lag than ROM measures of client functioning, as dropout rates require data on multiple clients over time. Dropout rates then can be used to stimulate reflection and analysis (e.g., are there differential dropout rates for particular types of clients the trainee or therapist is seeing?)

Information Obtained from Simulations

A third means of obtaining information about therapist performance is the use of simulations with actors who have been trained to present as clients with particular diagnoses or constellations of problems. (See Chapter 12 in this volume.) Objective structured clinical examinations, which employ standardized patients, have become widely used in medication education, including in psychiatry (Hodges, Hollenberg, McNaughton, Hanson, & Regehr, 2014). Although newer to psychology training, these examinations now are being used in that context as well (Sheen, McGillivray, Gurtman, & Boyd, 2015; Yap, Bearman, Thomas, & Hay, 2012). Anderson's measure of facilitative interpersonal skills (Anderson et al., 2009; Anderson, Patterson, & Weis, 2007) is a simulation that has been shown to have especially high levels of validity (Anderson, Crowley, Himawan, Holmberg, & Uhlin, 2016).

Simulations provide training-relevant information from two perspectives: (a) that of the supervisor or consultant who observes interactions with the standardized patient and (b) that of the standardized patient who reports what she or he observed in interaction with the therapist. To some extent, role-plays between trainee and supervisor or consultant can provide similar information and have the advantages of both spontaneity in response to a particular therapist sequence and cost. Their effectiveness, though, depends on the enactment skills of the supervisor or consultant. The costs of using standardized clients can be reduced by working with university drama departments, which might provide actors and actresses (Schram & Mudd, 2015).

Note that we are discussing simulations and role-plays as sources of information about performance. But they also can be used for training, as we discuss later.

Function 2: Identifying Gaps between Observed and Desired Performance

Assume that you review your records and find that over the past year, 25% of your clients have terminated treatment by their third session. Your interpretation of this will be very different if you know that this rate is much lower or much higher than that of therapists who are treating similar kinds of clients or if this rate is substantially higher or lower than you have had in prior years.

Information about a therapist's performance needs to be interpreted against some standard or benchmark. One of Ericsson's (2008) conditions for developing improved performance is that the individual be given "a task with a well-defined goal" (p. 991), against which his or her performance is then benchmarked. This is the basis for the feedback that supervisors and consultant will deliver. Some of those performance goals inevitably will be informed by the supervisor's or consultant's own theoretical model, for that is the mental map they bring to their work. But it is important as well that they incorporate goals that are more specific to the particular trainee or therapist.

When the trainee or therapist is being trained to proficiency, then training goals are defined by competence standards (e.g., Hatcher et al., 2013) or by level of fidelity to a particular treatment model (Prowse, Nagel, Meadows, & Enticott, 2015). But training goals are much more individualized for therapists who are working to develop increasing expertise. Defining those goals might begin, for example, with ROM data on a set of that therapist's clients who deteriorated in treatment or at least have done less well than expected and might proceed to examining other data (video recordings, data on alliance quality, qualitative information) to identify some aspect of the therapist's work that is contributing to these results. In this case, the goals for training are often co-constructed during interactions between supervisor and supervisee or consultant and therapist.

This process of evaluating therapist performance information against benchmarks not only affects the feedback that the supervisor or consultant will provide but helps trainees develop their own cognitive maps that enable self-monitoring of their performance. The ability to discriminate what constitutes a good or expected response is a prerequisite to being able to demonstrate that response (Carkhuff, 1969). As Kruger and Dunning (1999) observed, "Those with limited knowledge in a domain suffer a dual burden: Not only do they reach mistaken conclusions and make regrettable errors, but their incompetence robs them of the ability to realize it" (p. 1132).

Function 3: Providing Feedback

Having therapists' performance information and then having compared that performance to some standard sets the stage for delivering the feedback that is so essential to all therapists, regardless of experience levels. Tracey et al. (2014) observed that the unavailability of routine feedback contributes to therapists' overestimates of their level of performance (Walfish, McAlister, O'Donnell, & Lambert, 2012). The unavailability of feedback also results in their being poor judges both of the extent to which they are adhering to their intended treatment model (Martino, Ball, Nich, Frankforter, & Carroll, 2009) and of whether their clients are deteriorating (Hannan et al., 2005; Hatfield, McCullough, Frantz, & Krieger, 2010). And most important for our purposes, the unavailability of quality feedback is a barrier to developing expertise (Tracey et al., 2014).

Our use of the term *quality feedback* suggests that feedback varies in its usefulness. It is important that the supervisor or consultant provide "actionable feedback" (Larson, Patel, Evans, & Saiman, 2013) that will noticeably improve the therapist's performance. Hattie and Timperley's (2007) definition of feedback meets that criterion. They assert that feedback is information to another person that is intended "to reduce discrepancies between current understandings and performance and a goal . . . [and which] must answer three major questions . . . Where am I going? (What are the goals?), How am I going? (What progress is being made toward the goal?), and Where to next?" (p. 86).

The first rule supervisors and consultants should follow in making feedback actionable is to provide it on a regular and ongoing basis (i.e., timeliness). Other qualities of the feedback therapists receive are that it should be incremental, constructive, and specific.

Providing Timely Feedback

Brehaut et al. (2016) recommend that feedback be provided "as soon as possible and at a frequency informed by the number of new patient cases" (p. 436). There are several practices that supervisors and consultants can employ to help ensure that this occurs. One is making sure that the therapist is given ongoing access to, and the opportunity to process the meaning of, client progress data from ROM (Lambert, 2005). This enables the therapist to more objectively track the progress of individual clients as well as (depending on the data available at the particular work setting) the therapist's overall treatment success in comparison with peers in that setting. Timely feedback also can be provided when recordings of the therapist's work are a regular part of the supervision or consultation session. But the usefulness of those reviews depends on how the supervisor or consultant conducts them. For example, providing therapists with feedback that includes direct guidance is more effective (Kirchner, Sweller, & Clark, 2006) than discovery learning when reviewing recordings. It is fine if in observing a recording the therapist discovers particular things about his or her performance, but the supervisor or consultant needs to offer feedback as well. Therefore, the supervisor or consultant might ask questions like "What are you noticing in this session?" but then be sure to later provide his or her own feedback that links performance to agreed-upon learning goals. It may be that, as some have suggested (Kruse, 2012), this type of instruction is more usefully termed *feedforward*.

The issue of *when* to give the feedback is another aspect of timeliness. Usual practice is that supervisees receive feedback during supervision or consultation that occurs relatively soon after a therapy session. But Couchon and Bernard (1984) found that supervision delivered 4 hours prior to a counseling session had greater impact on counselor in-session behavior than supervision that occurred 2 days prior to the session. This is only one study, but it does offer a promising strategy for supervisors and consultants who work from the Expertise-Development Model to consider. Perhaps one way for a supervisor or consultant to capitalize on this finding would be to offer feedback and practice shortly after a session, then to offer coaching prior to a session where emerging skills are being demonstrated.

Providing Incremental Feedback

In the Expertise-Development Model, the supervisor or consultant provides feedback in digestible units that focus on performance goals that are just slightly beyond the learner's current level of functioning. For example, a supervisor or consultant may work to help a trainee develop stronger facilitative interpersonal skills (which are defined as "a person's ability to perceive, understand, and communicate a wide range of interpersonal messages, as well as a person's ability to persuade others with personal problems to apply suggested solutions to their problems and abandon maladaptive patterns," Anderson et al., 2009, p. 759). To do so, she or he may teach behavioral skills first (eye contact, body posture, etc.) and verbal skills afterward (careful listening, accurate reflection, etc.). Each set of skills might first be taught with the supervisor or coach role-playing a client who is friendly, approachable, and motivated for therapy. When the learner has succeeded with that role-play, the supervisor or coach could increase the difficultly by role-playing a client who is disagreeable and ambivalent about therapy—and, to further increase the difficulty, a client with psychotic symptoms.

No matter how carefully a supervisor or consultant titrates and processes feedback with the supervisee or consultee, there is the risk that she or he will misunderstand it. It is important, therefore, to ask supervisees and consultees to summarize the feedback they heard and its implications for their work. Doing this provides an opportunity to discuss missed or misunderstood information. The act of recounting it also aids in the cognitive consolidation of that feedback.

Providing Constructive Feedback

Feedback often creates a state of disequilibrium in the learner. It is important, therefore, that feedback not only be incremental, as noted, focusing on chunks that are manageable by the learner (Ericsson, 2006), but that it not elicit defensiveness or other forms of affective arousal that will interfere with how therapists hear and use it. To that end, supervisors and consultants often provide a "feedback sandwich" in which they cushion corrective feedback with positive feedback that both precedes and follows it: a positive-critical-positive sequence. But James (2015) questioned the utility of this approach, noting especially the danger of the supervisor or consultant coming up with vague or even patronizing statements as in this example.

> "I like your voice, BUT you have a tendency to out-pace your client . . . however, the therapy room was arranged really well." In this example, the opening statement is not specific enough (i.e. ideally, one needs to say what one liked about the therapist's voice). And the final statement is not related to the first two, perhaps indicating that one is struggling to say anything else positive about the trainee's mode of delivery. (p. 762)

James (2015) suggested the supervisors and consultants instead follow this seven-step sequence:

1. Ensuring the learners are aware of the purpose of the feedback.
2. Learners commenting about the goals they were trying to achieve during their task.
3. Learners stating what features of the task they thought they'd done well.
4. Supervisor stating what features were done well.
5. Learners stating what could be improved.
6. Supervisor stating what should be improved.
7. Agreeing on action plans for improvement. (p. 763)

Above all, it is important that feedback be delivered in descriptive rather than evaluative language. This is implied in the sequence that James (2015) described, but it is important that this be explicit.

Providing Specific Feedback Linked to Benchmarks

Too often the feedback supervisors provide is positive and global (Friedlander, Siegel, & Brenock, 1989). But actionable feedback needs to be simple and precise. So instead of focusing on global goals (i.e., "Try to build a stronger alliance with the client"), supervisors and consultants who use the Expertise-Development Model focus on isolating and practicing specific behavioral component skills within those goals.

At least one barrier to feedback specificity resides in supervisors' and consultants' own fears and difficulties in particular interpersonal circumstances. Hoffman, Hill, Holmes, and Freitas (2005) found, for example, that the discomfort supervisors felt as they anticipated giving difficult (i.e., corrective) feedback led them to become vague. Ironically, the effect is to deprive supervisees who could most use very clear feedback of the opportunity to receive it. Racial and ethnic differences between supervisor/consultant and supervisee/consultee also can contribute to difficulties in providing straightforward feedback (Burkard, Knox, Clarke, Phelps, & Inman, 2014; Constantine & Sue, 2007). The fact that supervisors and consultants have these difficulties speaks to the need for they themselves to receive consultation to guide *their* skill development.

Finally, we would observe that trainees and therapists often receive feedback in a group context. It is important for the facilitators of those groups to ensure feedback specificity as well. This means training the members at the outset about expectations for feedback delivery and then modeling it in the group.

Function 4: Facilitating Critical Reflection about Feedback

Once trainees and therapists have received feedback, they engage in a cognitive process to link this new knowledge to intended action. Supervisors and consultants usually help trainees and therapists to engage in this process as they deliver the feedback: These are not discrete processes. But we discuss this separately here to underscore its importance.

This processing often is considered under the framework of critical reflection, a concept Dewey (1910) introduced a century ago and that now has been declared a foundational competence for psychologists (Fouad et al., 2009). To us, the key word is "critical": It speaks to an analysis of what the feedback means to psychologists and how they will implement it. Supervisors or consultants can facilitate and even guide that critical reflective process as it moderates the impact of feedback on the intended action plan going forward (see Pelgrim, Kramer, Mokkink, & Van der Vleuten, 2013).

There also are variants of this cognitive processing that can apply in a deliberate practice paradigm. For example, Chow et al. (2015) included "[m]entally running through and reflecting on the past sessions in your mind" and "[m]entally running through and reflecting on what to do in future sessions" (page 340) as behaviors related to DP. And there also is a literature, especially in sports psychology, concerning the use of mental rehearsal as a form of deliberate practice (Cumming & Hall, 2002; Nordin, Cumming, Vincent, & McGrory, 2006).

Function 5: Facilitating Successive Skill Refinement

Skill acquisition and refinement requires considerable behavioral repetition (Ericsson & Charness, 1994). This stands in contrast to knowledge acquisition, which does not require behavioral repetition and is a focus of traditional supervision. (See Table 4.1.) As a result, supervisors and consultants using the Expertise-Development Model employ active learning methods, including simulation-based behavioral rehearsal: Learners practice skills rather than talk about theory. That action orientation occurs both during supervision and consultation and then in the assignments given to the trainee and the therapist during the week that follows.

Table 4.1 Traditional supervision or consultation versus simulation-based behavioral rehearsal

Traditional Supervision or Consultation	Simulation-Based Behavioral Rehearsal
Teaching about psychotherapy theory, models, etc.	Practicing skills via role-plays with coach or peers
Discussing or talking about theory, models, etc.	Learners practicing skills by reviewing and discussing videos of their sessions

Table 4.2 Examples of tasks assigned to trainees or therapists to achieve particular training goals.

Examples of Training Goals	Responses to Trainee or Therapist
Build a stronger alliance with the client	Notice each time the client breaks eye contact (taking into account possible cultural factors).
	Match the client's speech volume and pacing.
	Ask if the client thinks you understand what he/she just said.
Help the client get in touch with feelings	Ask the client to identify the emotion(s) he/she is having right now.
	Ask the client if any physical sensations accompany his/her emotions right now.
	Ask the client to notice if emotions are rising or falling in intensity or changing into other emotions.
Become more aware of countertransference	Notice if you have any feelings toward the client right now.
	Notice if there is anything about the client you wish you could change.
	Notice if the client reminds you of any people or situations in your current or past life.

During Supervision or Consultation Sessions

During their sessions with the trainee or therapist, supervisors or consultants are getting information about performance and providing feedback, as we have described. But this time together also affords the trainee or therapist the opportunity to intervene and begin practicing new skills. Earlier we gave the example of Coach Wooden who would, in one sequence, watch a player perform, give that player feedback about what was problematic in that performance, and then give instruction (both verbally and through modeling). Similar sequences occur during supervision and consultations sessions that are informed by the Expertise-Development Model. In Table 4.2, we provide some examples.

Also, consider this possible sequence as a more elaborate illustration:

- The therapist and consultant draw on a combination of clinical judgment, ROM data, and client verbal report to identify a case that is stuck.
- The therapist picks a video of a recent session with that client, then watches the video with the consultant to identify some aspect of the therapist's performance that could be improved.

- The consultant demonstrates the skill that might be improved by role-playing the therapist.
- They then switch roles, and the consultant role-plays the client while the therapist practices the new techniques. The consultant continues the role-play for 30 minutes, with increasingly challenging dialogues, until the therapist has demonstrated that mastery of the new techniques.
- Throughout the consultation, the supervisor aims to maximize the amount of time the supervisee is performing behavioral rehearsal rather than talking about the skills.
- At the end of the consultation session, the consultant assigns the homework to the therapist: "Spend an hour watching older videos of sessions with this client. Notice when this particular sequence we identified as challenging occurs. At that moment pause the video and practice responding to the client in the ways we have been rehearsing here."

DP Assignments for Between-Supervision/Consultation Sessions

Note that the consultant in the last example ended the session with a homework assignment. The original DP study of violinists found that solitary DP was to be only variable that predicted expertise: "There is complete correspondence between the skill level of the groups and their average accumulation of practice time alone with the violin" (Ericsson et al., 1993, p. 379). This means that it is incumbent on the supervisor or consultant, to work with the therapist to design exercises in which they might engage solitarily throughout the week.

Some of the work of the supervisor or consultant will, of course, focus on particular cases with whom the therapists are working. Hilsenroth and Diener (Chapter 8 of this volume) provide an excellent discussion of using feedback to guide skill development in that way. But one thing that sets the Expertise-Development Model apart is the use of drills or exercises that are separate from the routine performance of psychotherapy. There are several reasons why focusing only on routine performance is insufficient for expertise development.

- Focusing solely on routine practice continues to strengthen what the person already is doing. The maxim "Practice makes permanent, though not necessarily perfect" can apply in this case.
- The premise of deliberate practice is that the key to development is repetition in addressing increasingly challenging situations. But some events or processes occur only occasionally or even rarely in the routine practice of psychotherapy.
- As skills in any domain develop, they become increasingly automatized and function with reduced self-awareness. Csikszentmihályi (1990) discussed the related phenomenon of *flow* in which the person becomes so engaged with a task that she or he can lose track of time. But DP aims for the opposite of flow: a continuous process of disequilibrium that allows for continual improvement (Ericsson, 2006).

To enter a particular session armed with a supervisor's or consultant's feedback and directives can help disrupt automaticity and focus attention more deliberately. But even when trainees and therapists have the benefit of feedback, they still have to overcome the challenge of having infrequent opportunities to practice particular behaviors and sequences.

The alternative is exercises or drills that the supervisor or consultant works with the therapist to design. Often these exercises include therapists watching particular videos of their own therapy sessions and practicing specific skills related to the three domains of assessment, intervention, and self-awareness. In other words, therapists practice making assessments, saying interventions to the client in the video, and tuning in to their own experience while the video is playing (in real time). The therapist's level of development affects the way the task is structured, so beginners might do one of those domains at a time, rotating between them every 5–10–15 minutes, whereas experts would practice doing all domains simultaneously.

Skill Refinement and Skill Development

DP has two targets. One is to preserve and enhance already-mastered areas of functioning. The other is to engage in practice with new skills that stretch. We suggest that supervisors and consultants develop two types of exercises for the therapists with whom they are working.

One would be warm-ups in which therapists practice basic skills in which they already are competent. To practice these as separate exercises breaks up automaticity and allows for further refinement. The goal is to get therapists into the right frame of mind (treatment model and role) before engaging in work performance. These warm-ups can be short: 15 to 30 minutes.

The other would be skill development exercises, focusing on skills that are just beyond the therapist's current level of proficiency. These exercises might be longer, but we suggest that they not be shorter than the time of a typical therapy session because the goal is to build endurance.

Ericsson (2006) observed that "elite performers in many diverse domains have been found to practice, on the average, roughly the same amount every day, including weekends, and the amount of practice never consistently exceeds five hours per day" (p. 699). One lesson for psychotherapy supervisors and consultants, then, is to help therapists develop a routine that would occur at roughly the same time every day—and this also may involve helping them negotiate their work situations to free up that protected space. Those in salaried jobs, especially, will need the support of their superiors to have that space. While engaged in that routine, therapists should be engaged in the same way they would with work performance and should be undisturbed (e.g., turn off phones, internet access, etc.).

The other task is to continue to motivate and encourage therapists to maintain that routine. DP not as intrinsically enjoyable as the practice of psychotherapy. It is hard work, and even the "grittiest" (Duckworth & Eskreis-Winkler, 2013) psychotherapist will need support and encouragement to sustain it.

There also is the practical matter that separates psychotherapists from performers in other domains, such as athletics and music, who can spend hours each day engaged in DP: Psychotherapists have work demands that limit the time they can protect for DP and so they are unlikely to be able to give as much time to DP as, say, professional athletes. The important issue, though, is that there be some time set aside routinely and that it be protected.

Additional Issues Related to Implementing the Expertise-Development Model

Earlier we used Figure 4.2 to organize our discussion of the Expertise-Development Model. But several issues that did not logically fit into that organizational structure are important to address. These concern the roles that the supervisor or consultant might use, the domains of therapist functioning on which supervision and consultation might focus, matching supervisor's or therapist's own clinical expertise to training needs, and the importance of the therapist (initially) learning one model well.

Supervisor or Consultant Role

Although the Expertise-Development Model is focused on teaching, we do not intend to convey that the supervisor's or consultant's role is exclusively didactic. Bernard (1997) described the three primary roles that supervisors enact as those of teacher, consultant, and counselor or therapist; these roles correspond roughly to Friedlander and Ward's (1984) task-oriented, attractive, and interpersonally sensitive styles, respectively. The supervisors' or consultants' theoretical model will affect which of these roles and styles they emphasize more (Putney, Worthington, & McCullough, 1992). In the case of the Expertise-Development Model, the supervisor or consultant would rely heavily, but not exclusively, on the teacher role and a task-oriented style.

Effective teaching optimizes the balance between the extent to which the learner is challenged and that to which she or he is supported. This optimization can occur at a task structure level, so the learner is challenged with task to go just beyond his or her comfort zone. But it also means being available to support and encourage in what Bernard (1997) calls the consultant role, or even in the therapist role. This is especially important in deliberate practice, which requires ongoing, hard work: The supervisor's or consultant's encouragement can be important.

Matching Supervisor or Consultant Clinical Expertise to Therapist Training Needs

Ericsson, Prietula, and Cokely (2007) observed:

> [F]uture experts need different kinds of teachers at different stages of their development. In the beginning, most are coached by local teachers, people who can give generously of their time and praise. Later on, however, it is essential that performers seek out more-advanced teachers to keep improving their skills. Eventually, all top performers work closely with teachers who have themselves reached international levels of achievement. (p. 119)

This means that those of us who supervise and consult should be mindful of our own clinical skills and supervise or consult accordingly. Of course, if we are continually following our own personal paths toward ever-increasing expertise, the range of those with whom we can work will expand over time as well.

Also, much consultation is done as peer supervision. Therefore, an implication would seem to be that therapists should choose peers who are at least of an equal level of expertise development themselves.

Learning One Model Well Initially

The Expertise-Development Model assumes that as therapists becomes increasingly expert, they will develop an increasingly individualized model of practice. That is, in responding to the feedback they obtain about their performance, they inevitably will drift away from adherence to a particular model. But we assume that it is useful to begin by learning a particular model well. This can mean, for example, using treatment manuals early in training, as they provide very clear guidelines regarding desired responses for particular models of training. Therefore, they facilitate the development of discrimination skills (with respect to those models) and also the ability to execute the desired skills with fidelity.

But in using treatment manuals, supervisors who follow the Expertise-Development Model still will be attentive to client outcomes. So even as the person learns adherence or fidelity to the model, she or he also is learning to attend to the feedback on the impacts they have. As the supervisee gains experience, the supervisor will increasingly focus on appropriate responsiveness to the client and to feedback (Hatcher, 2015).

Conclusion

In the title we chose for this chapter, we intended to signal that expertise exists on a continuum and that the important issue is that the therapist is continually improving. The intent is for all therapists to focus their development on becoming their personal best rather than on their place in reference to other therapists (e.g., to become in the top X% of therapists).

The model presented in this chapter aims to join the expertise and clinical supervision literature. The idea of using deliberate practice to benefit supervision is new and was exciting for us to think through. But because it is new, there is much yet to be fleshed out. As increasing numbers of supervisors and consultants adopt this model, we hope gradually to be able to add more specificity to it.

Finally, we focus in this chapter on how supervisors and consultants can implement the Expertise-Development Model in order to help foster the continuing development of therapists. But the model applies just as well to their own work. We hope that those who provide supervision and consultation will commit not only to their own expertise development as therapists but also as supervisors or consultants who themselves should be working to become every day a little better as supervisors or consultants.

Questions from the Editors

Question #1. In this chapter, many examples of expertise in other areas (e.g., sports, music) are discussed. In those areas, there are identifiable experts (e.g., Michael Jordan in basketball, Lionel Messi in soccer, Pablo Casals in music), but they are very rare—most athletes and musicians are not in the elite categories but perform adequately. This raises the question of whether most therapists are good enough already and whether achieving expert status is worth the effort. Why should therapists strive to be experts? Said another way, why is competence not sufficient for most clinicians?

Answer from Authors: It is true that identifiable experts tend to be the very rare elite who typically comprise the top fraction of 1% of people in that particular domain. Certainly the principles and practices outlined in this book would apply to anyone striving for elite status. But this book is not written for them. Rather, it is intended for *all* therapists, regardless of how effective they might be at the point they read it. As this chapter's title suggests, expertise development is a lifelong process that involves commitment to the hard work necessary to attain ongoing improvement. In short, it assumes that as the therapists continue to improve, their point of reference will be their own performance rather than how they are ranking against the larger population of therapists.

The question ends by raising what surely is a value issue: Why is competence not sufficient for most clinicians? Certainly the large literature in psychology on competence implies that competence *is* sufficient. And, of course, we believe that it provides the essential foundation for moving ahead toward expertise. But we would assert that we as individual therapists have an ethical obligation to provide the best services we possibly can—and this means a commitment to continually improving.

Question #2. In many countries, particularly the United States, post licensure (credentialed/ registered), no supervision or consultation is required of practicing clinicians. What can be accomplished at the policy level to encourage supervision and/or consultation for practicing clinicians? And how can supervision and consultation involve more aspects of deliberate practice?

Answer from Authors: Policy change will occur to the extent that there are changes in attitudes. The competence movement in U.S. psychology provides a useful example: Over the past 15 years, professional organizations (especially the Association of Psychology and Postdoctoral Internship Centers and the American Psychological Association) sponsored conferences and commissioned follow-up papers. They both coincided with and further stimulated work by training programs to implement competence models. And then these changes eventually became codified in accreditation standards and in regulatory policy (as promoted then by the Association of State and Provincial Psychology Boards).

In short, this was a systemic change that resulted from a shift in attitudes that, in turn, was prompted by a larger national and international conversation about accountability in higher education. It would seem that these same mechanisms might be brought into play for actions to enact requirements for lifelong supervision.

The second part of this question concerns how we ensure that supervision and consultation practices embody more of the deliberate practice model we have discussed. As with the first part of this question, this will require attitude shifts. Fortunately, there already are conversations in the professional literature about the limited evidence that supervision affects client outcomes (e.g., Watkins, 2011). What we propose has the possibility of addressing that issue. And so the challenge now is to more widely disseminate the model—and to bolster it now with evidence of its effectiveness.

Question #3. It is not an easy matter to get supervisors and consultants trained to a deliberate practice orientation. How do you propose, in terms of education and training, to implement a deliberate practice model in psychotherapy in supervision and consultation?

Answer from Authors: In our response to the prior question, we addressed some of the attitudinal shifts that will have to occur. But those who teach supervision and consultation also need practical guidelines for how this might work. This chapter is intended to provide that. A useful follow-up would be videos to depict it in practice—and then opportunities to train the trainers in the model. We recommend such a program to ensure that those who teach supervision and consultation are themselves knowledgeable about this model.

References

American Psychological Association. (2015). Guidelines for clinical supervision in health service psychology. *American Psychologist, 70,* 33–46.

Anderson, T., Crowley, M.E.J., Himawan, L., Holmberg, K., & Uhlin, B. D. (2016). Therapist facilitative interpersonal skills and training status: A randomized clinical trial on alliance and outcome. *Psychotherapy Research, 26,* 511–529. doi:10.1080/10503307.2015.1049671

Anderson, T., Ogles, B. M., Patterson, C. L., Lambert, M. J., & Vermeersch, D. A. (2009). Therapist effects: Facilitative interpersonal skills as a predictor of therapist success. *Journal of Clinical Psychology, 65*(7), 755–768.

Anderson, T., Patterson, C. L., & Weis, A. C. (2007). *Facilitative interpersonal skills performance analysis rating method.* Unpublished coding manual, Department of Psychology, Ohio University, Athens, OH.

Association for Counselor Education and Supervision. (2011, April). *Best practices in clinical supervision.* Retrieved from http://www.acesonline.net/sites/default/files/ACES-Best-Practices-in-clinical-supervision-document-FINAL.pdf

Association of State and Provincial Psychology Boards. (2009). *Guidelines on practicum experience for licensure.* Retrieved from http://www.asppb.net/?page=Guidelines

Bambling, M., King, R., Raue, P., Schweitzer, R., & Lambert, W. (2006). Clinical supervision: Its influence on client-rated working alliance and client symptom reduction in the brief treatment of major depression. *Psychotherapy Research, 16*(3), 317–331.

Bernard, J. M. (1997). The discrimination model. In C. E. Watkins (Ed.), *Handbook of psychotherapy supervision* (pp. 310–327). New York, NY: Wiley.

Bernard, J. M., & Goodyear, R. K. (2014). *Fundamentals of clinical supervision* (5th ed.). Boston, MA: Merrill.

Beutler, L. E., & Howard, M. (2003). Training in psychotherapy: Why supervision does not work. *Clinical Psychologist, 56,* 12–16.

Borders, L. D., Glosoff, H. L., Welfare, L. E., Hays, D. G., DeKruyf, L., Fernando, D. M., & Page, B. (2014). Best practices in clinical supervision: Evolution of a counseling specialty. *Clinical Supervisor, 33,* 26–44. doi:10.1080/07325223.2014.905225

Brehaut, J. C., Colquhoun, H. L., Eva, K. W., Carroll, K., Sales, A., Michie, S., . . . Grimshaw, J. M. (2016). Practice feedback interventions: 15 suggestions for optimizing effectiveness. *Annals of Internal Medicine, 164*(6), 435–441. doi:10.7326/M15-2248

Burkard, A. W., Knox, S., Clarke, R. D., Phelps, D. L., & Inman, A. G. (2014). Supervisors' experiences of providing difficult feedback in cross-ethnic/racial supervision. *Counseling Psychologist, 42*(3), 314–344.

California Board of Behavioral Sciences. (2016, January). *Statutes and regulations relating to the practice of professional clinical counseling, marriage and family therapy, educational psychology, clinical social work.* Retrieved from http://www.bbs.ca.gov/pdf/publications/lawsregs.pdf

Callahan, J. L., Almstrom, C. M., Swift, J. K., Borja, S. E., & Heath, C. J. (2009). Exploring the contribution of supervisors to intervention outcomes. *Training and Education in Professional Psychology, 3*(2), 72–77.

Carkhuff, R. R. (1969). *Helping and human relations: A primer for lay and professional leaders. Volume I: Selection and training.* New York, NY: Holt, Rinehart and Winston.

Carroll, M. (2010). Supervision: Critical reflection for transformational learning (Part 2). *Clinical Supervisor, 29*(1), 1–19. doi:10.1080/07325221003730301

Chow, D. L., Miller, S. D., Seidel, J. A., Kane, R. T., Thornton, J. A., & Andrews, W. P. (2015). The role of deliberate practice in the development of highly effective psychotherapists. *Psychotherapy, 52*(3), 337–345.

Constantine, M. G., & Sue, D. W. (2007). Perceptions of racial microaggressions among black supervisees in cross-racial dyads. *Journal of Counseling Psychology, 54*(2), 142–153.

Couchon, W. D., & Bernard, J. M. (1984). Effects of timing of supervision on supervisor and counselor performance. *Clinical Supervisor, 2*(3), 3–20.

Csikszentmihályi, M. (1990). *Flow: The psychology of optimal performance.* New York, NY: Cambridge University Press.

Cumming, J., & Hall, C. (2002). Deliberate imagery practice: The development of imagery skills in competitive athletes. *Journal of Sports Sciences, 20*(2), 137–145.

Dewey, J. (1910). *How we think.* Boston, MA: D. C. Heath.

Duckworth, A. L., & Eskreis-Winkler, L. (2013). True grit. *Observer, 26*(4), 1–3. Retrieved from http://www.psychologicalscience.org/index.php/publications/observer/2013/april-13/true-grit.html

Duncan, B. L., & Reese, R. J. (2016). Using PCOMS technology to improve outcomes and accelerate counselor development. In T. Rousmaniere & E. Renfro-Michel (Eds.), *Using technology to enhance clinical supervision* (pp. 135–156). Washington, DC: American Counseling Association

Ellis, M. V., Berger, L., Hanus, A. E., Ayala, E. E., Swords, B. A., & Siembor, M. (2014). Inadequate and harmful clinical supervision: Testing a revised framework and assessing occurrence. *Counseling Psychologist, 42*, 434–472. doi:10.1177/0011000013508656

Ellis, M. V., & Ladany, N. (1997). Inferences concerning supervisees and clients in clinical supervision: An integrative review. In C. E. Watkins Jr. (Ed.), *Handbook of psychotherapy supervision* (pp. 447–507). New York, NY: Wiley.

Ericsson, K. A. (2006). The influence of experience and deliberate practice on the development of superior expert performance. In K. A. Ericsson, N. Charness, P. J. Feltovich, & R. R. Hoffman (Eds.), *The Cambridge handbook of expertise and expert performance* (pp. 685–705). New York, NY: Cambridge University Press.

Ericsson, K. A. (2008). Deliberate practice and acquisition of expert performance: A general overview. *Academic Emergency Medicine: Official Journal of the Society for Academic Emergency Medicine, 15*, 988–994. doi:10.1111/j.1553-2712.2008.00227.x

Ericsson, K. A. (2009). *Development of professional expertise: Toward measurement of expert performance and design of optimal learning environments.* New York, NY: Cambridge University Press.

Ericsson, K. A., & Charness, N. (1994). Expert performance: Its structure and acquisition. *American Psychologist, 49*(8), 725–747.

Ericsson, K. A., Krampe, R. T., & Tesch-Römer, C. (1993). The role of deliberate practice in the acquisition of expert performance. *Psychological Review, 100*(3), 363–406.

Ericsson, K. A., Prietula, M. J., & Cokely, E. T. (2007). The making of an expert. *Harvard Business Review, 85*(7/8), 114–120.

Fouad, N. A., Grus, C. L., Hatcher, R. L., Kaslow, N. J., Hutchings, P. S., Madson, M. B., . . . Crossman, R. E. (2009). Competency benchmarks: A model for understanding and measuring competence in professional psychology across training levels. *Training and Education in Professional Psychology, 3*(4, Suppl.), S5–S26. doi:10.1037/a0015832

Freitas, G. J. (2002). The impact of psychotherapy supervision on client outcome: A critical examination of 2 decades of research. *Psychotherapy: Theory, Research, Practice, Training, 39*(4), 354–367.

Friedlander, M. L., Siegel, S. M., & Brenock, K. (1989). Parallel processes in counseling and supervision: A case study. *Journal of Counseling Psychology, 36*(2), 149–157.

Friedlander, M. L., & Ward, L. G. (1984). Development and validation of the Supervisory Styles Inventory. *Journal of Counseling Psychology, 31*(4), 541–557.

Gallimore, R., & Tharp, R. (2004). What a coach can teach a teacher, 1975–2004: Reflections and reanalysis of John Wooden's teaching practices. *Sport Psychologist, 18,* 119–137.

Goldberg, R., Dixon, A., & Wolf, C. P. (2012). Facilitating effective triadic counseling supervision: An adapted model for an underutilized supervision approach. *Clinical Supervisor, 31*(1), 42–60.

Goodyear, R. K. (2015). Supervision as pedagogy: Attending to its essential instructional and learning processes. *Clinical Supervisor, 33*(1), 82–99.

Goodyear, R. K., Falender, C., & Rousmaniere, T. (in press). Ethics of supervision and consultation in private practice. In S. Walfish, J. Barnett, & J. Zimmerman (Eds.), *The handbook of private practice.* New York, NY: Oxford University Press.

Goodyear, R. K., & Nelson, M. L. (1997). The major supervision formats. In C. E. Watkins, *Handbook of psychotherapy supervision* (pp. 328–344).New York, NY: Wiley.

Goodyear, R. K., Wampold, B. E., Tracey, T. J., & Lichtenberg, J . W. (in press). Psychotherapy expertise should mean superior outcomes and demonstrable improvement over time. *Counseling Psychologist.*

Grant, J., Schofield, M. J., & Crawford, S. (2012). Managing difficulties in supervision: Supervisors' perspectives. *Journal of Counseling Psychology, 59*(4), 528–541.

Guest, P. D., & Beutler, L. E. (1988). Impact of psychotherapy supervision on therapist orientation and values. *Journal of Consulting and Clinical Psychology, 56*(5), 653–658.

Haggerty, G., & Hilsenroth, M. J. (2011). The use of video in psychotherapy supervision. *British Journal of Psychotherapy, 27,* 193–210.

Hannan, C., Lambert, M. J., Harmon, C., Nielsen, S. L., Smart, D., Shimokawa, K. W., & Sutton, S. W. (2005). A lab test and algorithms for identifying clients at risk for treatment failure. *Journal of Clinical Psychology: In Session, 61,* 155–163. doi:10.1002/jclp.20108

Hatcher, R. L. (2015). Interpersonal competencies: Responsiveness, technique, and training in psychotherapy. *American Psychologist, 70*(8), 747–757.

Hatcher, R. L., Fouad, N. A., Grus, C. L., Campbell, L. F., McCutcheon, S. R., & Leahy, K. L. (2013). Competency benchmarks: Practical steps toward a culture of competence. *Training and Education in Professional Psychology, 7*(2), 84–91.

Hatfield, D., McCullough, L., Frantz, S. H., & Krieger, K. (2010). Do we know when our clients get worse? An investigation of therapists' ability to detect negative client change. *Clinical Psychology & Psychotherapy, 17*(1), 25–32. doi:10.1002/cpp.656

Hattie, J., & Timperley, H. (2007). The power of feedback. *Review of Educational Research, 77*(1), 81–112.

Heesacker, M., Petty, R. E., & Cacioppo, J. T. (1983). Field dependence and attitude change: Source credibility can alter persuasion by affecting message-relevant thinking. *Journal of Personality, 51*(4), 653–666.

Hicks, K. M. (2009). *Postdoctoral supervision: An exploratory study of recent practices and experiences* (Doctoral dissertation). Oklahoma State University. Retrieved from http://hdl.handle.net/11244/7428

Hodges, B. D., Hollenberg, E., McNaughton, N., Hanson, M. D., & Regehr, G. (2014). The psychiatry OSCE: A 20-year retrospective. *Academic Psychiatry, 38*(1), 26–34.

Hoffman, M. A., Hill, C. E., Holmes, S. E., & Freitas, G. F. (2005). Supervisor perspective on the process and outcome of giving easy, difficult, or no feedback to supervisees. *Journal of Counseling Psychology, 52*(1), 3–13.

James, I. A. (2015). The rightful demise of the sh* t sandwich: Providing effective feedback. *Behavioural and Cognitive Psychotherapy, 43*(6), 759–766.

Katzeff, P. (2001, January 3). Basketball player Larry Bird grit and discipline helped him lead championship teams. *Investors' Business Daily*. Retrieved from http://www.investors.com/news/management/leaders-and-success/basketball-player-larry-bird-grit-and-discipline-helped-him-lead-championship-teams/

Killian, K. D. (2001). Differences making a difference: Cross-cultural interactions in supervisory relationships. *Journal of Feminist Family Therapy, 12*(2–3), 61–103.

Kirschner, P. A., Sweller, J., & Clark, R. E. (2006). Why minimal guidance during instruction does not work: An analysis of the failure of constructivist, discovery, problem-based, experiential, and inquiry-based teaching. *Educational Psychologist, 41*(2), 75–86.

Kruger, J., & Dunning, D. (1999). Unskilled and unaware of it: How difficulties in recognizing one's own incompetence lead to inflated self-assessments. *Journal of Personality and Social Psychology, 77*(6), 1121–1134.

Kruse, K. (2012, July 19). Stop giving feedback, instead give feedforward. *Forbes*. Retrieved from http://www.forbes.com/sites/kevinkruse/2012/07/19/feedforward-coaching-for-performance/#2bbfe44b78e0

Ladany, N., Hill, C. E., Corbett, M. M., & Nutt, E. A. (1996). Nature, extent, and importance of what psychotherapy trainees do not disclose to their supervisors. *Journal of Counseling Psychology, 43*(1), 10–24.

Ladany, N., & Inman, A. G. (2012). Training and supervision. In E. M. Altmeier & J. I. Hanson (Eds.), *Oxford handbook of counseling psychology* (pp. 179–207). New York, NY: Oxford University Press.

Ladany, N., Lehrman-Waterman, D., Molinaro, M., & Wolgast, B. (1999). Psychotherapy supervisor ethical practices adherence to guidelines, the supervisory working alliance, and supervisee satisfaction. *Counseling Psychologist, 27(3),* 443–475.

Lambert, M. J. (2005). Emerging methods for providing clinicians with timely feedback on treatment effectiveness: An introduction. *Journal of Clinical Psychology, 61*(2), 141–144.

Larson, E. L., Patel, S. J., Evans, D., & Saiman, L. (2013). Feedback as a strategy to change behaviour: The devil is in the details. *Journal of Evaluation in Clinical Practice, 19*(2), 230–234.

Lee, M. J. (2016). On patient safety: When are we too old to operate? *Clinical Orthopaedics and Related Research, 474*(4), 895–898.

Li, C. I., Fairhurst, S., Chege, C., Jenks, E. H., Tsong, Y., Golden, D., . . . Schmitt, S. S. (2016). Card-sorting as a tool for communicating the relative importance of supervisor interventions. *Clinical Supervisor, 35*(1), 80–97.

Lichtenberg, J. W., Goodyear, R. K., Overland, E. A., & Hutman, H. B. (2014, March). *A snapshot of counseling psychology: Stability and change in the roles, identities and functions (2001–2014).* Presentation at the Counseling Psychology National Conference, Atlanta, GA.

Macdonald, J., & Mellor-Clark, J. (2015). Correcting psychotherapists' blindsidedness: Formal feedback as a means of overcoming the natural limitations of therapists. *Clinical Psychology and Psychotherapy, 22*(3), 249–257. doi:10.1002/cpp.1887

Maeschalck, C., Bargmann, S., Miller, S. D., & Bertolino, B. (2012). *Manual 3: Feedback-informed supervision.* Chicago, IL: ICCE Press.

Manfred, T. (2013, February 22). Kobe Bryant says he counts every single made shot during shooting practice, stops when he gets to 400. *Business Insider.* Retrieved from http://www.businessinsider.com/kobe-bryant-describes-shooting-practice-routine-2013-2

Markman, K. D., & Tetlock, P. E. (2000). Accountability and close-call counterfactuals: The loser who nearly won and the winner who nearly lost. *Personality and Social Psychology Bulletin, 26*(10), 1213–1224.

Martino, S., Ball, S., Nich, C., Frankforter, T. L., & Carroll, K. M. (2009). Correspondence of motivational enhancement treatment integrity ratings among therapists, supervisors, and observers. *Psychotherapy Research, 19*(2), 181–193.

McGaghie, W. C., & Kristopaitis, T. (2015). Deliberate practice and mastery learning: Origins of expert medical performance. In J. Cleland & S. J. Durning (Eds.), *Researching medical education* (pp. 219–230). Oxford, UK: Wiley Blackwell.

Milne, D. L., Sheikh, A. I., Pattison, S., & Wilkinson, A. (2011). Evidence-based training for clinical supervisors: A systematic review of 11 controlled studies. *Clinical Supervisor, 30*(1), 53–71.

Nicholas, H., & Goodyear, R. K. (2015, August). *When credentialed psychologists are supervisees: Reports from a British sample.* Poster session at the annual meeting of the American Psychological Association, Toronto.

Nordin, S. M., Cumming, J., Vincent, J., & McGrory, S. (2006). Mental practice or spontaneous play? Examining which types of imagery constitute deliberate practice in sport. *Journal of Applied Sport Psychology, 18*(4), 345–362.

Orlinsky, D. E., & Rønnestad, M. H. (2005). *How psychotherapists develop: A study of therapeutic work and professional growth.* Washington, DC: American Psychological Association.

Pelgrim, E.A.M., Kramer, A.W.M., Mokkink, H.G.A., & Van der Vleuten, C.P.M. (2013). Reflection as a component of formative assessment appears to be instrumental in promoting the use of feedback: An observational study. *Medical Teacher, 35*(9), 772–778.

Prowse, P.T.D., Nagel, T., Meadows, G. N., & Enticott, J. C. (2015). Treatment fidelity over the last decade in psychosocial clinical trials outcome studies: A systematic review. *Journal of Psychiatry, 18*. Retrieved from http://www.omicsonline.com/open-access/treatment-fidelity-over-the-last-decade-in-psychosocial-clinical-trialsoutcome-studies-a-systematic-review-Psychiatry-1000258.pdf

Putney, M. W., Worthington, E. L., & McCullough, M. E. (1992). Effects of supervisor and supervisee theoretical orientation and supervisor-supervisee matching on interns' perceptions of supervision. *Journal of Counseling Psychology, 39*(2), 258–265.

Reese, R. J., Usher, E. L., Bowman, D. C., Norsworthy, L. A., Halstead, J. L., Rowlands, S. R., & Chisholm, R. R. (2009). Using client feedback in psychotherapy training: An analysis of its influence on supervision and counselor self-efficacy. *Training and Education in Professional Psychology, 3*(3), 157–168.

Rønnestad, M. H., Orlinsky, D. E., Parks, B. K., & Davis, J. D. (1997). Supervisors of psychotherapy. *European Psychologist, 2*(3), 191–201.

Rousmaniere, T., & Frederickson, J. (2013). Internet-based one-way-mirror supervision for advanced psychotherapy training. *Clinical Supervisor, 32*(1), 40–55.

Rousmaniere, T. G., Swift, J. K., Babins-Wagner, R., Whipple, J. L., & Berzins, S. (2016). Supervisor variance in psychotherapy outcome in routine practice. *Psychotherapy Research, 26*(2), 196–205.

Safran, J. D., Muran, J. C., & Proskurov, B. (2009). Alliance, negotiation and rupture resolution. In R. A. Levy & J. Stuart Ablon (Eds.), *Handbook of evidence-based psychodynamic therapy* (pp. 201–225). New York, NY: Humana Press.

Safran, J. D., Muran, J. C., Stevens, C., & Rothman, M. (2008). A relational approach to supervision: Addressing ruptures in the alliance. In C. A. Falender & E. P. Shafranske (Eds.), *Casebook for clinical supervision: A competency-based approach* (pp. 137–157). Washington, DC: American Psychological Association.

Schram, A. P., & Mudd, S. (2015). Implementing standardized patients within simulation in a nurse practitioner program. *Clinical Simulation in Nursing, 11*(4), 208–213.

Sears, E. S. (2015). *Running through the ages* (2nd ed.). Jefferson, NC: McFarland & Co.

Sheen, J., McGillivray, J., Gurtman, C., & Boyd, L. (2015). Assessing the clinical competence of psychology students through objective structured clinical examinations (OSCEs): Student and staff views. *Australian Psychologist, 50*(1), 51–59.

Swift, J. K., Callahan, J. L., Rousmaniere, T. G., Whipple, J. L., Dexter, K., & Wrape, E. R. (2015). Using client outcome monitoring as a tool for supervision. *Psychotherapy, 52*(2), 180–184.

Swift, J. K., & Greenberg, R. P. (2015). *What is premature termination, and why does it occur?* Washington, DC: American Psychological Association.

Tracey, T.J.G., Wampold, B. E., Lichtenberg, J. W., & Goodyear, R. K. (2014). Expertise in psychotherapy: An elusive goal? *American Psychologist, 69*, 218–229.

Walfish, S., McAlister, B., O'Donnell, P., & Lambert, M. J. (2012). An investigation of self-assessment bias in mental health providers. *Psychological Reports, 110,* 639–644.

Wampold, B. E., & Imel, Z. E. (2015). *The great psychotherapy debate: The evidence for what makes psychotherapy work.* New York, NY: Routledge.

Wampold, B. E., Lichtenberg, J. W., Goodyear, R. K., & Tracey, T.J.G. (in press). Clinical expertise: A critical issue in the age of evidence-based practice. In S. Dimidjian (Ed.), *Evidence-based practice in action.* New York, NY: Guilford Press.

Watkins, C. E., Jr. (2011). Does psychotherapy supervision contribute to patient outcomes? Considering thirty years of research. *Clinical Supervisor, 30*(2), 235–256. doi:10.1080/07325223.2011.619417

Watkins, C. E., Jr., Hook, J. N., Ramaeker, J., & Ramos, M. J. (2016). Repairing the ruptured supervisory alliance: Humility as a foundational virtue in clinical supervision. *Clinical Supervisor, 35(*1), 22–41.

Webb, C. A., DeRubeis, R. J., & Barber, J. P. (2010). Therapist adherence/competence and treatment outcome: A meta-analytic review. *Journal of Consulting and Clinical Psychology, 78*(2), 200–211.

Yap, K., Bearman, M., Thomas, N., & Hay, M. (2012). Clinical psychology students' experiences of a pilot objective structured clinical examination. *Australian Psychologist, 47*(3), 165–173.

Yourman, D. B., & Farber, B. A. (1996). Nondisclosure and distortion in psychotherapy supervison. *Psychotherapy: Theory, Research, Practice, Training, 33*(4), 567–575.

Part II

Tracking Performance

5

Qualitative Methods for Routine Outcome Measurement
John McLeod

This chapter explores the use of qualitative methods as a way of supporting the development of therapist expertise through deliberate practice. The concept of deliberate practice is understood as representing, on the part of a clinician, a sustained commitment, over extended periods of time, to a cyclical process of learning and continual improvement. (See Chapter 2 of this volume.) The key elements of deliberate practice consist of making use of reliable and valid methods to identify areas for further learning, taking time to reflect on feedback and receive relevant guidance from recognized, and implementing a systematic plan for improvement including repeated practice of specific skills until they become routine, in a situation in which gains in skill can be monitored. Adherence to a regime of deliberate practice or the Cycle of Excellence is a challenging and serious matter that requires clinicians to be willing to move beyond their professional comfort zone and make regular and systematic use of feedback from clients, colleagues, supervisors, and trainers, along with research evidence, on a regular basis (McLeod, 2016).

This chapter offers a brief account of the nature of qualitative inquiry and how it can represent a valuable source of information within the Cycle of Excellence process. Within the field of psychotherapy, training, research, and practice within the deliberate feedback paradigm have focused mainly on the use of quantitative feedback, generated by brief outcome and process measures (e.g., the Outcome Rating Scale and the Session Rating Scale; Miller, Prescott, & Maeschalck, 2017). In practice, quantitative feedback is generally accompanied by some type of informal qualitative data collection, in the form of therapist observation of the client and conversations around how therapy is progressing. In this sense, therapists function within their everyday practice as qualitative researchers. One of the aims of this chapter is to show how formal qualitative data collection and analysis methods can assist practitioners to gather and utilize qualitative data in more systematic ways.

The Cycle of Excellence: Using Deliberate Practice to Improve Supervision and Training,
First Edition. Edited by Tony Rousmaniere, Rodney K. Goodyear, Scott D. Miller, and Bruce E. Wampold.
© 2017 John Wiley & Sons, Ltd. Published 2017 by John Wiley & Sons, Ltd.

What Is Qualitative Methodology?

For many people, the difference between "qualitative" and "quantitative" research reduces to a distinction between words and numbers. This distinction both oversimplifies and misunderstands the underlying epistemological basis of each of these forms of inquiry. It oversimplifies because qualitative inquiry often makes use of numbers, and quantitative inquiry always makes use of verbal descriptions to convey the meaning of the numbers that are generated. But it also reveals a misunderstanding. Qualitative research seeks to generate ways of understanding a social, personal, and relational world that is complex, is layered, can be viewed from different perspectives, and is the result of purposeful human action. We construct our world through many forms of individual and collective action: talk and language (stories, conversations), systems of meaning, memory, rituals and institutions, and all the myriad ways in which the world is physically and materially shaped by human purposes. By contrast, mainstream quantitative scientific inquiry seeks to produce explanations based on causal mechanisms that do not take account of purposeful human action. Within the field of psychotherapy, as well as other human service professions such as healthcare, education, and social work, there is a broad acceptance that both types of research are necessary, through providing complementary ways of knowing (Bruner, 1986, 1990).

Qualitative methodology encompasses many different forms of inquiry, including interviews, observation, and textual/transcript analysis (McLeod, 2010). What is common to all of these types of qualitative research is that they seek to elucidate the meaning of some aspect of human experience, in terms of how that meaning is created. Transferred into the domain of deliberate practice of counseling and psychotherapy, this approach leads to a focus on how clients make sense of whether therapy has been helpful to them, how therapists make sense of what clients tell them about the helpfulness of therapy, and how the client and the therapist co-construct the meaning of their work together (McLeod, 2013). The underlying philosophical or values position adopted in qualitative research involves taking a critical perspective in relation to the operation of power and control in human relationships. Qualitative research also acknowledges that the primary inquirer (the person collecting and analyzing data) is never detached, neutral, and objective but instead is an active participant in the process of meaning-making in relation to the topic under investigation. As a result, valid qualitative inquiry always involves an element of disciplined reflexivity.

Further information about the nature of qualitative inquiry, and its contribution to psychotherapy research and practice, can be found in Hill, Chui, and Bauman (2013), Levitt (2015), and McLeod (2010, 2013).

Rationale for Qualitative Outcome Assessment

In recent years, the psychotherapy profession has generated a wide range of brief, user-friendly process and outcome measures that can be deployed to collect feedback from clients (e.g., Miller, Hubble, Chow, & Seidel, 2015; see also Chapter 6 in this volume). In many instances, these tools are cost-effective and time-efficient and may conveniently be delivered and analyzed using information technology. Why, then, do we need qualitative methods? There are two main reasons why qualitative information has the potential to play a vital role in the process of deliberate practice: validity and heuristic value.

The validity of a measurement or assessment instrument lies in its capacity to provide an accurate estimate of an aspect of the emotional, psychological or behavioral functioning of an individual. It is important to appreciate that no single source of feedback evidence (quantitative, qualitative, or clinical observation) has a claim to special validity. Within the field of psychological measurement, the concept of "method variance" is widely acknowledged—each data source provides a slightly different "take" on the phenomenon being investigated (Meyer et al., 2001). The implication here is that the clearest picture can be gained by comparing and combining information from different sources. Conflicting results across sources can be viewed as a stimulus to further reflection and dialogue.

There is plentiful evidence that, in some situations, qualitative data may provide an understanding of client functioning that differs from that generated by quantitative self-report measures. For example, systematic single-case research makes it possible to evaluate the validity of different sources of information in the context of a comprehensive analysis of a whole case. Case study reports by Elliott et al. (2009) and Stephen, Elliott, and Macleod (2011) include detailed analysis of discrepancies between outcome indicators derived from qualitative and quantitative sources. For the clients who were investigated in these studies, quantitative measures were not sufficiently sensitive to clients' idiosyncratic definition of their presenting problem. Self-report measures require clients to respond in terms of categories (and questions) that are derived from the frame of reference of professional psychologists and psychiatrists. Studies that have explored the ways in which clients themselves construct and evaluate outcome generally find that clients do not evaluate therapy in terms of symptom change (McLeod, 2010; see also Chapter 13 in this volume). This research suggests that, for at least some clients, feedback from quantitative measures may be misleading (and therefore not a helpful source of information in relation to deliberate practice) because it is too far removed from clients' own ways of making sense—the feedback measures may not be asking the right questions.

In an experimental study, Shedler, Mayman, and Manis (1993) compared estimates of mental health difficulties arising from administration of a standard self-report measure and a qualitative instrument. Although there emerged a high level of agreement across instruments in relation to some subjects, there appeared to be a substantial subgroup of clients who reported low levels of psychopathology on the quantitative self-report measure but were qualitatively assessed as having significant mental health problems. The accuracy of the qualitative estimate was supported by supplementary data from analysis of physiological data. Shedler et al. suggested that cultural pressures to appear mentally "healthy" may contribute to some individuals self-reporting "illusory mental health" when completing symptom measures. These findings suggest that, in some situations, qualitative instruments may be more sensitive than quantitative measures in regard to collecting feedback on therapeutic failure.

The distinctive heuristic value of qualitative feedback arises from the fact that clients' experiences typically are conveyed in the form of vivid and meaningful phrases, images, metaphors, and stories, which are memorable for the therapist and which connect up with other stories and actions that are part of the therapist's personal and professional identity. For example, a client may not be improving, in terms of weekly scores on an outcome scale. This is useful information. However, if the same client writes, in a weekly open-ended qualitative feedback form, that "I stopped myself from talking about how desperate I feel, because I was afraid that you would send me for a psychiatric assessment," the form conveys more specific information about what has been happening. This kind of concrete and individualized qualitative feedback could lead that therapist to review his or her approach to initial contracting with clients, in consultation with a clinical supervisor, leading to further training in suicide management skills and deliberate practice of more effective strategies for exploring the options that might be available if a client was to talk about being suicidal.

In the following sections of this chapter, I describe how qualitative methodologies can be used to enhance deliberate practice aimed at maximizing therapist expertise. To the best of my knowledge, there has been no research into the utility of qualitative outcome feedback in relation to therapist learning and development. Up to now, qualitative feedback tools have been used by therapists solely to inform their work with clients, through gathering information about clients' experiences of the process and outcome of therapy. It is therefore not possible, at the present time, to estimate the strengths and limitations of this approach in relation to the development of deliberate practice.

The ideas and examples presented in this chapter do not reflect a rejection of quantitative feedback measures or an argument that they should be replaced by qualitative instruments. Instead, what is being suggested is that qualitative tools can be used to supplement the existing toolkit of brief self-report scales.

Using Qualitative Feedback and Outcome Data Collection Methods in Routine Clinical Practice

A range of qualitative methodologies can be used to gather information on the outcome of therapy. In the discussion that follows, the concept of "outcome" is understood to refer to micro-outcomes, such as shifts occurring within a brief segment of a therapy session, as well as more substantial outcomes, defined as improvements in respect of the primary presenting issue for which the client has entered therapy. Micro-outcomes include steps toward the building of a collaborative alliance or bond between client and therapist.

Research into expert professional judgment and decision making suggests that practitioners largely make sense of their work in terms of "scripts" or "typical cases" that provide a template for how an intervention with a client might unfold over time (Fishman, 1999). Useful descriptions of this way of thinking, generated from qualitative interviews with practitioners, can be found in research by Gabbay and le May (2004) into "clinical mindlines" and by Mattingly (1998) on "narrative reasoning." From this perspective, feedback on the attainment of micro-outcomes is crucially important in allowing practitioners to assess whether the case is on track to achieve a positive ultimate outcome. It is also valuable as a means of enabling practitioners to calibrate and refine their sensitivity to micro-outcomes, including their awareness of different types of micro-outcomes.

Quantitative Outcome Measures Used as Conversational Tools

In recent years, many practical initiatives and research studies have been developed around the use of data from quantitative self-report outcome scales as feedback to therapists and sometimes also to their clients. Outcome measures used in such studies have included the Outcome Rating Scale/Session Rating Scale (Bertolino & Miller, 2012), the CORE-Outcome Measure (OM) (Barkham, Mellor-Clark, & Stiles, 2015), and the Outcome Questionnaire System (Lambert, 2015) as well as other scales. Other measures have been developed that rely on client-defined problem or goal statements (Alves, Sales, & Ashworth, 2013; Sales & Alves, 2012). Examples of such measures include PSYCHLOPS (Psychological Outcome Profiles; Ashworth et al., 2004; Robinson, Ashworth, Shepherd, & Evans, 2007) and the simplified Personal Questionnaire (Elliott, Mack, & Shapiro, 1999; Elliott et al., 2016). With these measures, clients write in their own items, usually following discussion with the therapist. In some applications, it is also possible for clients to change the wording of items or add further items. In such situations, client–therapist dialogue is intrinsic to the way that the measure operates rather than being merely an optional add-on. In a review of the use of goal attainment monitoring in psychotherapy, Lindhiem, Bennett, Orimoto, and Kolko (2016) found that goals forms were substantially more sensitive to change than scores from symptom checklists completed by the same clients. These findings imply that instruments that track shifts in client goal attainment may be particularly valuable sources of information for therapist development, because they provide more opportunities for therapist reflection on client change.

In some instances, the information gleaned from these measures is used solely by the therapist, as the psychological equivalent of a thermometer or blood pressure monitor reading. In other cases, therapists use the act of completing the scale, and the responses recorded on the scale, as the basis for conversations with clients. Rolf Sundet (2009, 2012) has characterized this latter form of practice as involving the use of "conversational tools" in which what is interesting and helpful is not so much the quantitative score but the conversation that it makes possible. The brief scales used in first-generation client monitoring and feedback systems, such as the OQ and CORE-OM, were originally developed as measurement instruments. Second-generation tools, such as the Outcome Rating Scale and the Session Rating Scale, were designed to function with a dual purpose: as measures and as a basis for collaborative conversation (Miller, Prescott, & Maeschalck, 2016). These second-generation tools had a qualitative dimension, but this was not explicitly highlighted.

More recently, what might be considered as a further, third generation of client feedback and monitoring measurement has started to emerge, aimed more at facilitating therapeutic dialogue than measuring change. An example of such an instrument is the Cooper-Norcross Inventory of Client Preferences (Bowen & Cooper, 2012; Cooper & Norcross, 2016). This scale comprises 18 items that invite clients to indicate preferred therapist behavior and style (e.g., "allow me to take a lead in therapy" versus "take a lead in therapy").

The use of therapeutic conversational tools can be regarded as similar to the strategy, in qualitative research, of asking informants to comment on some kind of artifact or object. This method can involve interviewer and informant working together to create something. For example, in a study of the experiences of individuals who had received treatment for substance misuse, Berends (2011) structured interviews around the co-construction of a timeline representing their treatment history. Rich qualitative data can be elicited through providing relevant images that stimulate reflection. In a study of the meaning of the workplace, Bahn and Barratt-Pugh (2013) found it difficult to get reticent young male participants to talk, until they came up with the idea of asking them to comment on photographs of work scenarios. A variant on this technique is the use of a "think-aloud" protocol. To learn about the ways that young black women in Britain thought about their sense of identity and body image, Ogden and Russell (2012) made audio recordings of research participants thinking aloud as they read "white" and "black" fashion magazines. The relevance of these studies, for the use of conversational tools in therapy, is that they involve a similar process of co-construction of meaning. In therapy, this process consists of working together to make sense of ratings on an outcome measure, using an artifact or stimulus object (e.g., a questionnaire form) to make it easier to explore issues that are hard to talk about, and an invitation to think aloud ("What was in your mind when you were answering the ORS today?"). Familiarity with the qualitative research literature therefore has the potential to help therapists recognize that quantitative feedback measures in therapy may be regarded as functioning as conversational tools.

Qualitative Self-Report Forms

A number of qualitative forms can be used to invite clients to write, in the closing minutes of a session, immediately after the session has finished, or between one session and the next, a brief account of what has been helpful in a session. Although it is feasible to devise a customized form for use within one's own practice, there can be advantages in using a form that has been applied in research studies. Standardized qualitative forms make it possible to compare feedback from one's own clients with similar feedback recorded from clients who have participated in research studies that have used the same instrument. The capacity to make such comparisons sensitizes clinicians to potential themes and to methods of interpreting such data. Some of the most widely used qualitative client self-report forms are summarized next.

Helpful Aspects of Therapy

The Helpful Aspects of Therapy (HAT) form (Elliott, 1993; Llewelyn, 1988; Llewelyn, Elliott, Shapiro, Hardy, & Firth-Cozens, 1988) includes these questions:

1. Of the events which occurred in this session, which one do you feel was the most helpful or important for you personally? (By "event" we mean something that happened in the session. It might be something you said or did, or something your therapist said or did.)
2. Please describe what made this event helpful/important and what you got out of it.
3. How helpful was this particular event (rated on a 9-point scale)?
4. About where in the session did this event occur?
5. About how long did the event last?

These instructions are repeated for an optional second helpful event and then for a hindering event.

Important Events Questionnaire

The Important Events Questionnaire (IEQ; Cummings, Martin, Hallberg, & Slemon, 1992) contains five questions:

1. What was the most important thing that happened in this session (i.e., what stood out for you?)?
2. Why was it important and how was it helpful or not helpful?
3. What thoughts and feelings do you recall experiencing/having during this time in the session?

These three questions are repeated for the second most important event in the session.

4. What did you find yourself thinking about or doing during the time in between sessions that related in any way to the last session?
5. Are you experiencing any change in yourself? If so, what? (p. 308)

Session Bridging Form

Different versions of the Session Bridging Form (SBF; Tsai et al., 2008) have been developed, drawing on these questions:

1. On a 10-point scale, how would you rate the helpfulness or effectiveness of our last session?
2. What stands out about our last session? What was helpful?
3. What would have made the session more helpful or a better experience?
4. What emotional risks did you take in the session/with your therapist and/or what progress did you make that can translate into your outside life?
5. Was there anything that bothered you? Anything you are reluctant to say?
6. What was your week like? How would you rate your mood on a 10-point scale?
7. What items, issues, challenges or positive changes do you want to put on the agenda for our next session?
8. What work, or conscious steps did you take or consider taking this week? Did you discover anything?
9. How open were you in answering the above questions (0–100%)?
10. Anything else you'd like to add? (p. 215)

Client Feedback Note

The Client Feedback Note (CFN; Haber, Carlson, & Braga, 2014) form was devised for use in family therapy and is intended to be relevant for both child and adult clients. Items include:

1. What are my feelings about the session?
2. What did I learn?
3. What did I not like?
4. What I wish would have happened. (p. 310)

Dialogical Feedback Tool

Devised for use in family therapy, the Dialogical Feedback Tool (Rober, Van Tricht, & Sundet, 2016) is intended to be relevant for both child and adult clients. The form comprises a single page, with two faces (one smiley, the other unhappy) linked to thought bubbles. The client is asked to write within each bubble: What would she (he) think about the session today?

Other, similar forms are available. Event-focused session report tools, similar to the HAT, have been developed for group therapy by Bloch and Reibstein (1980; Bloch, Reibstein, Crouch, Holroyd, & Themen, 1979), Moreno, Furhiman, and Hileman (1995), and Doxsee and Kivlighan (1994). A simplified version of the HAT has been used by Ekroll and Rønnestad (2016). A writing task for clients oriented toward the question of what they learned in therapy has been created by Burnett (1999).

In practice, these forms should be given to clients with instructions. For example, for some individuals, it may not be immediately obvious what is meant by the term *event*. It is also necessary to give careful consideration to the length, design, and layout of a form—for example, the amount of space allocated for the answer to each question. Most of these forms invite the client to identify specific events that have been helpful or unhelpful and to avoid any tendency on the part of the client to offer vague generalizations, such as "It was a good session." These forms also tend to acknowledge the reality of client ambivalence—the likelihood that there will positive as well as negative reactions and that both are of interest. Most of the published reports on the use of qualitative session forms refer to paper forms. However, there are important possibilities associated with completion of such forms on a tablet or a laptop or by email.

The most widely investigated qualitative session report forms have been the HAT and IEQ. Studies using the HAT, in particular, have generated taxonomies of categories of helpful events (Castonguay et al., 2010; Timulak, 2007, 2011) and case descriptions of how HAT responses change over the course of therapy (see, e.g., Elliott et al., 2009; Stephen et al., 2011). The findings of these studies provide important contextualizing information for clinicians using such tools for client feedback and deliberate practice. Studies that have collected HAT forms from large samples of clients show that a wide range of change processes and events are reported. An implication of this finding is that an absence of diversity in HAT descriptions across the caseload of a clinician may reflect a lack of responsiveness to clients. For example, if a therapist discovers over time that the descriptions of helpful events offered by clients predominantly fall within the "problem resolution" category (Timulak, 2011), it may be appropriate for that clinician to use supervision to reflect on possible reasons for the absence of relationship-oriented themes, such as "feeling understood."

The HAT does not appear to be particularly sensitive to unhelpful aspects of therapy: In the Castonguay et al. (2010) study, only 2% of HAT forms included accounts of hindering events. However, Cummings et al. (1994) found that the IEQ was able to differentiate between good- and poor-outcome cases. It is also possible to use IEQ session report data to go beyond merely categorizing types of change event, through interpretation of the underling metaphors expressed within the written responses (Cummings, 1998). In a further study, in which both clients and therapists completed the IEQ on a weekly basis, convergence in client–therapist identification of significance over the course of therapy was associated with outcome (Kivlighan & Arthur, 2000). This finding suggests that lack of convergence late in therapy may be an indicator of not-on-track cases and that the nature of the divergence (e.g., what the therapist is missing in relation to the client's view of what is helpful) may represent valuable information in respect to areas for reflection and deliberate practice.

The qualitative session report forms described in this section have been developed primarily as feedback tools, with the intent of providing the therapist with information about the client's experience. Such instruments generate contextualized and concrete information about when therapy goes wrong, in terms of the client's definition of therapist errors or omissions, in ways that may contribute to the initiation of a cycle of deliberate practice informed by consultation with colleagues or a clinical supervisor around the personal learning arising from such an episode.

Case 5.1 Using Qualitative Feedback in the Context of Other Sources of Information: The Case of Brian

Brian was an experienced therapist who had initially been trained within a psychodynamic approach to therapy. He was employed in a clinic that was committed to the Cycle of Excellence model and collected client data at each session using the CORE outcome measure, a goal attainment form, and the HAT. On analyzing his data over a 6-month period, Brian was able to identify a set of 12 poor-outcome cases and unplanned-ending cases that had exhibited no change or some deterioration at the point at which the client had ceased to attend. With the help of his clinical supervisor, Brian carried out an item analysis of CORE data from these clients, along with a thematic analysis of available HAT data. The CORE data did not reveal any consistent pattern. However, within the HAT data there were six unhelpful events, all of which reflected client dissatisfaction with Brian's capacity to engage with emotional pain arising from loss and trauma. These clients had also described therapeutic goals associated with the resolution of painful affect. A review of a sample of the good-outcome cases in his file showed that the positive results achieved by Brian largely occurred in cases in which clients were seeking behavior change and insight. In both the good-outcome and poor-outcome HAT data, clients indicated events in which they had felt supported by Brian, implying that his general capacity to form a therapeutic alliance was sound. In a further supervision meeting, Brian reviewed two of the poor-outcome cases, comparing his own clinical notes, his supervisor's notes on their previous discussion of the cases, and the HAT data. Taken as a whole, this information allowed them to see that Brian had a tendency to freeze when clients expressed deep vulnerability, fear, or loss. As a result of this review process, the clinic director agreed that Brian should be funded to attend a 1-year training program in affect phobia therapy (McCullough et al., 2003). In addition to the specialist supervision included in the affect phobia therapy training, Brian and his regular supervisor contracted to give specific attention to HAT feedback over the ensuing 18-month period.

Visual Methodologies

Historically, qualitative researchers have relied mainly on verbal sources, primarily from interviews. More recently, qualitative researchers have realized that some informants can be assisted to convey a more complete sense of the meaning of their experience through using drawing, object making, and photography as adjuncts to verbal reports (Clark & Morriss, 2015).

There is a long and thriving tradition of visual outcome evaluation in the field of art therapy, based on interpretation of the series of artwork created by the client over the course of therapy. However, there are also some visual techniques that can be incorporated into routine talk therapy that do not require access to a studio or facilitation by a clinician who has received training in art therapy. Life-space mapping (Rodgers, 2006) invites clients to create a picture of their lives at that point in time and then talk about what the image means to them. In photovoice, clients take photographs of aspects of their everyday lives that are significant to them, then bring these images into therapy and discuss them with the researcher (or, potentially, their therapist; Aldridge, 2014; Mizock, Russinova, & Shani, 2014; Sutton-Brown, 2014). When drawings are used in therapy, it may be clients who create the images (Oster & Crone, 2004), or clients and therapists may engage in a nonverbal dialogue on paper (Withers, 2009). From the perspective of client feedback and monitoring, these approaches lead to the collection of a series of images that provide a visual representation of change. A technique that has been used by some therapists has been to invite clients to compare images—for example, to place the picture of their life before the start of therapy alongside the picture of their life now—as a means of stimulating reflection and conversation around what has changed (or not changed).

In an important study within this approach, Rodgers (2006) asked clients to make a life-space map and also complete a standardized outcome measure, the CORE-OM. Clients were then asked at the end of therapy which method they found most relevant. Rodgers found that client views ranged across a wide spectrum, with some clients reporting that the pictures had been more effective in allowing them to express how they felt and others preferring the questionnaire measure. There was a subgroup of clients for whom the life-space mapping conversation presented a much more negative view of change than the CORE, probably because it allowed them more directly to access the complexity of their lived experience in a manner that was less shaped by social desirability or impression management. Although this finding needs to be tested and replicated in other studies, it does suggest that visual methodologies may be particularly effective in collecting information around hard-to-articulate aspects of therapy that may be vital to the process of deliberate practice.

Projective Techniques

Projective techniques are currently out of favor within mainstream counseling and psychotherapy practice, because they take time to administer and interpret and are regarded in psychometric terms as not possessing adequate levels of validity and reliability (Lilienfeld, Wood, & Garb, 2000). The strength of the evidence around the validity of projective techniques is perhaps not fully appreciated (Piotrowski, 2015; Weiner, 2004). Some projective techniques, such as the Rorschach or the Thematic Apperception Test, can be regarded as falling within the broad category of visual methodologies. However, other projective techniques, such as the sentence completion test, do not use visual materials. The underlying principle of any projective technique is that people are asked to engage with an ambiguous situation or task, for which there are an indefinite number of responses. The responses offered by the people can therefore be regarded as an indication, or projection, of their characteristic way of being in the world. The information provided by a projective technique comprises a sample of operant behavior (McClelland, 1980) or a performance measure (Weiner, 2004). In other words, whereas standard questionnaire measures place people in a position of reflecting on their actions, a projective technique places them in a position of being a purposeful agent.

The potential of projective techniques to provide unique and distinctive insights that contrast with the results of questionnaire measures has long been recognized and exploited within the fields of marketing research (Boddy, 2005; Steinman, 2009), health research (Jones, Magee, & Andrews, 2015; Walsh & Malson, 2010), and management selection (McClelland & Boyatzis, 1982). Within the domain of routinely collecting client feedback on the outcome and process of psychotherapy, few clinicians would opt to engage in weekly administration of the Rorschach or Thematic Apperception Test. However, there are many ways of adapting the underlying principles of projective methodology, as a form of qualitative inquiry, to meet the requirements of routine feedback monitoring. For example, the use of thought bubbles in the Dialogical Feedback Tool (Rober et al., 2016) is ultimately derived from market research (see, e.g., Boddy, 2004). A further promising line of development lies in the practice of collaborative interpretation of projective responses (Finn, Fischer, & Handler, 2012; Fischer, 2000).

Client Diaries

Some clients keep personal diaries and journals, which they may choose to share with their therapists. In other clinical situations, therapists may encourage clients to keep a diary, write in response to online or paper workbook or writing tasks, or communicate by email (Mackrill, 2008; Milligan, Bingley, & Gatrell, 2005). An example of the potential of diary methods to generate qualitative data that is relevant to an understanding of outcome can be found in a study by Kerr, Josyula, and Littenberg (2011) in which weekly solicited diaries were kept by participants in a mindfulness-based stress reduction group. Analysis of diary entries showed that it was relatively straightforward to differentiate between the narratives produced by clients who were engaging with the therapy process and those who were not on track. In addition, themes within the diaries of participants who struggled yet persevered provided valuable clues about areas in which the group facilitators might seek to develop further skills or alter their approach. In many respects, qualitative self-report forms (discussed earlier) are similar to diaries and merely require further guidelines for free writing between sessions in order to function as solicited diaries.

Case 5.2 Using Visual Data to Enable a Client to Offer Feedback around a Sensitive Topic: The Case of Gudrun

Within her private practice, Gudrun used an integrative approach to therapy that incorporated ideas and methods from a wide range of therapy traditions, including expressive arts. She asked clients to complete the Session Rating Scale and Outcome Rating Scale at each second session, as a means of tracking client satisfaction with the progress of therapy. In the sessions between, Gudrun invited clients to make a quick drawing that reflected their feelings at that moment about their life as a whole and the place of therapy within that life. Many of these drawings conveyed images of journeys, maps, climbing mountains, groups of people, and home. On one occasion, a young male client drew a picture in which he stood on open ground with a powerful searchlight focused on him. He was reluctant to say much about this image other than to comment "I guess it means I'm just feeling a bit exposed and raw." Two weeks later, he created a similar image. This time Gudrun asked whether it could, in some way, be related to how he felt about what was happening in therapy. "Well, yes," he replied, "it's like you keep staring at me. I can't cope with it. So much of what you are giving me is great. But I just wish you wouldn't look at me so intensely." Gudrun thanked him for this feedback and encouraged him to say more. Afterward, in supervision and in conversations with colleagues, she learned that most people who knew her were able to confirm that occasionally she did have a tendency to engage in eye contact for longer than was comfortable for them. She was then able to self-monitor this behavior and, when appropriate, check with clients whether they were experiencing her in that fashion.

Therapist Writing

There is very little research on how therapists evaluate outcome in the absence of data from client self-report measures. This is surprising and concerning, given that psychotherapy was in existence for many decades before client feedback and monitoring tools became available, and even today the majority of clinicians do not employ such tools. In a study by Daniel and McLeod (2006), therapists reported that they pay attention to three main sources of outcome data within sessions: what clients say about their lives (e.g., in respect of lapses or successes); how therapists feel in relation to clients (e.g., whether they have a sense of genuine interpersonal contact or of being drawn into a destructive "game"); and the extent to which what is happening within the session matches therapists' "script" or template for good therapy. It would appear, therefore, that clinicians are sophisticated observers of outcome-relevant information. Yet there is compelling evidence that therapists are not at all accurate at detecting negative outcome (Hatfield, McCullough, Frantz, & Krieger, 2010). It may be, therefore, that informal qualitative outcome data collected by clinicians are not being harnessed as effectively as they might be in relation to routine outcome monitoring and deliberate practice.

Within the field of qualitative research, open-ended participant writing is used as a means of collecting data (Richardson & St. Pierre, 2005). The activity of writing about an area of experience makes it possible for a person to document critical incidents and reflect on the personal meaning of incidents and events. Writing can therefore contribute to personal learning and development on the part of the author as well as providing information and insight for readers (Etherington, 2004). Within the world of qualitative research, the method of autoethnography (using autobiography to explore cultural themes) represents a rich source of ideas about how this can be accomplished (Muncey, 2010; Wall, 2008).

Within the psychotherapy literature, there are already many valuable examples of therapist writing that are relevant to an understanding of the process of learning from clients in ways that feed into deliberate practice. For instance, Kottler and Carlson (2005) have collected therapist accounts of "the client who changed me." Several of these narratives make clear links between experiences with clients and ensuing personal programs of deliberate practice. The autobiographies of John Marzillier (2010) and Iris Fodor (2001, 2010) document several phases of deliberate practice across the course of their professional careers. In the case of Marzillier, the early part of his career comprised training in behavior therapy and cognitive behavioral therapy, which was followed by training in psychodynamic therapy and finally the development of an integrative approach. In the case of Iris Fodor, initial training in psychoanalytic therapy was followed by a sequence of further training experiences in cognitive behavioral therapy, Gestalt therapy, and Buddhist practice. For both of these therapists, the decision to engage in additional training arose from deep personal reflection on the limitations of their prior skills and knowledge in relation to the needs of particular clients or client groups. Although each of them was active at a time when routine feedback tools were not available, they were acutely sensitive to therapeutic failure and highly proactive in engaging with professional communities in which rigorous training in new skills could be accessed.

Other therapists have written about the impact of specific events in therapy that were hard for them—for example, receiving a professional malpractice complaint (Geller, 2014) or working with a suicidal client (Webb, 2011). Such reflective personal accounts provide valuable evidence for the rest of us in relation to the lived reality of how feedback from therapy practice may lead to professional development. What is less clear, from these narratives, is the extent to which these clinicians found it helpful to write about their experience and the extent to which such writing may have formed a bridge between work with clients and reflective decision making around deliberate practice.

Participation in Case Study Research

The qualitative outcome methodologies discussed in earlier sections all refer to data that are collected at each session and used to map or track the progress of clients over the course of treatment. The advantage of these techniques is that they provide "real-time" feedback that is linked to what is happening week by week. From a deliberate practice perspective, these sources of information allow practitioners to highlight and reflect on difficulties or gaps in their competence and then to monitor their implementation of remedies for these gaps. However, another key aspect of deliberate practice involves taking stock of how one has functioned as a therapist over the course of a whole case, taking account of all aspects of the case. This kind of holistic outcome evaluation is hard to incorporate into routine clinical supervision, because it takes time. An effective means of creating a space for this kind of outcome evaluation and reflection is to engage in case study research. There have been important developments in recent years around the development of principles for conducting robust case study research in psychotherapy (McLeod, 2010). Key methodological strategies fundamental to good-quality case study research are: (a) the construction of a rich case record, including qualitative and quantitative sources of information on the process and outcome of the case, from both client and therapist perspectives; and (b) analysis of case data by a small team of researchers within a structure that encourages careful critical scrutiny of all possible interpretations of the data. For a therapist, participating as a member of a case study inquiry group that examines a case where one has been the therapist can be a profound learning experience that can act as a catalyst for further development. An increasing number of systematic case studies are being published in journals such as *Clinical Case Studies* and *Pragmatic Case Studies in Psychotherapy*. Typically, the therapist in the case is a coauthor of the study. It would be valuable to know more about the impact of this type of activity on personal and professional learning and on subsequent deliberate practice.

Conclusion: Issues and Challenges in Using Qualitative Outcome and Process Instruments to Inform Deliberate Practice

Both qualitative and quantitative outcome and process monitoring tools fulfill a range of functions. They provide feedback to clinicians, for example, on whether work with a client is on track. They operate as an intervention: Clients completing a feedback form may find themselves reflecting on their experience and current emotional state, comparing their current state to how they felt at previous sessions, and engaging in a collaborative conversation with their therapist. These processes can be highly meaningful for clients. Monitoring tools also have a function outside the work with any single client, in offering clues to possible directions for further personal and professional development on the part of the therapist (deliberate practice). It would be helpful to know more about the distinctive contribution of different types of monitoring instruments in respect of these functions. In terms of further research and reflection on practice, it is necessary to begin to build a framework for understanding the potential role of different types of feedback at different stages of professional development. For example, during the phase of initial training when therapists need to develop a wide range of skills, it may be most facilitative to seek generic feedback from clients and to focus on learning how to make use of feedback. By contrast, senior therapists are more likely to have developed clearer ideas about "learning projects" that they are pursuing at a particular point in time and, as a result, may find it more facilitative to seek feedback specifically linked to these goals. A further dimension of feedback is associated with the theoretical orientation of the therapists and the particular skills that are characteristic of their espoused model of practice.

It appears that the type of client feedback that is most useful for clinicians—how the client feels about the therapist, and whether the client's problems are getting worse—is the categories of information that clients find hardest to disclose (Blanchard & Farber, 2016).

Qualitative feedback tools may possess some strengths and advantages in relation to collecting data on such topics, because they provide structures that encourage shameful or confusing experiences to be communicated in a tentative, nuanced fashion. Qualitative data may also be more sensitive to detecting how clients feel about particular negative events that may be highly significant personally (Bowie, McLeod, & McLeod, 2016; Walls, McLeod, & McLeod, 2016). Finally, qualitative data may also have a distinctive role to play in respect of learning about the meaning and nature of positive transformational shifts in clients' lives or their experience of self (Ekroll & Rønnestad, 2016; Weiner, 2004). Although weekly administration of a symptom scale may make it possible to identify when a sudden gain has occurred, it is only through listening to a client's story that it becomes possible to know where the shift fits into the client's life as a whole. In addition, sudden gains measured by a symptom scale can only ever indicate a move from many symptoms to few symptoms and are not sensitive to episodes of self-actualization or epiphany that take clients beyond the floor (or ceiling) of the measure.

In seeking to understand the nature of expertise in psychotherapy, the Cycle of Excellence model and the concept of deliberate practice have drawn heavily on existing theory and research into the development of expertise in fields such as music, medicine, chess, and sports. This body of knowledge has provided an invaluable framework that has the potential to make a significant difference to therapy training, supervision, and practice in the coming years. At the same time, it is perhaps important to acknowledge some of the differences between psychotherapy and these other fields of practice. Psychotherapy is essentially a collaborative process that draws on the knowledge and resources of both the client and the clinician. In this respect it stands in contrast to practices in which the practitioner is in competition with the other (e.g., chess, tennis) or where the object of the practice plays a mainly or wholly passive role (e.g., surgery, mathematics). It seems likely, therefore, that there may exist some distinctive aspects of the structure of deliberate practice—for example, the degree of reflexive self-awareness of the clinician and the need to be able to interpret feedback as meaningful communication from another person—that can be fully understood only in the context of the relationship between client and therapist and the whole of what is happening within the process of therapy. These are domains in which qualitative inquiry may be able to make a particularly valuable contribution.

Qualitative outcome and process feedback monitoring is at an early stage of development. There are many possibilities but little evidence. Much more needs to be known about the effectiveness of different forms of qualitative data collection methodology, in terms of client and therapist experience and impact on the ultimate outcomes of therapy. It would also be helpful to know more about the type of training and supervision that would be necessary for clinicians to make best use of such tools. There is arguably a lack of attention in therapist training programs to the role of qualitative methods, projective techniques, and case study methods. For this reason, therapists may lack confidence in such approaches. Demonstrating the use of such approaches in deliberate practice may result in greater acknowledgment that such methodologies should be given more priority in basic training.

Questions from the Editors

Question #1. Time is a major constraint for most practitioners. Do qualitative instruments take longer to administer and interpret? If so, what is your advice regarding this?

Answer from Author: The issue of the time taken to complete any kind of feedback measure has been a central issue for many clinicians who have been considering adopting these procedures. Most therapists would tend to believe that they already do not have as much face-to-face time with their clients as they would wish, and they are reluctant to allocate any of that scarce time to activities that may not yield therapeutic gains. Within the field of quantitative feedback measures, massive efforts have been devoted to the development of online completion and analysis of measures that reduce the time burden on both clinician and client. This chapter has described a number of different qualitative feedback tools. Some of them are in early stages of development, and it seems highly likely that variants, and new qualitative instruments, will be produced in the future. It is therefore hard to generalize about the time demands associated with qualitative instruments. One consideration that needs to be kept in mind is that, at present, most of these instruments comprise paper forms that clients complete between sessions and hand over at their next meeting with their therapists. Within the session, the intention is not to interpret what clients have written in the sense of producing a summary score but to invite clients to comment on what they have written, and to respond to that, in a way that informs the therapy process. The more formal analysis of what clients have written—for example, in terms of what it means for therapist development and deliberate practice—takes place when clinicians write their notes and meet with their supervisors. Clearly, with qualitative instruments, clients can produce a written or visual response that is somewhat ambiguous and may take time to interpret. What is of primary importance here is what the response means to the clients, and it may be best just to ask them. Some qualitative techniques such as projective and art-based measures are particularly time-consuming. The question for clinicians here is whether the inclusion of such instruments makes sense to them in terms of their therapy approach as a whole. In some situations, it can be appropriate to administer more time-consuming qualitative feedback measures at intermittent review sessions rather than weekly.

Question #2. In the conclusion to your chapter, you briefly mention that there may be some distinctive aspects to deliberate practice when applied to psychotherapy. Can you elaborate?

Answer from Author: Deliberate practice is about doing better therapy that is more helpful for clients. The deliberate practice model suggests that an important way to improve therapist performance is through analyzing feedback on current effectiveness, identifying skills that require further refinement, and then practicing these skills under the guidance of an expert supervisor. For example, a therapist who uses two-chair interventions with depressed clients who exhibit destructive self-criticism might collect feedback that these interventions were not producing the expected results. Watching videos with a supervisor or trainer and then, for example, trying out better ways of explaining the intervention to the client, might lead to much better results. This kind of process, which seems to lie at the heart of the deliberate practice approach, strikes me as being completely sensible and a significant step forward in terms of understanding how to support clinicians to do their best work.

The deliberate practice model brings to the world of psychotherapy ideas and strategies that have been shown to be effective in domains such as medicine, sports, and music. What is distinctive about psychotherapy is the extensive evidence that, while unsatisfactory therapist performance may sometimes be the result of a deficit in skills and knowledge, it can also be the result of deficits in self-awareness and personal development. To return to the example of the therapist who records poor results when using two-chair work with clients who are paralyzed by harsh inner critics, it may be that this therapist has, in his own personal life, struggled to come to terms with their own inner critic and that the issues presented by such clients are just too close to home and trigger a self-protective response of emotional withdrawal from the clients. It is unlikely that skills practice will make much difference to the effectiveness of this therapist with these clients. What might help would be some kind of psychotherapeutic experience—for example, personal therapy, journaling, spiritual practice, or some other activity—that allows the therapists to move from a state of being paralyzed by a particular category of emotional or existential dilemma to a stage of "insider knowledge" gained through the achievement of personal healing within that domain.

The therapist with a harsh inner critic is a simplified example of what tends to be a complex process of lifelong learning in which therapist carries out work on self. This type of work has two purposes. First, it allows therapists to overcome their limitations. Second, it allows therapists to become more sensitively aware, through firsthand experience, of the nature of clients' contributions to the process of change and the specific challenges associated with resolving particular issues. An acceptance of the value of these general principles is exhibited in the almost universal acknowledgment of the importance of personal therapy in practitioners from all therapy approaches and in the development of specific learning strategies, such as the use of "self-practice" in cognitive behavioral therapy training (Bennett-Levy & Lee, 2014).

My own view is that, even if the benefits of skills-focused deliberate practice have been clearly exemplified in fields such as medicine, sports, and music, personal development is also relevant in these arenas. Commitment to excellence requires a willingness to sacrifice personal life in favor of professional work. Moreover, maintaining high levels of performance over the course of a career requires a capacity to continue to reengage with personal sources of motivation. My guess is that, while excellence in any field builds on deliberate practice, an ability to engage with deliberate practice is supported by a complex mix of personal, family, and cultural resources.

Although the personal dimension of therapy practice represents the main distinctive aspect of deliberate practice when applied to psychotherapy, there are also other dimensions that may also have some significance. First, the concept of "practice" is problematic for therapists. Musicians and athletes are often able to practice for many hours for performances that may be infrequent or brief in duration. Doctors can practice their skills in various types

of simulated patient scenarios. Compared to these occupations, the opportunities for therapists to engage in high-quality supervised practice may be viewed as being somewhat
restricted. Second, there is a certain amount of ambiguity in psychotherapy around being
able to differentiate reliably between success and failure. Finally, a substantial amount of the
contribution for change really belongs with clients rather than therapists. For me, the client
is the hero. There is a risk that a deliberate practice perspective could detract from an appre-
ciation of the client's role in change. These issues do not diminish the value of theory and
research into deliberate practice but merely remind us that we need to make it our own and
tailor it to the particular circumstances of psychotherapy.

Question #3. Can you provide some ideas for or comments on how practicing clinicians
employing qualitative methods can avoid finding what they are looking for rather than what
they need to find?

Answer from Author: I really liked this question, because it opens up new ways of thinking.
I assume that those who formulated the question were thinking that numerical feedback is
precise and "hard" whereas verbal or qualitative feedback can often be ambiguous and
open to interpretation. This is undoubtedly true, but whether that means that statistical
data are less likely to be selectively interpreted is another matter. There has been a great
deal of research in cognitive psychology into how different types of display are perceived
by people, in terms of the impact, intelligibility, and memorability of information. It would
be useful to apply some of these research designs to exploring the ways in which therapists
make sense of different types of client feedback. At the moment, we just do not know.
For example, a vivid phrase or image conveyed in client feedback may have the potential to
capture the attention and evoke reflection in ways that might not happen with a line on
a graph.

Another aspect of this question is related to the process of what a therapist is doing when he
or she scrutinizes feedback from client ratings on the Outcome Rating Scale or a similar
instrument. I do not know of any published studies that have examined what happens at these
moments, but two of my students have conducted studies in which they interviewed therapists around this topic. What they found was that therapists interpreted data from the measure in the context of other information that was available to them, such as their firsthand
observation of the client in the session. This is not surprising. Indeed, it would be alarming if
clinicians acted as if a brief measure provided them with an infallible and comprehensive
reading of the state of the client or of the client–therapist alliance. The point here is that the
transition from data to subsequent action always involves some kind of judgment or appraisal
process.

The existence of an appraisal process invites reflection on the meaning of the distinction
between "what clinicians are looking for" and "what they need to find." I would suggest that
both are necessary. It seems to me that, when a feedback system is functioning properly, it
involves an active, hypothesis-testing process. A clinician who is committed to continuous
improvement asks questions about his or her performance based on ideas about which

skills or areas of emotional responsiveness are operating well and which are less secure. These questions are informed by conversations with others, such as the supervisor and peers. This aspect of deliberate practice touches on wider issues within the organization of psychotherapy services regarding the balance between managerial control and clinical relevance in the implementation of feedback systems.

References

Aldridge, J. (2014). Working with vulnerable groups in social research: Dilemmas by default and design. *Qualitative Research, 14*, 112–130.

Alves, P.C.G., Sales, C.M.D., & Ashworth, M. (2013). Enhancing the patient involvement in outcomes: A study protocol of personalised outcome measurement in the treatment of substance misuse. *BMC Psychiatry, 13*, 337.

Ashworth, M., Shepherd, M., Christey, J., Matthews, V., Wright, K., Parmentier, H., . . . Godfrey, E. (2004). A client-generated psychometric instrument: The development of "PSYCHLOPS." *Counselling and Psychotherapy Research, 4*, 27–31.

Bahn, S., & Barratt-Pugh, L. (2013). Getting reticent young male participants to talk: Using artefact-mediated interviews to promote discursive interaction. *Qualitative Social Work, 12*, 186–199.

Barkham, M., Mellor-Clark, J., & Stiles, W. B. (2015). A CORE approach to progress monitoring and feedback: Enhancing evidence and improving practice. *Psychotherapy, 52*, 402–411.

Bennett-Levy, J., & Lee, N. (2014). Self-practice and self-reflection in cognitive behaviour therapy training: What factors influence trainees' engagement and experience of benefit? *Behavioural and Cognitive Psychotherapy, 42*, 48–64.

Berends, L. (2011). Embracing the visual: Using timelines with in-depth interviews on substance use and treatment. *Qualitative Report, 16*, 1–9.

Bertolino, B., & Miller, S. D. (Eds.). (2012). *ICCE manuals on feedback-informed treatment* (Vols. 1–6). Chicago, IL: ICCE Press.

Blanchard, M., & Farber, B. A. (2016). Lying in psychotherapy: Why and what clients don't tell their therapist about therapy and their relationship. *Counselling Psychology Quarterly, 29*, 90–112.

Bloch, S., & Reibstein, J. (1980). Perceptions by patients and therapists of therapeutic factors in group psychotherapy. *British Journal of Psychiatry, 137*, 274–278.

Bloch, S., Reibstein, J., Crouch, E., Holroyd, P., & Themen, J. (1979). A method for the study of therapeutic factors in group psychotherapy. *British Journal of Psychiatry, 134*, 257–263.

Boddy, C. R. (2004). From brand image research to teaching assessment: Using a projective technique borrowed from marketing research to aid an understanding of teaching effectiveness. *Quality Assurance in Education, 12*, 94–105.

Boddy, C. (2005). Projective techniques in market research: Valueless subjectivity or insightful reality? A look at the evidence for the usefulness, reliability and validity of projective techniques in market research. *International Journal of Market Research, 47*, 239–254.

Bowen, M., & Cooper, M. (2012). Development of a client feedback tool: A qualitative study of therapists' experiences of using the Therapy Personalisation Forms. *European Journal of Psychotherapy and Counselling, 14,* 47–62.

Bowie, C., McLeod, J., & McLeod, J. (2016). "It was almost like the opposite of what I needed": A qualitative exploration of client experiences of unhelpful therapy. *Counselling and Psychotherapy Research, 16,* 79–87.

Bruner, J. (1986). *Actual minds, possible worlds.* Cambridge, MA: Harvard University Press.

Bruner, J. (1990). *Acts of meaning.* Cambridge, MA: Harvard University Press.

Burnett, P. C. (1999). Assessing the structure of learning outcomes from counselling using the SOLO taxonomy: An exploratory study. *British Journal of Guidance and Counselling, 27,* 567–580.

Castonguay, L., Boswell, J. F., Zack, S. E., Baker, S., Boutselis, M. A., Chiswick, N. R., . . . Holtforth, M. G. (2010). Helpful and hindering events in psychotherapy: A Practice Research Network study. *Psychotherapy: Theory, Research, Practice, Training, 47,* 327–344.

Clark, A., & Morriss, L. (2015). The use of visual methodologies in social work research over the last decade: A narrative review and some questions for the future. *Qualitative Social Work.* doi:10.1177/1473325015601205

Cooper, M., & Norcross, J. C. (2016). A brief, multidimensional measure of clients' therapy preferences: The Cooper-Norcross Inventory of Preferences (C-NIP). *International Journal of Clinical and Health Psychology, 16,* 87–98.

Cummings, A. L. (1998). Helping clients uncover metaphoric understandings of bulimia. *Canadian Journal of Counselling, 32,* 230–241.

Cummings, A. L., Hallberg, E. T., & Slemon, A. G. (1994). Templates of client change in short-term counseling. *Journal of Counseling Psychology, 41,* 464–472.

Cummings, A. L., Martin, J., Hallberg, E. T., & Slemon, A. G. (1992). Memory for therapeutic events, session effectiveness, and working alliance in short-term counseling. *Journal of Counseling Psychology, 39,* 306–312.

Daniel, T., & McLeod, J. (2006). Weighing up the evidence: A qualitative analysis of how person-centred counsellors evaluate the effectiveness of their practice. *Counselling and Psychotherapy Research, 6,* 244–249.

Doxsee, D. J., & Kivlighan, D. M., Jr. (1994). Hindering events in interpersonal relations groups for counselor trainees. *Journal of Counseling and Development, 72,* 621–626.

Ekroll, V. B., & Rønnestad, M. H. (2016). Processes and changes experienced by clients during and after naturalistic good-outcome therapies conducted by experienced psychotherapists. *Psychotherapy Research.* doi:10.1080/10503307.2015.1119326

Elliott, R. (1993). *Helpful aspects of therapy form.* Retrieved from http://www.experiential-researchers.org/instruments/elliott/hat.pdf

Elliott, R., Mack, C., & Shapiro, D. (1999). *Simplified Personal Questionnaire procedure.* Retrieved from http://www.experiential-researchers .org/instruments/elliott/pqprocedure.html

Elliott, R., Partyka, R., Wagner, J., Alperin, R., Dobrenski, R., Messer, S. B., . . . Castonguay, L. G. (2009). An adjudicated hermeneutic single case efficacy design study of experiential therapy for panic/phobia. *Psychotherapy Research, 19,* 543–557.

Elliott, R., Wagner, J., Sales, C.D.M., Alves, P., Rodgers, B., & Café, M. J. (2016). Psychometrics of the Personal Questionnaire: A client-generated outcome measure. *Psychological Assessment, 28*, 263–278.

Etherington, K. (2004). Heuristic research as a vehicle for personal and professional development. *Counselling and Psychotherapy Research, 4*, 48–63.

Finn, S. E., Fischer, C. T., & Handler, L. (Eds.). (2012). *Collaborative/therapeutic assessment: A casebook and guide.* Hoboken, NJ: Wiley.

Fischer, C. T. (2000). Collaborative, individualized assessment. *Journal of Personality Assessment, 74*, 2–14.

Fishman, D. B. (1999). *The case for a pragmatic psychology.* New York, NY: New York University Press.

Fodor, I. E. (2001). Making meaning of therapy: A personal narrative of change over 4 decades. In M. R. Goldfried (Ed.), *How therapists change: Personal and professional reflections* (pp. 123–146). Washington, DC: American Psychological Association.

Fodor, I. G. (2010). On being and not being Jewish: From pink diapers to social activist/feminist. *Women and Therapy, 33*, 382–397.

Gabbay, J., & le May, A. (2010). *Practice-based evidence for healthcare: Clinical mindlines.* London, UK: Routledge.

Geller, J. D. (2014). Adult development and the transformative powers of psychotherapy. *Journal of Clinical Psychology: In Session, 70*, 768–779.

Haber, R., Carlson, R. G., & Braga, C. (2014). Use of an anecdotal Client Feedback Note in family therapy. *Family Process, 53*, 307–317.

Hatfield, D., McCullough, L., Frantz, S.H.B., & Krieger, K. (2010). Do we know when our clients get worse? An investigation of therapists' ability to detect negative client change. *Clinical Psychology and Psychotherapy, 17*, 25–32.

Hill, C. E., Chui, H., & Baumann, E. (2013). Revisiting and re-envisioning the outcome problem in psychotherapy: An argument to include individualized and qualitative measurement. *Psychotherapy, 50*, 68–76.

Jones, S. C., Magee, C., & Andrews, K. (2015). "I think other parents might . . .": Using a projective technique to explore parental supply of alcohol. *Drug and Alcohol Review, 34*, 309–315.

Kerr, C., Josyula, K., & Littenberg, R. (2011). Developing an observing attitude: An analysis of meditation diaries in an MBSR clinical trial. *Clinical Psychology and Psychotherapy, 18*, 80–93.

Kivlighan, D. M., Jr., & Arthur, E. G. (2000). Convergence in client and counselor recall of important session events. *Journal of Counseling Psychology, 47*, 79–84.

Kottler, J., & Carlson, J. (2005). *The client who changed me: Stories of therapist personal transformation.* New York, NY: Routledge.

Lambert, M. J. (2015). Progress feedback and the OQ-system: The past and the future. *Psychotherapy, 52*, 381–390.

Levitt, H. M. (2015). Qualitative psychotherapy research: The journey so far and future directions. *Psychotherapy, 52*, 31–37.

Lilienfeld, S. O., Wood, J. M., & Garb, H. N. (2000). The scientific status of projective techniques. *Psychological Science in the Public Interest, 1*, 27–66.

Lindhiem, O., Bennett, C. B., Orimoto, T. E., & Kolko, D. J. (2016). A meta-analysis of personalized treatment goals in psychotherapy: A preliminary report and call for more studies. *Clinical Psychology: Science and Practice, 23*, 165–167.

Llewelyn, S. P. (1988). Psychological therapy as viewed by clients and therapists. *British Journal of Clinical Psychology, 27*, 223–237.

Llewelyn, S. P., Elliott, R., Shapiro, D. A., Hardy, G., & Firth-Cozens, J. (1988). Client perceptions of significant events in prescriptive and exploratory periods of individual therapy. *British Journal of Clinical Psychology, 27*, 105–114.

Mackrill, T. (2008). Solicited diary studies of psychotherapeutic practice—pros and cons. *European Journal of Psychotherapy and Counselling, 10*, 5–18.

Marzillier, J. (2010). *The gossamer thread: My life as a psychotherapist.* London, UK: Karnac.

Mattingly, C. (1998). In search of the good: Narrative reasoning in clinical practice. *Medical Anthropology Quarterly, 12*, 273–297.

McClelland, D. C. (1980). Motive dispositions, the merits of operant and respondent measures. In L. Wheeler (Ed.), *Review of personality and social psychology* (pp. 214–237). Thousand Oaks, CA: Sage.

McClelland, D. C., & Boyatzis, R. E. (1982). Leadership motive pattern and long-term success in management. *Journal of Applied Psychology, 67*, 737–743.

McCullough, L., Kuhn, N., Andrews, S., Kaplan, A., Wolf, J., & Hurley, C. L. (2003). *Treating affect phobia: A manual for short-term dynamic psychotherapy.* New York, NY: Guilford Press.

McLeod, J. (2010). *Case study research in counselling and psychotherapy.* London, UK: Sage.

McLeod, J. (2011). *Qualitative research in counselling and psychotherapy* (2nd ed.). London, UK: Sage.

McLeod, J. (2013). Qualitative research: Methods and contributions. In M. J. Lambert (Ed.), *Bergin and Garfield's handbook of psychotherapy and behavior change* (5th ed., pp. 49–84). Hoboken, NJ: Wiley.

McLeod, J. (2016). *Using research in counselling and psychotherapy.* London, UK: Sage.

Meyer, G. J., Finn, S. E., Eyde, L. D., Kay, G. G., Moreland, K. L., Dies, R. R., . . . Reed, G. M. (2001). Psychological testing and psychological assessment: A review of evidence and issues. *American Psychologist, 56*, 128–165.

Miller, S. D., Hubble, M. A., Chow, D., & Seidel, J. (2015). Beyond measures and monitoring: Realizing the potential of feedback-informed treatment. *Psychotherapy, 52*, 449–457.

Miller, S. D., Prescott, D. S., & Maeschalck, C. (2016) *Reaching for excellence: Feedback-informed treatment in practice.* Washington, DC: APA Books.

Milligan, C., Bingley, A., & Gatrell, A. (2005). Digging deep: Using techniques to explore the place of health and well-being amongst older people. *Social Science and Medicine, 61*, 1882–1892.

Mizock, L., Russinova, Z., & Shani, R. (2014). New roads paved on losses: Photovoice perspectives about recovery from mental illness. *Qualitative Health Research, 24*, 1481–1491.

Moreno, J. K., Furhiman, A., & Hileman, E. (1995). Significant events in a psychodynamic psychotherapy group for eating disorders. *Group, 19*, 56–62.

Muncey, T. (2010). *Creating autoethnographies.* London, UK: Sage.

Ogden, J., & Russell, S. (2012). How Black women make sense of "White" and "Black" fashion magazines: A qualitative think aloud study. *Journal of Health Psychology, 18*, 1588–1600.

Oster, G. D., & Crone, P. G. (2004). *Using drawings in assessment and therapy* (2nd ed.). New York, NY: Routledge.

Piotrowski, C. (2015). On the decline of projective techniques in professional psychology training. *North American Journal of Psychology, 17*, 259–265.

Richardson, L., & St. Pierre, E. A. (2005). Writing: A method of inquiry. In N. K. Denzin, & Y. S. Lincoln (Eds.), *The Sage handbook of qualitative research* (3rd ed., pp. 959–978). Thousand Oaks, CA: Sage.

Rober, P., Van Tricht, K., & Sundet, R. (2016). *"One step up, but not there yet": Moving towards developing a feedback oriented family therapy.* Manuscript in preparation.

Robinson, S. I., Ashworth, M., Shepherd, M., & Evans, C. (2007). In their own words: A narrative-based classification of clients' problems on an idiographic outcome measure for talking therapy in primary care. *Primary Care Mental Health, 4*, 165–173.

Rodgers, B. (2006). Life space mapping: preliminary results from the development of a new method for investigating counselling outcomes. *Counselling and Psychotherapy Research, 6*, 227–232.

Sales, C.M.D., & Alves, P.C.G. (2012). Individualized patient-progress systems: Why we need to move towards a personalized evaluation of psychological treatments. *Canadian Psychology, 53*, 115–121.

Shedler, J., Mayman, M., & Manis, M. (1993). The *illusion* of mental health. *American Psychologist, 48*, 1117–1131.

Steinman, R. B. (2009). Projective techniques in consumer research. *International Bulletin of Business Administration, 5*, 37–45.

Stephen, S., Elliott, R., & Macleod, R. (2011). Person-centred therapy with a client experiencing social anxiety difficulties: A hermeneutic single case efficacy design. *Counselling and Psychotherapy Research, 11*, 55–66.

Sundet, R. (2009). Therapeutic collaboration and formalized feedback: Using perspectives from Vygotsky and Bakhtin to shed light on practices in a family therapy unit. *Clinical Child Psychology and Psychiatry, 15*, 81–95.

Sundet, R. (2012) Therapist perspectives on the use of feedback on process and outcome: Patient-focused research in practice. *Canadian Psychology, 53*, 122–130.

Sutton-Brown, C. A. (2014). Photovoice: A methodological guide. *Photography and Culture, 7*, 169–185.

Timulak, L. (2007). Identifying core categories of client identified impact of helpful events in psychotherapy: A qualitative meta-analysis. *Psychotherapy Research, 17*, 305–314.

Timulak, L. (2010). Significant events in psychotherapy: An update of research findings. *Psychology and Psychotherapy: Theory, Research and Practice, 83*, 421–427.

Tsai, M., Kohlenberg, R. J., Kanter, J. W., Kohlenberg, B., Follette, W. C., & Callaghan, G. M. (2008). *A guide to functional analytic psychotherapy: Awareness, courage, love, and behaviorism.* New York, NY: Springer.

Wall, S. (2008). Easier said than done: Writing an autoethnography. *International Journal of Qualitative Methods, 7*, 38–53.

Walls, J., McLeod, J., & McLeod, J. (2016). Client preferences in counselling for alcohol problems: A qualitative investigation. *Counselling and Psychotherapy Research, 16*, 109–118.

Walsh, E., & Malson, H. (2010). Discursive constructions of eating disorders: A story completion task. *Feminism and Psychology, 20*, 529–537.

Webb, K. B. (2011). Care of others and self: A suicidal patient's impact on the psychologist. *Professional Psychology: Research and Practice, 42*, 215–221.

Weiner, I. B. (2004). Monitoring psychotherapy with performance-based measures of personality functioning. *Journal of Personality Assessment, 83*, 323–333.

Withers, R. (2009). The therapeutic process of interactive drawing therapy. *New Zealand Journal of Counselling, 29*, 72–90.

6

Quantitative Performance Systems

Feedback-Informed Treatment

Norah A. Chapman, Stephanie Winkeljohn Black, Joanna M. Drinane,
Nicholas Bach, Patty Kuo, and Jesse J. Owen

Routine outcome monitoring (ROM) is a research-supported clinical practice that uses client feedback to therapists to reduce premature dropout and improve treatment outcomes (Lambert & Shimokawa, 2011; Miller, Hubble, Chow, & Seidel, 2013). Important to the purpose of this book, feedback also can provide essential guidance to therapists who engage in continuous performance improvement. This chapter describes the use of two of the ROM systems—Outcome Questionnaire System (OQ-45) and the Partners for Change Outcomes Management System (PCOMS)—for therapists' continuing professional development and provide brief information about a few other popular systems.

Therapists historically have relied on their own clinical judgment to assess client progress (Grove, Zald, Boyd, Snitz, & Nelson, 2000). But it is increasingly clear just how inadequate that judgment typically is (Chapman et. al., 2012; Hannan et al., 2005; Walfish, McAlister, O'Donnell, & Lambert, 2012). For example, therapists who rely only on clinical judgment may overlook clients who actually worsen in therapy (Chapman et al., 2012; Hannan et al., 2005). Hannan and colleagues (2005) found, for example, that of 944 predictions therapists made as to whether clients in their caseloads would worsen in treatment, only three predictions were that a client would deteriorate and only one of those three was accurate. The ROM system, however, successfully predicted 36 out of 40 deteriorating cases. Similar failures to predict clinical deterioration have been obtained in group therapy (Chapman et al., 2012). But despite these difficulties in discriminating whether a client is progressing in treatment, therapists tend to rate themselves as being substantially above average (Walfish et al., 2012). When therapists are left only to their own judgments, their overestimates of their ability will affect their motivation to improve, and their difficulty in discerning which clients are deteriorating will keep them from focusing on areas that may need improvement.

Using brief assessments to identify clients who are at risk for negative treatment outcomes enables clinicians to take steps to identify problems in the treatment that they can address. In the deliberate practice sequence that Miller, Hubble, and Chow describe in Chapter 2 of this volume, for example, those steps might include sitting down with a supervisor to review recordings of the sessions to determine what to attend to in subsequent work with that client and also having conversations with the client to modify the course of treatment in order to help the client get back on track toward a positive treatment outcome trajectory. ROM data give therapists an objective viewpoint about how their clients are progressing in treatment and from which to reflect on their clinical effectiveness with each individual client.

Overview of Select ROM Systems

In what is perhaps the most complete compendium, Lyon, Lewis, Boyd, Hendrix, and Liu (2016) summarized the systems and their characteristics. Given space limitations, this chapter focuses on the two systems that have the strongest research base, the OQ-45 and the PCOMS, with generally equivalent effects (Lambert & Shimokawa, 2011). We then briefly describe five other ROM systems that are widely used.

Outcome Questionnaire-45

The OQ-45 (Lambert et al., 2004) is the most used of the OQ System's measures. It is a 45-item measure of clients' global psychological functioning, intended to be administered every session. Three OQ-45 subscales assess personal well-being, social functioning, and interpersonal functioning (Lambert, 2015). Lambert (2012) indicated that clients can complete the OQ-45 in approximately 5 to 10 minutes (via online device or paper version).

Therapists can choose to simply hand score a paper-and-pencil version and keep the scores in their own personal databases or to use the electronic version and analyze client responses using the OQ-Analyst software (Lambert, 2012) every session. The OQ-Analyst is intended to identify individuals as either nonresponders, at risk of negative outcomes, or on track for positive treatment outcomes. Therapists are able to access the scores in approximately 18 seconds on a computer and evaluate if the client is on track (OT), progressing as expected, or not progressing as expected (NOT). Scores can be used to discuss the direction and needs of treatment to help improve outcomes.

A total score of 180 is possible on the OQ-45, although many therapists utilize subscale scores to tell them which areas of functioning are most problematic for each client with whom they are working (Lambert, 2012). Should clients or therapists view those areas as particularly salient and connected to their goals for treatment, they may use such scores to inform where to focus treatment planning. Further, the OQ-Analyst produces progress graphs every session to clearly show how the client is progressing in therapy every week. Such graphs can be entered into clinical records and used as points of accountability for both clients and therapists (Lambert, 2015).

But the OQ-45 is not the only measure in the OQ System, which also includes clinical support tools, including the Assessment for Signal Clients (ASC; Lambert, 2015; Slade, Lambert, Harmon, Smart, & Bailey, 2008; Whipple et al., 2003), which can be used to assess factors that may be contributing to a client's lack of progress. The ASC measures therapeutic alliance, motivation for change, life events, and level of social support. Its utility was validated in studies by Harmon et al. (2007) and Whipple et al. (2003). Each found that university counseling center clients who provided both OQ-45 and ASC feedback to their therapists did better than those who provided only OQ-45 feedback.

Reliable Change

The Reliable Change Index (Jacobson & Truax, 1991) is another indicator of how meaningful client change is. For the OQ-45, if a client's score changes by 14 or more points, the change is likely reliable (Lambert, 2015). Clients may experience reliable changes, however, in either positive or negative directions.

The OQ System classifies client scores and graphically represents such changes from the client's initial session. Viewing how clients change each week allows therapists to have a collaborative discussion with them about their progress. If a client is deteriorating, therapists may check in about how the client experiences treatment, therapeutic relationship, or motivation for therapy. Using the Clinical Support Tools alongside the OQ-45 in these instances may help to further clarify how clients are experiencing the therapeutic process. Having the data from the OQ-45 creates entry points for therapists to initiate discussion about how their clients are doing and why.

Change Categories

The OQ-45 cutoff score of 63/64 is a dividing line between clinical and nonclinical cases—in other words, clients more or less likely to show measureable benefit from treatment (Lambert, 2015). This threshold helps therapists to define a treatment success in an empirically supported way. In addition to this cutoff being clinically meaningful from an assessment perspective, it also creates an opportunity for discussion with clients about the aspects of therapy that are supporting changes in outcome and helping them to reach the defined goals. Clients may improve beyond the clinical cutoff and still may have goals to achieve that they want to work on, so the integration of these data into therapeutic interventions is essential and enhances the process. Lambert et al. (2004, 2015) suggested the next categories to characterize various degree of reliable change:

- **Recovered.** Clients whose scores have decreased by 14 or more points and also pass below the cutoff score of 64
- **Improved.** Clients whose scores have changed reliably but still remain above the clinical cutoff
- **Unchanged.** Clients whose scores have not varied by more than 14 points in either direction
- **Deteriorated.** Clients whose scores have become reliably worse and increased by 14 or more points

Research on the Impact of the OQ System

Several studies have investigated the OQ-45's utility in enhancing treatment outcomes by detecting clients at risk for treatment failure (i.e., signal alarm) early enough for their therapists to correct a potential negative outcome. These studies consistently have found OQ-45 client feedback to lead to significantly better outcomes than are obtained by therapists who do not use client feedback (i.e., treatment as usual; e.g., Crits-Cristoph et al., 2012; Harmon et al., 2007; Simon et al., 2013; Slade et al., 2008; Whipple et al., 2003).

These positive impacts have been documented across settings and type of client disorders. For example, Crits-Cristoph and colleagues (2012) found that for clients presenting with substance abuse problems, OQ-45 feedback enhanced outcomes for those who were at risk for treatment failure in terms of their overall well-being and their drug use (but not alcohol use). In a sample of adult clients being treated in an inpatient eating-disorder treatment program, Simon et al. (2013) found that 52.95% of those who had been randomly assigned to the feedback condition achieved clinically significant change compared to 28.6% of clients in the nonfeedback condition.

How the data are used also can be important. For example, Hawkins, Lambert, Vermeersch, Slade, and Tuttle (2004) analyzed the outcomes of clients in three conditions: no feedback, feedback to the therapist, and feedback to both the therapist *and* client. They found that clients in the therapist and client feedback condition had significantly better outcomes compared to the therapist-only feedback condition.

In short, obtaining client feedback using the measures of the OQ System improves outcomes for clients who are at risk of treatment failure. One drawback is that the OQ-45 itself does not provide feedback on the therapeutic alliance; obtaining that information requires an additional step of using the ASC. Another drawback is the length of the OQ-45, for it is sometimes a lot to ask a client to complete 45 items each session. In contrast, the tools of the PCOMS are quite brief and also retain the clinical utility of the OQ System.

Partners for Change Outcome Management System

The PCOMS is comprised of two four-item measures: (1) the Outcome Rating Scale (ORS; Miller, Duncan, Brown, Sparks, & Claud, 2003) and (2) the Session Rating Scale (SRS; Miller, Duncan, Brown, Sorrell, & Chalk, 2006). Both measures are designed for administration every session: the ORS at the beginning and the SRS at the end of the visit. Versions of the scales are available for adults, adolescents, and children, in a number of different languages at no cost to individual practitioners, at https://goo.gl/GqRwQT. Additionally, a growing number of computer-based applications are available that can simplify and expedite the process of administering, scoring, interpreting, and aggregating data from the scales. Such programs include web-based outcome management systems and smartphone apps (e.g., fit-outcomes. com, myoutcomes.com, pragmatictracker.com) as well as web services designed for integration into electronic health records (e.g., OpenFIT).[1] Following a thorough and systemic review of available research evidence by the Substance Abuse and Mental Health Services Agency, PCOMS was listed on the National Registry of Evidence-based Programs and Practice (2013).

Outcome Rating Scale
The ORS is a measure of global psychological functioning defined by four domains using a visual analog scale 10 cm in length to rate the degree to which clients experience distress in those areas. The four domains were based on and parallel the subscales of the OQ-45: individual (quality of personal well-being), social (quality of work, school, and friendships), interpersonal (quality of family and other close relationships), and overall (quality of general well-being) functioning.

---

[1] Detailed descriptions of the other applications can be found online at www.scottdmiller.com.

The ORS is administered before the start of each session and takes approximately 1 minute to complete. Clients are asked to reflect on their past week (or the time since their last visit) and rate how well they are doing on each of the domains. On the paper-and-pencil forms, an "X" or a hash mark is made on the line that best represents their level of functioning. In the computerized versions, the client touches the screen. In both cases, marks to the left of the page reflect lower levels of well-being and marks to the right reflect higher levels of well-being.

When using the measure in paper-and-pencil format, therapists are encouraged to score the ORS together with clients. Therapists score the ORS by using a ruler to measure the distance between the left end of the scale and the client's mark in centimeters to the nearest millimeter. A total score is obtained by adding the scores for all of the domains, with a maximum possible score of 40. Clients with ORS scores above 25 are considered to be functioning at levels similar to clients not in therapy, while clients with ORS scores below 25 are functioning at levels similar to clients in therapy, or with scores consistent with a clinical sample (Bertolino & Miller, 2012).

Importantly, clients who score below 25 are likely to show measured benefit from treatment while those falling above 25 at intake are *less* likely to show improvement and are, in fact, at higher risk of deterioration in care. With regard to the latter, available evidence indicates that between 25% to 33% of people presenting for treatment score *above* the clinical cut-off at intake (Bertolino & Miller, 2012).

The chief problem with using the Reliable Change Index to evaluate individual client progress is that it represents an average across all levels of client functioning. Thus, the statistic likely underestimates the amount of change needed to qualify as "reliable" when clients score very low and likely overestimates the amount of change with those enter treatment scoring higher.

Most recently, a set of predictive algorithms has been developed for determining whether client progress from session to session is associated with successful outcome at termination (Miller, Hubble, Chow, & Seidel, 2015). Unlike some formulas, which plot the average progress of all consumers, successful and not, these equations provide benchmarks for comparing individual consumer progress to both successful and unsuccessful treatment episodes.

Consider an analogy to the field of medicine. No one would be interested in a test for the effectiveness of a particular cancer treatment that compared an individual's progress with the average of all patients whether they lived or died. The important question is whether the person receiving treatment is responding like those who eventually survive. If those at risk for a null or negative outcome are identified, the chances of success can be improved by altering, augmenting, or even referring to other services or providers.

Figure 6.1 displays the ORS scores of a client over the course of six sessions. As the graph illustrates, all the scores fall in the bottom shaded area. Such scores, if not changed, are predictive of a null or negative outcome or dropout from services. Therapists are advised to check in with clients about the therapeutic relationship and their thoughts regarding the treatment process whenever scores fall in the bottom shaded area. Specific questions that may be helpful include: "I notice that we are not making the progress maybe you hoped we would when you first came in. What do you think you need or that we need to do differently to help

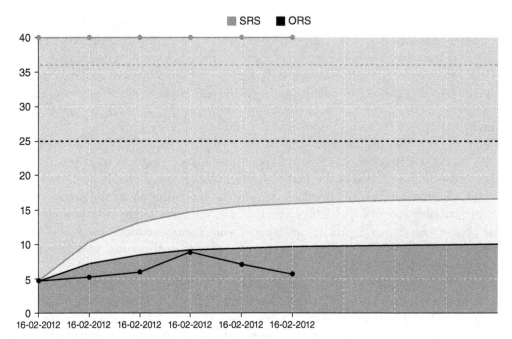

Figure 6.1 Graphical representation of client outcome data.
The top two-thirds shaded area represents successful outcomes; the bottom shaded area represents unsuccessful outcomes. The solid black line represents actual session-by-session ORS scores.
Screen shot courtesy of: www.fit-outcomes.com

you reach the goals you came into therapy to work toward?" Should no improvement occur, consultation and supervision are recommended. If such changes do not result in any improvement in client scores, therapists may want to consider referral to another program or provider.

Scores falling in the top two-thirds shaded area are predictive of success at termination. Therapists should reinforce the positive changes and collaborate with the client about ways to continue improving well-being. If clients further improve or plateau in future sessions, therapists may want to consider decreasing session frequency. As the reader may have surmised, scores in the middle shaded area indicate that caution is warranted as it is not possible to determine whether progress is indicative of success or failure.

Session Rating Scale

The SRS (Miller et al., 2006) measures the therapeutic alliance using Bordin's (1979) definition of the term. The SRS is comprised of four domains: *relationship* (how much clients feel heard by the therapist), *goals and topics* (how much clients feel they were able to work on goals and topics they wanted to work on), *approach or method* (match between therapist's approach and clients), and *overall fit of the session* (general quality of the session).

The SRS is administered at the end of every session and takes less than 1 minute to complete. In form, the measure resembles the ORS. Clients are asked to reflect on the visit and rate each domain. The SRS is designed to be scored and discussed with clients before they leave so that any concerns or problems can be addressed.

The clinical cutoff score for the SRS is 36. Scores below 36 indicate that there is a problem in the therapeutic relationship. However, scores below 9 on any of the four subscales, even when overall scores are 36 or above, can reflect problems as well. Thus, therapists should explore and process client experiences in therapy if SRS scores fall below 36 or if any subscale scores fall below 9. Furthermore, therapists may want to reflect on SRS scores with clients if there are no changes in ORS scores or if ORS scores deteriorate.

Interestingly, two studies have found that SRS scores that improve over time are associated with better outcomes (Miller, Hubble, & Duncan, n.d.; Owen, Miller, Borg, Seidel, & Chow, 2016). In a large study, adolescents who scored low on the SRS at the first session and then experienced an improvement in alliance scores had significantly better outcomes than clients whose SRS scores started high and stayed high throughout (Owen et al., 2016). For that reason, therapists are strongly encouraged to work early on at creating "a culture of feedback" in which consumers feel safe to share any and all concerns related to the therapy, the therapist, or the treatment context and then, of course, to address any specific feedback provided.

Research Support for the PCOMS

Miller, Prescott, and Maeschalck (2017) provided a comprehensive review of all research related to the ORS and SRS. Here, findings from several representative studies documenting the effectiveness of the system in individual, couples, and group therapy are reviewed.

Miller, Duncan, Brown, Sorrell, and Chalk (2006) conducted the first study of PCOMS. In it, the ORS and the SRS were administered to participants orally at the beginning and end of each telephonic-based counseling sessions. Client outcomes significantly improved from intake to termination, an effect that doubled in size when therapists had been using PCOMS in their practice for more than 6 months. In addition, when therapists had access to SRS data, their clients were three times more likely to return for another session than clients of therapists who did not have access to SRS data. An important validation of the value of PCOMS came from the therapists themselves: One year after their PCOMS training, 99% of the therapists at this center continued to use feedback measures regularly with clients.

Reese, Norsworthy, and Rowlands (2009) conducted two randomized clinical trials on PCOMS in a university counseling center and in a graduate training clinic. In both settings, clients in the feedback condition had significantly better outcomes than those in the no-feedback condition. Moreover, significantly more participants in the feedback condition met the criteria for reliable clinical change (i.e., an improvement of at least 5 points on the ORS, as discussed later). Unlike use of the OQ, use of the ORS and SRS was associated with improved outcomes for cases that were and were not progressing.

The fourth of these studies focused on whether PCOMS works with more distressed and impoverished clients. To do this, Reese, Duncan, Bohanske, Owen, and Minami (2014) compared the effectiveness of ORS feedback from clients in a large behavioral health center that served lower-income and more distressed clients with the effectiveness of other large-scale research studies for clients with depressive disorders. Results document that the outcomes of such clients were comparable to the benchmarks set in clinical trials.

Two studies have been conducted on the use of PCOMS in couples therapy, one in Norway (Anker, Duncan, & Sparks, 2009) and the other in the United States (Reese, Toland,

Slone, & Norsworthy, 2010). Couples in both studies were randomly assigned to either the feedback or the no-feedback condition. In both studies, couples in the feedback condition had significantly better outcomes than the no-feedback couples. In fact, Anker et al. (2009) found that the difference in outcome continued at a 6-month follow-up on the ORS, meaning that couples who provided feedback to their therapist were significantly less likely to separate or divorce (18.4% separation rate compared to no-feedback couples' 34.2% separation rate) 6 months after the study ended. Hannan and colleagues (2005) found, for example, that of 944 predictions therapists made as to who in their caseloads would worsen in treatment, only three predictions were that clients were deteriorating and only one of those three was accurate.

Two studies have evaluated the use of the ORS in group therapy. Schuman, Slone, Reese, and Duncan (2015) examined whether feedback via the ORS led to improved client outcomes, less deterioration, and lower rates of clients leaving before therapy was completed among a sample of Army soldiers referred to an outpatient group tailored for substance use. Slone, Reese, Matthews-Duvall, and Kodet (2015) evaluated the full PCOMS with a sample of college students in interpersonal process groups at a university counseling center. In both studies, clients in the feedback conditions had better outcomes and were also more likely to have achieved clinically reliable change. Additionally, clients in the feedback conditions were less likely to terminate prematurely (Schuman et al., 2015) and attended significantly more sessions than clients in the no-feedback groups (M = 8 sessions versus 6.6 sessions, respectively; Slone et al., 2015).

Additional Client Feedback Systems

Although the OQ System and PCOMS are the two ROM systems with the most research support, many others are in widespread use or have particular promise (Lyon et al., 2016). Four are described next.

CelestHealth Solutions

CelestHealth Solution is a ROM system that utilizes the Behavioral Health Measure-20 (Kopta & Lowry, 2002), a 20-item test of well-being, symptoms, and life functioning. This clinical outcome measure has three main clusters of items. First, the Well-Being cluster includes three items that assess overall distress, life satisfaction, and motivation. The Psychological Symptoms cluster has 14 items that measure clinical symptoms such as depression, anxiety, and substance use. The Life Functioning cluster includes three items that measure relationships, life enjoyment, and work/school functioning. More information on the BHM system can be found at http://www.celesthealth.com/.

ACORN Tookit

ACORN stands for "A Collaborative Outcomes Resource Network" and is comprised of a fairly large suite of validated measures. One routinely used with adults is the 13-item Brief Adult Outcome Questionnaire (Version 11) that assesses client symptom type, frequency, and intensity along with a measure of global distress among adults and adolescents who are seeking general outpatient and substance abuse services. It also includes an alliance measure.

The ACORN Toolkit also has an alliance measure available for use to check on the client's perceptions of the therapeutic relationship. Scores from the ACORN outcome measures are compared with projections of progress to evaluate if a client is on track with therapy or not. More information on the ACORN system can be found at http://www.psychoutcomes.org/COMMONS/WebHome.

CORE-Outcome Measure

The CORE-Outcome Measure (OM) has been adopted nationwide in the United Kingdom. It is a 34-item measure of global psychological distress across four domains that include well-being, symptoms, functioning, and risk. Several shorter measures can be used for routine monitoring or with special populations, such as students, adolescents, and those with learning disorders. The CORE-OM ROM system also has a goal attainment form as well as a therapeutic alliance measure available for use. A benefit of this system is that it is free and is available in several translations. More information on the ACORN system can be found at http://www.coreims.co.uk/index.html.

Treatment Outcome Package

The Treatment Outcome Package (TOP) is a ROM system for children, adolescents, and adults. The system is comprised of a 58-item outcome measure (adult version) that assesses 12 symptom and functional domains (e.g., anxiety, mania, sleep, quality of life). Benefits of this system include outcome monitoring across the life span and flexible electronic administration modalities for clients to respond either in or outside the office. More information about TOP can be found at http://www.outcomereferrals.com.

Using Client Feedback for Clinical Improvement

Although most ROM systems are relatively easy to use, some common issues arise, especially for those who are still new to using the systems. The remainder of the chapter addresses those issues. Because our own experiences are primarily with the PCOMS, that system is the basis for the examples we provide. However, most of what we describe is generalizable to other ROM systems.

Getting Started in Using ROM Feedback

Clinicians may begin using PCOMS as they would develop additional new competencies. Helpful readings prior to implementing the measures may be found in Miller et al. (2017) and in feedback-informed treatment manuals (Bertolino & Miller, 2012). The measures may be accessed for free at http://www.scottdmiller.com/performance-metrics/.

ROM Feedback and Therapist Theory

A common question concerns how client feedback systems work with a clinician's theoretical perspective. Like most of the other systems, PCOMS is designed to be atheoretical, permitting its use with a variety of theoretical perspectives. Reese, Slone, and Miserocchi

(2012), for example, used case examples to illustrate how PCOMS measures may facilitate the work of therapists working from an interpersonal process theory (Teyber, 2006). Owen, Lavin, Kuo, Winkeljohn Black, and Chapman (n.d.) similarly used a case study approach to examine how client feedback may facilitate tenets of psychodynamic psychotherapy.

Using Client Feedback Scores

A number of methods may be useful to process scores from the ORS and SRS. Methods may differ depending on if clients are on track or not with their treatment process. The next two examples illustrate possible responses.

Case 6.1 Client "On Track" for Treatment

Mary was an adolescent client who was referred to therapy by her mother after her father passed away. Mary's mother was concerned that Mary was grieving for her father but did not have a way to express her emotions. Mary's baseline ORS score was 23; the therapist and Mary explored her lower Individual and Interpersonal well-being marks. Mary revealed that while she was grieving over her father's death, she was not as affected by his death as others believed she was. Mary's mother and father had been divorced, and Mary had had a distant relationship with her father. Mary was frustrated that teachers at her school were making assumptions about how she felt. In essence, using the lower scores on these two domains on the ORS allowed Mary to define for herself the struggles she was having in these areas.

By the fourth session, Mary achieved reliably significant clinical change. Her ORS scores had increased to 26 by session 2 and then to 28 by the beginning of her fourth session. During the fourth session, the therapist pointed out the increase in ORS scores to Mary and asked her about her perceptions of her sense of well-being over the course of therapy. The therapist and Mary explored how being able to express her unspoken conflicted feelings for her father, and her tense relationship with her father's side of the family, had allowed her to process her guilt over her father's death. The therapist also asked Mary what she would like the therapist to continue doing to help her and what she would like the therapist to do differently. Mary informed the therapist that it had been helpful for her to hear her feelings and thoughts reflected back to her by the therapist and to feel that she was heard. Mary then initiated the conversation of having therapy once every 2 weeks before terminating therapy. The therapist and Mary explored the possibility of Mary experiencing a decrease in her well-being and Mary's feelings surrounding that possibility. The therapist and Mary had two more sessions before terminating; Mary's ORS score plateaued at the last session at a score of 31. Mary's SRS scores throughout therapy had been between 38 and 40, indicating that a positive therapeutic alliance was built and maintained across the course of treatment. During the last two sessions, the therapist and Mary processed what it was like for Mary to not be in weekly therapy sessions and how she continued to improve. The therapist and Mary agreed that Mary seemed ready for termination. Such collaborative discussions individualized the treatment process to Mary and isolated the reasons for what made therapy beneficial for her needs. The ORS scores also provided a tool to help support discussions around clinical decision making, including frequency of sessions and termination, given her progress.

Case 6.2 Client "Not on Track" for Treatment

Unfortunately, not all clinical progress can be as positive as Mary's. Fortunately, client feedback is especially useful when client change is not occurring or when clients actually are worsening in treatment. This is illustrated with the example of Shelly, a 36-year-old woman who entered therapy after an inpatient hospitalization for chronic suicidal ideation and severe anxiety. During her first therapy session, she obtained an ORS score of 11, which is in the clinical range of functioning. Her Individual domain was the lowest, and her Interpersonal and Social scores were close behind. After three treatment sessions, Shelly's scores had become slightly lower than when she first came in. An example of possible discussions that might occur between Shelly and her therapist follows.

> *THERAPIST:* Shelly, I see from your progress graph that your ORS scores are about the same as when you came in, and I feel concerned you are not getting what you hoped for when you came into therapy.
>
> *SHELLY:* I like coming in, but yeah, I am not feeling a lot different yet.
>
> *THERAPIST:* I imagine that feels frustrating. I see on your ORS scores that every area rated feels unmanageable right now. Is there an area that you think we could focus on or a direction of treatment that we could focus on that would help you to begin to work toward feeling improved? Or are there things about our relationship or the way we are working on your goals that could go differently for you so that this service would be more beneficial to you?

Discussing treatment progress in this manner communicates to the client that the therapist is hearing that they are not improving in treatment and facilitates a discussion to help understand from the client's perspective how they see change occurring. It also alerts the therapist to a need to change the manner in which treatment is being provided. Perhaps therapists can begin thinking about other referrals, such as an evaluation for medication, group therapy, support groups, or other avenues in which the client may benefit in addition to therapy.

Using Client Feedback in Therapy with Couples and Groups

Using client feedback in therapy that includes more than one client may require more creativity and logical consideration. PCOMS has been used successfully with couples and groups in research studies. The next recommendations are based on the protocols used in those studies.

Couples Therapy

It is recommended that the ORS and the SRS be administered to each partner and discussed in the context of their couples work. For example, a therapist may administer the ORS at the beginning of a couple's session to evaluate how each individual in the couple is progressing ovn the reasons they came in for couples therapy. Each individual may progress at a different rate and/or across different domains. Therapists can evaluate each session how progress is being made across the couple and process any changes, or the lack thereof, for each individual.

Doing so can benefit the couple by enabling each to hear from the other how he or she is doing and what is needed for each of them to move forward with their goals in therapy.

The same can be true at the end of the session with the SRS. Each individual can fill out the SRS as a way to process his or her experience of the couples session. It is hoped, of course, that both individuals would rate the session similarly and positively, so that the discussion could be focused on what about the session was a good fit for each of them and could be replicated in the future to ensure that therapy progressed in a way be beneficial for the couple. The next sample vignette is for when SRS scores are discrepant across couples, offering the therapist an opportunity to reflect on and understand how each individual perceived the session differently and to ascertain what may be needed from each of them to make the couples work a better fit for them both.

> *THERAPIST:* Stacy, I see that your SRS score today is a 30 and, Logan, your score is a 38. It seems as though you both saw the fit of this session a bit differently. Stacy, it seems like I could do some work to make sure this session is a better fit for you. Can you tell me what did not seem as helpful today and what I or we could do differently next time to help it improve?
>
> *STACY:* I just thought Logan got more time to talk today and I felt left out, as though what I brought to session did not matter as much. I guess I would like for there to be more equal time for us both to share.
>
> *THERAPIST:* Thank you for being honest about how you are feeling in the therapy session today. I'm sorry I didn't manage the time well, and I really appreciate you telling me. What ideas do you have for how we can share the time better during the session? What might be a good way to use our time?

This discussion focuses on what the clients need to benefit further from the service. Another conversation with Logan might have focused on what he perceived that he was taking away from the session that was beneficial. The scores provide a formal opportunity to reflect on the process of therapy every session and on what may be needed to change the course of treatment to improve outcomes and the therapist's effectiveness. In couples work, it can be beneficial too for each individual to have overt conversations about their experiences with progress and the service itself to facilitate open conversation and understanding of each perspective.

Group Therapy

Using PCOMS in a group may require creativity in how to use the ORS and SRS scores to best inform clinical decision making and reflection on the nature of the group process. In Slone et al. (2015), clients filled out the ORS before coming to group. Clients scored their own measures with rulers and plotted their total scores on a graph to evaluate their own progress before sharing it in the group. Doing so took approximately 2.5 minutes at the beginning of the group. Changes in ORS scores in the group can become a useful way to have a formalized check-in and also to evaluate who needs time that week to talk in the group. For example, if a client's scores do not improve or if they have remained unchanged, it may be beneficial for therapists to discuss in the group how the group could help that client make progress on his or her goals. When such conversations take place in the group, the group as a whole can support the client in moving forward.

In the PCOMS system, there is a group-specific measure of cohesion—the Group Session Rating Scale (GSRS; Duncan & Miller, 2007)—to be used in place of the SRS. Approximately 5 minutes before the group ends, therapists may facilitate clients filling out the GSRS. In Slone et al. (2015), clients measured their own GSRS scores and plotted the total scores on the graph to evaluate how group cohesion changed from the previous session. Therapists asked clients to share their progress in group cohesion as a means of a formal checkout process in the group. This gave clients an opportunity to share if they were not feeling particularly connected to the group that session or if there were any changes to their experience of group cohesion. If clients' scores had improved, the therapists would facilitate a discussion with the group that allowed everyone to hear what happened in the group that day to improve the experience of safety and connection. Conversely, members also heard what happened in the group that day that may have contributed to lower scores or experiences of disconnection. Members who do not feel connected may feel safer in returning knowing that they were heard and would have an opportunity to have a better experience the next time.

Some therapists reflected that such conversations about their scores may make clients feel rather vulnerable, particularly if scores have decreased on the ORS or the GSRS. In the Slone et al. (2015) study, clients were told they could share as much or as little as they wanted to about their scores in the group. Practicing such vulnerability could promote a corrective experience or an opportunity for that client to work on interpersonal effectiveness goals. If therapists integrate the ORS and the GSRS into the process of therapy, the systems become valuable tools that formalize the use of the here-and-now that is already occurring in the group.

Utilizing Client Feedback in Supervision

Client feedback is important to developing competence. But as Chapter 1 in this volume discusses, expertise builds on and is qualitatively different from competence: Competence is defined in terms of consensus about expected performance whereas expertise is defined in terms of client outcomes.

Developing Competence

Monitoring client outcome is an evidence-based practice and also an element of the competencies discussed as part of the American Psychological Association's Standards of Accreditation (2015). Training programs are encouraged to implement training in using client feedback systems with their students. Some training programs teach and/or require their trainees to use client feedback systems in their work and incorporate them into supervision, to ensure that assessment and therapy competencies are tracked and utilized together. For example, in the first author's (NC) university, students are required to present PCOMS progress graphs in their formal group supervision presentations. These data provide an important complement to those provided through video and case reports to evaluate treatment progress.

Students can also be trained to look for client ORS and SRS scores that indicate outcome and alliances that are not progressing as expected. Such indications on progress graphs may help supervisees and students know whom to prioritize talking about in supervision that week. Such a practice is consistent with DP, in that not only are clinicians reflecting on their effectiveness but supervisors also are supporting this formal time to help them improve their effectiveness with individual clients in a way that will best support client outcomes in treatment.

Developing Expertise: Helping Colleagues Understand the Need to Seek Client Feedback

Clinicians often will intimate that they have been doing this work for so long that they "just know" how well they and their clients are doing and would prefer not to include any more paperwork in their day. But as we reviewed at the outset of this chapter, the validity of those judgments is more illusory than real (Hannan et al., 2005; Walfish et al., 2012).

Fortunately, ROM systems and the research on them is getting increasing exposure, and this information eventually will reach practitioners. In the meantime, it is helpful to gently encourage clinicians to consider the research on self-perception bias: that while we may very well know our clients and their treatment progress, using ROM allows our clients' voices to guide the treatment progress in order to encourage practitioners to take the risk of dialogs with their clients about their experiences in therapy. We know that clients' perceptions of their experiences are the best predictor of treatment outcome (Horvath, Del Re, Flückiger, & Symonds, 2011).

Using a ROM system not only puts our clients in the drivers' seats with respect to their own care, but it also gives therapists a reliable and valid tool to formally check out how clients think they are progressing. Supervisors too change their perceptions of ROM data after using them with students. For example, one supervisor we know commented: "My immediate reaction was that it [a feedback system] would be cumbersome. . . . I discovered that I was wrong. . . . Most importantly, it facilitated our young clinicians in discussing the process of psychotherapy."

In short, the little time that is required to formally check on our clients' progress can make a big difference to the effectiveness of psychotherapy. For more information, guidance, and clinical examples on this topic, see Miller et al. (2017).

Limitations of ROM

Although this chapter has focused primarily on the benefits of using ROM data, it is important as well to acknowledge some of the limitations. Some recent studies show ROM to have less robust effects than previously touted in the literature (Miller et al., 2015). ROM works only when clinicians use the measures, are open to feedback, and successfully adjust their work as a result of the feedback (e.g., De Jong, Sluis, Nugter, & Heiser, 2012). Wampold (2015) noted that it is still unclear exactly how ROM benefits treatment. Wolpert (2013) raised concerns about ROM data being misused noncollaboratively with clinicians, which potentially could undermine treatment. These limits make it clear that ROM systems should be implemented thoughtfully, and that they are not a panacea that will save all clinicians and organizations from clients experiencing negative treatment outcomes (e.g., Miller et al., 2015).

Conclusion

ROM systems have made a significant impact on the way many therapists and organizations conduct and monitor psychotherapy services. However, it is worth emphasizing that obtaining routine outcome feedback from clients is also only half the practice. Therapists must be open to and hold a positive attitude toward hearing honest feedback from their clients *and* using such feedback to collaboratively make clinical decisions (De Jong, 2015). It is also imperative to remember *who* is receiving the feedback, regardless of the ROM system used. In many ways, ROM systems provide a window into a therapist's strengths and blind spots, which is a necessary component of deliberate practice. As Michael Lambert (2010) has often been quoted as saying, "Yes, it is time for clinicians to routinely collect client feedback."

Questions from the Editors

Question #1. You mention that it can be helpful for trainees to bring ROM progress graphs to supervision to supplement video and case reports. Please describe an example of how a trainee used ROM to gain insight about a client that would not have been available from a video or a case report.

Answer from Authors: In our (NC's) training program, students are required to integrate their ORS and SRS data graphs as part of a formal case presentation in group supervision. In general, the graphs are an excellent complement to the videos and case reports. They are a brief way of evaluating the global trajectory of treatment, whereas watching an entire therapy video and reading case reports is next to impossible every session to understand treatment progress across the duration of work. Certainly videos and case reports provide more depth and context to the nuanced processes that are captured in the graph, but the graph provides an opportunity for supervisors to gain a quick understanding of the *client's perception* of the outcome and alliance. Often video and reports are reviewed and written from the therapist's point of view. Although their perspectives are valuable as well, it is the client's perception of progress that tends to best predict their outcome in treatment.

One example of how a PCOMS graph was used in a presentation occurred when a student presented a client in group supervision with whom she felt stuck. The student provided basic demographic data and the presenting issue before sharing that she believed she was not making much progress with the client. This student showed the client's PCOMS graph, which displayed a line representing ORS scores that had not changed by more or less than 5 points. In essence, there had been no change from the client's perspective. The student shared that she had tried out different techniques from several different treatments, but nothing seemed to work. After seeing the graph, the supervisor asked the student to go back to view both the alliance and the outcome scores. The student noticed that the client's SRS score was between 30 and 35 each session. The student reflected that she and the client seemed to have a good relationship, but they "always seemed to run out of time to talk about the SRS." Given the client's scores, the supervisor suggested pushing pause on moving forward with the treatment techniques and going back to building rapport and gaining an understanding of the client's view of the alliance. The supervisor also encouraged the student to try to end the session a few minutes early to make it a priority to process the SRS scores at the end of session to further monitor the alliance. Evaluating both the alliance and outcome scores on the graph allowed the supervisor to be clued in to the potential for a lack of a therapeutic relationship before even seeing the video or reading a case report. The graph generated discussion about how the student felt in the room with the client and about in what ways the client might be interacting with the student or others in his life, and got the ball rolling, so to speak, as to uncovering part of what might be the reason the student felt stuck.

Question #2. Some therapists may have questions about when ROM data do not match up with clients' self-report of their well-being or symptoms in session. For example, the ROM data may indicate that a client is feeling better or worse than the client reports to the therapist in session. What is your advice for therapists regarding these situations?

Answer from Authors: This is a common question I get when I (NC) do talks about using ROM in clinical practice. I think instances such as these have a good deal to do with us as therapists in how we set up the framework around using ROM and how active of a participant we are in integrating those data into treatment. I believe that in order for ROM to be effective, we have to adequately inform clients that using these measures is a way for them to have a voice in their clinical care and for therapists to reflect on client progress, with the intention to help prevent negative treatment outcome. In most instances, when clients know that these measures are being used to help them get better and to have an opportunity for their therapists to receive a vital sign of their progress, most clients will be honest about their progress.

Occasionally I have clients whose scores do not seem to match up with how they describe their mood, circumstances of their week, and so on. In those cases, I will look for a pause at some point and say something to the effect of "You know, at the beginning of the session today your ORS score suggested that you were not feeling as good as you were last week. The way you are describing the changes in the past week do not seem to fit what you shared on your outcome measure." At that point, I will check in with clients to see if I understood their perception of their progress correctly or to ask them to reappraise their score. Sometimes clients will say that now that they have been talking about their week, they do see gains in ways perhaps that they were not giving themselves credit for or were not recognizing when they filled out the measure. In those cases, I would ask clients if they would like to rerate their ORS to be a more accurate representation of their progress. The same goes for when clients report declined progress. I am very clear to tell clients that I am not trying to influence their scores in any way, but rather I am trying to gain a score that is more accurate to their actual lived experiences so we have the best data from which to work.

I (SWB) find that some of the most meaningful conversations about therapeutic progress and goals occur when this discrepancy occurs. A discrepancy in either direction (high ROM score and low verbal reports in session or vice versa) gives me information about how clients see themselves, our therapeutic work, and the world. This gives me and the clients the opportunity to discuss what a "perfect score" would look and feel like for them. For some of my clients, a perfect score represents the absence of crisis rather than the experience of joy and contentment. Other clients may report high ORS scores out of a tendency to minimize or deny difficult experiences. By verbalizing the discrepancies I see in their ROM scores and in-session presentation, clients and I can begin to address how they see their own concerns and well-being.

I (NC) have had similar experiences with scoring the SRS. Sometimes clients will score the session consistently positively despite my take that sometimes the session did not flow, we did not seem to be connected or perhaps were on different pages with what to work on. If I continue to get high scores on those sessions, I will stop the session and check in more formally by saying, "You know, I do not want to change your scores or influence your decision here, but I know for me I felt like we might have been off today. I am wondering if we worked on what you hoped we would work on today." Most times when I open the door for clients to give me constructive feedback, they will approach it more honestly. At that time, I would ask them to rerate the SRS and thank them for being honest with me about how well the session fit for them. Doing so allows us to have a more honest conversation about how to move forward in a more helpful way the next session.

In our experiences, ROM data are best when we are vigilant about using the data to inform treatment. If we do not use the data, clients may not take their scores seriously. When clients know we highly value their perceptions of their progress, they are often motivated to give more accurate scores, in our experience. Another way we can use ROM data in the session to make them meaningful is to highlight dynamics in the session. For example, some clients who tend to be people pleasers have a very difficult time providing constructive feedback. In those instances, we use the data to check out perceptions of the session via the SRS and highlight the potential dynamic through process comments over time, welcoming the feedback and working to create a safe space for authentic and honest responses. In these cases, opening the door for constructive feedback can align well with the work of promoting a corrective experience for clients who may be working on this dynamic generally in their therapy and lives. When we become aware of inconsistencies or look for ways to use ROM data to inform treatment, we are sending the message that client perception is valuable to the progress of their work and that, in turn, we are dedicated to helping them improve.

Question #3. Have you tried using ROM data to track therapists' performance over time? If so, please describe your experiences. How was it helpful or not helpful? Do you think this process could be used to gain information about whether a trainee is improving their clinical effectiveness?

Answer from Authors: I (NC) have been using the PCOMS feedback system since I entered graduate school and began my practicum in 2009. My program required us to use PCOMS so I have never been without it in clinical practice across treatment formats, and I honestly cannot imagine not having a benchmark of my clients' perception of their progress. As a trainee at the time, I found it immensely helpful for me in growing in my professional clinical competencies from those whom I was learning how to serve most effectively. Specifically, it was helpful to me to understand when I was not using skills correctly or when I missed an understanding of my interpersonal dynamics with a client. ROM data gave me immediate feedback as to whether a technique worked or did not work for the particular client I was working with at the time. It allowed me to reflect immediately on my performance and training progress. The graph of my clients, particularly those who were not making progress as expected, became regular inclusions during my supervision meetings. I immediately knew whom to prioritize in supervision and in case conferences to get feedback on how to help my clients improve the next week, given their feedback. When ROM is used correctly and framed in service of clients getting what they need from services, I cannot imagine a scenario in which it is not helpful. That said, was it uncomfortable to get lower SRS scores or see flat ORS trajectories at times? Yes. And as a professional, it still is. However, ROM data give me a mechanism to formally check in and track progress over the course of treatment, and they help me to "just know." In essence, ROM data have promoted lifelong learning in the sense that I am always reflecting on my progress with clients and my performance as a therapist, all the while privileging my clients' voices in the process.

References

American Psychological Association. (2015). *Standards of accreditation for health service psychology.* Washington, DC: Author. Retrieved from http://www.apa.org/ed/accreditation/about/policies/standards-of-accreditation.pdf

Anker, M. G., Duncan, B. L., & Sparks, J. A. (2009). Using client feedback to improve couple therapy outcomes: A randomized clinical trial in a naturalistic setting. *Journal of Counseling and Clinical Psychology, 77*, 693–704.

Bertolino, B., & Miller, S. D. (Eds.). (2012). *ICCE manuals on feedback-informed treatment* (Vols. 1–6). Chicago, IL: ICCE Press.

Bordin, E. S. (1979). The generalizability of the psychoanalytic concept of the working alliance. *Psychotherapy: Theory, Research and Practice, 16*(3), 252–260. http://dx.doi.org/10.1037/h0085885

Chapman, C. L., Burlingame, G. M., Gleave, R., Rees, F., Beecher, M., & Porter, G. S. (2012). Clinical prediction in group psychotherapy. *Psychotherapy Research, 22*, 1–9. doi:10.1080/10503307.2012.702512

Crits-Cristoph, P., Ring-Kurtz, S., Hamilton, J. L., Lambert, M. J., Gallop, R., McClure, B., . . . Rotrosen, J. (2012). A preliminary study of the effects of individual patient-level feedback in outpatient substance abuse treatment programs. *Journal of Substance Abuse Treatment, 42*, 301–309. doi:10.1016/j.jsat.2011.09.003

De Jong, K., van Sluis, P., Nugter, M. A., & Heiser, W. J. (2012). Understanding the differential impact of outcome monitoring: Therapist variables that moderate feedback effects in a randomized clinical trial. *Psychotherapy Research, 22*(4), 464–474. doi:10.1080/10503307.2012.673023

Duncan, B. L. (2010). *On becoming a better therapist: Evidence-based practice one client at a time* (2nd ed.). Washington, DC: American Psychological Association.

Duncan, B. L., & Miller, S. D. (2007). *The group session rating scale.* Jensen Beach, FL: Author.

Grove, W. M., Zald, D. H., Boyd, L. S., Snitz, B. E., & Nelson, C. (2000). Clinical versus mechanical prediction: A meta-analysis. *Psychological Assessment, 12,* 19–30.

Hannan, C., Lambert, M. J., Harmon, C., Nielsen, S. L., Smart, D. W., Shimokawa, K., & Sutton, S. W. (2005). A lab test and algorithms for identifying clients at risk for treatment failure. *Journal of Clinical Psychology: In Session, 61,* 155–163.

Hawkins, E. J., Lambert, M. J., Vermeersch, D. A., Slade, K. L., & Tuttle, K. C. (2004). The therapeutic effects of providing patient progress information to therapists and patients. *Psychotherapy Research, 14,* 308–327. doi:10.1093/ptr/kph027

Horvath, A. O., Del Re, A. C., Flückiger, C., & Symonds, D. (2011). Alliance in individual psychotherapy. *Psychotherapy, 48*(1), 9–16. doi:10.1037/a0022186

Jacobson, N. S., & Truax, P. (1991). Clinical significance: A statistical approach to defining meaningful change in psychotherapy research. *Journal of Consulting and Clinical Psychology, 59,* 12–19. doi:10.1037/0022-006X.59.1.12

Kopta, S. M., & Lowry, J. L. (2002). Psychometric evaluation of the Behavioral Health Questionnaire-20: A brief instrument for assessing global mental health and the three phases of psychotherapy outcome. *Psychotherapy Research, 12,* 413–426.

Lambert, M. J. (2010). "Yes, it is time for clinicians to monitor treatment outcome." In B. L. Duncan, S. C. Miller, B. E. Wampold, & M. A. Hubble (Eds.), *Heart and soul of change: Delivering what works in therapy* (2nd ed., pp. 239–266). Washington, DC: American Psychological Association.

Lambert, M. J. (2012). Helping clinicians to use and learn from research-based systems: The OQ-Analyst. *Psychotherapy, 49,* 109–114. http://dx.doi.org/10.1037/a0027110

Lambert, M. J. (2015). Progress feedback and the OQ System: The past and the future. *Psychotherapy, 52,* 381–390. doi:10.1037/pst0000027

Lambert, M. J., Morton, J. J., Hatfield, D., Harmon, C., Hamilton, S., Reid, R. C., et al. (2004). *Administration and scoring manual for the Outcome Questionnaire (OQ-45.2).* Orem, UT: American Professional Credentialing Services.

Lambert, M. J., & Shimokawa, K. (2011). Collecting client feedback. *Psychotherapy, 48,* 72–79. doi:10.1037/a0022238

Lyon, A. R., Lewis, C. C., Boyd, M. R., Hendrix, E., & Liu, F. (2016). Capabilities and characteristics of digital measurement feedback systems: Results from a comprehensive review. *Administration and Policy in Mental Health and Mental Health Services Research, 43,* 441. doi:10.1007/s10488-016-0719-4

Miller, S. D., & Duncan, B. L. (2004). *The Outcome and Session Rating Scales: Administration and scoring manual.* Fort Lauderdale, FL: Author.

Miller, S. D., Duncan, B. L., Brown, J., Sorrell, R., & Chalk, M. B. (2006). Using formal client feedback to improve retention and outcome: Making ongoing, real-time assessment feasible, *Journal of Brief Therapy 5,* 5–22.

Miller, S. D., Duncan, B. L., Brown, J., Sparks, J., & Claud, D. (2003). The outcome rating scale: A preliminary study of the reliability, validity, and feasibility of a brief visual analog measure. *Journal of Brief Therapy, 2,* 91–100.

Miller, S. D., Hubble, M. A., Chow, D. L., & Seidel, J. A. (2013). The outcome of psychotherapy: Yesterday, today, and tomorrow. *Psychotherapy, 50,* 88–97. doi:10.1037/a0031097

Miller, S. D., Hubble, M. A., Chow, D., & Seidel, J. (2015). Beyond measures and monitoring: Realizing the potential of feedback-informed treatment. *Psychotherapy, 52*(4), 449–457. http://doi.org/10.1037/pst0000031

Miller, S. D., Hubble, M. A., & Duncan, B. L. (n.d.). The secrets of supershrinks: Pathways to clinical excellence. *Psychotherapy Networker.* Retrieved from http://www.scottdmiller.com/wp-content/uploads/2014/06/Supershrinks-Free-Report-1.pdf

Miller, S. D., Prescott, D., & Maeschalck, S. (2017). *Reaching for excellence: Feedback-informed treatment in practice.* Washington, DC: APA Books.

National Registry of Evidence-based Programs and Practices. (2013). *Intervention summary: Partners for Change Outcome Management System (PCOMS): International Center for Clinical Excellence.* Retrieved from https://goo.gl/kVH3bE

Owen, J., Lavin, K., Kuo, P., Winkeljohn Black, S., & Chapman, N. C. (n.d.). Case study of feedback-informed treatment. Manuscript in preparation.

Owen, J., Miller, S. D., Borg, V., Seidel, J. A., & Chow, D. L. (2016). The working alliance in treatment of military adolescents. *Journal of Consulting and Clinical Psychology, 84*(3), 200–210. http://dx.doi.org/10.1037/ccp0000035

Reese, R. J., Duncan, B. L., Bohanske, R. T., Owen, J. J., & Minami, T. (2014). Benchmarking outcomes in a public behavioral health setting: Feedback as a quality improvement strategy. *Journal of Counseling and Clinical Psychology, 82,* 731–742. doi:10.1037/a0036915

Reese, R. J., Norsworthy, L. A., & Rowlands, S. R. (2009). Does a continuous feedback system improve psychotherapy outcome? *Psychotherapy: Theory, Research, Practice, Training, 4,* 418–431. doi:10.1037/a0017901

Reese, R. J., Slone, N. C., & Miserocchi, K. M. (2012). Using client feedback in psychotherapy from an interpersonal process perspective. *Psychotherapy, 50,* 288–291. doi:10.1037/a0032522

Reese, R. J., Toland, M. D., Slone, N. C., & Norsworthy, L. A. (2010). Effect of client feedback on couple psychotherapy outcomes. *Psychotherapy: Theory, Research, Practice, Training, 47,* 616–630. doi:10.1037/a0021182

Schuman, D. L., Slone, N. C., Reese, R. J., & Duncan, B. (2015). Efficacy of client feedback in group psychotherapy with soldiers referred for substance abuse treatment. *Psychotherapy Research, 25,* 396–407. doi:10.1080/10503307.2014.900875

Simon, W., Lambert, M. J., Busath, G., Vazquez, A., Berkeljon, A., Hyer, K., . . . Berrett, M. (2013). Effects of providing patient progress feedback and clinical support tools to psychotherapists in an inpatient eating disorders treatment program: A randomized controlled study. *Psychotherapy Research, 23*(3), 287–300. doi:10.1080/10503307.2013.787497

Slade, K., Lambert, M. J., Harmon, S. C., Smart, D. W., & Bailey, R. (2008). Improving psychotherapy outcome: The use of immediate electronic feedback and revised clinical support tools. *Clinical Psychology and Psychotherapy, 15,* 287–303. doi:10.1002/cpp.594

Slone, N. C., Reese, R. J., Matthews-Duvall, S., & Kodet, K. (2015). Evaluating the efficacy of client feedback in group psychotherapy. *Group Dynamics: Theory, Research, Practice, 19,* 122–136. http://dx.doi.org/10.1037/gdn0000026

Teyber, E. (2006). *Interpersonal process in psychotherapy: A relational approach* (5th ed.). Pacific Grove, CA: Brooks/Cole.

Walfish, S., McAlister, B., O'Donnell, P., & Lambert, M. J. (2012). An investigation of self-assessment bias in mental health providers. *Psychological Reports, 110*(2), 639–644.

Wampold, B. E. (2015). Routine outcome monitoring: Coming of age—with the usual developmental challenges. *Psychotherapy, 52*(4), 458–462. doi:10.1037/pst0000037

Whipple, J. L., Lambert, M. J., Vermeersch, D. A., Smart, D. W., Nielsen, S. L., & Hawkins, E. J. (2003). Improving the effects of psychotherapy: The use of early identification of treatment failure and problem-solving strategies in routine practice. *Journal of Counseling Psychology, 50*, 59–68. doi:10.1037/0022–0167.50.1.59

Wolpert, M. (2013). Uses and abuses of patient reported outcome measures (PROMs): Potential iatrogenic impact of PROMs implementation and how it can be mitigated. *Administration and Policy in Mental Health and Mental Health Services Research, 41*(2), 141–145. http://doi.org/10.1007/s10488-013-0509-1

7

Routine Outcome Monitoring in Child and Adolescent Mental Health in the United Kingdom at the Individual and Systems Levels

Learning from the Child Outcomes Research Consortium

Miranda Wolpert, Kate Dalzell, Jenna Jacob, Jenny Bloxham, Matt Barnard, Emma Karwatzki, Duncan Law, Benjamin Ritchie, Isabelle Whelan, and Kate Martin

This chapter considers attempts to implement routine outcome monitoring both at the level of the individual and at the level of the system. We draw on learning from the Child Outcomes Research Consortium (CORC), the United Kingdom's (UK's) leading membership organization of mental health providers that supports members to collect and use evidence to improve children and young people's mental health and well-being.

CORC was established in 2002 by a group of frontline mental health professionals (psychologists, psychiatrists, therapists, and service managers) in the UK. The context in which they were working was publicly funded (largely National Health Service [NHS]) care for children and young people aged 0–24 and their families, focusing on problems that ranged from sleep problems and family relationship difficulties to psychotic episodes, eating disorders, and self-harm. Clinicians, working as part of a publicly funded service, were largely left to their own judgments about who was seen, for how long, and when to end a treatment. No benchmarking was available. Nor was attention being given to outcomes in routine practice. CORC's founding members were motivated to challenge themselves to better understand and reflect on their own practice to ensure they were providing the best help possible. They shared a desire to develop more data-informed and reflective practice in their services. In particular, they sought to embed the first two factors that Wampold identified in Chapter 3 of this volume as the necessary basis for developing deliberate practice: outcome measurement and national and international comparison.

CORC now includes members from over 65 provider organizations,[1] including publicly funded NHS providers, charity- and state-funded voluntary sector providers, schools, and publicly funded social care. Members of the collaboration have agreed to a common set of measures for people to consider using but no specific measures are mandated (CORC, 2015). Bickman, Lyon, and Wolpert (2016) described the CORC approach to using data and feedback as the cornerstone of "precision mental health," observing that it aligns with calls for "High Integrity Health" whereby patient preferences and coproduction are prioritized (Mulley, Richards, & Abbasi, 2015). This CORC approach has influenced UK government

---

[1] A full list of current members and the approach can be found at corc.uk.net.

The Cycle of Excellence: Using Deliberate Practice to Improve Supervision and Training,
First Edition. Edited by Tony Rousmaniere, Rodney K. Goodyear, Scott D. Miller, and Bruce E. Wampold.
© 2017 John Wiley & Sons, Ltd. Published 2017 by John Wiley & Sons, Ltd.

policy: It is now understood across publicly funded services in the UK that the use of outcome and feedback data along with relevant benchmarking to inform service delivery and improvement are best practices, although universal adoption of those practices is still some way off (Department of Health, Department for Education, & NHS England, 2015; Fleming, Jones, Bradley, & Wolpert, 2016).

A central team of CORC researchers and consultants continues to work closely with practitioners and service managers to try to help them address the challenges of embedding the approach and developing deliberate practice. They employ a range of means to do so, including convening regional and national meetings, helping share and apply learning, aggregating and reporting on outcome data, advising and training professionals in how to collect and use data, offering commissioning support, providing consultancy with interested parties, and advising governments and other relevant groups.

This chapter shares the CORC approach and learning in relation to seeking to embed deliberate practice at both the individual and the system levels.

Making Routine Outcome Monitoring a Central Part of Direct Work with Clients

As in other parts of the world, child mental health practitioners in the UK do not learn during their primary training either how to use outcome and feedback measures or how to usefully undertake comparison with national and international data. Nor are they trained in models of deliberate practice. The fact that this learning often has to happen later in people's careers brings with it particular challenges.

CORC has developed a range of approaches for working directly with individual practitioners. These include drawing on learning and quality improvement methodology (Health Foundation, 2012) to support a mind-set aimed at outcomes improvement, and the motivation to engage in active reflection and to consider areas for improvement. Examples of three of these approaches are the use of Plan Do Study Act (PDSA) cycles, the provision of post-qualification training, and consideration of research findings.

Use of Plan Do Study Act Cycles

CORC recommends practitioner use of the PDSA logbook, as shown in Figure 7.1 (Evidence Based Practice Unit, 2012) or others that have been developed based on this (Me First, 2015). Such materials encourage practitioners to:

- **Plan** one new thing they want to try (e.g., raising a particular issue with a given client).
- **Do** that one thing, noting any changes (e.g., how they actually raised the issues).
- **Study** the experience: Note how it went and any reflections on its impact.
- **Act** on this learning; given what we learned, what will we try next time?

The aim of using a PDSA logbook is to encourage rapid trial and review of practice. As part of a funded project in four child mental health services across England in 2013, 23 practitioners completed over 300 PDSAs in which they reviewed their attempts to use new

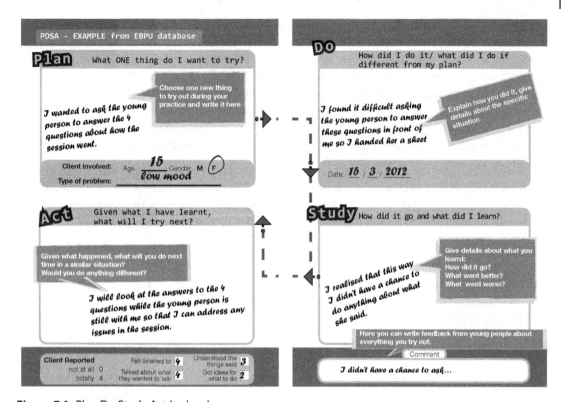

Figure 7.1 Plan Do Study Act logbook.
Source: Created by the Child Outcomes Research Consortium and the Evidence Based Practice Unit, both of which own the copyright.

approaches and tools, including routine outcome measures, to support greater shared decision making with children, young people, and families (Abrines-Jaume et al., 2016; Wolpert et al., 2012). Practitioners used the logbook to reflect on their attempt to make use of a brief session feedback, "the 4 questions."[2]

> I wanted to plan goals, with the young person. Help them scale the goals and ask them to answer the 4 questions about how the session went. I found it difficult asking the young person to answer these questions in front of me. I handed her a sheet but then I realized that I didn't have a chance to do anything about those. I will look at the answers to the 4 questions while the young person is still with me so that I can address any issues in the session. I am just not sure how honest the YP can be answering in front of me. (Abrines-Jaume et al., 2016, p. 6)

Analysis of the logbooks identified three experiential states in terms of trying to implement new approaches, including use of outcome measures: apprehension, "feeling clunky,"

---

[2] Did I feel listened to; did I understand what was said; did I take away ideas to work on; did I talk about what I wanted to talk about?

and integration (Abrines-Jaume et al., 2016). It was common for practitioners to note worries about the possible consequences of introducing the questionnaires, including the possible risks of using new approaches and concerns that the questionnaires might not help their practice, often causing them to procrastinate and avoid trying this. When they did attempt to use the questionnaires, they reported that they felt clumsy or clunky as they were uncertain how to introduce or explain the questionnaires to children and young people or they forgot to do certain actions or parts of the process, causing them to feel deskilled. Over time new approaches began to feel a natural part of practice and integrated:

> Discussed client's goals in context of how it would be useful to spend our time together and what client would like to achieve/what she's motivated to do. It felt like a natural part of the conversation and a way of focusing what she wants to achieve as well as a way for me to find out what motivates her. (Abrines-Jaume et al., 2016, p. 6)

It should be noted that while those involved said they found using the PDSA logbooks helpful, they also pointed out the burden of completing the logbooks amid the other demands on their time (Wolpert et al., 2012). It is not clear that this is sustainable beyond funded projects, unless it is built into supervision or other systems as required by funders or service managers.

Provision of Postqualification Training

Postqualification training can help practitioners move through the process of feeling apprehensive, clunky, and deskilled, to enabling them to integrate feedback and outcomes tools into their practice and to form the basis for deliberate practice. Therefore, CORC has developed a set of postqualification training packages to support practitioners with tools to develop and undertake deliberate practice, including Using Patient Reported Outcome Measurement to Inform Service Effectiveness (UPROMISE), a three-day training course with a focus on developing a mind-set that will encourage the development of a habit of deliberate practice. The course is co-run by mental health-trained professionals and those who represent young people with experience of mental health issues and service use. The overarching emphasis is on supporting the challenge of orthodoxies and the development of a stance of neutral curiosity rather than professional defensiveness about what outcomes are, and can be, achieved. The course structure allows practitioners to try new approaches and to review their practice with tutors and peers.

The course helps practitioners understand how feedback and outcome data can inform practice from the young person's viewpoint. Box 7.1 gives examples of feedback from young people garnered from consultations undertaken by Common Room, a service user advocacy group.

Practitioners are introduced to the ideas of Tversky and Kahneman (1974), which stress how, without challenge, people will naturally seek out ways to confirm their prior beliefs and assumptions and how this can undermine improvements in practice (Gray, 2001). Attendees are encouraged to think about how detailed consideration and tracking of progress can help them review their work. During the training, practitioners are supported to practice these skills through role-play. The training days are usually spaced three to four

---

Box 7.1 Young People's Experience of Feedback and Outcome Tools in Therapy

"They can help to normalize difficult feelings . . . you know you're not the only one."

"The first time I did a measure on depression . . . It's got a question in it like 'do you cry.' It had answers like 'sometimes, a lot, all the time, I feel like I want to cry but I can't'. It made me realize that feeling like I wanted to cry but couldn't was a valid way to feel, that it didn't mean I wasn't depressed."

"I can see what's changed, how far I've come."

"It's like losing weight, it can be so gradual, it can feel like nothing is changing. It's good to have something to help see what's changed . . . how far I've come."

"I kept all my papers from when I was first in [service]. I look back on them when I feel like I haven't made any progress and I can see that I really have."

"I find it hard to say how I feel . . . it takes me a while. I hate the scale 1–9 thing. I like the ones with words."

"Sometimes it's easier to have things on paper or written down. It makes things explicit between you and can be easier than trying to weave something into a conversation. If you're just talking about something, it's hard to know what you are or aren't allowed to say or what they've understood."

"It can help you to say how you're feeling without having to say it out loud. You can tick a box . . . and then they talk to you about it.

"At the moment I'm doing a piece of work [using feedback tools] with my doctor in CAMHS [Child and Adolescent Mental Health Services] and it's learning for both of us . . . This is a piece of work that hasn't been done much before . . . and she's only done it once or twice before, and we're both learning from each other but that's better."

---

weeks apart to enable practitioners to set goals, practice, and refine their skills using the Plan Do Study Act cycle and logbooks between training days. They are encouraged to film their practice and discuss this in supervision and with colleagues. At the end of the course, tutors join team meetings to explore embedded practice of how outcomes are being discussed and reviewed and to help to challenge or consider changes in practice, with a frequent focus on case endings. The result of this training has been practitioners' improved self-efficacy (Edbrooke-Childs, Wolpert, & Deighton, 2016), although the impact on outcomes achieved with children and families is not yet known.

Consideration of Research Findings

As a practice-research network, CORC collates data from members, which it analyzes to help develop their learning and understanding of what constitutes effective practice. CORC holds data on over 400,000 episodes of care from children and young people, and includes demographic and outcomes information collected between 2006 and 2016. This is the largest collection of data of its kind in Europe.

CORC's mission in relation to research is to undertake research that will benefit practice and to help support deliberate practice. For example, a recent publication explored how young people and their parents reported experiences of making treatment decisions with their clinicians in relation to how they reported their improvement. Children who made joint decisions with clinicians about their own mental healthcare reported higher levels of improvement in treatment results, as did parents who contributed to decisions about care for their children. However, child-reported experience of shared decision making was associated with higher levels of child-reported improvement only when their parents also reported higher levels of shared decision making (Edbrooke-Childs, Jacob et al., 2016).

Making Routine Outcome Monitoring a Central Part of Practitioner Development

A key way to support deliberate practice in practitioners as part of their ongoing professional development is via supervision, in which therapists' anxieties and concerns can be addressed, new skills can be practiced, and therapists can be supported to consider feedback and outcome data as a key part of case review.

Supervision that is used to support deliberate practice (see both Chapters 2 and 4) should encompass at least:

- feedback based on video review of the therapist's work,
- comparison of outcomes to expected trajectories,
- review of therapeutic alliance and therapist skill, and
- encouragement of the repetition of skills that, informed by feedback from those supervision sessions, lead to increased expertise.

Supervision can be used to reflect, identify errors, develop, and rehearse and execute plans for improvement. In supervision, therapists can use review of feedback and outcomes data to consider changes to the therapeutic approach or potential changes of therapist. Supervision can also support appropriate choice in the use of outcome and feedback metrics and measures, and how best to introduce measures to children, young people, and their families. A key current role for supervision, while outcome measures are still novel to many therapists, is to encourage supervisees to "have a go" and to address their anxieties and uncertainties about measurement and use of measures. In this regard, it is crucial that, wherever possible, supervisors lead by example: modeling use of deliberate practice in their own work and supervision—for example, by using feedback tools for supervision to understand the experience and model how to introduce and how to explore feedback from supervisee, and to engage in the practice of skills that are just outside their comfort zone.

A specific version of UPROMISE training for supervisors has been trialed and found to have positive effects on supervisors' self-efficacy and attitudes toward using outcome data (Fullerton et al., 2017). Checklists have been developed to help supervisors review and enhance their own practice in this regard. Some case examples are provided next.

Case 7.1 Using Supervision to Consider Multiple Forms of Outcomes Feedback

Julie is a 15-year-old girl with anxiety difficulties. The therapist has seen her for six individual sessions. The supervisor wants to discuss Julie as she has noticed that although Julie's anxiety symptoms seem to have improved, her feedback on the goals-based outcome indicates she seems no closer to reaching her goal "to not feel so worried about bad things happening."

SUPERVISOR: Julie seems to be making really good progress with respect to her symptoms and you as a therapist are receiving positive feedback. So that's really fantastic. One thing I did notice is that she seems to have stagnated in her progress toward her goals, and I wondered if this might be worth discussing. How did you go about setting goals with Julie?

THERAPIST: I remember it taking quite some time, as Julie felt underconfident about her ability to make changes to her current situation, and overwhelmed. Her mum tried to set goals for her, but, with help, Julie was able to think about what might be realistically achievable, if we were able to work together in partnership.

SUPERVISOR: And does the feedback on the tools fit with your experiences within therapy sessions?

THERAPIST: Her anxiety levels are reported to be low on the symptom checklist, and she doesn't seem anxious within sessions. And she is giving positive feedback about her experience of me as a therapist; she feels we are working well together.

SUPERVISOR: I was interested in the differences between the feedback on the symptom tracker and the goals. They don't seem to be improving at a similar rate, and I'm curious about that, what it might mean. Maybe we could come up with some ideas to help make sense of that . . . What do her parents feel about the progress she is making?

THERAPIST: They feel she is staying in her room a lot, but she is happy there.

SUPERVISOR: So it's possible she's avoiding situations, resulting in her anxiety not being triggered? How might we consider that idea further?

THERAPIST: Maybe we could look at the symptom tracker and the goals progress sheet together in session.

SUPERVISOR: Would it be useful for us to look at that in detail, and role-play the scenario together?

Therapist suggests supervisor takes role of Julie.

THERAPIST: Julie, I've been doing some really careful thinking about how our work together has been going and have been talking this through with my supervisor. I've been feeling a bit confused about whether things are moving in the right direction for you, and wondered if we could look at this in some detail today?

JULIE: Oh, I thought things were going well, I'm sorry I haven't been working hard enough, I'll try harder.

THERAPIST: Sorry if it felt like I was criticizing you . . . (Tails off, unsure how to proceed.)

Therapist and supervisor talk together about the ways in which the therapist introduced the idea and decide to switch roles, to give the therapist the opportunity to consider a different perspective.

Therapist: Sorry if it felt like I was criticizing you, I had intended to think about our work together and how things are moving forward in our work as a team. It is important that you don't feel that you are solely responsible. Maybe it would help if I got out the goals sheets we have been using and the checklists you have been filling in each session. Would it be useful to summarize these on a sheet of paper to help us look at development over time?

Therapist and supervisor reflect on how this might have felt for Julie and the pros and cons of each approach. They acknowledge the challenge for the therapist in learning a new skill, and discuss that video review of the next session may help to support further learning.

Case 7.2 Using Supervision to Consider Differing Parent and Child Views on Symptom Tracker Questionnaires

Robert is a 17-year-old boy wanting help with his low mood. At his first appointment, Robert clearly demonstrated a preference for individual work. The case was discussed some weeks ago in supervision, and it is being brought back for further discussion, because although Robert's symptoms appear to be improving, according to information provided on the parent feedback tool, there has been an increase in his low mood symptoms over time.

Supervisor: I think when we met a few weeks ago, you talked about wanting to start some family therapy sessions with Robert and his parents, as he had been talking about the challenges in family relationships. In reviewing goals and symptoms at that point, it appeared that the individual work didn't seem to be moving things forward. It seemed that you were both feeling quite stuck, and it was felt that involving the parents in sessions may help bring additional ideas to the work.

Therapist: That's right; we've had four sessions of family work now. But I've been feeling quite confused and don't understand how to make sense of the symptom tracker scores. Robert's ratings on the symptom tracker have started to improve over recent weeks, after a period of stagnation, but I feel confused, as his parents' feedback on the symptom tracker suggests he is deteriorating. It feels confusing, as they are giving very positive feedback about the sessions themselves. They feel we have a good working relationship and that we are focusing on the relevant issues—that is, improving communication and sharing feelings. And they certainly seem to understand more about how Robert feels.

Supervisor: It's curious. I wonder what could be going on here. If you look at the parents' and Robert's feedback together, it's interesting that they are scoring his symptoms at around the same level, at this point. What might this mean?

Therapist: I suppose that they are starting to see things in a similar way. Maybe his parents are starting to realize how significant his problems are. I mean, that would fit with the kinds of conversations we are having in sessions. So maybe it's a case that things are not in fact deteriorating, more that they understand more about how he is feeling.

Supervisor: If this were the case, what predictions would we make about how the symptom tracker scores would adapt over time?

Therapist: I guess they might stay in line more with one another and that as Robert feels more and more understood, his symptoms may start to decrease further.

Supervisor: How might you begin to discuss these ideas with Robert and his family? Would they agree with the ideas we have generated, or might they have an alternative point of view?

Therapist: I wonder whether it would be helpful to share the graph with the family and ask what sense they make of it. Maybe I could also talk to them about the conversation we have been having.

Supervisor: Shall we have a go at practicing that now, in supervision?

The therapist expresses reluctance, stating that he has a number of other priorities for supervision. They discuss together the value of in-depth exploration and the learning that may follow on, and the therapist agrees to trial it. The therapist asks the supervisor to take on the role of therapist initially, which the supervisor agrees to, in an attempt to scaffold learning. They then swap roles and give detailed feedback to one another on the process.

Therapist (to family): I've been fascinated by the feedback you have all given on your checklists each session and have found it really helpful to draw this out, to help me make sense of it . . . Would you be interested in looking at this with me in more detail?

Parents: If Robert's happy to, then that's okay with us.

Robert: Umm, I suppose so.

The "therapist" proceeds to ask Robert for help in summarizing the scores from the symptom tracker questionnaires and stops to reflect at regular points with the family, asking for their ideas on what sense they make of the changes in reported symptom levels. This is subsequently mirrored, when the supervisor de-roles and asks the therapist to reflect on what worked well and less well about the process and to practice having a go themselves, in supervision. The supervisor provides detailed feedback about aspects of the role-play that worked well and reenacts areas that seem to require further development. They also reflect on the process of in-depth role-play and when this may be applied in future supervision sessions.

Using Client Feedback as a Central Part of Service Review

CORC has been analyzing and feeding back routinely collected information from its members since 2007. Each year, members submit their aggregated team-level data to the central team for analysis and benchmark reporting. The central team of researchers produces reports that allow members to review their outcomes relative to other teams across the country. Figures 7.2 to 7.5 show three sample pages from an anonymized CORC report.

Funnel plots are a way of presenting data taking into account varying numbers of cases. The aim is to compare services to an overall average and to each other, while accounting for the number of cases that each service has submitted.

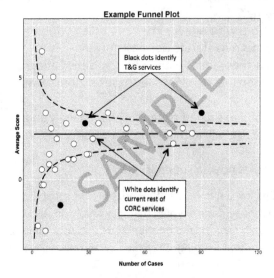

Example Funnel Plot

Black dots identify T&G services

White dots identify current rest of CORC services

What can I see on the plot?

The horizontal line represents the overall average score for all organizations whose data fell within the reporting period (in this case, close to 2.4 points).

Each service has a dot representing its average score (higher than average is above the line, lower is below), and size (services with fewer cases submitted are to the left, more cases to the right). **T&G services** in this report will be identified as **black dots**, and current rest of CORC services as white dots.

How do we know if a service is significantly higher, or lower, than the average?

If the service is outside of the dashed lines, then there is evidence that their average is significantly different from the overall average.

Why are the dashed lines wider towards the left-hand side?

We expect there to be more 'unusual' cases in services submitting fewer cases than in those submitting more cases, so the dashed lines account for this random variation.

Figure 7.2 How the report compares services across the learning collaboration using funnel plots, which prevent overinterpretation of fluctuations in outcomes due to small data sets.
Source: Created by the Child Outcomes Research Consortium and the Evidence Based Practice Unit, both of which own the copyright.

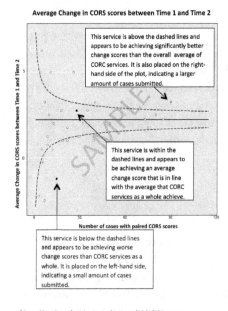

Average Change in CORS scores between Time 1 and Time 2

This service is above the dashed lines and appears to be achieving significantly better change scores than the overall average of CORC services. It is also placed on the right-hand side of the plot, indicating a larger amount of cases submitted.

This service is within the dashed lines and appears to be achieving an average change score that is in line with the average that CORC services as a whole achieve.

This service is below the dashed lines and appears to be achieving worse change scores than CORC services as a whole. It is placed on the left-hand side, indicating a small amount of cases submitted.

A worked example of a service 'below the funnel', for average change in CORS scores between Time 1 and Time 2:

Using a 'directed discussion' approach[1], we would want to spend 25% of discussion time investigating possible data issues, such as:

- Are there service characteristics or processes that could have had an impact on the results? (e.g. completion rates, case complexity, length of interventions, type of service)
  For example: *The service is placed on the left-hand side of the plot, indicating that the average is based on a small number of cases and therefore the results may not be applicable to all children and young people seen by the service as a whole*
- Are the right measures being used with the right service users at the right times?
  For example: *Perhaps the CORS is too broad a measure to pick up specific symptom changes that some service users may be looking to achieve*

We would then want to spend 75% of time discussing 'If these data are showing issues in our practice, how can we investigate and rectify them?':

- What kind of change would you be expecting to see?
  For example: *Depending on case complexity, a risk management approach, rather than a focus on improving mental health, may be used, in which case we would not expect to see large changes in outcomes as measured by the CORS*
- Does your service use regular outcome monitoring to inform interventions and supervision?
  For example: *Checking in regularly with service users on their progress and thinking collaboratively about the intervention using this feedback is key*
- Are the interventions being offered evidence-based?
  For example: *Ensuring that the most appropriate and evidenced interventions are offered increases the likelihood of achieving better outcomes*
- Does your service share best practice with other similar services?
  For example: *Linking in with similar services and sharing information and learning is hugely important for fostering best practice*

[1] http://qualitysafety.bmj.com/content/23/4/272.extract

Figure 7.3 How to interpret a funnel plot: a worked example.
Source: Created by the Child Outcomes Research Consortium and the Evidence Based Practice Unit, both of which own the copyright.

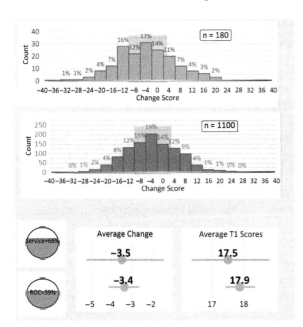

Results included
Any paired scores for the Child SDQ for your service (n = 180) and the rest of CORC sample (n = 1100)

How representative is this sample?
66% of those with a time 1 score, had a corresponding time 2 score at Erinsborough. For the RoC sample this figure was 59%. The follow-up rate suggests the sample is representative of around 60% of the children and young people who completed the SDQ at the first time point in Erinsborough and rest of CORC services.

What do the plots show us?
The change scores look very similar for your service and the rest of CORC. The top quarter improve their scores, the bottom quarter deteriorate, and the middle 50% do not change or improve by up to 10 points (on a scale of 1 to 40). On average, children started at an SDQ score of about 18. This was about the same for Service and ROC. By the end of treatment, the average improvement in SDQ score was around 3.5 in both Service and ROC.

Conclusion
The C&YP we have data for appear to progress at a similar rate to those in the rest of CORC sample. With a higher follow-up rate, these results could be generalizable to all children and young people who completed the SDQ at a first time point in your service and the rest of CORC services.

Figure 7.4 Change scores for the service for one particular outcome measure compared with those from the rest of CORC.
Source: Created by the Child Outcomes Research Consortium and the Evidence Based Practice Unit, both of which own the copyright.

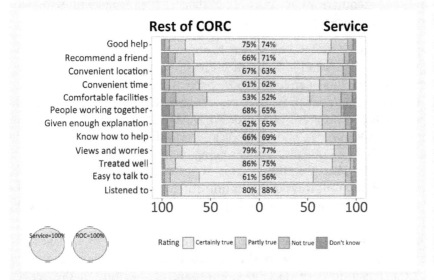

Results included
Any child-reported ESQ with at least one item completed: Service n = 579, Rest of CORC n = 8761.

How representative is this sample?
Children and young people were asked to complete the ESQ 6 months after first contact or at case closure, if this was sooner. The completeness rates suggest that the samples may not be representative of all children seen by Erinsborough and by the rest of CORC services.

What do the responses show?
Children's and young people's responses at Erinsborough were similar to those in the rest of CORC services. The most positively-rated item was 'Listened to', rated by 88% of children and young people as 'certainly true', compared to 80% in the RoC sample.

Figure 7.5 Service experience data.
Source: Created by the Child Outcomes Research Consortium and the Evidence Based Practice Unit, both of which own the copyright.

Once a report has been produced, the researchers meet with the service providers to help them reflect on the implications of the results using the MINDFUL approach (Wolpert et al., 2014). This comprises:

1. **Multiple perspectives.** Reminding members of the need to consider child, parent, and practitioner perspectives separately as it is known they do not highly correlate.
2. **Interpretation level.** Agreeing on the appropriate unit of analysis to consider the right level of granularity (individuals, practitioners, teams, or a whole system of care).
3. **Negative differences.** Spending energy first on any indications that the agreed interpretation level in question (individual/team/system) is achieving worse outcomes than relevant benchmarks.
4. **Directed discussions (75%–25% rule).** In view of the human tendency to ascribe any uncomfortable findings to flaws in the data, members are encouraged to spend 75% or more of the time allocated to discussion of the results planning potential improvements in light of them, and 25% or less on discussing ways in which the data may be flawed.
5. **Funnel plots.** To avoid unnecessary discussion of differences that are most likely due to fluctuations in small data sets, members are encouraged to consider funnel plots (see Figures 7.2 and 7.3) as the way of presenting key data for considering comparisons across services.
6. **Uncertainty.** Members are advised never to make decisions on the data in the report alone but always to consider the wider context and other data.
7. **Learning collaborations:** members are encouraged to discuss the results with wider collaborations including service users and funders.

Feedback about reports from CORC members has been positive, with many saying that different aspects are particularly useful for different professional groups. For example, the experience of the service section has been found to be particularly helpful to practitioners who want to change the service they are providing; key changes that have been made in the light of such data have included different offers for appointment times and information available prior to being seen. One service chose to look at service feedback at the level of the individual practitioner, which led to one practitioner being identified as an outlier in terms of particularly poor feedback. This practitioner was supported in supervision to consider the comments and find different ways of communicating with clients. To the surprise of the senior manager, the practitioner welcomed the feedback and the opportunity for improvement.

Discussion of both outcomes achieved and type of children seen, as shown in a CORC report with a community service, showed that the service saw lower severity of symptoms/difficulties at baseline than its CORC comparators. Although the service also saw a greater improvement across all outcome measure subscales, this led to a senior management review of appropriateness of referrals and of whether the right children were being seen. This resulted in an audit of this aspect of the work, which is ongoing.

Making Routine Outcome Monitoring a Central Part of System-Level Quality Improvement

In the United Kingdom, there is an increasing emphasis on working across a range of systems to support child mental health (Department of Health et al., 2015; Wolpert et al., 2015). In this context, there are growing efforts to improve the "whole system," which refers to the collective contribution of health, education, social care, voluntary, public health, and youth justice services (Department of Health et al., 2015). Experience from initiatives to integrate health and social care suggests there are a wide range of barriers to and facilitators of improvements at this level. Notable facilitating factors include partner organizations having a joint sense of accountability for outcomes, clear understanding of the intended benefits of changes to working, and integrated data systems (Damberg et al., 2009; Ling, Brereton, Conklin, Newbould, & Roland, 2012). In alignment with these factors, the support offered by CORC is developing along two interrelating lines of work.

First, we bring together representatives from different sectors (e.g., health, education, social care) to operationalize "shared outcomes frameworks." These outcomes frameworks usually consist of statements of what the system aims to achieve with children and young people, endorsed by those commissioning, delivering, and using services. CORC's input includes helping partnerships to appraise the strengths and weaknesses of different measures and indicators and to interpret and act on the information they yield. It has been helpful to encourage partnerships to draw on existing routinely collected data where possible, to avoid additional data collection burden falling on service users and providers. Implementation challenges to overcome include bridging the different perspectives of practitioners working in different sectors toward the relevance of particular types of information, such as goal-based outcomes (Law & Jacob, 2015).

Second, CORC supports partner organizations with data linkage, which is the supplementation of person-level data held by one organization with person-level data held by another organization, along with the data-sharing approaches and agreements that allow it to occur. This enables partnerships to consider the outcomes of multiple service input, which is arguably the perspective of most relevance to children and young people using advice and help from different parts of the system. Learning to date indicates that success is dependent on partners having a clear understanding of the purpose (e.g., as facilitated by a shared outcomes framework), strong commitment to that purpose, and willingness to allocate resources to addressing challenges of a legal, technical, and organizational relationship nature.

This work is still at the stage of initial implementation and proof of concept, and we do not yet know if routine outcome monitoring at this level of the system will enhance outcomes for children and young people.

Conclusion

In conclusion, in the United Kingdom at least, there is a long way to go before routine outcome monitoring is embedded as part of the culture of child and young mental health services. However, the discussion in this chapter indicates some practical case examples of how practitioners and service leaders across England are seeking to create the conditions in which deliberate practice can flourish, in order to enhance and support the well-being of children and young people facing the challenges of mental health issues.

Questions from the Editors

Question #1. You discuss the important role supervisors can play in therapist professional development. Do you have any specific suggestions for how the field can better prepare supervisors to be more effective in this capacity? What key skills do supervisors need to help therapists improve, and how can supervisors better acquire those skills?

Answer from Authors: Supervisors play a key role in developing therapist skill and practice, despite often being disconnected from organizational decision-making processes, which can have a direct impact on their effectiveness. In our experiences of working closely with supervisors through the UPROMISE project, the following aspects have been important:

- Enabling supervisor access to decision-making processes at higher levels of the organization (such as training budget spend, target setting, making sense of data).
- Providing sufficient time in clinician and supervisor job plans to enable opportunities to review videotapes of clinical sessions, and client-related data.
- Accredited supervisor training programs and support networks, both virtual and face to face, delivered to several supervisors within an organization.
- Supervisor awareness of models of supervision, service development, and organizational change.
- Supervision for supervisors—opportunities to reflect on their own biases and to receive feedback on their supervisory and clinical practice.
- Ongoing connection into the latest research and evidence base in the field.

Question #2. Focusing on outcomes will inevitably lead therapists to see more clearly which clients are not benefiting from treatment. While accepting the limits of treatment is valuable, some therapists may risk becoming discouraged by their clients who do not improve. Do you have any advice for therapists regarding how to sustain or enhance their desire for professional development and drive to acquire new skills while also accepting the realistic limits of treatment?

Answer from Authors: It is important for supervisors to acknowledge that self-reflection and skills development can be an unsettling and challenging process, and organizations also need to get behind this message. An explicit conversation about anxieties and concerns is an important starting point; otherwise, these issues may fuel partial engagement with the process or unhelpful obstructions. Supervisors need to demonstrate willingness to place themselves in a "vulnerable" position by showing that they are keen to respond to feedback and develop their own practice. For example, they may use a feedback tool with supervisees to collect data about their supervisory practice and use their own supervision to highlight areas for development.

The language that is used around "success" or "failure" is an important consideration when implementing this way of working. Supervisor and organizational language, focusing on concepts such as "development" or "excellence," and demonstrating curiosity about the ways in which client feedback may be understood, also provides a more motivating context, which can offset disappointment or discouragement. It is valuable for the supervisor to highlight that a focus on outcomes enables clinicians to target their efforts more specifically. Clinicians subsequently are in a more informed position, reducing the risk of them operating in a "blind" way or via more intuitive and subjective sources.

Question #3. How can the programs described in your chapter help with the problem of therapist burnout in the United Kingdom? Do you have any suggestions for how to use professional development to prevent or heal burnout at a systems level, beyond encouraging therapists to accept that they cannot help all clients?

Answer from Authors: The organizational systems that clinicians and supervisors operate within can have a marked impact on practice. The values and messages that organizations convey may motivate clinicians to invest more in skill development and practice. The following systemic components are likely to provide the optimum conditions:

- Organizational investment in infrastructure (information technology, recording equipment, support staff to help interpret data).
- Management systems that devolve decision making to frontline workers and value clinicians who take steps to innovate.
- Therapist networks and peer-support groups that aim to share good practice and acknowledge the challenges in adopting new ways of working.
- Communication flow through the system—direct links with key stakeholders, both within and external to the system.

References

Abrines-Jaume, N., Midgley, N., Hopkins, K., Hoffman, J., Martin, K., Law, D., & Wolpert, M. (2016). A qualitative analysis of implementing shared decision making in child and adolescent mental health services in the United Kingdom: Stages and facilitators. *Clinical Child Psychology and Psychiatry, 21*(1), 19–31. doi:10.1177/1359104514547596

Bickman, L., Lyon, A. R., & Wolpert, M. (2016). Achieving precision mental health through effective assessment, monitoring, and feedback processes: Introduction to the special issue. *Administration and Policy in Mental Health and Mental Health Services Research, 43*(3), 271–276. doi:10.1007/s10488-016-0718-5

Child Outcomes Research Consortium. (2015). Homepage. Retrieved from http://www.corc.uk.net/

Damberg, C. L., Sorbero, M. E., Hussey, P. S., Lovejoy, S., Liu, H., & Mehrotra, A. (2009). Exploring episode-based approaches for Medicare performance measurement, accountability and payment. Final report. Santa Monica, CA: RAND.

Department of Health, Department for Education, & NHS England. (2015). *Future in mind: Promoting, protecting and improving our children and young people's mental health and well-being.* London, UK: Department of Health.

Edbrooke-Childs, J., Jacob, J., Argent, R., Patalay, P., Deighton, J., & Wolpert, M. (2016). The relationship between child- and parent-reported shared decision making and child-, parent-, and clinician-reported treatment outcome in routinely collected child mental health services data. *Clinical Child Psychology and Psychiatry, 21*(2), 324–338. doi:10.1177/1359104515591226

Edbrooke-Childs, J., Wolpert, M., & Deighton, J. (2016). Using Patient Reported Outcome Measures to Improve Service Effectiveness (UPROMISE): Training clinicians to use outcome measures in child mental health. *Administration and Policy in Mental Health and Mental Health Services Research, 43*(3), 302–308. doi:10.1007/s10488-014-0600-2

Evidence Based Practice Unit. (2012). *EBPU log book.* London, UK: CAMHS Press.

Fleming, I., Jones, M., Bradley, J., & Wolpert, M. (2016). Learning from a learning collaboration: The CORC approach to combining research, evaluation and practice in child mental health. *Administration and Policy in Mental Health and Mental Health Services Research, 43*(3), 297–301. doi:10.1007/s10488-014-0592-y

Fullerton, M., Edbrooke-Childs, J., Law, D., Martin, K., Whelan, I., & Wolpert, M. (2017). Using patient-reported outcome measures to improve service effectiveness for supervisors: A mixed-methods evaluation of supervisors' attitudes and self-efficacy after training to use outcome measures in child mental health. *Child and Adolescent Mental Health* doi:10.1111/camh.12206

Gray, J.A.M. (2001). *Evidence-based health care.* Edinburgh, UK: Churchill Livingstone.

Health Foundation. (2012). *Quality improvement training for healthcare professionals.* London, UK: Author.

Law, D. & Jacob, J. (2015). *Goals and goal based outcomes (GBOs): some useful information* (3rd ed.). London, UK: CAMHS Press.

Ling, T., Brereton, L., Conklin, A., Newbould, J., & Roland, M. (2012). Barriers and facilitators to integrating care: Experiences from the English Integrated Care Pilots. *International Journal of Integrated Care, 12*(129), 1–12. doi:10.5334/ijic.982

Me First. (2015). *PDSA logbook.* London, UK: Author.

Mulley, A., Richards, T., & Abbasi, K. (2015). Delivering health with integrity of purpose. *British Medical Journal, 351.* doi:10.1136/bmj.h4448

Tversky, A., & Kahneman, D. (1974). Judgment under uncertainty: Heuristics and biases. *Science, 185*(4157), 1124–1131. doi:10.1126/science.185.4157.1124

Wolpert, M., Deighton, J., De Francesco, D., Martin, P., Fonagy, P., & Ford, T. (2014). From "reckless" to "mindful" in the use of outcome data to inform service-level performance management: Perspectives from child mental health. *British Medical Journal Quality & Safety, 23*(4), 272–276. doi:10.1136/bmjqs-2013-002557

Wolpert, M., Harris, R., Hodges, S., Fuggle, P., James, R., Wiener, A., . . . Fonagy, P. (2015). *THRIVE Elaborated.* London, UK: CAMHS Press.

Wolpert, M., Hoffman, J., Abrines, N., Feltham, A., Baird, L., Law, D., . . . Hopkins, K. (2012). *Closing the gap through changing relationships: Final report.* London, UK: Health Foundation.

Part III

Applications for Integrating Deliberate Practice into Supervision

8

Some Effective Strategies for the Supervision of Psychodynamic Psychotherapy

Mark J. Hilsenroth and Marc J. Diener

Theorists and researchers have provided a rich literature illustrating the clinical applications of evidence for various processes, context, and treatments used by *therapists* to promote beneficial patient outcomes (Wampold & Imel, 2015). Guidance for clinical *supervisors* in training therapists, by contrast, has received less attention. The research we review in this chapter comes primarily from empirical investigations conducted by the lab group of the first author, specifically from a programmatic study of psychodynamic psychotherapy delivered by graduate clinicians in a university-based community outpatient psychological training clinic, using a hybrid effectiveness/efficacy research model and video recordings of sessions (Hilsenroth, 2007). Given the nature of the study's methodology, specifically the systematic, structured, and comprehensive training of the study therapists (graduate clinicians), these findings provide at least some, albeit limited, empirical evidence for the results of one approach to deliberate practice in the supervision of psychodynamic psychotherapy. These issues fall into four categories, each of which we discuss in turn: (a) psychodynamic techniques associated with outcome, (b) psychodynamic techniques associated with alliance, (c) empirical research on graduate trainees learning psychodynamic psychotherapy, and (d) methods for training therapists in psychodynamic psychotherapy.

Techniques/Processes Associated with Outcome in Psychodynamic Psychotherapy

In one of the initial set of results from this research program specifically examining outcomes in the treatment of depression, Hilsenroth, Ackerman, Blagys, Baity, and Mooney (2003) identified psychodynamic technique, both at the global level and in relation to specific interventions, that predicted reliable change in depressive symptoms at outcome. The Comparative Psychotherapy Process Scale (CPPS; Hilsenroth, Blagys, Ackerman, Bonge, & Blais, 2005) was used to measure mean levels of therapist activity and psychotherapy techniques across the treatment. Using CPPS ratings provided by independent

The Cycle of Excellence: Using Deliberate Practice to Improve Supervision and Training,
First Edition. Edited by Tony Rousmaniere, Rodney K. Goodyear, Scott D. Miller, and Bruce E. Wampold.
© 2017 John Wiley & Sons, Ltd. Published 2017 by John Wiley & Sons, Ltd.

judges to predict outcomes, results demonstrated that greater use of psychodynamic-interpersonal (PI) techniques across treatment was associated with improvements in depressive symptoms. (These symptoms were rated by both clinicians and the patients themselves.) Affect-focused techniques were specific ones that predicted change, such as the CPPS item "The therapist encourages the patient to experience and express feelings in the session" and "The therapist addresses the patient's avoidance of important topics and shifts in mood."

In later studies, this research program examined the relations between psychodynamic techniques and outcome at different points in treatment for patients diagnosed with *anxiety* disorders (Pitman, Slavin-Mulford, & Hilsenroth, 2014; Slavin-Mulford, Hilsenroth, Weinberger, & Gold, 2011). Results indicated that use of PI techniques at the third or fourth treatment session predicted improvement in anxiety symptoms (Slavin-Mulford et al., 2011). Therapist use of specific psychodynamic techniques at this point in treatment that were significantly associated with change included "Links current feelings or perceptions to past," "Suggests alternative ways to understand experiences not previously recognized by patient (i.e., interpretation)," and "Focuses on wishes, fantasies, dreams, early memories."

Pitman et al. (2014) extended the findings of Slavin-Mulford et al. (2011), using the same sample of patients with anxiety disorders, but this time examining relations between therapist technique/process with outcome at a *subsequent* point in early treatment (session 9) as well as between technique/process aggregated across these early points in treatment (sessions 3 and 9) with outcome. Results of the Pitman et al. (2014) study were highly consistent with those of Slavin-Mulford et al. (2011), indicating that greater overall use of PI technique predicted patient improvement. Analyses of *specific* PI techniques demonstrated that therapist focus on cyclical intrapersonal patterns in patient actions, feelings, or experience, as well as suggestions of alternative ways to understand these experiences or events not previously recognized by the patient (i.e., interpretation) at one or more of these time periods, predicted better anxiety outcomes.

Subsequent studies by Hilsenroth and colleagues extended the previously discussed research further, by examining interactions between alliance and technique in predicting postsession gains (Owen & Hilsenroth, 2011; Owen, Hilsenroth, & Rodolfa, 2013) or processes (Owen, Quirk, Hilsenroth & Rodolfa, 2012). In these studies, the researchers used specific data analyses to control for the fact that some therapists have better patient outcomes than others. In the first of these studies, Owen and Hilsenroth (2011) found that patient-rated alliance predicted improvement on a broad-band measure of functioning. Furthermore, several *individual* psychodynamic techniques exploring cyclical patterns of relating interacted with alliance in predicting outcome, such as (a) linking current feelings or perceptions to the past; (b) focusing attention on similarities among patient's relationships repeated over time, settings, or people; and (c) identifying recurrent patterns in patient's actions, feelings, and experiences.

In the Owen et al. (2013) study, the authors examined postsession gains in a counseling center in which the theoretical orientation was integrative. Results demonstrated a three-way interaction among clients' perceptions of the alliance, PI techniques and cognitive behavioral (CB) techniques, with postsession changes. Specifically, (a) more PI *and* more CB techniques, and (b) more PI but fewer CB techniques were associated with better postsession changes in the context of stronger alliances. However, (a) more CB techniques but fewer PI techniques, and (b) fewer PI *and* fewer CB techniques were not significantly associated with postsession changes in the context of stronger (or weaker) alliances. These findings suggest that clients' perceptions of PI techniques in the context of stronger alliances were most beneficial for postsession outcomes. Thus, consistent with Owen and Hilsenroth (2011), a strong alliance will likely maximize the impact of PI techniques. In addition, clients who rated their therapist as being relatively inactive reported fewer positive postsession outcomes, suggesting that an idle therapeutic approach is not advantageous.

An additional study by Kuutmann and Hilsenroth (2012) that examined the association between specific PI technique and interaction effects illustrates a more complex approach to understanding the use of PI technique. In this study, Kuutmann and Hilsenroth (2012) used pre–post change in a measure of cold/distant interpersonal problems. Results indicated that a greater focus on the in-session therapeutic relationship ("The therapist focuses on the relationship between the therapist and patient"; Hilsenroth et al., 2005) was associated with greater change in cold/distant relational problems, interpersonal problems in general and that for those patients with less impaired levels of object representations, a greater focus on the in-session therapeutic relationship was associated with outcome change to a greater extent than for patients with more impaired object relations. Finally, Levy, Hilsenroth, and Owen (2015) shed further light on the association between specific PI technique and outcome, using an approach that allowed for consideration of the potential impact of other variables. Levy et al. examined the ability to predict change in the overall severity of psychiatric symptoms using (a) pretreatment levels of psychiatric symptoms, (b) a measure of personality disorder severity, (c) degree of pretreatment patient insight, (d) quality of object relations, (e) alliance, and (f) therapist use of interpretation (i.e., use of CPPS item #13, "The therapist suggests alternative ways to understand experiences or events not previously recognized by the patient"; Hilsenroth et al., 2005). Results indicated that when all variables were examined and therapist effects were controlled for, pretreatment symptomatology and use of early treatment interpretations were the only two variables that reliably predicted global symptomatic improvement.

The previously reviewed research demonstrated the relations between adherence to PI technique and outcomes (posttreatment or postsession). At the same time, however, meta-analytic results presented by Webb, DeRubeis, and Barber (2010) suggested that treatment adherence is related only very weakly to therapy outcomes, indicating that the relation between adherence and outcome is not consistently linear and can be affected by additional variables (see Owen & Hilsenroth, 2014). This finding also further underlines a larger pervasive problem in otherwise sophisticated and well-designed randomized clinical trials, where adherence/competence is being prized in and of itself, without examination of the direct relationship these treatment fidelity variables assessed during the trial have on actual client outcomes.

Techniques/Processes Associated with Therapeutic Alliance in Psychodynamic Psychotherapy

Previous meta-analytic research has demonstrated a relatively strong association between therapeutic alliance and treatment outcome (Horvath, Del Re, Flückiger, & Symond, 2011; Martin et al., 2000), a relation considered reflective of the power of alliance as "the most robust predictor of treatment success" (Safran & Muran, 2000, p. 1). Given these empirical findings, it is important to identify the degree to which psychotherapy techniques are associated with therapeutic alliance. (For a more complete review of the relation between techniques from a variety of theoretical orientations and alliance, see Hilsenroth, Cromer, & Ackerman, 2012.)

Therapist Techniques that Contributed Positively to the Alliance over the Course of Therapy

Colli and Lingairdi (2009) incorporated a transcript-based method for the assessment of therapeutic alliance ruptures and identified nine specific therapist interventions that were positively related to a collaborative treatment process. These interventions included verbalizations where the therapist focused on the here and now of the relationship, explored a patient's emotion, admitted to his/her participation in a rupture process, and self-disclosed countertransference feelings. Those findings are consistent with most of the available evidence, which supports the conclusion that therapist engagement with the patient enhances subsequent alliance levels (Dolinksy, Vaughan, Luber, Mellman, & Roose, 1998; Gaston & Ring, 1992; Saunders, Howard, & Orlinsky, 1989; Sexton, Hembre, & Kvarme, 1996). In general, when therapist activities convey a sense of understanding, connectedness, and collaboration in the therapeutic process, a greater sense of partnership and trust may transpire in the therapeutic relationship (Coady & Marziali, 1994; Crits-Christoph et al., 1998; Joyce & Piper, 1998; Price & Jones, 1998; Saunders et al., 1989).

Crits-Christoph, Barber, and Kurcias (1993) examined the degree to which accuracy of therapist interpretations—measured by judges' ratings of how closely the interpretation matched the patients' Core Conflictual Relationship Theme—predicted changes in therapeutic alliance. A Core Conflictual Relationship Theme is a thematic pattern that consists of a wish (i.e., what the patient desires in a relationship), a response of other (i.e., how others respond to the wish), and how the patient responds to the conflict between the wish and the response of other (Book, 1998; Luborsky, 1984). Results indicated that accuracy of therapist interpretation of the wish and the response of other (ratings were aggregated) predicted better treatment alliance measured late in therapy. Accuracy for interpretations of the response of self, however, did not reliably predict treatment alliance.

Although they did not examine accuracy of interpretations, Ogrodniczuk and Piper (1999) studied the degree to which frequency of, and adherence to, psychodynamic interpretive technique predicted alliance scores in two forms of short-term psychodynamic psychotherapy (i.e., short-term interpretive therapy and short-term supportive therapy). Greater frequency of interpretive technique (measured by the degree therapist emphasis of interpretive techniques, such as encouraging exploration of uncomfortable emotion and making interpretations) predicted stronger therapist-rated alliance in the short-term interpretive therapy condition. Therapist adherence to interpretive technique (measured by the relative emphasis of interpretive versus supportive technique) was also associated with stronger therapist-rated alliance across both therapy conditions.

This Ogrodniczuk and Piper (1999) study, however, did not examine use of specific interpretive techniques and their relation with alliance. Allen et al. (1996) provided this more specific type of data. They studied a number of techniques, including interpretation ("explanatory statements linking two or more elements into a new relationship") and confrontation ("addressing the patient's avoidance, minimization, or denial; or sharply underscoring an affect or content that the patient is overlooking"). Results indicated that a greater proportion of therapist interpretations generally predicted stronger alliance, whereas proportion of confrontations did not reliably predict any of the alliance ratings.

In their study of brief dynamic therapy for late-life depression, Gaston and Ring (1992) examined the association of overall exploratory techniques and therapist contribution to alliance. Overall exploratory techniques included therapist techniques that addressed the patient's problematic defenses, emotions, and cognitions. Therapist contribution to the alliance was measured using the Therapist Understanding and Involvement Scale of the California Psychotherapy Alliance Scale (Marmar, Gaston, Gallagher, & Thompson, 1989). Although use of exploratory techniques did not reliably predict alliance when examining all of the patients in the brief dynamic treatment arm together, it did predict stronger alliance for patients who were classified as improved. In the *un*improved group, by contrast, use of exploratory techniques did *not* reliably predict alliance. These findings suggest that therapists used more exploratory techniques for improved patients when they had stronger alliances (see also Owen & Hilsenroth, 2011; Ryum, Stiles, Svartberg, & McCullough, 2010), but that there was no reliable association between exploratory techniques and alliance for patients who did not improve.

Therapist Techniques that Contributed Negatively to the Alliance over the Course of Therapy

In a small-sample study of time-limited psychodynamic psychotherapy, Coady and Marziali (1994) examined the associations between therapist behaviors and alliance. Therapist behaviors were rated using the Structural Analysis of Social Behavior (Benjamin, 1974), and results indicated that ratings of therapists' "Disclosing/Expressing" behavior predicted weaker client-rated and therapist-rated alliance (these therapist behaviors did not, however, reliably predict judges' ratings of alliance), suggesting that therapists' focus on self, perhaps disclosure of their own emotional conflicts, is associated with weaker alliance.

Although the previously reviewed research demonstrates how and when therapist technique is related to alliance and symptom change, it is important to contextualize these findings. Individual techniques have been found to be associated with various outcome changes, but we are not suggesting that any one set of techniques used in isolation would constitute a treatment per se for any disorder. To do so would be a very concrete interpretation of the data reviewed here and clinically unsophisticated. What these data do suggest is that, within a psychodynamic model of treatment, delivered in an optimally responsive manner and in which patient alliance was found to be high (see Hilsenroth, 2007; Hilsenroth, Peters & Ackerman, 2004), the use of these specific interventions at moderate levels was related to greater degrees of symptom reduction during the course of therapy. Thus, the current findings provide support for accentuating some specific therapeutic techniques within a comprehensive approach that is consistent with psychodynamic theory, research, and practice. Specifically, these results should not be interpreted to suggest that therapists adhere rigidly to psychodynamic technique in general or to any particular psychodynamic technique. Instead, therapists need to consider the unique needs of individual patients and tailor their interventions accordingly.

This flexibility is supported by further findings from Owen and Hilsenroth (2014), who studied the association of within-case differences in adherence to PI techniques and outcome, after controlling for (a) alliance, (b) between-case differences in PI adherence, and (c) therapist effects. Their results demonstrated that greater within-case PI adherence variation predicted better outcomes. These findings provide greater specificity in understanding the role of PI techniques in predicting outcome, and they suggest that therapists who demonstrate greater adherence flexibility in their use of PI technique within a given treatment appear to have better outcomes across their caseload than therapists who are less flexible with their interventions at the individual patient level. In order to determine how to flexibly intervene with their patients, specific training experiences are needed to guide therapists accordingly. Again, this finding runs counter to a pervasive sentiment in the research training literature that more or higher levels of adherence necessarily lead to better outcomes, and ignores extant research that asymmetrical fluctuations in session process across treatment may even be quite important with regard to eventual outcomes (Aderka, Nickerson, Bøe, & Hofmann, 2012; Flückiger, Grosse Holtforth, Del Re, & Lutz, 2013).

Empirical Research on Graduate Trainees Learning Psychodynamic Psychotherapy

Two empirical studies have recently been published using advanced statistical methods to examine changes in alliance and psychodynamic technique use of graduate trainees across patients and time (Hill et al., 2015; Hilsenroth, Kivlighan, & Slavin-Mulford, 2015). Although there is a lot of interest in the relationship of training with alliance and psychodynamic technique, these are two of the very few studies to examine these issues empirically, with advanced statistical methods, and they lend support to an earlier study examining the same constructs with similar analyses (Multon, Kivlighan, & Gold, 1996). The findings were generally quite positive, although not without some differences, and help to lay the groundwork for future investigations in this area as well as offering ideas for additional hypotheses to be tested.

First, all three studies demonstrated that trainees improved in patient-rated alliance over time (Hill et al., 2015; Hilsenroth et al 2015; Multon et al., 1996). This is very exciting because it seems that there is something about the process these trainees received in gaining more experience that translates into patients feeling stronger alliances with their graduate therapists. However, this finding may not have to do exclusively with supervision or training but also with clinical maturation and experience as well as other therapist and patient characteristics. For instance, in Hilsenroth et al. (2015), we found that the slopes of these changes in patient alliance over time was inconsistent across trainees (i.e., variable slopes), supporting prior findings by Multon and colleagues (1996). This suggests there are likely multiple pathways for trainees to obtain higher patient-rated alliances. Although one of these ways is very likely supervision or training, there are likely multiple ways to achieve these results. The Hill et al. (2015) study used a different type of statistical analysis, and so it is unclear if their findings are similar to those of Hilsenroth et al. (2015) and Multon et al. (1996). Still, this finding of different degree of changes across time occurring between student therapists is very informative and may help direct future research in the area of training with alliance (i.e., the need to examine variables beyond supervision), as it seems important to discern this relationship between training and patient alliance with a broader sampling of variables before it can be clearly related to supervision per se. In the end, however, there may be something about the larger process of classwork, training completed in the graduate program, clinical experience, supervision, and other factors (patient, therapist, interaction, etc.) that seemed to have had a positive effect on patient-rated alliances in their treatment with graduate trainees. So, although we cannot quite say what "it" was that led to patient increases in alliance, "it" happened during the course of the data collection, and "it" was likely different for different trainees. Such findings open up the possibility for exploring models that examine trainee–training interactions. In sum, though, this is still a very important finding, given the relative absence of research in this area. It seems useful to know at least that "trainees improved in patient-rated alliances over cases/time," even if we cannot yet specify what caused that improvement.

Second, two of the studies (Hilsenroth et al., 2015; Multon et al., 1996) found significant changes in therapist technique early in treatment across sessions (Multon et al., 1996) and cases (Hilsenroth et al., 2015), with consistent slopes of change when examining therapist skill acquisition. That is, individual trainees demonstrated improvement in technique in similar and consistent ways. This finding suggests that the trainees were responding with similar patterns of gains on techniques consistent with their psychodynamic psychotherapy training in supervision, and in the Hilsenroth et al. (2015) study, not with alternative techniques (i.e., CB techniques) that were not a focus of in their training. Although the Hill et al. (2015) study did not find changes in PD technique across time, these authors noted that this was likely due to limited power, with only 12 therapists in those analyses. However, a close comparison of the Hilsenroth et al. (2015) and Hill et al. (2015) studies suggests that an unintended and rough "dismantling" aspect of supervision methods may have occurred across the two studies in relation to technique. That is, trainees in the Hilsenroth et al. (2015) study had twice as much weekly supervision, that focused much more heavily on both the videotape review of the sessions and the use of manuals in training. These training issues may have important ramifications, consistent with Ericsson's model on building expertise (2008), since our trainees had more time and focus on the deliberate practice of PD interventions that was well defined, specific, where task performance was followed by immediate feedback, and where there was an opportunity for repetition (i.e., pause and rewind of videotape). It seems that hours of supervision, amount of time/use of videotape and manuals in supervision would be important variables to assess in future studies examining the impact of psychotherapy training.

Methods for Training Therapists in Psychodynamic Psychotherapy

As discussed, Ericsson (2008) has developed a model of expertise and expert performance over several years and across various disciplines. A key aspect of this model is that expert performance does not occur simply from exposure, repetition of performance, or reflection. Rational or intuitive processing alone does not result in expert performance, but actual task-specific actions and behaviors are required instead. In other words, you cannot "think" your way to expertise; you must "do" your way there. That does not mean that thoughtful reflection on experience is not a useful endeavor, but it must be coupled with actual focused and deliberate practice.

In addition, deliberate practice presents performers with tasks (i.e., challenges) that are initially outside their current realm of reliable performance or level of achievement yet can be mastered through practice by concentrating on critical aspects and gradually refining performance through repetitions after feedback. Thus, skill acquisition is viewed as a series of gradual changes in observable performance that show associated improvements in target behaviors. It is also important to note that when we use the term *performance*, we mean therapists achieving better outcomes across a broad band of patient functioning. Adherence, competency, and expertise in the delivery of any set of therapeutic interventions are relevant only if this results in better outcomes for patients. In other words, achieving adherence and competence through supervision are tools or penultimate steps toward patients achieving better clinical outcomes, not necessarily goals in themselves.

We now discuss five aspects of Ericsson's model (2008) of deliberate practice in relation to effective strategies for the psychodynamic supervision of technique and alliance that were employed in the training research study described previously (Hilsenroth et al., 2015):

1. A safe learning environment
2. Engagement in well-defined, specific tasks
3. Obtaining feedback about performance
4. Repetition of tasks in a way that facilitates refinement of performance
5. Exploiting opportunities for improvement that are afforded by errors.

Next we detail the application of these components in the context of training therapists in psychodynamic treatment.

Creating a Safe Learning Environment

Although a safe learning environment may not be necessary for trainees to develop expertise in a given content area, it likely has some relevance for the discipline of psychotherapy. There are, in fact, some empirical data to support this notion that a safe learning environment may have specific importance to the supervision of trainees in psychodynamic psychotherapy (DePue, Lambie, Liu & Gonzalez, 2016; Watkins 2014). Examining how the quality of the supervisory working alliance might be related to the quality of the therapeutic alliance and the acquisition of skills from a psychodynamic treatment model, Patton and Kivlighan (1997) asked graduate trainees to complete a supervisory alliance measure after supervision sessions; their clients completed an alliance measure after each therapy session and independent raters coded videotape of the sessions for psychodynamic techniques. Patton and Kivlighan's findings demonstrated that trainees who perceived their alliance with their supervisor as stronger tended to have patients who perceived the therapeutic alliance as stronger as well. In addition, trainees who perceived their alliance with their supervisor as stronger demonstrated greater acquisition of psychodynamic technique. That is, the more graduate trainees felt they were in a supportive, safe, collaborative, skill-focused, and facilitative supervisory environment, the more likely they were to employ psychodynamic techniques in their sessions, and the more likely their clients were to report a positive therapeutic alliance.

The obvious question then becomes: *"How does one increase a sense of positive supervisory alliance?"* Based on our review of optimizing therapeutic alliance within treatment, and specific aspects related to the supervision provided in our training program, we offer these suggestions to supervisors on how to help facilitate a supportive learning environment:

- Lead by example.
- Affirm your commitment and focus during supervisory sessions by limiting distractions.
- Clearly and collaboratively identify the goals of each supervisory relationship and the tasks to achieve those goals.
- Develop a sense of bond in supervision.
- Be mindful of and discuss your own experience and contribution to the supervision process.
- Be engaged and active in the technique training at hand.

Lead by Example
First, we believe that supervisors need to lead by example, and we offer some specific suggestions of what this means in relation to providing a positive professional role model for their trainees. We suggest that supervisors not ask trainees to do something they are not willing to do themselves. One example of this would be to provide trainees the opportunity to observe their own (i.e., the supervisor's) clinical work. In today's training clinics, there are ample opportunities for faculty to take on training cases through the clinic and use these in conjunction with audio/videotape to provide ongoing case conference or just illustrative examples of their own clinical process. We have found that students greatly value such experiences and report gaining a great deal of insight regarding the use of technique. Furthermore, we believe these types of interchanges offer supervisors the opportunity to model reflection and complexity with regard to constructive feedback.

Affirm Your Commitment and Focus during Supervisory Sessions by Limiting Distractions
Additionally, we encourage supervisors to affirm their commitment and focus during supervisory sessions by limiting distractions. Chief among these, do not answer your phone, text or email. Make it clear that your time, effort, and energy are completely focused on your students' needs during supervision.

Clearly and Collaboratively Identify the Goals of Each Supervisory Relationship and the Tasks to Achieve Those Goals
Similar to the discussion of the components of therapeutic alliance in psychotherapy, we believe that clearly and collaboratively identifying the goals of each supervisory

relationship and the tasks to achieve those goals often is overlooked. We recommend that in the first meeting of the supervisory relationship, an explicit discussion of goals and tasks take place—that is, a discussion with trainees about their goals and what is most important for them to achieve during the supervision. Some useful questions to help facilitate such a conversation can be: *What will be most important to you during our supervision together? What aspect or area of your work would you most like to see change between now and the end of our supervision together?* and *How will you know if supervision has been effective?* In addition, it is important for both parties to try to explicitly outline their expectations for the time and focus of supervision. And if there are any discrepancies in these expectations, it is vital that they be collaboratively worked through to resolution.

Develop a Sense of Bond in Supervision

Related to the first two components of therapeutic alliance, goals and tasks, it is important to also develop a sense of bond in supervision. Given that all supervisors are also legally responsible for the treatment of their supervisee's patients, this fostering of a collective, shared experience and purpose seems like a natural development that needs to be embraced. Along with the development of this supervisory bond, appropriate support needs to be provided to trainees. It is important to recognize that psychotherapy is hard work, hard to do, and even harder to master. With this empathic position in mind, it will be important to recognize this struggle, as well as successes along the way. Accordingly, it will also be necessary for supervisors to normalize these varied experiences along the way to help put them in the appropriate context and perspective. One manner in which to do this is to explore possible alternatives in the supervisee's choices of technique in a curious and nonhostile manner.

Be Mindful of and Discuss Your Own Experience and Contribution to the Supervision Process

In a related vein, we encourage supervisors to be mindful of and discuss their own experience and contribution to the supervision process. However, we stress the need to be respectful of a supervisee's boundaries during any discussion of process. Of course, any facilitative, supportive, learning environment may also be experienced as therapeutic. While in such environments personal exploration can occur in natural useful ways, it is important to remember that supervision should not be treated as a supervisee's personal therapy.

Be Engaged and Active in the Technique Training at Hand

In parallel with a focus on the supervisory alliance, supervisors need to be engaged and active in the technique training at hand. It is useful to avoid jargon and the use of metapsychology when explaining different concepts and technical interventions. Instead use clear and experience-near language when discussing technical interventions and issues related to treatment. This does not mean to suggest that theoretical issues are not useful, but that—as we see later in the process of skill development and expertise—there is a need for clear, well-defined, and specific tasks during the training process if it is to be most effective.

Engagement in Well-Defined, Specific Tasks

Psychodynamic treatment manuals (e.g., Book, 1998; Luborsky, 1984; Malan, 1979; McCullough et al., 2003; Strupp & Binder, 1984) provide useful operational definitions of dynamic interventions as well as guidelines for when and how to apply them. Psychodynamic treatment manuals focus on specific techniques, interventions, and skills that can be successfully used to organize, aid, and inform the therapy rather than prescribe treatment in a rigid manner. Although using these manuals does not guarantee that supervisees will *skillfully* execute dynamic interventions, such training can provide well-articulated explanations for the basic components of psychodynamic techniques in a systematic and clear manner (Binder, 1999).

One example is in regard to interpretation. There are multiple definitions of what an interpretation is and how to best communicate this information within psychodynamic theory. Take, for example, the Core Conflictual Relationship Theme (CCRT) method for supportive-expressive dynamic therapy (Luborsky, 1984). Interpersonal themes and processes are a key area of focus in the patient narrative material, and they are important in organizing therapist responses. Patient relational episodes are evaluated with regard to the identification of, and response to, relevant case-specific formulations. These relational narratives can then be explored, organized, and formulated into the identification of patterns in thoughts, experiences, actions, feelings, and interactions with regard to factors contributing to the maintenance-of-life problems.

As part of this training in psychodynamic therapy (i.e., Hilsenroth et al., 2015), therapist interventions were guided by their use of the CCRT, which involves identifying and exploring recurrent interpersonal patterns. As briefly noted earlier, these patterns consist of a wish (W; what the patient desires in a relationship), a response of other (RO; how the other person actually responded; or how the patient anticipates, expects or imagines others will respond to the wish), and a response of self (RS; what the patient feels, his/her predominant affect,and how s/he behaves or acts after the W and RO; or when there is a conflict between the wish and the response of other). For instance, one example of a CCRT interpretation from a depressed patient in our study was *"In that moment you described wanting a deeper connection and more support from your mother* (W), *but instead experienced her as rejecting and neglectful toward you* (RO). *This led you to withdraw from her* [RS-Action], *feeling sad, hopeless that she will ever be concerned about your needs, and also . . . even 'a **little angry***' [RS-Affect]" (emphasis added). Luborsky's (1984) and Book's (1998) manuals provide clear definitions of the CCRT components, guidelines for using the CCRT to organize therapist interpretive interventions, theoretical background, and case examples demonstrating use of the CCRT.

Systematic and structured training in psychodynamic treatment can include the use of such treatment manual, in order to provide therapists with the necessary understanding of theoretical concepts, guidelines for execution of technical interventions, and opportunities for engagement in well-defined specific therapeutic tasks. Several studies have examined outcomes in psychodynamic therapy that included use of therapy manuals to facilitate these components of deliberate practice.

To illustrate how a supervisor can use engagement in well-defined, specific tasks as part of the process of deliberate practice, consider the following clinical example. The trainee, whom we will call "Sigmund,"[1] reports during supervision that he had difficulty figuring out how to make an interpretation during a recent session with his patient, "Anna." The supervisor asks Sigmund to cue the videotape to the relevant portion of the session. After watching the segment of the session describing a relational interchange between Anna and her father, the supervisor asks Sigmund to review the different components of the CCRT—that is, the wish, the response of other, and the response of self relevant to the patient. The supervisor explains that an important step in formulating interpretation involves working with the patient to explicitly identify the CCRT components (Book, 1998; Luborsky, 1984). The supervisor then asks Sigmund which component of a CCRT was most salient in Anna's narrative of the specific relationship episode, and Sigmund responds by identifying the patient's affective response of self. The supervisor can then work with Sigmund to refine or clarify the response of self, followed by a similar process for the remaining CCRT components (i.e., soliciting Sigmund's hypothesis regarding the CCRT component and then collaboratively working with Sigmund to refine it).

Obtaining Feedback about Performance

The use of audio/videotape allows for deliberate practice of interventions that are well defined, specific and in which task performance can be followed by immediate feedback as well as opportunity for repetition (i.e., pause and rewind). Haggerty and Hilsenroth (2011), basing their conclusions on the findings of social and cognitive psychology research (e.g., Bower, 1992; Garry, Manning, Loftus, & Sherman, 1996; Schachter, 1999; Schachter & Addis, 2007), noted the important limitations of memory and, because of this, maintained that supervision that solely depends on secondhand reporting of session events in supervision could be equally limited. Additionally, secondhand reporting and audiotapes of session material are often not able to shed adequate light on the nonverbal behavior exhibited by patient and therapist. Use of audio/videotape in supervision, by contrast, allows for stop-frame analysis of specific interactions of actual session content and provides opportunities for both supervisor and supervisee to "think out loud" about what occurred in the session. In addition, recordings allow a supervisor to evaluate the actual session material as it happened during the session, allowing for more precise supervision of actual session content and more targeted psychotherapy training.

Now, some reading this may be thinking, "I don't have any grant funding or research resources; how can I use audio or videotape in my supervision?" The answer, both surprising and inexpensive, is currently in your smartphone, tablet, or laptop. Given current technology, it is now possible to use these devices to record sessions, and to do so in an encrypted, safe, and HIPAA-compliant manner. Thus, for example, one could record the session with a laptop and share it with a supervisor using Dropbox Business (https://www.dropbox.com/business), assuming that a few conditions are met, including (a) obtaining a business associates agreement from Dropbox Business, (b) using adequate firewall and antivirus on the therapist's and supervisor's devices, (c) encrypting the devices of the therapist and supervisor (see Huggins, 2017b for details), and (d) deleting the recording from Dropbox Business

---

[1] Throughout this chapter, all vignettes consist of fictitious, composite, or modified examples of actual therapist–patient and supervisor–supervisee interactions. In all cases, identifying information has been removed to protect confidentiality.

once it has been downloaded by the supervisor (Huggins, 2016, 2017a). This technology may presage emerging uses of psychotherapy process scales via the same format (Imel et al., 2014).

In the previously reviewed studies of short-term dynamic psychotherapy by Hilsenroth and colleagues at a university-based outpatient community clinic, individual and group supervision each week focused heavily on the review of videotaped case material and technical interventions designed to facilitate the appropriate use of psychodynamic interventions (Hilsenroth, 2007). Examination of these treatment vignettes was structured to provide specific and direct feedback to supervisees (e.g., focusing on the CCRT, perspective shifts, and linking the supervisory discussion to the readings in the treatment manuals and other key training texts). During individual supervision, supervisor and supervisee identified key vignettes that illustrated specific content, both positive and negative. These recorded vignettes were reviewed during group supervision meetings, providing further opportunities for feedback and reflection (i.e., experience multiplier). Support, encouragement, and praise were actively provided to trainees. This positive feedback, however, was consistently linked to specific treatment interventions or training experiences (practice interventions, case-relevant formulations, etc.) during the supervisory session (see also Henry, Strupp, Butler, Schacht, & Binder, 1993). As part of this process, it was important to help supervisees clarify or understand "why" they chose to make the interventions they did. Supervision sessions included a significant focus on these technical choice points. More specifically, supervisees were encouraged to articulate their thoughts, feelings, and decision-making process in attending to particular content or not doing so (i.e., *"What would have needed to be different in order to follow that other issue instead?"*). This supervisory process aimed to clarify the plan for treatment, refine case formulations, and provide a framework to aid trainees' decision making.

Returning to the above-mentioned clinical example of Sigmund's treatment with Anna, the next interaction took place between Sigmund and his supervisor during a review of the video from a particularly intense therapy session. His supervisor noted a shift in the topic of discussion between Sigmund and Anna. Specifically, the supervisor pointed out that Sigmund and Anna had been exploring Anna's relationship with her father when, rather abruptly, Anna shifted to talking about an interaction she had with an older male teacher. Sigmund's supervisor asked him if, in fact, Sigmund noticed this transition during the session. Sigmund acknowledged that he had but that he was unsure how to directly address it. The supervisor then collaboratively worked with Sigmund to identify potential interventions for doing so.

In Hilsenroth and colleagues' (2015) study of training in short-term dynamic therapy, the supervisory focus was applied equally—and at times more often—to trainees' experiences, process, and use of interventions as to patient dynamics. Thus, for example, supervisory discussion focused on trainees' process reactions to the particular session and exploration of the features that contributed to whether an intervention or session was effective *("What was different about today's session?," "What about it made it a good session?"*). In the supervision example of Anna's shift in discussion content during her session, the supervisor asked Sigmund what his experience was during that shift. Sigmund responded that although he knew that something important had just happened in the session, he was hesitant to discuss it directly with Anna. Sigmund's supervisor asked him if, given that Sigmund had discussed previously in supervision his reluctance to "redirect," "refocus," or "explore" these affective or thematic shifts in a session, a similar process might help them understand Sigmund's reluctance to engage his patient in addressing the shift. As part of the subsequent supervisory discussion, Sigmund and his supervisor worked to identify ways that Sigmund could anticipate similar future interactions with his patient as well as ways of most effectively managing them (e.g., *"I think what you just mentioned seems very important and wonder if we could explore it a little more"*; *"I wonder if we could circle back around to this issue of 'X'. Could you tell me a little more about that?"*; *"You know I can't help but notice we were discussing the issue of 'X' in relation to your father, and then we were talking about your teacher. Is there any way . . . there might be some sort of relationship between the two?"*; *"Or a clear difference between them?"*).

Also of note, some of our psychodynamic colleagues have expressed fears to us that the use of audio/video recordings might foreclose an opportunity to discuss parallel process or countertransference with trainees. We actually find the opposite to be true. Prior to reviewing the tape of a session, we find it incredibly useful to ask trainees for their recollections and experiences of the session, the patient, and themselves. When discrepancies occur while we are reviewing the recordings, we have a very fertile area for supervisees to better explore their self-perceptions or biases. It has been our experience that trainees are often far too hard on themselves, and critical, in basing their evaluation of their work on memory recall alone. Observing recorded material of the actual session provides an unequivocal perspective that often helps to improve their perception of the skills and abilities they possess.

Repetition of Tasks in a Way that Facilitates Refinement of Performance

Supervision and training experiences in our programmatic study of short-term psychodynamic psychotherapy included explicit focus on repetition of tasks to facilitate refinement of trainee performance (Hilsenroth, 2015). Specifically, technical interventions were reviewed and rehearsed during individual and group supervision, with exploration of several alternative options (see, e.g., Wachtel, 1993, as well as McCullough et al., 2003). During these discussions, trainees were often encouraged to explore (a) what they most wanted to communicate to their patients, (b) how they could communicate that in a way patients will be most able to hear and use, (c) what are some different or related ways of communicating this information, and (d) what—if anything—may have gotten in the way of their communication attempts (Hilsenroth et al., 2015).

Take the example of the supervision session with Sigmund, where the supervisor worked with Sigmund to explore how to address Anna's shift from discussing her relationship with her father to reporting an interaction she had with her teacher. To explore this process effectively, Sigmund's supervisor asked him to identify the key message he might want to communicate to Anna at that point in the session. Sigmund stated that he would have wanted to direct Anna's attention to the avoidant nature of the shift in discussion, that is, the way in which Anna moved abruptly from the topic of her relationship with her father— a topic previously discussed in sessions as one laden with conflicting and intense emotions—to a more benign discussion of an interaction with her teacher.

Sigmund's supervisor then collaboratively worked with him to frame and explore this shift in a way that would not further increase Anna's avoidance (Wachtel, 1993).

Specifically, they considered a number of alternative interventions. The first one that emerged in the discussion was *"It seems like it's easier to talk about your teacher than your father."* In discussing this framing of the interpretation, Sigmund and his supervisor decided to explore this intervention along several other different lines as well, such as: *"Given that we've noticed together in the past how hard it can be at times, and uncomfortable, to discuss the difficulties you've had with your father, it makes sense to move toward focusing on what happened with your teacher the other week."* And perhaps even more simply, just observe: *"Sometimes it's easier to talk about your relationship with your father than others"* or *"Relationships with a lot of intense emotions are challenging for anyone to talk about."* Finally, Sigmund's supervisor encouraged him to consider factors that may have contributed to his reluctance to directly address during the session Anna's shift in topics, as detailed earlier.

Exploit Opportunity for Improvement Afforded by Errors

It is important to recognize that supervisors communicate an attitude or perspective on the process of psychotherapy. In addition to the attention given to clarifying and refining trainee responses and interventions, we believe it is important to frame clinical "errors" as opportunities for improvement. That is, it is important to recognize that it is not only okay—and inevitable—to make mistakes along the way but that there are important lessons to be learned in any misstep that can help pave the way for later success. And in many respects, it is essential to convey the attitude that one cannot hope to "get it right" without "getting it wrong" sometimes during the course of treatment. As stated previously, we find that trainees are quite often excessively self-critical of their work, and an important part of supervision therefore involves helping supervisees trust themselves more. When asked, for example, *"What do you most want to communicate to the patient right now?,"* many trainees seemingly know what they want to say and often have a very good idea of how to say it, but too often we see that, early in their training, supervisees talk themselves out of their response because of worry or fear that they may be wrong or not 100% accurate. Early on in training, therefore, supervisees often seem inhibited by the belief that if they are not 100% sure about what to say, then they should say nothing at all. In response, we try to communicate that intervening in psychotherapy is not akin to a very long-range sniper shot that only allows for a single opportunity and that has to be perfectly calibrated in order to be successful. Instead, we underscore that psychotherapy is an asymmetric process full of stops and starts, and the cyclical nature of pathology is such that if an opportunity is not fully capitalized on or missed, it will come back around until the issue is addressed therapeutically. And even then, it will need to be worked on, and through, several times more before functional changes may occur. In conveying this attitude, we hope to facilitate trainees' acceptance of being "good enough" rather than needing to be perfect, as well as the importance of not being afraid to make a mistake. Relatedly, we try to impart the message that session process is all grist for the mill and that good therapists can find a way to use any misstep productively.

An example of a supervisory interaction with Sigmund can illustrate the usefulness of repetitive practice. Sigmund described to his supervisor a relationship episode that Anna discussed during the previous session. Sigmund explained that he had an intuitive sense of what he wanted to do at that juncture in the session but that he felt stuck when he was unable to communicate it in a "highly articulate" way. Sigmund's supervisor asked him to "just give it a shot now" during the supervision in terms of how he might intervene in that session and then worked with Sigmund to refine and modify the intervention. Next, Sigmund's supervisor asked him for another instance in which he felt stuck and reluctant to respond to Anna during a recent session. Again, Sigmund and his supervisor worked together to formulate a therapeutic response. Sigmund's supervisor noted that they should keep an eye out for future instances in which such reluctance occurs, so that they could continue to practice effective therapeutic interventions.

In the collaborative process between supervisor and trainee, supervision in this programmatic research on short-term dynamic therapy included emphasis on positively exploiting such experiences of therapist "mistakes" to better understand the factors contributing to such "errors." Supervisees were encouraged to reflect on different content markers as well as cyclical relational patterns that may have influenced the therapist's choice, or manner, of executing particular interventions. As before, supervision emphasized that being "off" when responding to a patient provides a collaborative opportunity to work together with the patient to "get it right." That is the very definition of collaboration—*the action of working with someone to produce or create something.* This definition implies that it is not the therapists' responsibility to do all of the work and that therapists do not always need to be right or accurate in what they say; instead, therapists and patients can figure things out together. Such collaborative interactions can strengthen the alliance and pave the way for constructive therapeutic endeavors. At the same time, exploration of clinical missteps was considered important in terms of communicating to trainees that they do not need to have unqualified certainty before intervening. Instead, they were encouraged to use their case conceptualization, understanding of the therapeutic process, and intervention skills to respond in a reasonable way, without becoming inhibited by undue fears of making a mistake.

During another supervision session, Sigmund discussed an intervention with Anna in which she had bristled at his use of the word *anger* in describing her response to an interaction with her father. ("*I'm not angry,*" she said rather loudly.) After Sigmund expressed his guilt and worry over his "insensitive" choice of this word, Sigmund's supervisor asked him to cue the videotape to the portion of the session that Sigmund had referred. In watching the videotape, his supervisor noticed that Anna's negative affective response did seem as extreme as Sigmund had originally described. After review and replaying of the videotape segment several times, examining voice tone, facial expressions, and nonverbal behavior, it seemed clear to Sigmund that his perception may well have been accurate, except that the use of the word *anger* was something Anna seemed to resist most. Next, Sigmund's supervisor encouraged him to consider multiple different ways to explore with Anna her negative reactions in a way that she might hear better. His supervisor recommended first that Sigmund acknowledged that he had heard her state she was not angry and then that Sigmund try to create some phenomenological space around the concept of "anger" with Anna. For instance, Sigmund and his supervisor discussed exploring a range of different related labels, such as "miffed," "frustrated," "irritated," and so on. During the next session, Sigmund revisited this issue with Anna, and she was able to use and acknowledge a sense of "frustration" with her father, which then led to an exploration of how frustration differs from anger, when she has been the most and least frustrated with her father, and ultimately back to what would it mean *if she ever was angry instead of frustrated* with her father and expressed this in some way to him.

Conclusion

In this chapter, we have laid out some pragmatic guideposts to help increase the structure and focus of psychodynamic supervision in a manner consistent with Ericsson's (2008) model of deliberate practice and expertise development. And, again, we would highlight, consistent with Ericsson's model, that the ultimate goal of expertise developed through psychotherapy supervision is better broad band treatment outcomes of patients, *not* higher ratings on treatment adherence or competency scales. We recognize that such a model (i.e., one that uses deliberate, structured, and repetitive tasks), as well as some of the processes regarding its implementation (i.e., use of treatment manuals, videotape, process and outcome assessments), may be experienced as anathema by some in the psychodynamic training community. And it seems reasonable to us that supervisors who have never been exposed to these methods, have not seen them modeled or used these various aids to training, would be hesitant to employ them. We humbly offer this encouragement for those who are in this situation but who also are curious to explore the kinds of methods described. First, we encourage supervisors to attend a workshop or seminar on a contemporary approach to psychodynamic treatment that utilizes videotape sessions as part of that training experience. Second, we encourage supervisors to undertake training with one of the many brief progress monitoring and feedback systems currently available (e.g., Bertolino & Miller, 2012; Duncan & Reese, 2015; Lambert, 2015; Wampold, 2015). Web-based versions of progress monitoring systems are available with a subscription fee (e.g., http://www.myoutcomes.com/); conditions needed to maintain HIPAA compliance are similar to those noted earlier regarding sharing recordings with supervisors (e.g., use of a business associates agreement, encryption of the therapist's device, etc). Third, we recommend that supervisors consider familiarizing themselves with a psychodynamic treatment manual, including reading, reviewing, and practicing the implementation of some of the material covered. Fourth, we have found that the best way to gain familiarity with the use of audio or videotaping is to use it, so we suggest beginning a case where informed consent has been provided to use recordings. (Digital audio recording machines are now readily available and quite inexpensive.) Fifth, we suggest that supervisors consider participating in a practice research network, either locally through a university, hospital, or nationally (e.g., Tasca et al., 2015). Such experiences will help to provide some important exposure to the methods discussed in this chapter and to facilitate the methods described in this supervisory process.

It also seems timely and prudent that the focus of training in psychotherapy actively expand beyond only technical interventions, to also include issues involving the therapeutic alliance, relationship, and empathy (Horvath et al., 2011; Falkenstrom et al., 2013, 2016; Xu & Tracey, 2015; Zilcha-Mano & Errázuriz, 2015, Zilcha-Mano et al., 2014, 2016). That is, if supervision that increases adherence, competence, and expertise in the interventions of a given treatment approach does not show a relationship with better patient outcomes, then the field needs to radically shift focus to those trainable skills that do demonstrate consistent links to improvement across a broad range of outcomes in psychotherapy. In addition to the research reported earlier, an emerging literature suggests that there may be pathways between training and patients' perception of the alliance and empathic response (Bambling, King, Raue, Schweitzer, & Lambert, 2006; Berkhout & Malouff, 2015; Crits-Christoph et al., 2006; Crits-Christoph et al., 1998; Hilsenroth et al., 2002; Hilsenroth et al., 2015; Multon et al., 1996). In sum, we find ourselves at a pivotal time in the field with regard to evolving demands and focus in psychotherapy training. The operative question is not "if" these changes in the status quo of supervision are coming, but rather "when" and "what" emerging strategies in that process will be included to ultimately most effect patient change.

Questions from the Editors

Question #1. What role, if any, can you see for supervisors formally soliciting feedback regarding the quality of the supervisory alliance? If none, why? Is there any research on this topic?

Answer from Authors: Although a substantial literature has emerged that has examined soliciting feedback on the quality of the therapeutic alliance (Horvath et al., 2011), there has been relatively little attention to obtaining feedback on the supervisory alliance. There are, however, some findings that would seem to support the importance of doing so.

As discussed in the chapter, Patton and Kivlighan (1997) asked graduate trainees to complete a supervisory alliance measure after supervision sessions; their clients completed an alliance measure after each therapy session, and independent raters coded videotape of the sessions for psychodynamic techniques. Their findings demonstrated that trainees who perceived their alliance with their supervisor as stronger tended to have patients who perceived the therapeutic alliance stronger as well. In addition, such trainees tended to demonstrate greater acquisition of psychodynamic technique. That is, the more graduate trainees felt they were in a supportive, safe, collaborative, skill-focused, and facilitative supervisory environment, the more likely they were to employ psychodynamic techniques in their sessions, and the more likely their clients were to report a positive therapeutic alliance!

Additionally, in Marmarosh et al.'s (2013) study of novice therapists, results demonstrated that stronger supervisory alliance was significant associated with a greater degree of trainee self-efficacy. Related, Mesrie (2016) found that for novice therapists, higher attachment insecurity in the supervisee–supervisor relationship correlated with decreased trainee self-efficacy. Given the strong positive association found between supervisory alliance and attachment to supervisor (Marmarosh et al., 2013), the results of Mesrie (2016) would seem to indirectly support the importance of supervisory alliance for trainee self-efficacy as well.

Nevertheless, the crucial issue in determining the relevance of obtaining feedback on supervisory alliance would be the degree to which this alliance predicts broad band patient outcomes. As we emphasized throughout the chapter, the most important factor in developing clinical guidelines based on any of the research we have reviewed is the connection between therapist and supervisor technique/process with functional patient outcomes. In the context of supervisory alliance, however, we are not aware of research that has specifically examined the relation between such techniques/processes with outcomes.

Question #2. What suggestions can you give to clinicians and supervisors to help them avoid being overwhelmed when reviewing information-rich audio and video recordings?

Answer from Authors: Use of audio/videotape recordings in supervision can provide a wealth of clinical material as it happened during the session, allowing for more precise discussion of actual content and more targeted psychotherapy training. However, this can also lead to the very sobering questions of what to watch, as well as how much to watch during the time available. We have a few suggestions that may help in this process of most efficiently organizing the audio/videotape material available.

First, we have generally found that when they have audio/videotape material available, trainees will often watch their sessions prior to supervision, regardless of whether they are explicitly asked to do so. So we suggest promoting a training culture where supervisees are actively engaged in self-observation and reflection. One thing we often communicate to our trainees is that reviewing session recordings by oneself is highly useful to professional growth and skill development. That is, even without a supervisor present, supervisees are quite capable of observing and recognizing important moments in the session, exploring alternative interventions to those they undertook, as well as identifying adaptive interactions and effective interventions they have made.

Second, we often ask supervisees to review the recording prior to the supervision meeting and select parts of the session that they found to be particularly important (e.g., positive, negative, difficult, challenging, odd). We request that, when supervisees do so, they note the time stamps so that these segments can be quickly cued up during supervision. This can help make the most efficient use of the supervisory session.

Third, as the number of cases and/or supervisees expands, there will be less time available to watch larger sections of any one treatment. We generally recommend watching the first and last 5 minutes of the session to get a sense of how the therapeutic dyad comes together and then separates. And then two or three 5- to 10-minute segments that supervisees have identified as being particularly important (e.g., positive, negative, difficult, challenging, odd) in the session to be reviewed.

Finally, after supervision of a session is over, we often encourage trainees to go back to very intense or important segments (e.g., positive, negative, difficult, challenging, odd) in the session to further review and reflect on these with the new information gained during supervision. Most important, we suggest that supervisees ask themselves "why" and "what" about the therapeutic interaction or segment made it so "good," "different," "difficult," "uplifting," "intense," and so on.

Question #3. When would clinicians' efforts to improve via deliberate practice necessitate their reaching outside of the psychodynamic tradition?

Answer from Authors: As discussed in the chapter, findings from Owen and Hilsenroth (2014) suggest that therapists who demonstrate greater *adherence flexibility* in their use of PI technique within a given treatment appear to have better outcomes across their caseload, in comparison to therapists who are less flexible with their interventions at the individual patient level. That is, technical flexibility is important in predicting positive outcomes, and rigid adherence to technique is likely contraindicated.

In a related study, Goldman, Hilsenroth, Owen, and Gold (2013) found the integration of PI and CB techniques was significantly related to higher patient alliance subscales of Goals and Task Agreement as well as Confident Collaboration during a psychodynamic treatment. That is, when some traditional CB elements, such as providing patients with explicit information and rationale about their symptoms and treatment, are presented from a psychodynamic perspective (i.e., relational, affective, intrapsychic, etc.), patients may have more confidence to face their challenges and a greater sense of collaboration with their therapist. By providing this type of psychoeducation and increased therapist activity within a psychodynamic session, clinicians were also able to facilitate a stronger emphasis on goals and tasks aspects of the alliance. Therefore, psychodynamic clinicians may want to consider having an explicit discussion regarding how psychodynamic psychotherapy works, and how this approach might offer specific aid to the patients' functioning in order to enhance the goals and tasks aspects of the alliance.

These findings recently have been extended to the outcomes of this sample (Goldman, Hilsenroth, Gold, Owen, & Levy, in press). Results indicated that the relation between integrative PI and CB technique use with reliable change in global symptoms differed at different levels of the alliance subscales, specific to Goals and Task Agreement as well as Confident Collaboration, where higher levels of these alliance subscales were related to better outcomes.

Question #4. Your chapter focuses on developing competence. What would it look like if you took it to the next level toward developing expertise?

Answer from Authors: Actually, as we discussed in the section of the chapter titled "Methods for Training Therapists in Psychodynamic Psychotherapy," we delineated several specific aspects of our training/research program that were consistent with—and capitalize on—the different components of Ericsson's model of expertise development.

In addition, the discrepancy between findings from our research program and that of Hill et al. (2015) may be a function of aspects in our supervision/training that more effectively actualized the components of Ericsson's model of expertise development. That is, future training research needs to examine important variables, such as hours of supervision (group and individual), use/hours of videotape review, and use/hours of treatment manual review, and investigate these variables in relation to patient outcomes. In addition, supervisor as well as therapist effects should be evaluated. In this manner, we will have a better sense of what supervision variables most impact the performance (i.e., patient broad band outcomes) of supervisees across different levels of training.

References

Aderka, I. M., Nickerson, A., Bøe, H. J., & Hofmann, S. G. (2012). Sudden gains during psychological treatments of anxiety and depression: A meta-analysis. *Journal of Consulting and Clinical Psychology, 80,* 93–101.

Allen, J. G., Coyne, L., Colson, D. B., Horwitz, L., Gabbard, G. O., Frieswyk, S. H., & Newson, G. (1996). Pattern of therapist interventions associated with patient collaboration. *Psychotherapy, 33,* 254–261. doi:10.1037/0033-3204.33.2.254

Bambling, M., King, R., Raue, P., Schweitzer, R., & Lambert, W. (2006). Clinical supervision: Its influence on client-rated working alliance and client symptom reduction in the brief treatment of major depression. *Psychotherapy Research, 16,* 317–331.

Benjamin, L. S. (1974). Structural analysis of social behavior. *Psychological Review, 81,* 392–425. doi:10.1037/h0037024

Berkhout, E., & Malouff, J. (2015). The efficacy of empathy training: A meta-analysis of randomized controlled trials. *Journal of Counseling Psychology, 63,* 32–41.

Bertolino, B., & Miller, S. D. (Eds.) (2012). *ICCE manuals on feedback-informed treatment* (Vols. 1–6). Chicago, IL: ICCE Press.

Binder, J. L. (1999). Issues in teaching and learning time-limited psychodynamic psychotherapy. *Clinical Psychology Review, 19,* 705–719. doi:10.1016/S0272-7358(98)00078-6

Book, H. (1998). *How to practice brief psychodynamic psychotherapy: The core conflictual relationship theme method.* Washington, DC: American Psychological Association.

Bower, G. H. (1992). How might emotions affect learning? In S. A. Christianson (Ed.), *The handbook of emotion and memory: Research and theory* (pp. 3–31). Hillsdale, NJ: Erlbaum.

Coady, N. F., & Marziali, E. (1994). The association between global and specific measures of the therapeutic relationship. *Psychotherapy, 31,* 17–27. doi:10.1037/0033-3204.31.1.17

Colli, A., & Lingiardi, V. (2009). The collaborative interactions scale: A new transcript-based method for the assessment of therapeutic alliance ruptures and resolutions in psychotherapy. *Psychotherapy Research, 19,* 718–734. doi:10.1080/10503300903121098

Crits-Christoph, P., Barber, J. P., & Kurcias, J. S. (1993). The accuracy of therapists' interpretations and the development of the therapeutic alliance. *Psychotherapy Research, 3,* 25–35. doi:10.1080/10503309312331333639

Crits-Christoph, P., Gibbons, M.B.C., Crits-Christoph, K., Narducci, J., Schramberger, M., & Gallop, R. (2006). Can therapists be trained to improve their alliances? A preliminary study of alliance-fostering psychotherapy. *Psychotherapy Research, 16,* 268–281.

Crits-Christoph, P., Siqueland, L., Chittams, J., Barber, J. P., Beck, A. T., Frank, A., . . .Woody, G. (1998). Training in cognitive, supportive-expressive, and drug counseling therapies for cocaine dependence. *Journal of Consulting and Clinical Psychology, 66,* 484–492. doi:10.1037/0022-006X.66.3.484

DePue, M. K., Lambie G. W., Liu, R., & Gonzalez, J. (2016). Investigating supervisory relationships and therapeutic alliances using structural equation modeling. *Counselor Education and Supervision, 55*(4), 263–277.

Dolinsky, A., Vaughan, S. C., Luber, B., Mellman, L., & Roose, S. (1998). A match made in heaven? *Journal of Psychotherapy Practice and Research, 2,* 119–125.

Duncan, B. L., & Reese, J. (2015). The partners for change outcome management system (PCOMS) revisiting the client's frame of reference. *Psychotherapy, 52,* 391–401.

Ericsson, K. A. (2008). Deliberate practice and acquisition of expert performance: A general overview. *Academic Emergency Medicine: Official Journal of the Society for Academic Emergency Medicine, 15,* 988–994. doi:10.1111/j.1553-2712.2008.00227.x

Falkenström, F., Ekeblad, A., & Holmqvist, R. (2016). Improvement of the working alliance in one treatment session predicts improvement of depressive symptoms by the next session. *Journal of Consulting and Clinical Psychology, 84,* 738–751.

Falkenström, F., Granström, F., & Holmqvist, R. (2013). Therapeutic alliance predicts symptomatic improvement session by session. *Journal of Counseling Psychology, 60,* 317–328.

Flückiger, C., Grosse Holtforth, M., Del Re, A. C., & Lutz, W. (2013). Working along sudden gains: Responsiveness on small and subtle early changes and exceptions. *Psychotherapy, 50,* 292–297.

Garry, M., Manning, C. G., Loftus, E. F. & Sherman, J. (1996) Imagination inflation: Imagining a childhood event inflates confidence that it occurred. *Psychonomic Bulletin & Review, 3,* 208–214.

Gaston, L., & Ring, J. M. (1992). Preliminary results on the Inventory of Therapeutic Strategies. *Journal of Psychotherapy Practice and Research, 1,* 135–146. Retrieved from http://www.ncbi.nlm.nih.gov/pmc/journals/1745/

Gibbons, M. B. C., Thompson, S. M., Scott, K., Schauble, L. A., Mooney, T., Thompson, D., Green, P., MacArthur, M. J., & Crits-Christoph, P. (2012). Supportive-expressive dynamic psychotherapy in the community mental health system: a pilot effectiveness trial for the treatment of depression. *Psychotherapy, 49*(3), 303.

Goldman, R. E., Hilsenroth, M., Gold, J., Owen, J., & Levy, S. (2016, October 20). Psychotherapy integration and alliance: An examination across treatment outcomes. *Journal of Psychotherapy Integration.* doi:http://dx.doi.org/10.1037/int0000060.

Goldman, R. E., Hilsenroth, M. J., Owen, J. J., & Gold, J. R. (2013). Psychotherapy integration and alliance: Use of cognitive-behavioral techniques within a short-term psychodynamic treatment model. *Journal of Psychotherapy Integration, 23*(4), 373.

Haggerty, G., & Hilsenroth, M. J. (2011). The use of video in psychotherapy supervision. *British Journal of Psychotherapy, 27,* 193–210. doi:10.1111/j.1752-0118.2011.01232.x

Henry, W. P., Strupp, H. H., Butler, S. F., Schacht, T. E., & Binder, J. L. (1993). Effects of training in time-limited dynamic psychotherapy: Changes in therapist behavior. *Journal of Consulting and Clinical Psychology, 61,* 434.

Hill, C. E., Baumann, E., Shafran, N., Gupta, S., Morrison, A., Rojas, A. E., . . . Gelso, C. J. (2015). Is training effective? A study of counseling psychology doctoral trainees in a psychodynamic/interpersonal training clinic. *Journal of Counseling Psychology, 62,* 184–201.

Hilsenroth, M. J. (2007). A programmatic study of short-term psychodynamic psychotherapy: Assessment, process, outcome, and training. *Psychotherapy Research, 17,* 31–45. doi:10.1080/10503300600953504

Hilsenroth, M. J., Ackerman, S. J., Blagys, M. D., Baity, M. R., & Mooney, M. A. (2003). Short-term psychodynamic psychotherapy for depression: An examination of statistical, clinically significant, and technique-specific change. *Journal of Nervous and Mental Disease, 191,* 349–357. doi:10.1097/00005053-200306000-00001

Hilsenroth, M. J., Ackerman, S. J., Clemence, A. J., Strassle, C. G., & Handler, L. (2002). Effects of structured clinician training on patient and therapist perspectives of alliance early in psychotherapy. *Psychotherapy, 39,* 309–323.

Hilsenroth, M. J., Blagys, M. D., Ackerman, S. J., Bonge, D. R., & Blais, M. A. (2005). Measuring psychodynamic-interpersonal and cognitive-behavioral techniques: Development of the Comparative Psychotherapy Process Scale. *Psychotherapy, 42,* 340–356. doi:10.1037/0033-3204.42.3.340

Hilsenroth, M. J., Cromer, T. D., & Ackerman, S. J. (2012). How to make practical use of therapeutic alliance research in your clinical work. In R. A. Levy, J. S. Ablon, H. Kächele, R. A. Levy, J. S. Ablon, & H. Kächele (Eds.), *Psychodynamic psychotherapy research: Evidence-based practice and practice-based evidence* (pp. 361–380). Totowa, NJ: Humana Press.

Hilsenroth, M. J., Kivlighan, D. J., & Slavin-Mulford, J. (2015). Structured supervision of graduate clinicians in psychodynamic psychotherapy: Alliance and technique. *Journal of Counseling Psychology, 62,* 173–183. doi:10.1037/cou0000058

Hilsenroth, M., Peters, E., & Ackerman, S. (2004). The development of the therapeutic alliance during psychological assessment: Patient and therapist perspectives across treatment. *Journal of Personality Assessment, 83,* 332–344.

Horvath, A. O., Del Re, A. C., Flückiger, C., & Symonds, D. (2011). Alliance in individual psychotherapy. *Psychotherapy, 48,* 9–16. doi:10.1037/a0022186

Huggins, R. (2016, December 9). Session 84: HIPAA audit scam, passwords, sending videos, online backup, and more. Retrieved from https://personcenteredtech.com/office-hours-session/december-9th-2016/

Huggins, R. (2017a, January 6). Session 88: Shared WiFi in office buildings and coffee shops, VPNs, connecting computers across the Internet, and much more. Retrieved from https://personcenteredtech.com/office-hours-session/january-6th-2017/

Huggins, R. (2017b, January 8). Easy safe harbor from HIPAA breach notification: Now on your computer and smartphone. Retrieved from https://personcenteredtech.com/2013/04/05/hipaa-safe-harbor-for-your-computer-the-ultimate-in-hipaa-compliance-the-compleat-guide/

Imel, Z. E., Barco, J. S., Brown, H., Baucom, B. R., Baer, J. S., Kircher, J., & Atkins, D. C. (2014). Synchrony in vocally encoded arousal as an indicator of therapist empathy in motivational interviewing. *Journal of Counseling Psychology, 61,* 146–153.

Joyce, A. S., & Piper, W. E. (1998). Expectancy, the therapeutic alliance, and treatment outcome in short-term individual psychotherapy. *Journal of Psychotherapy Practice and Research, 7,* 236–248.

Kuutmann, K., & Hilsenroth, M. J. (2012). Exploring in-session focus on the patient–therapist relationship: Patient characteristics, process and outcome. *Clinical Psychology & Psychotherapy, 19,* 187–202. doi:10.1002/cpp.743

Lambert, M. (2015). Progress feedback and OQ-System: The past and the future. *Psychotherapy, 52*, 381–390.

Levy, S. R., Hilsenroth, M. J., & Owen, J. J. (2015). Relationship between interpretation, alliance, and outcome in psychodynamic psychotherapy: Control of therapist effects and assessment of moderator variable impact. *Journal of Nervous and Mental Disease, 203*, 418–424. doi:10.1097/NMD.0000000000000302

Luborsky, L. (1984). *Principles of psychoanalytic psychotherapy: A manual for supportive/expressive treatment.* New York, NY: Basic Books.

Malan, D. (1979). *Individual psychotherapy and the science of psychodynamics.* London, UK: Butterworths.

Marmar, C. R., Gaston, L., Gallagher, D., & Thompson, L. W. (1989). Alliance and outcome in late-life depression. *Journal of Nervous and Mental Disease, 177*, 464–472. doi:10.1097/00005053-198908000-00003

Marmarosh, C. L., Nikityn, M., Moehringer, J., Ferraioli, L., Kahn, S., Cerkevich, A., . . . Reisch, E. (2013). Adult attachment, attachment to the supervisor, and the supervisory alliance: How they relate to novice therapists' perceived counseling self-efficacy. *Psychotherapy, 50*, 178–188. doi:10.1037/a0033028

Martin, D., Garske, J., & Davis, M. (2000). Relation of the therapeutic alliance with outcome and other variables: A meta-analytic review. *Journal of Consulting and Clinical Psychology, 68*, 438–450. doi:10.1037/0022-006X.68.3.438

McCullough, L., Kuhn, N., Andrews, S., Kaplan, A., Wolf, J., & Hurley, C. (2003). *Treating affect phobia: A manual for short-term dynamic psychotherapy.* New York, NY: Guilford Press.

Mesrie, V. (2016). *Trainee attachment to supervisor and perceptions of novice therapist self-efficacy: The moderating role of level of experience.* (Unpublished doctoral dissertation). Long Island University-Post, Brookville, NY.

Multon, K., Kivlighan, D., & Gold, P. (1996). Changes in counselor adherence over the course of training. *Journal of Counseling Psychology, 43*, 356–363.

Ogrodniczuk, J. S., & Piper, W. E. (1999). Measuring therapist technique in psychodynamic psychotherapies: Development and use of a new scale. *Journal of Psychotherapy Practice & Research, 8*, 142–154.

Owen, J., & Hilsenroth, M. J. (2011). Interaction between alliance and technique in predicting patient outcome during psychodynamic psychotherapy. *Journal of Nervous and Mental Disease, 199*, 384–389. doi:10.1097/NMD.0b013e31821cd28a

Owen, J., & Hilsenroth, M. J. (2014). Treatment adherence: The importance of therapist flexibility in relation to therapy outcomes. *Journal of Counseling Psychology, 61*, 280–288. doi:10.1037/a0035753

Owen, J., Hilsenroth, M. J., & Rodolfa, E. (2013). Interaction among alliance, psychodynamic–interpersonal and cognitive–behavioural techniques in the prediction of post-session change. *Clinical Psychology & Psychotherapy, 20*, 513–522.

Owen, J., Quirk, K., Hilsenroth, M. J., & Rodolfa, E. R. (2012). Working through: In-session processes that promote between-session thoughts and activities. *Journal of Counseling Psychology, 59*, 161–167.

Patton, M., & Kivlighan, D. (1997). Relevance of the supervisory alliance to the counseling alliance and to treatment adherence in counselor training. *Journal of Counseling Psychology, 44*, 108–115.

Pitman, S., Slavin-Mulford, J., & Hilsenroth, M. (2014). Psychodynamic techniques related to outcome for anxiety disorder patients at different points in treatment. *Journal of Nervous and Mental Disease, 202*, 391–396. doi:10.1097/NMD.0000000000000137

Price, P. B., & Jones, E. E. (1998). Examining the alliance using the Psychotherapy Process Q-Set. *Psychotherapy, 35*, 392–404. doi:10.1037/h0087654

Ryum, T., Stiles, T., Svartberg, M., & McCullough, L. (2010). The role of transference work, the therapeutic alliance, and their interaction in reducing interpersonal problems among psychotherapy patients with Cluster C personality disorders. *Psychotherapy, 47*, 442–453.

Safran, J. D., & Muran, J. C. (2000). *Negotiating the therapeutic alliance: A relational treatment guide*. New York, NY: Guilford Press.

Saunders, S. M., Howard, K. I., & Orlinsky, D. E. (1989). The Therapeutic Bond Scales: Psychometric characteristics and relationship to treatment effectiveness. *Psychological Assessment: A Journal of Consulting and Clinical Psychology, 1*, 323–330. doi:10.1037/1040-3590.1.4.323

Schacter, D. L. (1999). The seven sins of memory: Insights from psychology and cognitive neuroscience. *American Psychologist, 54*, 182–203.

Schacter, D. L., & Addis, D. R. (2007). The cognitive neuroscience of constructive memory: Remembering the past and imagining the future. *Philosophical Transactions of the Royal Society (B), 362*, 773–786.

Sexton, H. C., Hembre, K., & Kvarme, G. (1996). The interaction of the alliance and therapy microprocess: A sequential analysis. *Journal of Consulting and Clinical Psychology, 64*, 471–480. doi:10.1037/0022-006X.64.3.471

Slavin-Mulford, J., Hilsenroth, M., Weinberger, J., & Gold, J. (2011). Therapeutic interventions related to outcome in psychodynamic psychotherapy for anxiety disorder patients. *Journal of Nervous and Mental Disease, 199*, 214–221. doi:10.1097/NMD.0b013e3182125d60

Strupp, H. H., & Binder, J. (1984). *Psychotherapy in a new key*. New York, NY: Basic Books.

Tasca, G.A., Sylvestre, J., Balfour, L., Chyurlia, L., Evans, J., Fortin-Langelier, B., . . . Wilson, B. (2015). What clinicians want: Findings from a psychotherapy practice research network survey. *Psychotherapy, 52*, 1–11.

Wachtel, P. L. (1993). *Therapeutic communication: Principles and effective practice*. New York, NY: Guilford Press.

Wampold, B. E. (2015). Routine outcome monitoring: Coming of age—with the usual developmental challenges. *Psychotherapy, 52*, 458–462.

Wampold, B. E., & Imel, Z. E. (2015). *The great psychotherapy debate: The research evidence for what works in psychotherapy* (2nd ed.). New York, NY: Routledge.

Watkins, C. E., Jr. (2014). The supervisory alliance: A half century of theory, practice, and research in critical perspective. *American Journal of Psychotherapy, 68*, 19–55.

Webb, C. A., DeRubeis, R. J., & Barber, J. P. (2010). Therapist adherence/competence and treatment outcome: A meta-analytic review. *Journal of Consulting and Clinical Psychology, 78*, 200–211. doi:10.1037/a0018912

Xu, H., & Tracey, T.J.G. (2015). Reciprocal influence model of working alliance and therapeutic outcome over individual therapy course. *Journal of Counseling Psychology, 62,* 351–359.

Zilcha-Mano, S., Dinger, U., McCarthy, K. S., & Barber, J. P. (2014). Does alliance predict symptoms throughout treatment, or is it the other way around? *Journal of Consulting and Clinical Psychology, 82,* 931–935.

Zilcha-Mano, S., & Errázuriz, P. (2015). One size does not fit all: Examining heterogeneity and identifying moderators of the alliance–outcome association. *Journal of Counseling Psychology, 62,* 579–591.

Zilcha-Mano, S., Muran, J., Hungr, C., Eubanks, C., Safran, J., & Winston, A. (2016). The relationship between alliance and outcome: Analysis of a two-person perspective on alliance and session outcome. *Journal of Consulting and Clinical Psychology, 84*(6), 484–496.

9

Nurturing Therapeutic Mastery in Cognitive Behavioral Therapy and Beyond

An Interview with Donald Meichenbaum

Cognitive behavioral therapy (CBT) is the most widely researched and disseminated psychotherapy approach in existence. Studies have found the approach effective for a variety of presenting complaints and treatment populations compared to no-treatment controls (Hofmann, Asnaani, Vonk, Sawyer, & Fang, 2012). Around the world, the approach dominates official lists of scientifically sanctioned mental health treatments, including the National Institute for Health and Clinical Excellence in the United Kingdom and the National Registry of Evidence Based Practices and Programs in the United States (Wampold & Imel, 2015).

The CBT model posits that mental health problems result from dysfunctional beliefs and information-processing errors and accompanying emotional dysregulation (Beck, Rush, Shaw, & Emery, 1979). Over the years, a number of CBT techniques and treatment protocols have been developed and standardized. Each aims at helping people identify, evaluate, and modify the distorted thinking believed to be at the core of various disorders. Behavioral strategies designed to enhance cognitive and emotional skills and to increase engagement in activities associated with improved mood and functioning also are included.

Popularity and overall efficacy notwithstanding, research has failed to provide evidence that CBT is more effective than most other treatments or that it works through the purported mechanisms of change (Wampold & Imel, 2015). When CBT is compared directly with other therapies designed to be therapeutic, no differences in effectiveness are found (Wampold & Imel, 2015). Moreover, dismantling studies to date have not found that any specific ingredient is critical to the benefits of CBT (Ahn & Wampold, 2001; Bell, Marcus, & Goodlad, 2013). This evidence suggests that an emphasis on adherence to any one method or treatment protocol as a means of improving the quality of mental health services is misguided (Evans, 2013). As presented in previous chapters of this volume, there are a number of critical therapeutic skills unrelated to particular protocols that, if practiced and mastered, would improve outcomes.

In the United Kingdom, large amounts of money have been spent over the last five years training clinicians to use CBT. The expenditure is part of a well-intentioned government program aimed at improving access to effective mental health services (Griffiths & Steen, 2013).

The Cycle of Excellence: Using Deliberate Practice to Improve Supervision and Training,
First Edition. Edited by Tony Rousmaniere, Rodney K. Goodyear, Scott D. Miller, and Bruce E. Wampold.
© 2017 John Wiley & Sons, Ltd. Published 2017 by John Wiley & Sons, Ltd.

And yet the benefit of these expenditures is questionable (Mukuria et al., 2013). Consider a recent study by Branson, Shafran, and Myles (2015) that investigated 43 clinicians who participated in a year-long "high-intensity" CBT training that included more than 300 hours of training, supervision, and practice in CBT. The outcomes of 1,247 service users were tracked using standardized measures administered at regular intervals. Not surprisingly, adherence to and competence in delivering CBT improved significantly throughout the training. However, contrary to expectations, results showed that greater adherence and competence, acquired through this CBT-specific training, did *not* result in better outcomes. The therapists were, in other words, no more effective following the training than they were before.

Although one might hope such findings would lead to questions regarding the relationship between the treatment method and the outcome, the researchers chose instead to question whether "patient outcome should . . . be used as a metric of competence" (Branson et al., 2015, p. 27). Said another way, despite the results, adhering to protocol still was viewed as more important than whether adherence improved outcomes.

Given our understanding of the evidence about CBT, as volume editors we were eager to have a chapter about developing expertise in CBT with improving outcomes as the goal. We approached Donald Meichenbaum, PhD, to gain some insight into this process. Meichenbaum is one the most prominent founders of CBT. Early on, he began studying transtheoretical patterns associated with expert performance in psychotherapy. In time, he developed a model of therapeutic expertise, identifying a core set of tasks that effective therapists use.

We were pleased that Meichenbaum agreed to be interviewed about his model of expertise and how his thinking about psychotherapy evolved from CBT to an emphasis on improving outcomes through deliberate practice.

Interview

EDITORS (EDS.) We are pleased to have you contribute to our discussion of how to nurture expertise in psychotherapists.

DM I am honored to be invited to contribute. This is a challenging issue that I have been struggling with for some time. I have been involved in training psychotherapists for over 40 years, as a clinical supervisor, as a consultant to various psychiatric treatment centers where the clientele range from children to the elderly. In addition, I have been offering continuing education for over 30 years. I have been concerned about what trainees and what participants take away from my instruction and supervision.

EDS. You are considered one of the founders of cognitive behavioral therapy, and you initially conducted a number of innovative treatment outcome studies designed to determine the relative efficacy of such therapeutic procedures as self-instructional training, stress inoculation training, cognitive restructuring procedures, and problem-solving approaches. How did your clinical research lead you to a more generic concern with the concept of "expertise" of psychotherapists?

DM You are correct in noting my professional trajectory. In fact, recently I was invited by Routledge Publishers to conduct a retrospective of my publications over 40 years

(Meichenbaum, 2017). This was an opportunity to reflect on my ongoing preoccupation with what constitutes the core tasks that "expert" psychotherapists engage in.

EDS. How did you come to this position?

DM The answer comes in three parts. First, I was impressed by the marked variability in the treatment outcomes of the therapists we were working with. Some therapists consistently achieved better outcomes than others. This finding is in accord with the findings of a number of researchers (Baldwin & Imel, 2013; Dawes, 1994; Wampold, 2001, 2006; Wampold & Imel, 2015). Second, as a consultant to various treatment programs and as a provider of continuing education, I had a strong desire to be an "honest broker" and advocate for evidence-based interventions. My presentations were tempered, however, by the finding that all treatments that are intended to be therapeutic seem to be approximately equally effective. Thus, my interest turned to what are the behavior change principles and core psychotherapeutic tasks that are common to these varied treatment approaches.

The third and most critical contribution to my evolving views of expertise and psychotherapy was that I also wear a "professional hat" of being a developmental psychologist. With a colleague, Andy Biemiller, we wanted to better understand why smart children in school keep getting smarter, and other students fall further and further behind. For example, by the time students reach high school, the spread between high- and low-achieving students could be as much as six grade levels. In some sense, the high-achieving students are "experts" in negotiating the demands of the school system (Meichenbaum & Biemiller, 1998).

EDS. How did your work on students' academic performance link with your training of psychotherapists?

DM In our work with students, I reviewed the research on the acquisition and structure of expertise (Ericsson & Charness, 1994; Ericsson, Charness, Feltovich, & Hoffman, 2006; Shanteau, 1992). In fact, Neil Charness was a colleague at the University of Waterloo, in Ontario, Canada, where I worked for 40 years.

As a result of a number of observational studies of independent student learners (socalled budding experts), we developed a theoretical model that could be applied to the acquisition of expertise, including psychotherapy (Biemiller & Meichenbaum, 1992).

EDS. That is interesting. Can you describe the model and discuss its implications for the training of psychotherapists?

DM Figure 9.1 provides a pictorial presentation of the Model of Mastery. It is a three-dimensional framework that includes an x-axis (horizontal), a y-axis (vertical), and a z-axis (diagonal). The x-axis represents a tutee's movement from easy to more difficult tasks that require more knowledge and skills. For school students, this may reflect moving from simple math problems to more difficult problems. For novice psychotherapists, this may entail taking on patients with less complex, straightforward adjustment disorders than more complex high-demand, traumatized patients with chronic co-occurring disorders who have few social supports. The critical feature in moving along the x-axis is the nature of the "fit" between the tutee's competence and the task

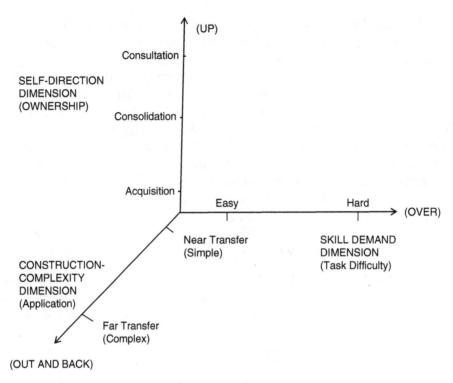

Figure 9.1 Model of Mastery.

demands. An effective teacher or clinical supervisor attempts to match, and slightly challenge the tutee and "scaffold" instruction, providing necessary supports and then reducing guidance and fading them as the tutee acquires skills.

The vertical y-axis reflects further steps in the development of mastery. A tutee (either student or psychotherapist) moves from an initial point of being a complete novice (lack of knowledge, skills, experience) by means of deliberate practice to the point of task efficiency, where he or she can consolidate skills and performance. Such deliberate practice is goal-directed in achieving well-defined specific tasks that the tutee seeks to master. It includes multiple repetitive opportunities to engage in the tasks and affords immediate feedback, highlighted errors, and represents "teachable moments." As automaticity develops the tutee can learn to perform more than one skill set at a time.

In school, students may have opportunities to do and redo a particular academic task. For a psychotherapist, it may be working on ways to establish, maintain, and monitor a therapeutic alliance or deal with "ruptures" to such an alliance. Therapists can use session-by-session patient input to monitor the perceived fit and effectiveness of the therapeutic alliance and alter the psychotherapeutic approach accordingly (Lambert, 2010; Lambert & Shimokawa, 2011).

One of the goals of this deliberate practice is to help automatize performance (put the tutee on "auto-pilot"), so it frees up mental capacity. This consolidation process should be revisited on a regular basis when feedback indicates that performance errors have occurred.

But engaging in deliberate practice in moving from initial steps of acquisition to consolidation is *not sufficient* to evidence mastery and develop expertise. The tutee needs to continue up the y-axis to the point of becoming a mindful, reflective, deliberate consultant, to themselves and to others. It is in this consultative role that situational awareness develops, as the tutee can self-monitor, observe, and "own" his/her skills. In order to develop mastery, the student or psychotherapist needs to develop conditional strategic knowledge, knowing when and how to implement the skill set, and also must be able to describe the process and even teach it to others. The learner must come to spontaneously use language or some other form of mental representation (diagrams, semantic webs) in a way to direct others and him- or herself.

As the tutee moves up the y-axis with more and more difficult demanding tasks (moving concurrently along the x-axis), he or she calls upon meta-cognitive, executive skills, and can even shift goals.

But the journey to expertise is *not* yet complete. The tutee needs to learn how to apply the acquired skills to new tasks, in new situations, and in innovative ways. In short, the tutee (student or psychotherapist) needs to move along the z-axis. There are two ways to negotiate the z-axis (OUT and BACK). The training sessions can take the form of what is called near transfer. The training opportunities can closely approximate the initial training tasks that were used in the acquisition of the skill set. Users can "criterion cheat," making the training tasks similar to the transfer tasks. In this way, the tutee can apply his or her knowledge and skills in a methodical and perhaps innovative manner to new tasks, settings, and patients.

A second way to negotiate the z-axis is to confront the student or psychotherapist with an "authentic" challenging task and have the tutee deduce, infer, and problem-solve ways to figure out and apply his or her knowledge and skills, which is called far transfer.

The z (OUT) dimension denotes the planning and application complexity of a task, as tutees apply their knowledge and skills to new tasks in novel situations. The learners acquire or generate strategies for planning new tasks—transferring or generalizing their knowledge and skills. As noted, the tasks may vary from near transfer (tasks and contents similar to training) to far transfer ("authentic" applied tasks that require high levels of skill integration and complex decision making). Tutees move from merely consuming knowledge to constructing knowledge, tasks and procedures.

Tutees may move OUT from the initial simplified learning settings to complex "authentic" tasks. They may also move BACK from "authentic" complex tasks to focusing on the acquisition of further needed skills and strategies. This bidirectional movement is a dynamic interactive process.

In summary, the proposed Model of Mastery means that in order to develop "expertise," individuals need to:

1. move from simple to more complex difficult tasks (patients) (x-axis);
2. move from being a novice to becoming proficient by means of deliberate practice, to the point whereby they consolidate their skills that frees up mental capacity all the way to the point of becoming a consultant to themselves as well as to others. In this way, they now come to own their skill set and can teach them to others (y-axis).

3. apply and extend their knowledge and skill sets to new tasks (patients), settings, and to do so in innovative, creative ways. They can do so by applying their skills to an increasing challenging set of transfer tasks, or they can do so by engaging in "authentic" real-life tasks, even inventing new applications. In order to become an "expert" in any area, an individual needs to move OVER, UP, and OUT along the three dimensions proposed by the Model of Mastery. If you want to become an "expert" at something, the individual has to learn to perform more challenging tasks, on their own, as a result of deliberate practice and apply these skills in new ways on novel tasks in different settings. According to this analysis, deliberate practice is embedded in the journey toward expertise.

The development of such expertise by means of deliberate practice in implementing the core tasks of psychotherapy will contribute to the ultimate objective of helping patients achieve their treatment goals that they have collaboratively established with their therapists.

Eds. How did the three-dimensional Model of Mastery contribute to your training of psychotherapists?

DM In order to answer your question, let us take one axis at a time. Keep in mind that when the contributors to this volume call for deliberate practice, the critical question is what specific skill sets should psychotherapists deliberately practice?

Eds. Exactly!

DM Research indicates that the most robust predictor of therapy outcomes is the quality of the therapeutic alliance (TA). The amount of change attributable to TA is seven times that of the specific treatment model or specific treatment techniques. In fact, the specific treatment accounts for no more than 15% of variance of treatment outcomes. In comparison, some 36% of the treatment outcome is attributed to the person of the therapist, which is three to four times that of the specific treatment approach (Sperry & Carlson, 2013). But as Miller, Hubble, and Duncan (2008) highlighted, it is the availability of timely quality feedback from patients on a session-by-session basis that is critical to the development of expertise in any area.

In terms of the Model of Mastery, this translates into the need for psychotherapists to engage in deliberate practice with more and more challenging patients (namely, across the x-axis of level of difficulty) and to actively solicit patient feedback on an ongoing basis.

But a big feature of developing a good therapeutic alliance is for the patient and therapist to mutually agree on the treatment goals and methods by which to achieve the patient's goals ("pathways thinking" and being "practically optimistic" in order to nurture the patient's level of hopefulness) (Bordin, 1979; Horvath, Del Re, Flückiger, & Symonds, 2011).

Thus, a second core set of tasks that psychotherapists need to deliberately practice are motivational interviewing and collaborative goal-setting procedures. As Goldfried (2012) observed, the patient should hold the belief "My therapist really understands and cares about me," and the therapist should hold the belief "I really enjoy working with this patient." The patient's trust and confidence in the therapist that he/she is competent and interested in the patient's well-being is predictive of outcome (Norcross, 2002; Skovholt & Jennings, 2004).

An effective TA may develop as early as the first session, but an effective TA must be firmly in place by the third session, if treatment is to be successful (Sperry & Carlson, 2013). It is the therapist and not the treatment that influences the amount of therapeutic alliance that occurs. Relationship skills at developing a therapeutic alliance is the cornerstone of therapeutic alliance.

The use of patient rating scales and Socratic probes, and the therapist's adjustment of treatment accordingly, are predictive of treatment outcomes.

It is the adjustment of treatment interventions that are in response to patient feedback that is a critical aspect of being a successful psychotherapist. Expert therapists tend to be more reflective and work harder between sessions, seeking mentoring opportunities (Miller et al., 2008). In terms of the proposed Model of Mastery, in order to develop expertise individuals have to move up the y-axis to the point of being a "consultant" to themselves as well as to others (including their patients). Both the therapist and the patient have to "own" their newly developed skills and, moreover, take credit for the changes they have brought about. A core task for psychotherapists is to deliberately practice ways to have their patients engage in self-attributional training that nurtures personal agency and self-efficacy. Patients need to see the connections between their efforts and resultant changes and become more situationally aware of the consequences of their efforts and interventions (Duncan, Miller, Wampold, & Hubble, 2010; Messer & Wampold, 2002).

In short, therapists who achieve better outcomes have developed a way of teaching their patients how to become their own therapists. Expert therapists teach their patients how to take the therapist's voice with them. For instance, the therapist teaches patients how to become "experts" in achieving their treatment goals and ways to improve the quality of their lives. Consider the potential value of psychotherapists asking their patients the following question: "Let me ask you a somewhat different question. Do you [the patient] ever find yourself, in your everyday experiences, asking yourself the kind of questions that we ask each other right here?"

The Model of Mastery highlights that there is a need to have psychotherapists not only move across the x-axis and up the y-axis but to also move out and back along the z-axis. In order to truly become an "expert" at any skill, there is a need to apply, extend, generalize, and invent new and creative applications of their skill sets. Psychotherapists need to apply their knowledge and skills to "authentic" challenging new and complex cases. Psychotherapists require knowledge of and skills on how to increase the likelihood of transfer and generalization in order to help their patients achieve lasting changes. Expert therapists do not merely train and hope for such transfer, but they build in specific ways their patients can move out along the z-axis (Meichenbaum & Biemiller, 1998).

Eds. Let us see if we have captured what you are proposing. You have highlighted three main features that characterize psychotherapists who achieve better treatment outcomes:

1. The development, maintenance and monitoring of the quality of the therapeutic alliance with more and more challenging patients.
2. The self-reflective activity to use such patient feedback on an ongoing basis to adjust their treatment approach accordingly, in order to become more meta-cognitively active, or what you call being in a consultative role with themselves, as well as with others, including their patients. Interestingly, you are proposing that therapists who achieve better results teach their patients how to become "experts" themselves, in using the principles of deliberate practice.
3. Finally, you have proposed that effective therapists challenge, cajole, nurture, and support their patients to undertake these activities in new and challenging tasks, in new situations and settings with significant others.

DM Indeed, three basic features characterize "expert" psychotherapists who obtain better treatment outcomes, namely, (a) the ability to establish, maintain, and monitor on an ongoing basis the quality of the therapeutic alliance that has been implemented in a culturally sensitive manner, (b) the ability to become more strategically knowledgeable, self-aware, and reflective as they operate in a consultative role to their patients and to themselves in order to alter treatment accordingly, and (c) the ability to increase the likelihood of their patients achieving lasting changes by their incorporating into their treatment protocols behavioral generalization guidelines. Insofar as psychotherapists deliberately practice implementing these core tasks of psychotherapy, they will improve their patients' treatment outcomes.

"Expert" psychotherapists do not view themselves as experts but continually seek feedback from their patients, colleagues, and supervisors on their personal journey to becoming more effective catalysts of change.

References

Ahn, H., & Wampold, B. E. (2001). A meta-analysis of component studies: Where is the evidence for the specificity of psychotherapy? *Journal of Counseling Psychology, 48*, 251–257.

Baldwin, S. A., & Imel, Z. E. (2013). Therapist effects: Finding and methods. In M. J. Lambert (Ed.), *Bergin and Garfield's handbook of psychotherapy and behavior change* (6th ed., pp. 258–297). Hoboken, NJ: Wiley.

Beck, A. T., Rush, A. J., Shaw, B. F., & Emery, G. (1979). *Cognitive therapy of depression.* New York, NY: Guilford Press.

Bell, E. C., Marcus, D. K., & Goodlad, J. K. (2013). Are the parts as good as the whole? A meta-analysis of component treatment studies. *Journal of Consulting and Clinical Psychology, 81*(4), 722–736. doi:10.1037/a0033004

Biemiller, A., & Meichenbaum, D. (1992). The nature and nurture of self-directed learner. *Educational Leadership, 50*, 75–80.

Bordin, T. S. (1979). The generalizability of the psychoanalytic concept of the working alliance. *Psychotherapy: Research and Practice, 16*, 252–260.

Branson, A., Shafran, R., & Myles, P. (2015). Investigating the relationship between competence and patient outcome with CBT. *Behaviour Research and Therapy, 68*, 19–26. doi:10.1016/j.brat.2015.03.002

Dawes, R. M. (1994). *House of cards: Psychology and psychiatry, built on a myth.* New York, NY: Free Press.

Duncan, B. L., Miller, B. E., Wampold, B. E. & Hubble, M. A. (Eds). (2010). *The heart and soul of change: Delivering what works in therapy.* Washington, DC: American Psychological Association.

Ericsson, K. A., & Charness, N. (1994). Expert performance: Its structure and acquisition. *American Psychologist, 49*, 725–747.

Ericsson, K. A., Charness, N., Feltovich, P. J., & Hoffman, R. R. (2006). *The Cambridge handbook of expertise and expert performance.* Cambridge, UK. Cambridge University Press.

Evans, J. (2013). *David Clark on Improving Access for Psychological Therapy (IAPT).* Retrieved from https://goo.gl/p3Zahc

Goldfried, M. (2012). The corrective experience: A core principle for therapeutic change. In L. Castonguay & C. Hill (Eds.), *Transformation in psychotherapy* (pp. 13–29). Washington, DC: American Psychological Association.

Griffiths, S., and Steen, S. (2013). Improving Access to Psychological Therapies (IAPT) programme: Scrutinizing IAPT cost estimates to support effective commissioning. *Journal of Psychological Therapies in Primary Care, 2*, 142–156.

Hofmann, S. G., Asnaani, A., Vonk, I.J.J., Sawyer, A. T., & Fang, A. (2012). The efficacy of cognitive behavioral therapy: A review of meta-analyses. *Cognitive Therapy and Research, 36*(5), 427–440.

Horvath, A., Del Re, A. C., Flückiger, C & Symonds, D. (2011). Alliance in individual psychotherapy. *Psychotherapy, 48*, 9–16.

Lambert, M. J. (2010). *Prevention of treatment failure: The use of measuring, monitoring and feedback in clinical practice.* Washington, DC: American Psychological Association.

Lambert, M. J., & Shimokawa, K. (2011). Collecting client feedback. *Psychotherapy, 48*, 72–79.

Meichenbaum, D. (2017). *The evolution of cognitive behavior therapy: A personal and professional journey with Don Meichenbaum.* New York, NY: Routledge.

Meichenbaum, D., & Biemiller, A. (1998). *Nurturing independent learners: Helping students take charge of their learning.* Cambridge, MA: Brookline Books.

Messer, S. B., & Wampold, B. S. (2002). Let's face facts: Common factors are more potent than specific ingredients. *Clinical Psychology: Science and Practice, 9*, 21–25.

Miller, S. D., Hubble, M., & Duncan, B. (2008). Supershrinks: What is the secret of their success? *Psychotherapy in Australia, 14*, 14–22.

Mukuria, C., Brazier, J., Barkham, M., Connell, J., Hardy, G., Hutten, R., . . .Parry, G. (2013). Cost-effectiveness of an improving access to psychological therapies service. *British Journal of Psychiatry, 202*(3), 220–227. dx.doi:https://doi.org/10.1192/bjp.bp.111.107888

Norcross, J. (Ed.). (2002). *Psychotherapy relationships that work. Therapist contributions and responsiveness to patients.* New York, NY: Oxford University Press.

Shanteau, J. (1992). Competence in experts: The role of task characteristics. *Organizational Behavior and Human Decision Processes, 53*, 252–266.

Skovholt, J. M., & Jennings, L. (2004). *Master therapists: Exploring expertise in therapy and counseling.* Boston, MA: Allyn & Bacon.

Sperry, L., & Carlson, J. (2013). *How master therapists work.* New York, NY: Routledge.

Tracey, T. J., Wampold, B. E., Lichtenberg, J. W., & Goodyear, R. K. (2014). Expertise in psychotherapy: An elusive goal. *American Psychologist, 69,* 218–229.

Wampold, B. E. (2001). *The great psychotherapy debate: Models, methods, and findings.* Mahwah, NJ: Erlbaum.

Wampold, B. E. (2006). The psychotherapist. In J. C. Norcross, L. E. Butler, & R. F. Levant (Eds.), *Evidence-based practices in mental health: Debate and dialogue on fundamental questions* (pp. 200–208). Washington, DC: American Psychological Association.

Wampold, B. E., & Imel, Z. E. (2015). *The great psychotherapy debate: The research evidence for what works in psychotherapy* (2nd ed.). New York, NY: Routledge.

10

Nurturing Expertise at Mental Health Agencies
Simon B. Goldberg, Robbie Babins-Wagner, and Scott D. Miller

There is no end point. We are either creeping gradually toward success, inching toward improvement, or losing ground. So, support must be constant, always connecting process to results and back again, because this isn't easy. It's hard work.
  —Cathy Keough, Director of Counseling, Calgary Counselling Centre

It is a difficult moment in history to be running a mental health agency. Despite clear evidence for the benefits of psychotherapy (Seligman, 1995; Wampold & Imel, 2015), mental healthcare agencies have come under increased scrutiny and pressure in recent years and funding for mental health services has decreased in the United States (National Alliance on Mental Illness, 2011). Under these conditions, agencies offering psychotherapy have faced particular challenges. Since 1998, individuals seeking mental health treatment have increasingly received medications instead of psychotherapy (Olfson & Marcus, 2010). Those who do receive psychotherapy receive fewer annual visits, with lower mean expenditures per visit and a declining proportion of mental health budgets allocated to psychotherapy (Olfson & Marcus, 2010). Perhaps surprisingly, declines in psychotherapy utilization relative to pharmacotherapy utilization are occurring despite clear evidence that mental health consumers would prefer to receive psychotherapy (McHugh, Whitton, Peckham, Welge, & Otto, 2013).

Against this backdrop of economic shifts and treatment utilization trends, pressures are also present from within the world of psychotherapy. Over the past two decades, psychotherapy providers have faced pressure to provide therapies drawn from lists of evidence-based treatments (Chambless & Hollon, 1998). Many of these treatments are manualized (i.e., based on a treatment manual) and time-limited in nature (e.g., Cognitive Processing Therapy, Prolonged Exposure; Resick, Nishith, Weaver, Astin, & Feuer, 2002), and providers may be expected to treat long-standing and complex psychiatric conditions in as few as 9 to 12 sessions. Although there is strong evidence that relatively brief treatments can be effective (Chambless & Hollon, 1998), the movement toward promoting and expecting brief, manualized treatments forces agencies to operate within tighter constraints.

The Cycle of Excellence: Using Deliberate Practice to Improve Supervision and Training,
First Edition. Edited by Tony Rousmaniere, Rodney K. Goodyear, Scott D. Miller, and Bruce E. Wampold.
© 2017 John Wiley & Sons, Ltd. Published 2017 by John Wiley & Sons, Ltd.

The passage of the Affordable Care Act in the United States has increased the culture of accountability within the healthcare system (Fisher & Shortell, 2010), which, although potentially of benefit to clients and healthcare systems in the long run, can further increase pressures on treatment providers and agencies to perform.

There are a number of ways that mental health agencies traditionally respond to these forces. One common approach is to track and report static outcomes, such as the number of clients served or the amount of treatment provided. This approach can be effective, particularly for communicating with stakeholders and potential funders who can easily appreciate the import of simply providing a larger *quantity* of care. However, such outcomes are limited in that they do not reflect the *quality* or impact of services provided. In addition, mental health agencies can invest in the training and supervision of their staff. Although training and supervision are an industry standard within mental health agencies, particularly for unlicensed clinicians, these efforts are costly and can take clinician time away from being able to provide clinical services (Proctor et al., 2007). More important, there is limited evidence that the supervision and training typically provided within mental health agencies actually lead to improved outcomes for clients (Rousmaniere, Swift, Babins-Wagner, Whipple, & Berzins, 2016; Watkins, 2011).

This chapter explores the efforts and subsequent results of one mental health agency seeking to improve its outcomes. This agency—Calgary Counselling Centre—has faced a number of the challenges outlined here: static funding for mental healthcare despite increases in clients seeking services; more clients seeking services and requiring subsidies to pay for their services; and limited improvement due to traditional training and supervision. The innovative ways in which the agency has responded to these pressures may serve as a model for other agencies facing the same challenges.

Calgary Counselling Centre

Calgary Counselling Centre (CCC), founded in Calgary, Canada, in 1962, has a very simple mission statement: Improving the well-being of individuals and families and strengthening communities by delivering best practices in counseling, training, and research. CCC leadership wanted to be sure that the agency was doing all that it could to uphold this mission. CCC is dependent on funding from fees for services, the United Way, the municipal government, and private donations (which come primarily from the local business community). Thus, it is vital, in CCC's view, to ensure that clients achieve the results they are looking for and to demonstrate to clients and funders that there is a valuable return on their investment in the CCC. Toward this end, CCC leadership has striven to create a culture in which the CCC staff could thrive, both clinically and personally, thereby optimizing outcomes for clients. This chapter explores these efforts and their results.

Description of CCC

CCC offers a full range of individual, couple, family, and group counseling services to the community at large. Client referrals are primarily self-referrals, but many clients are also referred from physicians, school counselors, the provincial court (for domestic violence), and child protective services. CCC has 24 full-time staff counselors. In addition, 25 trainees pursuing graduate training in the provision of psychotherapy also provide services along with 20 unlicensed providers who have finished their graduate training and are accruing supervised hours for licensure. The clinical staff at CCC are multidisciplinary, including psychologists, registered marriage and family therapists, registered social workers, pastoral counselors, and dieticians. Approximately 8,500 individuals receive services each year at CCC. The clinical team provides approximately 29,000 hours of treatment every year. Over 86,288 clients have received services at the CCC since 2000.

CCC is deeply embedded in the local community that it serves and works to provide innovative services to clients. It has established partnerships with 33 other community agencies and mental/social health organizations within the greater Calgary area. The partnerships provide referral sources and coordination of services and help avoid duplication of services. Among the family violence-serving agencies, there is a coordinating body that has a broad mandate to enhance communication and interagency collaboration and look at strategic issues that arise from time to time. The family violence community has worked this way for more than 30 years. As a result, services to victims and offenders are well coordinated, and very few have wait lists. In its depression program, CCC has used its outcome data to change the structure of therapy. Traditionally clients would receive individual therapy. The data suggest that although many individuals experience change, many leave counseling with significant levels of distress. When CCC looked at the pattern of counseling for those depression clients who did both individual and group therapy, the data suggested that clients did best when they participated in an average of six sessions of individual therapy followed by a 14-week depression group.

Engagement in training and research are core missions of the agency. Since the inception of the CCC in 1962, providing prevention programs and training counseling professionals have been core parts of the mission. Training at CCC is focused on developing and enhancing practice skills of master's level practicum students in social work, psychology, and marriage and family therapy. CCC is also a registered educational institution and provides a postgraduate training program for those who are completing their hours for licensure as psychologists, social workers, and marriage and family therapists. The focus of this program is to prepare clinicians for employment as therapists. Students in both programs attend a weekly three-hour seminar. Over the past three years, we have been transitioning the training from a traditional passive instruction-based seminar to one that is focused on experiential exercises and trainees' practice skills and on role-play situations they are likely to see in practice.

What CCC Did to Improve Outcomes

CCC's efforts to improve outcomes were based on research on the development of expertise and were conducted in collaboration with leaders in the field of psychotherapy training and supervision. The central feature of these efforts was measuring outcomes (Shimokawa, Lambert, & Smart, 2010). Once outcomes were being measured, CCC provided opportunities for feeding these outcomes back to center counseling staff. Then, with support from within the agency and through collaborations with outside consultants, CCC clinicians were provided clear instruction on ways to modify their behavior and deliberately practice therapeutic skills that have been shown empirically to improve outcomes. Details of these efforts over time are provided here in chronological order to highlight the process of change that has occurred at CCC over the past 15 years.

Prepilot Phase (2000–2004)

The notion of measuring outcomes was not embraced by the nonprofit sector in North America when initially proposed by funding bodies almost 20 years ago (Plantz, Greenway, & Hendricks, 1997). The introduction of the conversation about outcome measurement brought with it fear of potential funding cuts, limitations of service to clients, and concerns that outcomes of interest to funding bodies would not be the same as those of interest to practitioners and their clients. Some of this remains true today. Although there is increased knowledge about outcome measurement and more agencies are collecting some data, outcome measurement has, for the most part, not been included in the operational DNA of most organizations; nor is it typically infused in practitioners' clinical thinking. CCC's interest in collecting outcomes was driven internally, not by funder request or requirement. At an agency level, CCC was interested in learning more about how it could help clients benefit from services and improve the well-being of those who seek services.

The agency director and some key staff had been reading articles about the benefits of routine outcome measurement (ROM). "Here was a way," director Robbie Babins-Wagner reported, "to not only find out if we were effective but potentially improve outcomes while simultaneously preserving clinical diversity and freedom. We'd taken the research documenting equivalence between treatment approaches seriously. If dictating which treatment approaches staff would use was not viable, we had to find another way to get better results." Director of counseling Cathy Keough said, "It was clear from the research and clinical experience that our clients benefit from a variety of methods. As a result, as managers, we did not want to prescribe or proscribe *how* clinicians worked. We wanted everyone to be 'miniresearchers,' with all contributing to the body of knowledge."

CCC first became interested in developing a pilot project for the use of routine outcome measures in early 2000. (Of note, they eschewed the more commonly used term *monitoring* and instead viewed this as routine outcome *measurement*.) It commissioned some initial research to see what measures were being used in other agencies in Canada and the United States and tried to understand the process of implementation. Its pilot project began in early 2002. CCC collected data for two years, compared two measures, looked at whether the data were collectible and usable. In September 2004, it began routine collection of Outcome Questionnaire 45.2 (OQ-45; Lambert et al., 2004) and Session Rating Scale 2.1 (Johnson, 2005).

Phase I Implementation (2004–2008)

For the first 4 years, between September 2004 and September 2008, CCC simply asked counselors to collect OQ data prior to every session and Session Rating Scale data toward the end of the session. Data were used to produce statistical reports once per year at the end of December to report client outcomes. These reports were for the agency's own purposes; no external driver or funding body asked for these data. From the outset, the center made a commitment to the staff that counselor outcomes from these measures would not be used for performance management and would not appear on any yearly performance plan or report.

Overall, CCC administrators and staff were pleased with the results as they revealed that client outcomes were at least as good as benchmarks established in research (Hansen, Lambert, & Forman, 2002); at times, on average greater percentages of clients were improving or recovering based on the measure. A segment of the counseling team adopted the use of the measures and were curious about their personal outcomes. "I immediately saw the benefit," recalled Marcus Pankiew, a counselor and intern. "When I first heard about ROM at a two-day workshop, I was intrigued by the practice of getting feedback. Most important, however, when I started doing it, clients stayed engaged and I could see myself growing as a therapist." A larger segment of the team did not adopt the measures, and the leadership team was confused by the lack of adoption.

In the fall of 2008, CCC did an analysis of data, reviewed client outcomes over a 12-month period and learned, to their surprise, that it had data for only 40% of clients. Counselors were not offering the questionnaire to over 60% of the clients. CCC began some internal discussion about the poor compliance with outcome measurement and determined that it had to do something different and transformative to increase the percentage of clients who completed the measures. CCC administrators naively believed that simply bringing the research results to the counselors would increase utilization; clearly, this was not the case. When queried, those counselors not using the tools provided many reasons why (e.g., the use of the measures interfered with their counseling sessions, or negatively impacted alliance formation with their clients). "There were lots of concerns raised 'around the water fountain,'" Marcus Pankiew noted. "'More paperwork' was a common theme, as was 'the clients won't like it,' and 'I already ask for feedback, so why are we being asked to do this?'" Boswell, Kraus, Miller, and Lambert (2015) noted similar objections. After a year of discussion with CCC staff and the lack of improvement in the percentage of clients who used the measures, it was clear that something more needed to be done. The barriers to completing the measures were client literacy issues—reading levels below grade 6 and not having English as their first language.

Phase II Implementation (2008–2011)

In the fall of 2008, the policy supporting the use of measures was changed. The new policy stated explicitly that all counselors were expected to provide the measures to all clients. Counselors could not opt out of the use of the measures with the clients. The new policy added a counselor performance measure which said that counselor use of measures would be tracked and individual counselors would be held accountable for clients' completion of the measures. Thus, CCC administration began tracking the percentage of each therapist's clients who completed the measures at each counseling session; CCC administration remained committed to not using client outcomes for performance measurement. "This was a very challenging phase," Babins-Wagner remembered. "While there were virtually no complaints from consumers, it was a huge cultural shift for counselors. Routinely and formally asking for feedback was so different from what they were used to. At university, diagnosis and models of treatment are the focus. ROM shifted the focus to outcome."

Within four months of the implementation of the policy that required use of measures in all cases, almost 40% of the licensed professionals on staff resigned to either move into private practice or work for provincial health services with the explicit intention of not collecting outcomes as part of their work. Although the CCC administrators were not surprised by the resignations, they wondered if they could recruit licensed professionals to join their team. A new strategy for staff recruitment was developed with the intention of selecting staff who were interested in collecting and using outcomes in routine practice. Within 4 months, CCC was fully staffed. Looking back, Babins-Wagner concluded: "Simply put, we in management had not been clear. The staff were kind, generous people who were doing what they thought was right. It was up to us to set the standard, hold people accountable for a new standard."

From the time the measures were first introduced, clients had the choice as to whether they wanted to complete the measures. Very few clients declined the invitation to complete the measures, and most appreciated seeing the graphs of their scores as it provided them with an objective visual representation of their progress or lack thereof. Although this was a choice for clients, it was not a choice that was provided to the counselors. To work or train at the CCC, one had to complete and use the outcome data in practice. According to Babins-Wagner, "The policy became 'If you are not interested in learning or ensuring your clients get the results they are seeking, you are not a good fit.'" Director of counseling Cathy Keough similarly recalled that "the question we were faced with was how to make ROM come alive, how to integrate measurement, tracking, and feedback into every aspect of CCC practice and culture."

So, at the time of the policy change, CCC also added monthly clinical consultations with an external consultant to discuss cases and build a culture of feedback. For consultation purposes, the counseling team was divided into two groups: a staff team and a student team. Consultations were two hours long and took place over Skype. Counselors were asked to each provide a graph for a case for discussion. The graphs were provided to the counselors and were sent in advance to the consultant. In the Skype consultations, a camera with a wide-angle lens was used so that the consultant could see the team on his screen and they could all see the consultant. For the first eight months or so, the cases whose graphs were being presented for the live consultation were ones that appeared to be going well. The graphs, even though most were showing improvement, provided a context where the counselors could begin to discuss cases with the full group and begin the process of building trust and support within the consultation team. However, CCC administrators were aware that, if outcomes were to improve, focus needed to shift to cases that were not progressing. "Once again, practices were changing. We were being pushed," Staff Counselor Michele Keough recalled, "to reflect on our practice in an entirely new way. It required being vulnerable, openly sharing in front of peers what wasn't working."

Such "error-centric consultation" differs from traditional supervision in at least three key ways (Bernard & Goodyear, 2014). First, the process is focused on and organized around outcomes. A phrase commonly used in these meetings was first shared by our consultant, Scott Miller: "outcome holds process on a leash." In other words, therapeutic process (e.g., methods, strategies) was valued only to the degree it related to improving outcome. Improving results was the goal of the consultation; data were the proof of its value. These meetings were focused on clients and on working with clients in whatever way was most likely to improve their outcomes. Graphical displays of client scores on the outcome measure were the primary means of tracking progress and sharing results with other staff and the outside consultant.

The second key feature was that consultation was transtheoretical. CCC clinicians were not being trained in a particular treatment modality (e.g., cognitive behavioral therapy, psychodynamic therapy). Rather, the consultant encouraged clinicians to use whatever theoretical orientation they preferred—provided it was ethical and met community standards for practice—as long as it helped the client. When a graph showed progress was limited or a client's scores were getting worse from session to session, the consultant used the feedback-informed treatment supervision model to provide guidance (Bertolino & Miller, 2012). Briefly, this approach focuses on aspects of therapy common across theoretical orientations (e.g., mutually and collaboratively determined goals and means, core relational processes [i.e., empathy, respect, genuineness], and connection of methods and therapist role with client culture, values, and preferences). Typically, the consultant worked with the counselor to identify changes in therapeutic process that would increase clients' engagement in whatever specific therapeutic actions the given theory involved.

The third key feature, one that is described in more detail later, was focusing on cases that were not making progress. Importantly, this did not mean focusing on cases that merely had interactional difficulties (e.g., interpersonally challenging cases) but rather those in which the client's OQ scores were not improving. "Other avenues for sharing successes were already, and had always been, available," observed Cathy Keough. "The purpose of consultation was to get help with those clients we were not helping."

At the eight-month point, the CCC administrators became aware that some therapists were presenting only those cases that were progressing well. At that point, the administrators put in place a new policy that required that counselors present cases that, based on the data and graphs, were not going well. The consultant was well versed in the OQ and asked specific questions about the progress or lack thereof in each specific case. Over time, the case consultations became more and more focused on what was not working well in the therapy or in the relationship between the clinician and the client. As counselors took risks and implemented suggestions discussed in the consultations, client scores began to improve. These positive changes impacted the use of measures in other cases and across counselors in both consultation groups. This was a very slow and deliberate process. Staff Counselor Michele Keough recalled, "Even if you are willing, the process is challenging. There you are, in front of everyone, with 'no clothes on.' It requires a shift in what it means to be 'competent,' going from being able to explain what and why you are doing what you are doing, from attributing blame to yourself or the client when it doesn't work, to constantly reflecting on how you can do better."

With the implementation of these changes, once again some staff left because of their dislike of collecting and using outcome data. This time, only four staff left, less than half the size of the previous group. It is interesting to note that while CCC was going through these changes, initial data suggested that overall agency outcomes were improving (perhaps, as will be discussed, because they were losing lower-performing therapists; Imel, Sheng, Baldwin, & Atkins, 2015). CCC had the opportunity to further refine its recruitment strategy and were pleased to discover that the number of qualified applicants for vacancies exceeded available spaces.

Phase III Implementation (2011–2015)

As CCC administrators began to see small changes in both their counseling team and their student team, they became more deliberate in the structure of the consultations and began developing themes for them. CCC administrators asked that counselors bring cases that were not improving and that focused on depression, relationship distress, anxiety, poor alliance, and more. As the conversations in the consultations became more focused, counselors became more engaged in them. Another factor that led to increased engagement occurred when counselors started using the feedback they received in consultations. As the feedback helped them produce results, they slowly became more open to using the specific skills in other clinical situations. When asked what accounted for the change, Cathy Keough reported, "I think it's due to the consistent message staff were receiving from management and the support we were providing. Policy was lined up with practice. Everyone was now using ROM, bringing cases, sharing their struggles. Everyone, from line staff to senior manager, was equal. From that emerged open, nonjudgmental conversations and curiosity."

During this phase, CCC became increasingly deliberate about all its activities related to outcomes. Administrators began redeveloping their internal software systems to assist staff in managing caseloads with a focus on client outcomes. Staff teams were engaged in the development of software tools and signals that allowed them to focus on metrics they understood. For example, staff developed *clinical dashboards* that summarized each therapist's clinical outcomes in comparison with the average outcomes from all of the therapists at CCC. (See Figure 10.1) The dashboards are given to staff every 4 months as a tool to gauge their own effectiveness.

As staff began to experience the benefits of these outcome-focused changes directly, the culture of feedback began to take deeper roots within the agency. On this score, it is interesting to note that nearly all of the staff contacted regarding the implementation of ROM at CCC for this chapter concluded the interview by asking "Did you get what you needed?" and "Is there anything else I can do to be of help?"

Changes in Outcomes at CCC over Time

CCC made a committed and concerted effort over the course of a decade. These efforts were not without costs, both financial and in terms of staff turnover. Were these efforts worth the costs? Did these changes actually impact client outcomes?

A recent study examined outcomes at the CCC over the past seven years during which they were consistently measured (Goldberg, Babins-Wagner et al., 2016). This study aimed to address the basic question of whether outcomes, in fact, improved as a result of the efforts at CCC. Further, if such improvements were observed, the study explored whether it was due to the therapists showing improved outcomes over time (i.e., within-therapist improvement) or whether the therapists hired later in time were more effective than the therapists hired earlier (i.e., the agency was hiring better therapists or losing poorer-performing therapists).

Outcome Summary
Female Post Graduate Student
Closed Cases January 1, 2015 – August 31, 2015

Counsellor:

Average Number of Sessions (Single Sessions Included)				Average Number of Sessions (Excluding Single Sessions)		
Number of Cases	Average Number of Sessions	CCC Average Residents 2015		Number of Cases	Average Number of Sessions	CCC Average Residents 2015
86	5.37	5.26		69	6.45	6.41

*Average number of sessions based on clients with First and Last OQ data

Average Change Score

	Your Scores for 2015	CCC Average for Residents 2015
Average first session OQ	73.81	74.76
Average last session OQ	57.26	60.61
Average Change Score	−16.55	−14.16

Effect Size

		CCC Average Effect Size (Agency)
Your Effect Size for 2015	0.58	0.55
Severity Adjusted Effect Size	0.60	0.50

Reminders:

*In instances when there are less than 30 cases, the effect size calculation is not valid.

Reliable Change Score (RCI) for the OQ is 14

Effect size: "Effect size" is simply a way of quantifying the size of the difference between groups. It is particularly valuable for quantifying the effectiveness of a particular intervention, relative to some comparison. Effect size is an important tool in reporting and interpreting effectiveness.

Relative Size of Effect Size
negligible effect (>= −0.15 and <.15)
small effect (>=.15 and <.40)
medium effect (>=.40 and <.75)
large effect (>=.75 and <1.10)

Figure 10.1 Clinical dashboard.

At the outset of this study, there was no promise that outcomes would improve. In fact, the preponderance of the evidence—from the psychotherapy literature as well as from the expertise literature—suggested that psychotherapists would not be likely to improve over time. Research on expertise suggests that expertise can develop when: (a) the environment is predictable and outcomes are explicit, and (b) there are opportunities to learn from decisions, based on having access to quality information (Shanteau, 1992). These kinds of conditions are present in some occupations, such as accounting, mathematics, and astronomy. Indeed, individuals in these professions do improve as they gain experience (Shanteau, 1992). These conditions may not be present for therapists, however. Of course, psychotherapy can be far from predictable. And psychotherapists rarely have high-quality feedback with which to assess the decisions they make in treatment (Tracey, Wampold, Lichtenberg, & Goodyear, 2014).

Empirically, there is little evidence that therapists in general tend to improve over time. A recent longitudinal study in a large sample of clients ($n = 6,591$) and psychotherapists ($n = 170$) suggested that therapists on average do not improve simply by gaining increased experience working with clients (Goldberg, Rousmaniere et al., 2016). In fact, results from this study showed small decreases in outcomes across time, suggesting that, on average, these clinicians showed poorer outcomes as experience accrued. In this particular sample, clinicians even had access to their clients' self-reported symptoms, suggesting that mere access to outcomes is insufficient to guarantee improvements over time.

Nonetheless, CCC was interested in seeing if their outcomes improved across time. To do this, CCC collected seven years of data, representing 5,128 clients seen by 153 therapists. These clients completed the Outcome Questionnaire 45.2 (OQ-45; Lambert et al., 2004) before each session of therapy. The OQ-45 is a 45-item self-report measure that was designed to capture changes that occur during the course of therapy. The measure has items representing three areas: (a) Symptom Distress (e.g., "I feel no interest in things," "I feel nervous"); (b) Interpersonal Relations (e.g., "I am concerned about family troubles," "I have trouble getting along with friends and close acquaintances"); and (c) Social Role Performance (e.g., "I feel that I am not doing well at work/school," "I feel stressed at work/school"). The sample used in the analysis was in the clinical range at the beginning of treatment, meaning that patients' OQ-45 scores were similar to those drawn from clinical populations. To be sure that each therapist included had enough clients to get a good estimate of their outcomes, a minimum of 10 clients per therapist was required.

A series of statistical models was used to examine changes in outcomes across time. The first of these asked the primary question of whether outcomes improved across time within the agency overall. Results from this initial model suggested that outcomes at the CCC were improving each year. That is to say, clients who came to the CCC in 2014 would be predicted to have larger gains over the course of treatment than those who came in 2010. This was, of course, good news.

This initial finding was promising and provided the warrant for seeking to understand more deeply what may be accounting for this improvement over time. The question of interest was whether improvements in outcome were occurring in individual therapists. A previous study using this same method in another agency suggested that therapists do not necessarily improve simply due to gaining more experience (Goldberg, Rousmaniere et al., 2016). In the CCC data, however, therapists *were* getting better over time. According to the results of this model, a client seen by a given therapist in the therapist's fifth year at the agency would be expected to show larger drops in reported symptoms over the course of therapy than a client seen by that same therapist in the therapist's first year at the agency.

Although this result suggested that the improvement within the agency may be attributed to the therapists improving over time, it was important to also explore the possibility that the agency's outcomes were improving simply due to hiring higher-performing therapists (or to losing lower-performing therapists; Imel et al., 2015). To explore this question, another analysis was conducted that predicted clients' outcomes from their therapists' start date at the agency. The results from this model did not suggest that the therapists who began at CCC later had higher overall outcomes than those who began there earlier. Thus, it appeared that the agency-level improvement may be best explained by the therapists themselves improving over time rather than by the hiring of therapists who began as high-performing (or losing therapists who began as low-performing).

Although the results from the CCC represent the outcomes of just one agency, they prove an important point: Therapists *can* improve over time. Improving over time is far from promised in the profession of psychotherapy (Goldberg, Rousmaniere et al., 2016; Tracey et al., 2014). Moreover, the focused efforts taken at the CCC provide some clear suggestions as to what an agency can do to improve outcomes.

Costs to Implement

CCC is a success story. The agency was committed to improving outcomes, put efforts into place to do so, and has demonstrated that its clients have benefited as a result. This rosy picture, however, can belie the considerable costs these efforts can exact at both the management and the staff levels.

For Managers

Babins-Wagner was fortunate to have a board and a close circle of colleagues who were similarly interested in measuring outcomes and using these data to improve practice at the CCC. These efforts were not made in response to external pressure but rather were motivated from within the agency (i.e., they were more intrinsically motivated; Ryan & Deci, 2000). Yet the implementation of these efforts required immense commitment. Overall, the change management required exceeded everyone's expectations; clinicians seem to be socialized through their graduate training to believe that they know what works for clients, and shifting this perception took considerable effort on the part of management. As noted, the decision to make the use of outcome measures mandatory at every session was a significant practical and philosophical decision as the CCC team. Clients as well as staff were impacted when 40% of the staff left CCC following the implementation of this policy. Sticking with the plan when 40% of the staff left CCC was tough; management had to affirm its commitment to moving the agency in this direction. CCC management had, to its advantage, the chief executive's experience and familiarity with psychotherapy research coupled with preliminary results from the CCC's data suggesting that clients were making progress with the implementation of ROM. These initial data were critical in CCC management being able to make the case, for itself, that data had to be collected for all clients who provided consent.

Along with the labor (emotional and otherwise) associated with implementing an (at first) controversial policy change, CCC management were also charged with clarifying how ROM would not be used. Deciding to not use counselor outcomes for performance measurement was a critical decision, and one that required time and energy. Managers had to attend closely to the way that language was used to describe these policies. For example, as noted previously, CCC uses the term *outcome measurement* rather than *outcome monitoring* in order to avoid the connotation of "monitoring" with performance evaluation. Working to create a culture of learning and change took precisely this kind of attention and sensitivity on the part of CCC management.

In addition to the costs of time, energy, and attention associated with implementing a policy change, there is also the very real financial burden of providing the infrastructure for measuring outcomes, the time for reviewing these outcomes, and the resources for bringing in consultants who are well versed in using outcomes as a part of training.

For Staff

The staff turnover that occurred at the CCC during the various phases of the implementation of outcome measurement is indicative of the costs to staff. In 2008, when CCC changed its policy to require the measurement outcomes for all clients, almost 40% of the licensed professionals on staff resigned. These clinicians felt that the measuring of their outcomes by the agency was not in their own best interests. These clinicians did not perceive these efforts as being designed to support their own growth and improve outcomes. Similar staff turnover occurred when agency policy changed again to require that clinicians present cases that were not improving during consultation meetings.

It is worth noting that CCC staff members certainly are not alone in their discomfort at having their outcomes measured. Boswell et al. (2015) highlighted seven practical and philosophical obstacles that frequently arise during attempts to implement outcome measurement. Of the seven obstacles Boswell et al. recognize, perhaps the most germane to the CCC staff was fear and mistrust regarding why outcomes were being measured and how this information would be used. Many clinicians value the freedom and autonomy inherent in clinical work and therefore dislike external control exerted by agency administrators through measuring outcomes. Clinicians may not appreciate what they perceive as "big brother" efforts (p. 12) in the form of administrators measuring their clients' symptoms. Further, clinicians may dislike having their clients' outcomes compared with other therapists', in part out of fear of appearing incompetent (Youn, Kraus, & Castonguay, 2012). Bear in mind that these reactions occurred at the CCC even though there was explicit reassurance from CCC administrators that outcomes would not be used for performance evaluation.

Possibility of Change

The costs outlined here are very real. And, more broadly, one can point to significant dangers in moving mental healthcare toward a culture of accountability through outcome measuring (Imel et al., 2015). Yet the data from CCC are compelling—clients showed larger benefits from psychotherapy over the years that CCC administrators, supervisors, and clinicians worked together to improve outcomes. And, importantly, these gains appeared within the therapist, indicating that therapists themselves were improving with the kind of outcome measuring, supervision, and the culture of feedback developed at CCC.

It is important to highlight that these cultural (and quantitative) changes at CCC did not occur overnight. As described, there was a gradual shift in attitude toward feedback-informed treatment. A few major shifts were vital in this process. The first was staff members seeing that outcomes were truly not going to be used against them. Although staff members had been reassured that this was the case, it was necessary for them to see their outcomes measured and not experience negative consequences. The second was seeing that outcome measurement could be helpful. This shift occurred most strikingly through meetings with the outside consultant, in which the clinicians at CCC were able not only to see their outcomes but have them explored by the group in ways that supported their growth as psychotherapists. Staff members were able to learn from the feedback and were given concrete ways of moving the work forward. Slowly, and over the years, staff members were able to see the fruits of these efforts, with clients showing gains in treatment in cases that otherwise seemed hopeless. Thus, CCC staff developed an increased trust in the process of outcome measurement coupled with feedback-informed supervision. The natural hesitation and resistance gave way to a curiosity as credibility increased.

Reality Check

The specific costs to managers and staff of creating the kind of work environment developed at the CCC can explain why so few agencies go this direction. Many agencies are simply trying to stay afloat: to keep in the black financially, to avoid lawsuits, to retain staff (and administrators' mental health) in a profession at risk for burnout (Bernard & Goodyear, 2014). In the spirit of acknowledging what might get in the way of making change, a deeper resistance to these efforts is also worth highlighting. That force is human beings' natural tendency to resist self-regulation and self-control. Muraven and Baumeister (2000) defined self-control as "the exertion of control over the self by the self" (p. 247). They noted that in the absence of self-control, individuals carry out the "normal, typical, or desired behavior" (p. 247). In contrast, self-control "involves overriding or inhibiting competing urges, behaviors, or desires" (p. 247). Decades of research in social psychology has explored the vital importance of self-control for so many human behaviors (including most social interactions) as well as the significant costs of engaging self-control (Hagger, Wood, Stiff, & Chatzisarantis, 2010; Inzlicht, Schmeichel, & Macrae, 2014; Muraven, Tice, & Baumeister, 1998). Put simply, it is often easier to continue doing things the way we tend to do them (i.e., the normal, typical way) than to change. Changing our behavior requires an investment of psychological resources, and we, as humans, tend to be motivated to avoid this when possible.

Clearly, invoking the specter of our limited self-regulatory resources is not intended to say change is not possible. Indeed, this chapter is founded on the basic assumption that change *is* possible: for clients, for staff, for agencies. And, likewise, social psychological research also suggests that factors can be implemented to protect against self-regulatory exhaustion. These factors include providing motivational incentives (i.e., rewards), training that promotes increased self-regulation, and glucose supplementation (Hagger et al., 2010). We do not expect that mental health agencies will begin pairing their outcome-measuring protocols with snacks to increase blood glucose levels anytime soon. However, it is worth considering ways in which staff involvement in the potentially arduous and taxing process of improving outcomes can be rewarded. Indeed, the shift discussed in this chapter during which clinicians began to see improved outcomes as a result of the training efforts is a clear example of a motivational incentive.

Summary and Conclusion: A Culture of Excellence

The last 10 years have been an important time for the CCC. Against a backdrop of significant challenges that are facing mental health agencies, particularly agencies focused on the provision of psychotherapy, CCC has devoted itself to improving outcomes for the clients it serves. Managers within CCC engaged in several specific steps in this process, based on research on both the development of expertise (Tracey et al., 2014) and the factors that make psychotherapy work (Wampold & Imel, 2015). The key components of these efforts have involved implementing ROM; providing feedback to clinicians on their clients' outcomes; and giving staff regular, ongoing opportunities to receive supervision and training focused on these outcomes.

The efforts paid off: Over the last seven years, outcomes have improved at the CCC. And, even when outcomes are examined within a given therapist's caseload, there is evidence that the therapists themselves are getting better outcomes over time (Goldberg, Babins-Wagner et al., 2016).

These clinical and training successes have not, however, been without significant challenges, both for agency administrators and for staff clinicians. They have required a committed effort, attention, and investment of time and financial resources from agency administrators. Administrators have had to weather staff turnover and discomfort as new policies have been written to support this process. Likewise, CCC staff have undergone the sometimes uncomfortable shift toward having their outcomes measured, followed by sharing their outcomes with their peers and supervisors, followed by sharing their cases that were not progressing. And staff have invested their own time, self-regulatory resources, and mental and psychological energy in working to learn from this process and change their practice with clients. Some staff members decided that these changes were too uncomfortable for them to remain at CCC while others embraced the opportunities for clinical skill development. In short, CCC administrators and staff have grown and have experienced the struggle and rewards that inevitably accompany this process.

In summary, CCC provides a clear and we feel compelling case study of how an agency may go about trying to improve. Further, CCC provides clear evidence that these efforts can make a difference, for clients as well as for staff. These changes, like so many changes that occur in the context of psychotherapy, took time, dedication, patience, and effort. This is hard work, but it is unquestionably work well worth the investment.

Questions from the Editors

Question #1. You describe consultation with your staff as having begun during Phase II Implementation (2008–2011) with an external consultant who worked via teleconferencing with groups of CCC staff. As you go forward from here, what would you envision as an optimal supervision or consultation model? Specifically, what are the relative merits and limitations of using an external supervisor/consultant versus someone who is internal to the agency? And regardless of which seems the better fit for you, what are some of the considerations you would have in choosing a supervisor or consultant?

Answer from Authors: At this point, we have no plan to end the external consultations. Although we don't "need" to use an external consultant (there are CCC staff with sufficient expertise to provide consultation), using an external consultant has some advantages. For one, this individual is less immersed in the ongoing, day-to-day operation of CCC and is therefore more naturally able to see broader perspectives. Having an individual whose primary professional interest is training also allows a level of clarity, a focus on process as opposed to content, and a model for how supervision/consultation can be done. The cross-fertilization we have had from having an outside person involved in this way has been valuable and generally well received. In addition, an outside consultant, not being a local supervisor, can at times have the license to take greater risks in the kinds of feedback provided to staff, which has been important. We have not yet identified criteria for supervisors at CCC, but we expect these qualities will be similar to those of good clinicians: curiosity, flexibility, clarity of personal practice framework, good boundaries, understanding the difference between process and content, and having an interest in focusing on process (Ackerman & Hilsenroth, 2003).

As we move forward, we have a number of strategies in development to support our supervision framework. By early 2017, we plan to have an explicit CCC framework for supervision in place. The framework will outline a process and structure for supervision at CCC that is aligned with best practices from the research literature. In particular, supervision will be focused on assisting the supervisee with cases that are not progressing as identified by our software algorithms (Shimokawa et al., 2010). It will also focus on ensuring that for cases that are progressing well, a clear plan toward termination is established. Therapy sessions with stuck cases will be digitally recorded so that they can be reviewed by supervisees and supervisors. In addition to identifying cases that are not progressing as they might, we are working to identify supervisees who are not progressing as we would hope so that we can assist their skill development with live supervision and skill coaching. Supervision will be focused on client outcomes (i.e., graphs) and increasing the skill and capacity of counselors to work with a variety of cases with different presenting problems. Even outside of the ongoing supervision with our external consultant, all CCC supervisors will be expected to support and adhere to this new framework. We will test this framework for eight to 12 months and then revisit the process and structure and edit as required.

Question #2. Also, what you describe is a group format for supervision or consultation. From an agency management perspective, what is the feasibility of moving beyond the group format to provide more focused training or coaching to individuals or smaller groups?

Answer from Authors: Yes, we plan to do both. We currently provide both individual and group supervision through our local CCC supervisors (which is in addition to our use of our external consultant). However, at this time, most supervision is "supportive" and administrative (e.g., is the counselor's paperwork being done as expected). Supervision is not sufficiently focused on cases and especially not focused on cases that are not on track toward a positive outcome. By early 2017, we plan to have electronic dashboards in place on our intranet that will provide each supervisor and counselor with the status of all open cases. The dashboard will form the basis of decision making on clinical priorities for supervision. We also have plans to individualize supervision and training for each trainee and counselor so that their specific needs can be met. As mentioned previously, one way we plan to do this is through tracking clinicians' outcomes and providing additional supervisory support (e.g., review of recorded sessions) when indicated. We are also planning to reboot a project we started a few years back where we collected measures from supervisees' regarding their experience of supervision. This project was suspended due to supervisors' discomfort hearing potentially critical feedback from their supervisees. Incidentally, this was quite consistent with our initial experience when we introduced outcome measures for patients to complete. We expect to have these supervisee ratings reintroduced in either January or May 2017, consistent with our intention of building a culture of feedback at several levels within the agency.

Question #3. You also report having a relatively large number of trainees. To what extent does working with them seem to have induced a contagion effect on the training programs that send you those students so that the way their training is conducted has been affected? If so, have you noticed any particular factors that seemed to particularly encourage this?

Answer from Authors: As we have relatively little interaction with the training programs that send us students, it is hard to assess the degree of "contagion" that has occurred within those training programs. There has, however, been some measure of contagion within our agency from trainees to staff. Trainees have been, in general, ahead of the staff counselors in their interest and adoption of the external consultation model (i.e., feedback-informed treatment), and this is at a time where there is good adoption by the counseling staff. We hope that the contagion effect is functioning to support the further development of both clinical and supervisory skills on the team of staff counselors.

It is worth pointing out that trainees are well informed in the interview phase about our use of feedback-informed treatment within CCC and that tracking outcomes is mandatory. We also talk about the benefits of these practices to them and their clients and begin coaching in the use of the measures from the first session onward. That is not to say that some trainees do not struggle with the measures or the philosophy of their use. As these practices have become more integrated into the culture at CCC, there is more positive feedback about their use. Trainees also seem to like the fact that all the outcome scales are now completed on tablets, and the graphs are automatically generated and sent to the printer for use with clients in session.

Question #4. Your consultant does not encourage therapists to employ any particular theoretical model. Please comment on what you have observed in terms of the longer-term effects of that consultation on the evolution of therapists' models and styles as they focus on outcomes rather than processes. (Your observation that "outcome holds process on a leash" is so vivid.) For example, one possibility would be that each therapist becomes increasingly unique in style/model as she or he focuses on outcomes. Yet the other therapists in the consultation group and the consultant inevitably bring perspectives and emphases they could offer instead, increasing convergence in models across therapists.

Answer from Authors: Based on the philosophy of CCC, we feel it is not the consultant's place to determine what theoretical models the agency and our staff use. We have observed, however, that consultation has generally supported the therapists to be more grounded in whatever particular theoretical orientation they tend to use (perhaps leading to an increasingly unique style, as you suggested). This is not always the case—at times consultation has encouraged therapists to question their own use of a particular model with a particular client and attempt something new (sometimes leading to increasing convergence, as you noted, when therapists adopt styles or models from their peers or the consultant). The modeling of different perspectives brings forth a richness of ideas and perspectives that can bring new information forward to the therapist and opens space for consideration of new strategies to help a client who is stuck and not progressing. The comparison of theoretical models is not a primary factor in the consultation, and the intention is that everyone feels respected for their choice of model.

References

Bernard, J. M., & Goodyear, R. K. (2014). *Fundamentals of clinical supervision* (5th ed.). Upper Saddle River, NJ: Merrill.

Bertolino, B., & Miller, S. D. (Eds.). (2012). *ICCE manuals on feedback-informed treatment* (Vols. 1–6). Chicago, IL: ICCE Press.

Boswell, J. F., Kraus, D. R., Miller, S. D., & Lambert, M. J. (2015). Implementing routine outcome monitoring in clinical practice: Benefits, challenges, and solutions. *Psychotherapy Research, 25*(1), 6–19. doi:10.1080/10503307.2013.817696

Chambless, D. L., Baker, M. J., Baucom, D. H., Beutler, L. E., Calhoun, K. S., Crits-Christoph, P., . . . Woody, S. R. (1998). Update on empirically validated therapies, II. *Clinical Psychologist, 51*(1), 3–16.

Chambless, D. L., & Hollon, S. D. (1998). Defining empirically supported therapies. *Journal of Consulting and Clinical Psychology, 66*(1), 7–18. doi:10.1037/0022-006X.66.1.7

Fisher, E. S., & Shortell, S. M. (2010). Accountable care organizations: Accountable for what, to whom, and how. *Journal of the American Medical Association, 304*(15), 1715–1716.

Goldberg, S. B., Babins-Wagner, R., Rousmaniere, T., Berzins, S., Hoyt, W. T., Whipple, J. L., . . . Wampold, B. E. (2016). Creating a climate for therapist improvement: A case study of an agency focused on outcomes and deliberate practice. *Psychotherapy, 53*(3), 367–375. doi:10 .1037/pst0000060

Goldberg, S. B., Rousmaniere, T., Miller, S. D., Whipple, J., Nielsen, S. L., Hoyt, W. T., & Wampold, B. E. (2016). Do psychotherapists improve with time and experience? A longitudinal analysis of outcomes in a clinical setting. *Journal of Counseling Psychology, 63*(1), 1–11. doi:10.1037/cou0000131

Hagger, M. S., Wood, C., Stiff, C., & Chatzisarantis, N.L.D. (2010). Ego depletion and the strength model of self-control: A meta-analysis. *Psychological Bulletin, 136*(4), 495–525. doi:10.1037/a0019486

Hansen, N. B., Lambert, M. J., & Forman, E. M. (2002). The psychotherapy dose-response effect and its implications for treatment delivery services. *Clinical Psychology: Science and Practice, 9,* 329–343.

Imel, Z. E., Sheng, E., Baldwin, S. A., & Atkins, D. C. (2015). Removing very low-performing therapists: A simulation of performance-based retention in psychotherapy. *Psychotherapy, 52*(3), 329–336.

Inzlicht, M., Schmeichel, B. J., & Macrae, C. N. (2014). Why self-control seems (but may not be) limited. *Trends in Cognitive Sciences, 18*(3), 127–133. doi:10.1016/j.tics.2013.12.009

Johnson, L. (2005). *Psychotherapy in the age of accountability.* New York, NY: Norton.

Lambert, M. J., Morton, J. J., Hatfield, D., Harmon, C., Hamilton, S., Reid, R. C., . . . Burlingame, G. B. (2004). *Administration and scoring manual for the Outcome Questionnaire-45.* Orem, UT: American Professional Credentialing Services.

McHugh, R. K., Whitton, S. W., Peckham, A. D., Welge, J. A., & Otto, M. W. (2013). Patient preference for psychological vs. pharmacological treatment of psychiatric disorders: A meta-analytic review. *Journal of Clinical Psychiatry, 74*(6), 595–602. doi:10.4088/JCP.12r07757

Muraven, M., & Baumeister, R. F. (2000). Self-regulation and depletion of limited resources: Does self-control resemble a muscle? *Psychological Bulletin, 126*(2), 247–259. doi:10.1037//0033-2909.126.2.247

Muraven, M., Tice, D. M., & Baumeister, R. F. (1998). Self-control as a limited resource: Regulatory depletion patterns. *Journal of Personality and Social Psychology, 74*(3), 774–789.

National Alliance on Mental Illness. (2011). *State mental health cuts: The continuing crisis.* Arlington, VA: Author.

Olfson, M., & Marcus, S. C. (2010). National trends in outpatient psychotherapy. *American Journal of Psychiatry, 167*(12), 1456–1463.

Plantz, M. C., Greenway, M. T., & Hendricks, M. (1997). Outcome measurement: Showing results in the nonprofit sector. *New Directions for Evaluation, 75,* 15–30.

Proctor, E. K., Knudsen, K. J., Fedoravicius, N., Hovmand, P., Rosen, A., & Perron, B. (2007). Implementation of evidence-based practice in community behavioral health: Agency director perspectives. *Administration and Policy in Mental Health and Mental Health Services Research, 34,* 479–488. doi:10.1007/s10488-007-0129-8

Resick, P. A., Nishith, P., Weaver, T. L., Astin, M. C., & Feuer, C. A. (2002). A comparison of cognitive-processing therapy with prolonged exposure and a waiting condition for the treatment of chronic posttraumatic stress disorder in female rape victims. *Journal of Consulting and Clinical Psychology, 70*(4), 867–897.

Rousmaniere, T. G., Swift, J. K., Babins-Wagner, R., Whipple, J. L., & Berzins, S. (2016). Supervisor variance in psychotherapy outcome in routine practice. *Psychotherapy Research, 26*(2), 195–205. doi:10.1080/10503307.2014.963730

Ryan, R. M., & Deci, E. L. (2000). Self-determination theory and the facilitation of intrinsic motivation, social development, and well-being. *American Psychologist, 55*(1), 68–78.

Seligman, M.E.P. (1995). The effectiveness of psychotherapy: The *Consumer Reports* study. *American Psychologist, 50*(12), 965–974.

Shanteau, J. (1992). Competence in experts: The role of task characteristics. *Organizational Behavior and Human Decision Processes, 53*, 252–266.

Shimokawa, K., Lambert, M. J., & Smart, D. W. (2010). Enhancing treatment outcome of patients at risk of treatment failure: Meta-analytic and mega-analytic review of a psychotherapy quality assurance system. *Journal of Consulting and Clinical Psychology, 78*(3), 298–311. doi:10.1037/a0019247

Tracey, T.J.G., Wampold, B. E., Lichtenberg, J. W., & Goodyear, R. K. (2014). Expertise in psychotherapy: An elusive goal? *American Psychologist, 69*(3), 218–229. doi:10.1037/a0035099

Wampold, B., & Imel, Z. E. (2015). *The great psychotherapy debate: The evidence for what makes psychotherapy work* (2nd ed.). New York, NY: Routledge.

Watkins, C. E. (2011). Does psychotherapy supervision contribute to patient outcomes? Considering thirty years of research. *Clinical Supervisor, 30*(2), 235–256. doi:10.1080/07325223.2011.619417

Youn, S. J., Kraus, D. R., & Castonguay, L. G. (2012). The treatment outcome package: Facilitating practice and clinically relevant research. *Psychotherapy, 49*(2), 115–122.

11

The Ongoing Evolution of Continuing Education

Past, Present, and Future

Jennifer M. Taylor and Greg J. Neimeyer

Participation in lifelong learning activities serves as the bridge that joins graduate training with ongoing professional competence. But just as the landscapes of graduate training and professional practice have been transformed across time, so too has the bridge that joins them. In this chapter, we discuss the evolution of the processes and procedures that jointly constitute what can be called continuing professional development (CPD), a loosely federated, and continuously evolving, set of practices that range widely in their form and function but collectively serve to maintain and enhance professional competence.

We begin this chapter with a brief history of formal continuing education (CE), the primary regulatory form of lifelong learning, and distinguish it from a range of related practices that together support our ongoing efforts to remain current and competent in relation to the services we provide. We then examine contemporary best practices before describing what CPD could become if it is to more fully realize its potential to maximize ongoing professional development and enhance the delivery of services and clinical outcomes associated with psychotherapy services.

Laying the Groundwork

At the outset, it is important to distinguish among, and tease apart, several key terms while discussing the processes and procedures that sustain and enhance ongoing professional competence; these include the concepts of lifelong learning, continuing professional development, and continuing education. One way to think of these three processes is within the context of a Venn diagram with three concentric circles. Lifelong learning (LLL) is the largest of the three circles, and subsumes the other two. LLL can be defined as an active, continuous quest for knowledge, growth, and development (Taylor & Neimeyer, 2015a), and it draws from the full range human experience. LLL runs the gamut from the most deliberate, focused, intentional efforts to learn (as in learning a new language), to those

The Cycle of Excellence: Using Deliberate Practice to Improve Supervision and Training,
First Edition. Edited by Tony Rousmaniere, Rodney K. Goodyear, Scott D. Miller, and Bruce E. Wampold.
© 2017 John Wiley & Sons, Ltd. Published 2017 by John Wiley & Sons, Ltd.

inchoate lessons that are associated with increased "worldliness" (as in a cultural immersion experience), "maturity" (e.g., breadth of vision), or "wisdom" (Skovolt, 2011). In its broadest form, LLL can be understood as a series of regulated efforts to profit from personal experiences in ways that enrich, enhance, or extend an understanding of the world and more capable navigation though it. Many therapists nominate their clinical experience itself as the critical crucible in which they forge much of their clinically relevant LLL, with accumulating experience giving rise to "clinical wisdom" (Skovolt & Starkey, 2012) over the course of time.

By contrast, continuing professional development (CPD) can be understood as a loosely federated assortment of processes and procedures with the express goal of maintaining or enhancing professional functioning or competence (Neimeyer & Taylor, 2014). CPD is a narrower concept than LLL, not only because it is ordinarily focused on professional values, knowledge, skills, and capacities but because it targets specific outcomes (e.g., increased competence and enhanced service delivery). Although they share common goals, these CPD activities can vary markedly in their degree of formality. They can be informal (e.g., reading professional journals or books), incidental (secondary to some other, primary purpose, like the learning that comes from reviewing a manuscript or teaching a course), or formal (e.g., the completion of a course or a certification program). But in all cases, the purposes, processes, and procedures that constitute CPD are more focused on professional processes and outcomes than in LLL, locating CPD as a circle within the broader circle of LLL that subsumes it.

In this chapter, we concentrate on CPD and one of the primary mechanisms associated with it: formal continuing education (CE). CE can be understood as a regulatory expression of CPD that is designed to support a "compact of competence" between therapists and the public(s) we serve. As such, CE has specific objectives as well as recognized processes and procedures associated with accountability.

The American Psychological Association (APA; 2015) defines CE as

> an ongoing process consisting of formal learning activities that (1) are relevant to psychological practice, education, and science, (2) enable psychologists to keep pace with emerging issues and technologies, and (3) allow psychologists to maintain, develop, and increase competencies in order to improve services to the public and enhance contributions to the profession. (p. 2)

These objectives inform and constrain the processes and procedures associated with formal CE. Formal CE commonly situates the therapist in the role of the learner, provides an opportunity to reflect on or evaluate what is learned, and engages the learner in evaluating the nature of the learning experience as well so that it can be continuously improved in future iterations. Formal CE concludes with formal documentation of the completion of a CE activity, provided by an approved agency or provider, under the auspices of an accrediting organization, such as the APA, the National Board of Certified Counselors, or the National Association of Social Work. Specific processes, procedures, and requirements for CE vary widely across disciplines and around the world.

Continuing Professional Development: Early Groundwork

Attention to issues of ongoing professional competence varies by profession; each has a distinct trajectory in relation to the evolution of its practices and mechanisms of accountability. As an example, early in the development of professional psychology, Hunter (1941) issued a call to the profession to address issues related to continuing professional competence. When the initial proposal for an official code of ethics for psychology was first published in 1947, the foremost responsibility that it identified was to provide competent services to the public (see APA, 1947). This ethical imperative naturally spawned mechanisms designed to fulfill that objective, which in turn gave rise to the concept of formal CE and the various regulatory mechanisms designed to support its implementation and objectives.

In 1957, Maryland enacted the first CE mandate for psychologists in the United States, intending it as a mechanism to ensure continuing professional competence. Two years later, the first code of ethics was formally recognized by the APA. Its second principle addressed the importance of professional competence to the integrity of the field, thus setting the stage for the field to consider methods for ensuring this competence across the course of the professional life span. Issues of knowledge obsolescence were already gaining attention across a broad spectrum of professional services as the era of accountability associated with social activism and the demand for professional regulation grew. Citizens urged mental health providers to demonstrate their professional competence, the special skills and competencies associated with specialized knowledge, and the advanced application of that knowledge in effective psychological practice.

An era of professional accountability was emerging. In the early 1970s, the Association of State and Provincial Psychology Boards (ASPPB), urged member boards to create CE requirements for license renewal. By 1975, three states had adopted CE mandates, and one year later, the APA Board of Directors voted to develop a program for CE within its central office. Nineteen states had adopted CE mandates within the field of psychology by 1990 (VandeCreek, Knapp, & Brace, 1990), and the number of state licensing boards adopting similar mandates continued to grow to the point where 46 U.S. licensing jurisdictions now have CE mandates for psychology license renewal. Although each of the allied mental health professions has a distinctive trajectory in relation to the development of its CE requirements, they share to this day the absence of the uniformity and universal mandates associated with other health-related professions, such as medicine, nursing, and pharmacy (Neimeyer & Taylor, 2014).

Because individual state licensing boards retain sovereignty in relation to CE regulations for licensees within their jurisdictions, there is little consistency in CE requirements across different states or professions (Adams & Sharkin, 2012). Some states require school counselors to engage in specific coursework in areas like school violence prevention while other states allow full flexibility in courses taken. And whereas the United States has some mandates on CE for mental health providers, other countries, such as Australia, the United Kingdom, Ireland, and Canada, have moved to a broader LLL requirement in within the field of CPD.

Notwithstanding the regulatory mechanisms themselves, the need for CE and CPD has long animated discussions within the literatures regarding continuing professional competence. Early advocates of CE outlined a range of issues that required attention. Webster (1971), in particular, suggested four issues that needed particular attention in the early days of this discussion.

1. **Program planning.** Webster (1971) suggested that the APA, the National Institute of Mental Health, ASPPB, the National Science Foundation, and other professional organizations increase involvement in quality CE by establishing mechanisms for promulgating CE and CPD training standards and for developing programming that would provide access to quality training opportunities.
2. **Creating leadership to provide CE and CPD training and to recruit and promote instructional excellence to sustain excellent postdoctoral education.** Webster (1971) noted that universities, with their agenda of integrating practitioners with researchers, could play an important role with respect to addressing this issue, effectively "seeding" the ranks of competent presenters and then "training the trainers" to develop a sufficient, effective workforce for providing CPD programs.
3. **Identifying and offering high-priority content areas for CE and CPD.** Because professional development content cannot always be comprehensive, Webster (1971) encouraged the field to identify and prioritize the most crucial professional development content areas on an ongoing basis.
4. **Developing an ongoing research agenda related to CE and CPD in the mental health fields.** Webster (1971) called for both basic research on adult learning, communication, and organizational behavior and the ongoing evaluation of professional development program outcomes. It stands as a contemporary testament to Webster's prescience that these issues still occupy positions of centrality in the contemporary literatures in CE, where concerns regarding access to CE, the evaluation of instructor quality, ongoing needs assessments, and the demonstrated outcomes associated with CE are all ongoing topics of discussion and concern (Mazmanian, Berens, Wetzel, Feldman, & Dow, 2012; Neimeyer, Taylor, & Cox, 2012; Neimeyer, Taylor, & Philip, 2010).

Contemporary Landscape of Continuing Professional Development

The typical U.S. psychologist completes more than 22 formal CE credits each year (Neimeyer, Taylor, & Wear, 2009; Neimeyer, Taylor, & Philip, 2010; Wise et al., 2010). In addition, psychologists, counselors, therapists, and other mental health professionals complete hundreds of hours of informal CPD every year (Brown, Leichtman, Blass, & Fleisher, 1982; Neimeyer, Taylor, & Cox, 2012). Taylor, Neimeyer, Wear, and Linder-Crow (2012) found, for example, that the average U.S. psychologist completed 135 hours of informal CE per year and more than 23 hours of formal CE. This broad commitment to ongoing professional development is shared across the related helping professions. Ongoing professional development is mandated in social work (see Social Workers Registration Board, 2016) and counseling (see National Board for Certified Counselors, 2016), for example. In fact, clinical mental health counselors and master addictions counselors are required to take 25% to 50% of their continuing coursework in specific areas relevant to their specialties (e.g., testing and appraisal, group counseling, family addictions counseling). In New Zealand, for example, researchers surveyed 285 social workers and found that 90% of them reported that they had participated in one or more days of continuing professional education over the past year and approximately two-thirds reported that they were in the process of completing some form of continuing professional education (CPE) (Beddoe & Henrickson, 2005). In another survey of 1,000 New Zealand social workers, three-fourths of them noted that they had engaged in CPE since completing their general educational requirements and over two-thirds reported interest in engaging in more CPE (Staniforth, 2010).

Calvert and colleagues (2007) compared the continuing professional development experiences of social workers in New Zealand, the United States, and Canada and found that social workers in Canada and New Zealand reported a good deal more previous specialized training in specific areas of psychotherapy than social workers in the United States (94%, 80%, and 47%, respectively). However, their current specialized training did not significantly differ.

Satisfaction with CE

In general, mental health professionals in the United States report being satisfied with the quality of their CE programming. Sharkin and Plageman (2003) found that 69% of participants were satisfied with CE quality, and Fagan, Ax, Liss, Resnick, and Moody (2007) and Neimeyer, Taylor, and Wear (2009) reported that 79% of their participants described their CE experiences as good or excellent.

Less is known empirically about the participation and practices of mental health providers in countries outside of the United States. However, Calvert and colleagues (2007) found that among their samples of North American, Canadian, and New Zealand social workers, the impact of courses and seminars on professional development was perceived as less substantial than that of receiving supervision and on-the-job training, for all three groups. Among both Canadian and American social workers, receiving personal therapy was also viewed as more impactful than CPD courses for their professional development and competence. Furthermore, among American social workers, informal case discussions were viewed as more impactful than CPD coursework.

Although this study pointed to the effectiveness of alternative forms of professional development over formal CPD programming, Gao and colleagues (2010) surveyed psychiatrists, clinical psychologists, psychiatric nurses, and counselors in China and found, disconcertingly, that many mental health practitioners felt underprepared for their field. Nearly three-fourths of mental health professionals held a bachelor's degree or less, approximately two-thirds of them did not major in psychology, and over half were employed only part time. Less than half of them were certified, and nearly half were not affiliated with a professional organization. When asked about CPD and training, most surveyed Chinese mental health providers described CPD programs as theory-based and short-term and stated that they rarely included learning assessments or any other points of contact following the training experiences. Many mental health professionals also reported challenges regarding access to supervision and consultation, thus perpetuating the need for access to high-quality CPD programming for ongoing competence.

Regardless of the reported satisfaction, or dissatisfaction, with CE and CPD programs, satisfaction surveys themselves have their own limitations. Satisfaction can result from many factors (e.g., the convenience of the location, the quality of the venue or refreshments) and is therefore not necessarily related to effectiveness, particularly enhanced clinical effectiveness. Nevertheless, satisfaction surveys remain the most commonly used outcome measures in CE research. This finding supports the observation of Neimeyer and colleagues (2009) that there is "an inverse relationship between the strength of the outcomes utilized in the field of CE and the frequency with which these outcomes are utilized" (p. 622). Satisfaction surveys give us little information about the particular effectiveness of programs and do not adequately address the critical questions surrounding the objectives or outcomes attributed to CE.

Does CE Work?

CE research in psychology and other mental health professions has focused so heavily on satisfaction as an outcome that we know little of its effects on practice. It can be useful, then, to look to the literatures of allied health professions. Particularly important is *Redesigning Continuing Education in the Health Professions* from the Institute on Medicine (IOM; 2010), which reviewed over 18,000 articles related to CE, learning among adults, and the translation of knowledge and skills to clinical practice. The authors concluded: "Although CE research is fragmented and may focus too heavily on learning outside of clinical settings, there is evidence that CE works, in some cases, to improve clinical practice and patient outcomes" (p. 39). The broad endorsement reflected in this conclusion, however, implicitly recognizes a range of ongoing concerns and questions that follow from the limitations of the field in its current state of development.

Limitations of the Status Quo

Limitations of CE as it is currently offered include its cost and inconvenience, the quality and availability of CE programs, and the lack of empirical evidence that CE is effective in improving clinical practice (Melnyk et al., 2001; Neimeyer, Taylor, & Philip, 2010; Neimeyer, Taylor, & Wear, 2009, 2010; Zemansky, 2012). CE programs can cost practitioners thousands of dollars annually and cause them to accrue significant indirect costs associated with travel (airfare, hotel, and meal costs) and loss of work.

Some have wondered whether the benefits of CE are sufficient to outweigh these limitations. Yet the public has high expectations, and maintains a robustly favorably appraisal, of CE (Taylor & Neimeyer, 2015b). In a recent study of the public's perceptions of CE within professional psychology, 742 people rated 10 different forms of CPD for the extent to which they met the three principal objectives of CE: to maintain competence, improve outcomes, and protect the public (Taylor & Neimeyer, 2015b). Respondents rated CE highly with respect to all three objectives, underscoring the role of CE in helping to satisfy the profession's compact with the public to maximize its service through continuing professional competence. Moreover, as Neimeyer and colleagues (2009) noted, within professional psychology, the absence of the demonstrated outcomes of CE on practice behaviors and outcomes is more the result of failing to assess these impacts than it is of failing to find them, and for that reason, the field is largely left to extrapolate the impact of CE from the findings in other, allied fields of health.

> The mental health professions still need more research that follows the outcomes of CE mandates and the outcomes of specific programming. (See Daniels & Walter, 2002; Neimeyer, Taylor, & Wear, 2009.) As Neimeyer, Taylor, and Wear (2009) concluded, research in CE remains in its infancy and can best be described as a pre-experimental patchwork of isolated surveys conducted largely on localized samples of convenience. These efforts have not yet risen to the level of programmatic research and for that reason have not yet demonstrated the methodological progression or systematic knowledge gains that would ordinarily accompany a sustained program of research. (p. 18)

But here is what we do know: The majority of CE programs are offered as didactic seminars (Taylor & Neimeyer, 2016), even though research indicates that passive learning from didactic presentation does not facilitate long-term learning and registers minimal impact on skill acquisition or client outcomes (Bloom, 2005; IOM, 2010). In fact, didactic programs are the equivalent of a spray-and-pray method in which the teacher "sprays" information to the learners and "prays" that some of it sticks (Shern, 2010).

Dunning, Heath, and Suls (2004) also noted that more interactive programs are more beneficial for long-term retention of knowledge and skills than are those that use the didactic method. The IOM (2010) concurred, noting that

> health professionals often need multiple learning opportunities and multiple methods of education, such as practicing self-reflection in the workplace, reading journal articles that report new clinical evidence, and participating in formal CE lectures, if they are to most effectively change their performance and, in turn, improve patient outcomes. (p. 47)

Because there is limited research on CE in psychology, many researchers have relied on the evidence of effective continuing medical education programs among physicians. In a randomized clinical trial assessing the effectiveness of an interactive, skill-based continuing medical education program on cardiovascular and cancer treatment for physicians, researchers found that physicians who received the interactive, skill-based training performed the recommended procedures more frequently than those who did not receive the training and that those differences were maintained over a yearlong follow-up period (Jennett et al., 1988). Bloom (2005) concluded from his extensive review of 20 years of controlled research on continuing medical education effectiveness that interactive methods were most effective at improving physician care and patient outcomes, whereas didactic programs had "little or no beneficial effect in changing physician practice" (p. 380). (See also IOM, 2010.) Thus, all CE programs may not be created equal; some may be more effective than others (see Slotnick & Shershneva, 2002), a conclusion that has prompted an ongoing quest for identifying "best practices" within the field (IOM, 2010; Neimeyer & Taylor, 2014).

Providing professionals the opportunity to learn and practice techniques or skills is likely one of the most effective forms of training when effectiveness is understood as improved clinical practices or outcomes. Davis, Thomson, Oxman, and Haynes (1995) noted that interactive techniques, simulations, and online learning experiences tend to be effective, especially when they are combined with learning across several occasions or learning through various instructional formats.

Interactive workshops that combine demonstration, discussion, opportunities to practice skills through simulations, and direct feedback also tend to enhance the CPD experience. (See IOM, 2010; O'Brien et al., 2001; also Chapter 12 in this volume.) This interactivity can extend to online CPD programs, as well. E-learning opportunities can facilitate translation of learning and application of skills through factors such as interactivity, feedback, repeated exposures to the material, and the use of multimedia (IOM, 2010).

This finding is consistent with those of Neimeyer, Taylor, and Webber (2016); their study highlighted the potential value of utilizing multiple media channels in enhancing learning. Neimeyer and colleagues conducted a randomized clinical trial of online CE, where participants were randomly assigned to three different versions of an online training program concerning problematic internet use: audio-only, text-only, and audio-visual CE programs, the last of which included interactive learning. Although participants in every group showed improved learning after objective posttest assessments, results revealed that those in the audio-visual group performed better at the posttest than did those in the other two conditions, highlighting the importance of multimedia in engagement and facilitation of learning. Researchers from the United Kingdom also pointed to the value of e-learning. Blackmore, Tantam, and van Deurzen (2008) explored both face-to-face and online CPD learning experiences for European postgraduates and found that online training programs were associated with similar satisfaction ratings from participants, in comparison to on-site programs. The researchers further found that the anonymity of online learning was associated with greater self-disclosure from participants, and self-disclosure has been found to be an important tool for engagement in learning and professional competence. (See also St. Jean, 2012.)

It is important to note, however, that the movement toward online CPD experiences must not come at the expense of peer interaction. In their recent qualitative study, researchers in England found that career advisers valued webinars as convenient, accessible, and engaging in their own right, but the advisers also expressed concerns regarding the lack of peer-to-peer interaction that typically occurs in on-site CPD sessions (Yates, 2014). Concerns were further expressed regarding the current unfamiliarity and unreliability of technology as a learning medium.

Given the current state of CPD programs, what can be done to improve current CPD offerings? The IOM (2010) suggested that CE programs need to include five things:

1. Needs assessments to determine which CE programs are most crucial
2. Interactive components (e.g., opportunities to practice skill development, group reflection)
3. Feedback solicited from participants to enhance their involvement in the learning process
4. Various forms of learning that are utilized, together with time for learners to process the material
5. Clinical simulation opportunities during CE sessions

We provide additional suggestions in the section titled "Recommendations for More Effective Continuing Professional Development."

Continuing Education Worldwide

There are important lessons to learn from CE requirements in a range of international contexts. In Ontario, Canada, for example, the Quality Assurance Program of the College of Psychologists of Ontario requires that psychologists create a personalized self-assessment guide and professional development plan (Morris, 2012). Psychologists work through a sequence of questions, designed to explore their strengths, weaknesses, and areas in need of remediation. Following their completion of the self-assessment measure, professionals build a personalized proposal to build, enhance, and remediate their professional competencies. They share this plan with a colleague who reads through it and provides feedback, prior to an attestation to the board regarding the completion of the self-assessment. The board then audits the completion of these self-assessments and, upon review, provides constructive feedback regarding incomplete assessments or other licensing actions in cases of significant neglect of statutory requirements.

New Zealand also enacted a similar policy for social workers, through its Competence Assessment and Competence Recertification programs. (See Social Workers Registration Board, 2016.) Social workers are required to complete a form that not only tracks their CPD experiences but requires learners to reflect on the usefulness and relevance of the CPD programs to their clinical activities. Supervisors or managers are also required to provide feedback and sign off the forms.

England's Health and Care Professions Council outlined details on their CPD (CPD) expectations for their members. The council highlighted five CPD requirements for members:

1. Keep a current and ongoing log of their CPD experiences.
2. Show that their CPD activities are applicable to both their current and future clinical practice.
3. Confirm that their CPD experiences have promoted more effective clinical practice and delivery.
4. Demonstrate that their CPD experiences have helped their clients directly.
5. Provide a hard copy with evidence of their CPD experiences, in case they are requested by the council (Newby, 2013).

In Germany, psychotherapists have been mandated for more than 15 years to participate in a three- to five-year certified postgraduate training program. This involves theory-based or knowledge-based lessons and practical-based lessons (e.g., working in a clinical setting with individual clients), self-experience, and participating as a client in therapy (Vollmer, Spada, Caspar, & Burri, 2013). After completing this postgraduate requirement, psychotherapists can participate in independent practice. To maintain licensure, however, German psychotherapists must participate in CPD coursework.

CE courses may be particularly important for mental health professionals who are not recent graduates. Disconcertingly, Vollemer and colleagues (2013) found, in their study of German therapists, that experienced therapists (those in practice for at least 10 years) scored significantly lower on clinical and basic psychological knowledge tests than did trainees, suggesting that our knowledge base may have a "shelf life." (See also Neimeyer,

Taylor, & Rozensky, 2012; Neimeyer, Taylor, Rozensky, & Cox, 2014; Neimeyer, Taylor, Wear et al., 2012.) Although the relationship between clinical knowledge and practice outcomes remains unclear, it seems likely that the former is necessary, but not sufficient, for the latter, and a growing literature is beginning to attest to knowledge atrophy across time. (See Neimeyer, Taylor, & Rozensky, 2012; Neimeyer et al., 2014; Vollmer et al., 2013.)

When therapists find that they lack sufficient knowledge to address the concerns they are presented with, the most common response is to seek further training in those areas of need, a finding noted in a study of the Australian psychologists (Byrne & Davenport, 2005). In that study, when therapists noticed perceived deficits in their training, they reported that they most often turned to formal CE, followed by informal CE, conferences, and supervision for remediation. Neimeyer, Taylor, and colleagues (2012) found similar preferences among their sample of 1,606 board-certified North American psychologists, with the majority noting that they utilize informal CE, formal CE, peer consultation, outcome assessments, conferences, and courses as their primary forms of CPD.

Redesigning Continuing Professional Development

Because so many psychotherapists turn to LLL programs to keep up with new developments in their professions and to remediate areas of weakness, it is vital that strong programs, designed to enhance competence, are developed. As noted earlier, research suggests that not all CPD programs are equally effective at generating their stipulated outcomes (Bloom, 2005; Dunning et al., 2004; IOM, 2010; Neimeyer et al., 2016; Shern, 2010). What components, then, make for an effective CPD program? If an ideal form of CPD could be created, what would it look like? What sort of training positively impacts knowledge and skill retention, application of course concepts, and improved clinical outcomes?

Recommendations for More Effective CPD

In the remainder of this chapter, we offer practices that, if adopted, could lead to more effective mechanisms for facilitating ongoing professional development. We propose a multimodal, multifaceted, extended, applied form of CPD that follows the recommendations appearing in the literature on adult learning. Our 14 recommendations can be used as guidelines for enhancing the quality of training opportunities and the likelihood that training would generate greater learner comprehension, retention, and application in practice. Although no single CE activity would necessarily utilize all of these recommendations, selective attention to as many of these features as possible likely would contribute to the acquisition of new knowledge and enhance the transfer of that knowledge into practice. After discussion of these 14 guidelines for more effective CPD, we conclude with an example that incorporates many of these features and illustrates their utility in CPD.

1. Identify Training Levels CPD Offerings Are Intended to Address

One challenge many practitioners face when choosing a CE program is determining which experiences might best build on their current knowledge and skills. CE programs may be strengthened by organizing the courses by training levels (e.g., introductory, intermediate, advanced). The training needs of an advanced clinical child psychologist in the area of pediatric bariatric surgery, for example, may differ substantially from the needs of a general clinical psychologist who may see children only in the context of school counseling or family therapy. Likewise, the training needs of a school counselor who has spent 20 years working at an urban school district may be quite different from the needs of an early-career school counselor who practices in a rural context. (For an example from a different profession, see Çalışkan & Acar, 2016.) If courses are clearly identified as being introductory, intermediate, or advanced, mental health professionals can make more informed decisions regarding what programs will best meet their needs and expectations.

2. Build on Previous Learning Experiences

In addition to creating CPD programming that specifies its instructional level, sequential, cumulative, and directive training represents a critical component of skill development. However, these features are uncommon aspects of CPD as it is usually practiced. Research from the field of education suggests that learning is enhanced by assessing the learner's prior knowledge of the material and any assumptions currently held (see Recommendation 1) while also deliberately integrating new knowledge and skills gained from the course into the learner's existing repertoire (Dolezal, Welsh, Pressley, & Vincent, 2003). Building on high-connection learning (i.e., providing learners with opportunities to connect their previous knowledge and skills to the topics at hand in the CE workshop) is much more effective than simply using low-connection learning, or presenting material without exploring the learner's previous knowledge or experience with the material or the relevant area of training. (See Education Queensland, 2002.)

As a single example of the application of this guideline, instructors could send out a short survey, prior to the learning session, asking participants about their current knowledge and skills in relation to the targeted area of training and any particular areas or topics they would like to address that would build their skills or knowledge base in directions that are relevant to their practice.

3. Develop Diverse Teaching Methods

Instructors can also use multiple methods of instruction to engage different learning modalities. Several learning styles have been proposed through different learning theories, and one way to address these varying learning styles may be to provide opportunities for learners to engage with *multiple* learning methods. Utilizing videos, role-plays, case demonstrations, and small-group discussions in addition to the didactic or written presentation of information may be helpful to engage CPD learners. An example comes from the field of continuing medical education, where nearly 300 physicians and personnel viewed a CE video about the medical, social, and legal components of interpersonal violence. Utilizing pre- and posttests to determine the effectiveness of the video, which included role-plays to illustrate challenging client encounters, researchers found that the video was related to greater knowledge and improved attitudes regarding elder, child, domestic, and sexual violence at the posttest (McCauley, Jenckes, & McNutt, 2003).

4. Focus on Skill Application and Outcomes

As noted in Recommendation 3, engaging learners in multiple learning methods can be useful for skill development and enhancement. However, research from the field of medicine has demonstrated that the majority of CPD activities are geared toward *knowledge* retention rather than *skill* acquisition. In fact, among 110 accredited CPD activities, only 26% targeted skill improvement (Légaré et al., 2015).

Providing CE learners the opportunity to practice that translation of learning into clinical practice in the CE classroom, in advance of them directly applying their knowledge with clients, could be particularly useful. Extending the knowledge-acquisition focus that many CE programs utilize and focusing on learner skill acquisition would likely enhance the CE learner's experience. Instructors should encourage learners to apply and adapt the material rather than simply learn it. In CPD courses, this might take the form of inviting learners to practice techniques from that day with a partner who is also part of the CPD course; or the CPD instructor may enlist, in advance, other experts in the field to work with small groups in the CPD program, providing them with personalized feedback on their skill development. At the end of the day, CE and CPD sponsors should be able to answer this question: How do knowledge and skill acquisition in this course translate into clinical practice for each of my learners? They also should approach program development with that question in mind.

5. Create Interactivity to Foster Experiential Learning, Retention, and Application

Many CPD programs utilize only didactic learning (Dunning et al., 2004), even though engagement and active learning is critical for knowledge retention and translation to practice (Dunning et al., 2004; Sholomskas et al., 2005). Griscti and Jacono (2005), for example, concluded from their extensive literature review exploring the effectiveness of CE programs in nursing that the typical didactic CE programs are ineffective and that programs should instead involve more learner participation.

Sholomskas and colleagues (2005) examined the impact of technology in LLL and compared three training programs provided to clinical psychologists. One program involved reading a manual to learn; the second program involved a manual and online learning; and the third program involved a manual, a training seminar, and supervision of practice. The most effective learning program was the third one, the seminar/supervision program. This was followed by the second program, the online program, and then the first one, the manual program. The psychologists who attended the seminar/supervision program and the online program maintained or enhanced their professional skills, while the professional skills of those who were in the manual group tended to decrease or remain the same. These studies highlight the importance of not only actively engaging with learners but providing the sort of monitoring and feedback that are stressed throughout this book.

Monitoring learning throughout CPD programs may take different forms, depending on the topic at hand. Feedback may be delivered through demonstrations, group reflections, case conceptualizations, discussions, audience polls or clickers, periodic pop quizzes during the course, skills rehearsal opportunities, and direct feedback from the instructor or peers (see Davis et al., 1995; IOM, 2010; O'Brien et al., 2001; Slotnick & Shershneva, 2002).

6. Include Knowledge and Skill Assessments

Currently, learning gained from CE and CPD is assessed primarily through simple satisfaction surveys, which tell us much more about the activities in which psychotherapists participated and the number of hours they sat in a chair than the amount of information gained from such activities and its translation to practice. CPD evaluations could be revamped from satisfaction surveys to 360-degree assessments that are more directly grounded in impact on client care (see Kaslow et al., 2009). These assessments might include:

1. Client outcome data (rather than subjective psychotherapist self-assessment of their skills; see Chapters 5, 6, and 7)
2. Benchmarking (which might involve behavioral anchors to create more specificity and objectivity to learning and attained goals from CE courses)
3. Cultivating a culture of mindfulness (focusing on present learning needs)
4. Peer assessment
5. Reviewing past performance (see also Dunning et al., 2004).

7. Provide Performance Feedback

Feedback is critical for knowledge and skill retention and for making adjustments as necessary (Piazza-Waggoner, Karazsia, Hommel, & Modi, 2015; Violato, Lockyer, & Fidler, 2008). The delivery of feedback in supervision and consultation has been addressed directly in Chapters 2 and 4. Additionally, in their study exploring the most effective teaching methods for counseling skill development in Turkey, Aladağ, Yaka, and Koç (2014) found that video recording, modeling, evaluation of records, self-observation, practice, and receiving feedback were considered some of the most important methods for skill development.

The emphasis on collaboration and supervision is key. As the research suggests, the most effective of these ways to deliver feedback to CPD learners is often through supervision or consultation, perhaps using technology. For example, all workshop participants might have access to a website that connects them to a private discussion board or chat room with the workshop instructors and colleagues from the course. Learning could also be reinforced through the use of technology. Simulated "clients" with preprogrammed responses through either virtual simulations or hired actors could be utilized so that mental health professionals could practice different techniques and receive feedback. (See Chapter 12 for a discussion of simulations in medical training.) Sessions with clients could even be taped via webcams and given to the workshop instructors to provide feedback to the student, or other attendees could view the sessions for peer consultation or feedback.

In fact, in a comparative study, social workers from New Zealand rated supervision as the most seminal experience in their professional development, more so than on-the-job training with the clients they serve or even courses and seminars (Calvert et al., 2007). North American and Canadian social workers also rated supervision as important, more important than courses and seminars, but not as important as direct clinical services. Similar findings were noted in an international study of 4,000 psychotherapists (Orlinsky, Botermans, & Rønnestad, 2001). Supervision, direct work with clients, and personal therapy were also noted as more important than CPD courses or reading books or journals. Because supervision has been reported as a seminal form of training, it follows that CPD programs could be enhanced to include a supervisory component.

In medicine, multisource feedback (i.e., from questionnaires answered by patients, medical colleagues, and coworkers) is common and has been shown to improve a wide range of outcome-related factors, including office print materials, staff psychosocial skills, and patient care (Andrews, Violato, Ansari, Donnon, & Pugliese, 2013; Fidler, Lockyer, Toews, & Violato, 1999; Violato et al., 2008). Discussion and feedback among colleagues has also been shown to improve communication, and peer feedback has been found to be particularly useful when the focus is on pinpointing challenges the practitioner faces rather than highlighting the practitioner's flaws (Eva & Regehr, 2013).

Given the fact that psychotherapists are not immune to "unconscious incompetence" (see L. Adams, 2011; O'Donovan, Bain, & Dyck, 2005; Vollmer et al., 2013), soliciting feedback from instructors and colleagues may be particularly beneficial in support of maintenance and enhancement of competence. Learners could invite instructors and colleagues directly to provide feedback to them on their growth areas, or CPD providers could facilitate this feedback exchange.

8. Allow Time to Process the Content

Providing sufficient time for learners to process the learning content and experiment with its application remain critical to knowledge and skill development, and instructors need to allow for this time. Learning may be improved by short pauses throughout the CE trainings that invite participants to ask questions, reflect on content, or answer knowledge- or application-based questions about the content. Alternatively, learning may be distributed across time, accompanied by periodic prompts that invite learners to reflect on, and respond to, learning material. As an example, the APA experimented with a "booster learning" online instructional method in 2015. The program, dedicated to the topic of professional ethics, began with a live video webcast of a presentation on ethics, followed by intermittent "prompts" over the course of the subsequent two weeks that were "pushed" out to participants via email. The prompts boosted learning by providing participants with short videos, exercises, polls, or reflective questions for them to respond to. These were followed by a second live video webcast that served as a capstone learning experience where participants could interact with the instructor, share their experiences, and solicit feedback about their experiences and application of the course material. The experiment was evaluated very positively, in part because it provided learners with sufficient time to process and apply the new material within their various workplace settings.

9. Create Longitudinal Programs with Multiple Touch Points

To enhance knowledge retention and translation to skilled practice, longitudinal learning may be superior to the traditional one-and-done approach. Research suggests that knowledge and skill development gained from CE workshops diminishes over time when refresher courses are not offered on a consistent basis (Guardini, Talamini, Fiorillo, Lirutti, & Palese, 2008). Researchers also found that CE participants scored higher on posttests that contained topics or material that they likely put into practice following the workshop than they scored on posttests with material they likely had not yet applied in the real world (Guardini et al., 2008). This finding underscores the importance of learning over the course of time, with opportunities to engage in skill building and the application of the material serving as important sources of learning and retention. The use of "nudges" that invite learners to reflect on, apply, or extend their knowledge in some ways has demonstrated consistent improvements not only with knowledge comprehension and retention but also application and transfer to practice contexts (see Carpenter, 2012; Roediger & Karpicke, 2006). Longitudinal training opportunities provide greater opportunities for multiple touch points.

10. Create a Community of Learners

Fostering a community around learning could encourage consultations between attendees and may also help buffer against burnout and stress, which are often noted as issues therapists face (see Recommendation 14). Also, as the editors of this volume note in Chapter 1, commitment to ongoing professional development is sufficiently hard work, and that motivation can be difficult to sustain. Deci, Vallerand, Pelletier, and Ryan (1991) provided a useful conceptual frame for understanding that motivation. Using self-determination theory, they proposed that the three needs of (1) competence, (2) relatedness, and (3) autonomy all must to be considered. Developing a LLL community can positively affect the psychological need for relatedness and may help psychotherapists engage in more meaningful conversations with their colleagues about the material during training, during breaks, or after the CE training has concluded. Creating a community around learning may, for example, involve trainers engaging learners with their peers in training activities and/or subsequent follow-up.

11. Utilize the Buddy System

An extension of this community of learners is the buddy system. In this colleagueship development method, therapists could be paired with others from the skill-based trainings or sustained trainings in which they are participating. Colleagues would be responsible for following up after the training concludes and holding each other accountable for how they utilize what they learned in practice. These buddies could also enhance learning by opening a door for consultation with each other when the need arises. The value of the buddy system may best be underscored by the experiences of psychologists in Ontario, many of whom collaborate with colleagues to give and receive feedback on their CPD plans (Morris, 2012). And when colleagues share mutual professional development interests, they sometimes join forces on learning activities to complete their professional development plans (Morris, 2012). Utilizing a buddy system may naturally invite greater accountability, social comparison (see discussion of benchmarking in Recommendation 13), and opportunity to deepen or extend learning through sharing and discussion.

12. Offer Mentoring and Consultation

Butterworth, Hayes, and Zimmerman (2011) studied the impact of mentors on distance learning continuing medical education and found that physicians who were mentored demonstrated higher-quality reflection of their learning than did those who were not mentored. Interactive, web-based CPD programs have been enacted and proven effective in British Columbia (Stanton, 2001). Researchers found that computer-mediated conferencing allowed for greater discussion and reflection of client concerns than did in-class discussions (Stanton, 2001).

Within the realm of psychotherapy, technology could be used to facilitate more specific and tailored feedback to therapists. Sessions with clients or with mock clients could be taped (with client consent). The therapist could then send the tapes to an expert, who would explore the videos and identify instances in which the therapist performed well and instances in need of improvement. Through this expert monitoring, the learner would receive specific, skill-focused consultation on cases and would be provided with a much richer learning experience than would be the case with a traditional one-and-done approach to CE.

13. Engage the Learner in Self-Reflection and Self-Assessment

In addition to the value gained from peers and mentor feedback, borrowing from Ontario's CPD model, CE could be improved by incorporating a self-reflective component or master plan for skill improvement within the CE offering. Research suggests that people retain information and apply skills best when they perceive themselves as having an internal locus of control (Mantesso, Petrucka, & Bassendowski, 2008). By encouraging learners to feel a sense of responsibility toward their learning and to feel an obligation to carefully consider what their needs are, learners recognize that they are active, not passive, participants in their ongoing professional development.

Accurate self-assessment is an important precursor to effective self-directed learning and lifelong maintenance of competence (Candy, 1991; Morris, 2012). Researchers have found that ongoing competence, improved by critical self-assessment, is related to effective clinical practice and clinical outcomes (Beutler, Crago, & Arizendi, 1986). Indeed, the importance of feedback mechanisms to facilitate self-assessment is a central theme of this volume.

But how good are helping professionals at assessing their competence? Davis and colleagues (2006) performed a systematic literature review of 725 articles on the accuracy of physician self-assessment. The researchers then closely examined the 17 most relevant studies and those that employed the strongest empirical rigor. Of concern, over half of the comparisons that were made between self-assessment and objective assessment demonstrated little, no, or inverse relationships between self- and objective assessments. Even more troubling, those who performed the poorest, as measured through objective assessments, had some of the most inaccurate self-assessments. Thus, professionals who are least competent may be least able to recognize, and correct, their deficiencies and areas in need of remediation. Parker, Alford, and Passmore (2004) discovered similar findings, as residents who scored in the lowest quartile of a family practice knowledge-based examination assessed their learning needs least accurately. Dunning and colleagues (2004) also highlighted this concern, noting that the incompetent have "deficits [that] cause them to make errors and also prevent them from gaining insight into their errors" (p. 73). In concluding their assessment, Dunning and colleagues noted, "When one looks at the accuracy of self-assessment in the workplace, from the office cubicle to the executive boardroom, one sees that people tend to hold overly inflated self-views that are modestly related to actual performance" (p. 90).

Several activities may be useful in enhancing the accuracy of self-assessment, however. Research suggests that when residents watch videotapes of their previous performance, their self-assessment accuracy is enhanced (Lane & Gottlieb, 2004). Their accuracy is strengthened even more when they watch the tapes with a faculty member. Additionally, when students rate their own performance and later meet with a faculty member who conducts a separate assessment of the students' competence, their skill appraisals become more accurate (Cochran & Spears, 1980). Thus, mental health professionals may benefit from watching their practice tapes, utilizing skills from the CE session, and receiving feedback from other professionals (e.g., peers at the CE session, instructor).

Another strategy that can increase the accuracy of self-assessment is benchmarking, which involves comparing a professional's performance with the performance of others (Martin, Regehr, Hodges, & McNaugton, 1998). As one example of benchmarking, family practice residents mock-interviewed a mother who potentially physically abused her child and then were asked to rate their performance. Then the residents watched their videotaped interview, in addition to watching four benchmark interviews with varying competence levels. After they watched the benchmark interviews, the relationship between the residents' self-ratings and supervisor ratings was significantly stronger. When appraisal from supervisors and benchmarking is not available, peer assessment can be a useful tool to increase self-assessment accuracy (see Falchikov & Goldfinch, 2000; Topping, 1998).

In addition to feedback from colleagues and benchmarking, Epstein (1999) suggested that professionals practice mindfulness through a nonjudgmental awareness of their mental and physical processes throughout the day. Mindfulness creates stronger self-understanding and decreases the likelihood that a professional will remain unaware of expectations, prejudices, and other processes that arise when a professional is not in the moment.

14. Promote Therapist Self-Care

As a natural extension of self-assessment and self-reflection, therapist self-care may also positively impact a therapist's competence. There is a growing understanding in the field of psychology that personal and professional lives are intertwined (Taylor, Neimeyer, & Wear, 2012). To understand and assess professional competence requires an understanding of the impact of a psychotherapist's personal life. Thus, engagement in self-care is crucial for professional competence and ethical practice (APA, 2010; Wise et al., 2010).

For many reasons, psychotherapists often undergo a significant amount of stress. Research suggests that mental health providers have the highest suicide rate among a number of professions (Ukens, 1995). Many mental health providers have experienced childhood trauma (Pope & Tabachnick, 1994), and most report burnout, relationship issues, and depression during their professional careers (Brodie & Robinson, 1991; Rupert, Stevanovic, & Hunley, 2009; Wood, Klein, Cross, Lammers, & Elliott, 1985). In fact, approximately 10% of psychotherapists report suicide ideation or attempts, and 7% report substance abuse issues (Brodie & Robinson, 1991; Rupert et al., 2009; Wood et al., 1985; see also Good, Thoreson, & Shaughnessy, 1995; Laliotis & Grayson, 1985; Smith, Moss, & Burton, 2009). In addition to their own personal issues, psychotherapists may suffer from compassion fatigue, which occurs when mental health providers experience burnout from an ongoing "caring cycle of empathy, client attachment, and ending the therapeutic relationship" (Figley, 1995). And aside from stress *within* the workplace, stress *from* the workplace may trickle into home life. Research suggests that work–family conflict is related to higher levels of emotional exhaustion, negative attitudes toward clients, and fewer feelings of accomplishment (Rupert et al., 2009).

Given the impact of stress on mental health providers, Smith and colleagues (2009) urged greater attention to, and research exploring, issues of psychological distress, substance abuse, depression, and burnout among psychotherapists. In two large-scale studies among both American doctoral students in psychology and board-certified psychologists, research has demonstrated that a higher level of stress is related to a lower level of professional competence (Taylor, Latorre, Fouad, Santana, & Berkey, 2016; Taylor, Neimeyer, & Cox, 2016), supporting Wise's (2008) assertion that competence and professional development include personal factors, such as interpersonal relationship skills, positive attitudes and personality traits, self-care, and self-awareness.

In allied health fields (e.g., nursing, medicine), it is understood that distress and impairment exist among professionals, and programs were developed to combat these issues as early as the 1970s (Laliotis & Grayson, 1985). However, the field of psychology began to acknowledge the impact of personal distress on professional competence in recent years. The Advisory Committee on the Impaired Psychologist, now termed the Advisory Committee on Colleague Assistance, was developed in 1986 to support psychologists who are experiencing psychological distress. Nonetheless, no comprehensive methods exist to tackle the impact of psychological distress on a professional's functioning. (See Smith et al., 2009.) Layman and McNamara (1997) urged researchers to devote more attention to exploring the impact of colleague support programs. Additionally, offering trainings on self-care or incorporating self-care into curricula could be useful for a wide range of psychotherapists.

Illustration of Effective Continuing Professional Development

The effectiveness of any CPD experience is necessarily gauged against its objectives and aspirations, and for this reason there is no single best form of effective training. Trainings devoted to providing an update on the side effect profiles of the latest psychopharmacological medications might be very different from those that are designed to assist therapists to do more effective assessment of intellectual abilities or to learn to conduct emotion-focused therapy. All forms of educational methods and teaching techniques arguably have a place in the field of CPD, but a single example of a novel professional development experience may help to underscore the integration of several of the recommended guidelines into actual practice.

The "Walk a Mile" program (United Way, 2016) provides one such example. The purpose of the Walk a Mile program is to provide therapists and others in the helping professions with a deeper, lived experience of the social service network that many clients experience as a consequence of the positions they find themselves in their lives. Many therapists are broadly aware of the range of social services that their potential clients may eligible for, or participate in, including services related to food, housing, transportation, home visitation, and other medical and social services. But relatively few therapists have extensive experience or familiarity with navigating their way through the network of social service applications in support of recruiting those resources for themselves and their families, and that experience can be highly relevant, even critical, to the provision of effective psychotherapeutic or counseling services because it may serve as a backdrop for those services. Clients who have experienced frustration, disappointment, discrimination, or microaggressions and other marginalizing experiences may naturally bring with them feelings of mistrust, exasperation, or learned helplessness, all of which could have a significant impact on effective service delivery.

The Walk a Mile program is designed to provide participants with direct experience of navigating the social service system in support of acquiring the goods and services that would provide them with the levels of support essential to their daily needs and effective functioning. As an immersive, hands-on activity, the experience involves giving a minimum of 30 individuals an opportunity to occupy a variety of different roles, including being a member (child, parent, other adult) of a family that is at or below the poverty line and must struggle to make difficult decisions while coping with a lack of resources and a confusing support system. If you did not have enough money to feed your children, what would you do? Sell your household goods? Not pay rent and face eviction? Take a predatory loan? The Walk a Mile experience assigns participants to "families." These "families" engage in the center of the room, surrounded by tables representing community services (bank, grocery store, school, nonprofit organizations) and are challenged to secure the services needed to provide for their families, with the ultimate goal of getting themselves out of crisis and achieving self-sufficiency. The Walk a Mile experience serves as a flipped classroom experience insofar as it is followed by an extensive debriefing session where participants discuss their thoughts, feelings, and perceptions and share what they learned from the experience.

The Walk a Mile experience embodies several of the recommended features of ideal CPD experiences. Participants with minimal knowledge and direct experience of soliciting social services are recruited to participate, making the experience an introductory training experience. Their participation is highly interactive and represents a form of experiential learning. It builds on participants' prior, usually rudimentary, knowledge of social service systems, enhancing and enriching their prior levels of familiarity in this content domain. Immersion into a shared learning experience with a community of learners allows participants to learn together and to benefit from one another's learning, and their assignment into families constitutes a variation on the buddy system. Participants are actively engaged in self-reflection and self-assessment during the debriefing session too, where they also are asked to identify what they have learned and to reflect on how that learning might transfer to subsequent work with clients.

It should be noted that not every recommended best practice for CPD needs to be incorporated into every learning experience; indeed, specific recommendations are more appropriate to the objectives of experiences than to others. The Walk a Mile experience does not utilize performance feedback nor skill assessment per se, because its objectives are not primarily to develop skills so much as to enhance awareness, empathy, and familiarity with social service systems that may enable them to more fully understand the experiences and lives of the clients they seek to serve. But the judicious inclusion of select best practices from among the 14 recommendations covered in this chapter can at least begin to serve as guideposts toward more personally meaningful and professionally relevant CPD activities.

Concluding Remarks

In this chapter we have explored the development of CE within the helping professions, the benefits and current limitations associated with the field of CPD, and challenges related to further development within the field. Although research on effective mechanisms for facilitating ongoing professional development is still growing, we can learn from the real-world experience of our colleagues in other disciplines and countries in their efforts to support the continuing competence of providers while protecting the public they serve. Building on empirical research from the fields of education, medicine, social work, counseling, and psychology, considerations for improving CE were suggested. A set of 14 suggested best practices were identified and illustrated with the hope that they may serve as useful guidelines to facilitate the translation of new learning into practice in ways that support ongoing professional competence and enhance the quality of our professional services and the outcomes that they generate.

Questions from the Editors

Question #1: Currently, in the United States, those states that have CE requirements stipulate that, for licensure renewal, one does not have to demonstrate skill development but rather has only to show evidence of having attended a particular number of hours of CE that were offered by a person or group that was certified or accredited in some way, and sometimes addressing particular topics (e.g., ethics). If licensure and other regulatory boards came to you for advice about how to create a process to evaluate whether CE activities truly demonstrate skill development, what would you advise and why?

Answer from Authors: CE is designed to fulfill a variety of interrelated functions. These include the maintenance of competence, the enhancement service delivery and outcomes, and the protection of the public (Neimeyer, Taylor, & Cox, 2012; Neimeyer, Taylor, & Wear, 2009; Taylor & Neimeyer, 2015b). Ongoing skill development is a critical element in relation to these objectives, joined by a variety of other elements in an effort to create the safety net that effectively satisfies the professional compact that the profession has entered into in relation to the public that it serves. Beyond skill development, other elements include knowledge updates regarding advances in substantive areas of practice as well as ongoing awareness of broader social, cultural, legal, and regulatory developments that carry direct implications for ongoing competence and effective practice. Because of the rapid proliferation of new knowledge in the field, and the corresponding diminishing durability of knowledge (Neimeyer, Taylor, & Rozensky, 2012; Neimeyer et al., 2014), considerable time and attention are dedicated to substantive knowledge updates. Rapid advances in psychopharmacology, for example, require that practicing professionals understand the range of late-breaking advances in those medications, together with the side effect profiles associated with them. Likewise, developments in regulatory areas, such as changes in CE requirements, insurance reimbursement, or payment models, all require ongoing knowledge updates as vital strands in the safety net of CE.

The traditional model of utilizing a clock-hour approach to regulating CE can be viewed as broadly consistent with CE's multiple objectives; it fits well the idea that professionals are engaged in ongoing learning that is subject to both independent verification and evaluation. Verification helps fulfill the public compact by providing accountability (see Taylor & Neimeyer, 2015b), and evaluation provides the opportunity for the learner to reflect on, and assess, his or her learning while also providing feedback that can be critical to the ongoing revision and improvement of the professional training experience.

Skill development is an important, and often underutilized, element of CPD. Although skill development is often the target of ongoing training, it is rarely required or assessed. Knowledge tests are common elements (as in all home study courses), but the direct assessment of behavioral skills is uncommon, not only because often they are not the target of training but also because of the significant dedication of resources required to conduct such evaluations. Recent efforts to include translation-to-practice questions in CE evaluations are designed to approximate this assessment but provide neither independent verification of these skills nor any sort of mandated level of competency in order to satisfy the CE requirements.

The bottom line is that the most frequently used assessments in the area of CPD are the weakest ones (i.e., satisfaction ratings) while progressively more rigorous measures (e.g., knowledge tests, competency assessments, measures of translation into actual practice, improved clinical outcomes, and improved protection of the public) are correspondingly less common elements that are more often assumed than demonstrated and optional rather than required (Neimeyer & Taylor, 2014). In the context of ongoing CPD, however, professionals regularly learn to score and interpret new tests, acquire new statistical, methodological, conceptual, diagnostic, and technological skills, and develop proficiencies related to their areas of interest and practice. The requirement that they demonstrate these competencies as a prerequisite to satisfying their license renewal requirements (e.g., as in mandated CE) would require the infusion of considerable resources into the mechanisms of ongoing CE.

Licensing or registration boards are charged with implementing professional regulations in support of stipulated professional objectives. In most cases, these objectives include the maintenance of competence, the improved delivery of services, and the protection of the public. Documented professional skill development may be a necessary, if not sufficient, element of ongoing professional development activities designed to fulfill those objectives. One mechanism for assessing the effectiveness of these activities in relation to their activities would be to ask trainers/presenters to specify whether the objectives of their training efforts included (a) substantive knowledge gains, (b) focused skill development, and/or (c) broader regulatory, legal, technological, or other awareness, and then require that participants evaluate themselves along those dimensions at the end of the training. Because best practices include skill rehearsal and feedback (IOM, 2010), peer assessments and/or instructor assessments could be encouraged, or mandated, as inclusions in relevant CE activities. The American Board of Professional Psychology has recently moved to a maintenance of competency demonstration for its ongoing board certification, and licensing boards could consider adopting this model or some variant on it. According to the new stipulations, every seven years a board-certified psychologist would need to undergo a portfolio assessment and knowledge examination in support of his or her continuing certification. Although the effects of such competency assessments remain indeterminate, provisional correlational data are consistent with the fact that board certification in psychology is associated with a range of positive professional outcomes that may suggest superior competence, performance, or accomplishment (Neimeyer & Taylor, 2014; Taylor & Neimeyer, 2016). Cause and effect have yet to be determined, however. It remains unclear whether board certification simply filters for more competent professionals, for example, or whether the ongoing demonstration of that competence and performance drives continuing improvements, or some combination of both. All in all, the role of skill development in the maintenance of professional competence and the delivery of more effective services deserves careful, sustained, controlled research, not unlike the programmatic research efforts that have informed the field of psychotherapy research for the last several decades. As it stands, the empirical study of CE (best practices and outcomes) remains a full generation behind the field of psychotherapy research (Neimeyer, Taylor, & Wear, 2009; Taylor & Neimeyer, 2016).

Question #2: Reforms to mandated continuing professional development (whether labeled CE or something else) must originate from the government agencies or professional associations that regulate practice (e.g., the APA). Thus, an implementation of the more effective practices you describe would necessitate changes in these larger entities. Are you aware of any larger entities, anywhere, that have successfully made the shifts toward these more effective practices? If so, what lessons are there for making changes in other regulatory groups?

Answer from Authors: Reforms to mandated CPD necessarily must originate with, or articulate with, regulating organizations, agencies, or professional associations. Changes within the interests and operations of those organizations are essential to moving the needle in relation to significant shifts in the way in which the objectives of CPD are met. A number of significant developments are occurring that converge on the cultivation of best practices. Changes within the APA, changes within the ASPPB, changes within the American Board of Professional Psychology, and changes formulated by the Institute of Medicine (IOM, 2010) all represent examples of seismic shifts in the field of CPD.

The APA recently approved as a matter of policy a resolution addressing quality professional development and continuing education. This resolution emphasizes the important of an evidence-based approach to CE, supporting best practices in training and education, and measuring outcomes following from it. Consistent with this resolution, APA now requires a self-assessment of both the extent to which individuals have engaged in new learning resulting from their professional development experience and the extent to which they view it as likely to transfer into their actual practice. The Office of Continuing Education in Psychology at the APA now specifically assesses the integration of best practices into all CPD that it offers in order to determine the relationship between best practices and learning outcomes. Moreover, it includes hands-on skill building as a key ingredient of the review process to determine the selection of CE programs to be developed or delivered. These changes are designed to align the delivery of CE both with best practices, as they are currently understood, and with the era of accountability in which they operate.

A complementary set of developments is occurring within the ASPPB, which has advanced a Maintenance of Competence for Licensure (MOCL) system that serves as a complement to traditional CE (Webb & Horn, 2012). The MOCL system conceptualizes CPD as consisting of a loosely federated network of educational experiences that range widely in their degree of formality and accountability but converge on broadening the nature of ongoing professional training and tilting it decidedly toward on-the-job training and incidental learning, in contrast to formal and/or didactic education. According to the MOCL model, credentialed professional development activities would consist of experiences such as engaging in peer consultation, conducting outcome monitoring of service delivery, sitting on professional boards, taking or teaching courses or trainings, publishing professional works, and the like. Formal CE would constitute only a subset of the creditable CPD activities in this model, which ostensibly aims to enhance the real-world value and, presumably, the translation to practice of the new learning that occurs through these experiences.

Although the MOCL system represents a creative initiative designed to broaden the range of creditable CPD activities, it raises some important considerations and questions as well. Many of its proposed CPD activities would not be subject to independent verification (e.g., collecting client outcomes, self-directed learning), for example, and other of its activities would appear to bear only an oblique relationship to relevant professional skill development per se (e.g., sitting on boards). Moreover, as Neimeyer, Taylor, and Wear (2009) noted, in the absence of any evaluation or feedback, there is no mechanism for determining the nature of whatever learning they may have generated or any way to improve those experiences based on feedback.

A further development that is squarely consistent with the ongoing assurance of professional competence is the American Board of Professional Psychology's recent decision to begin requiring ongoing competency assessments for its continuing board certifications. Previous board certification was a one-and-done competency assessment, lacking any requirement to demonstrate competency at any point beyond the initial assessments. Recent changes now require a recertification process every seven years, based on a portfolio review and other demonstrations of professional competence.

These developments can all be viewed as broadly consistent with the IOM's (2010) recent efforts to redesign CE in the health professions. The IOM recognized the field's overreliance on didactic presentations as a mechanism for maintaining competence and contrasted those methods with known best practices based on the science of learning and adult education literatures, which place a premium on (a) multiple exposures to new information, (b) the use of multimedia in presenting information, (c) exploration and interactivity in relation to the new content, and (d) skill rehearsal and feedback as critical mechanisms likely to enhance the comprehension and retention as well as the transfer and utilization of new learning in actual practice.

Taken collectively, these disparate efforts by various regulatory agencies and organizations signal a common interest in moving the field toward generating, and demonstrating, relevant outcomes central to the objectives of CE: the maintenance of competence, the improvement of services delivered, and the protection of the public.

Question #3. As you look at various mental health disciplines and countries, what models for continuing professional development come closest to an ideal (e.g., you already mention Ontario's system—is it the best)? What aspects of that system are especially good? And if you were advising that regulatory entity to further improve that system, what would your advice be?

Answer from Authors: An ideal system has yet to be created, but the IOM's (2010) recommendations are instructive in this regard. Its vision includes a multidisciplinary private–public partnership in the form of a Center for Interdisciplinary Continuing Professional Development. The center would be tasked with developing, implementing, and evaluating the educational and training programs and experiences that it furnishes. Ongoing research would focus on the continuing quest for excellence and the identification and utilization of best practices in the field's CPD efforts. In this vision, didactic presentations would be reserved for those experiences to which they are best suited (e.g., informational updates) while interactive, multimedia trainings with opportunity for skills-based rehearsal and feedback would become the more modal practice.

And while instructors can improve CPD programs by offering interactive, engaging experiences, rather than the typical didactic presentation, students may improve their CPD experiences by taking time to self-reflect and carefully consider their CPD needs. As noted earlier in the chapter, the College of Psychologists in Ontario offers a self-assessment guide and professional development plan that invites mental health providers to consider how familiar they are with various mental health laws, the ethics code, their work relative to various important areas of professional practice, and their developing needs in relation to their other professional responsibilities (e.g., teaching/training, research, supervision), current specialty areas, and anticipated specialty areas (Morris, 2012). Mental health professionals are then encouraged to share their professional development plan with colleagues, and this collaborative process results in two important outcomes: feedback and accountability. The process of self-reflection and collaboration with colleagues offers psychotherapists the opportunity to be accountable for the value gained from their CPD experiences, thus supporting their ongoing maintenance of competence.

References

Adams, A., & Sharkin, B. S. (2012). Should continuing education be mandatory for re-licensure? In G. J. Neimeyer & J. M. Taylor (Eds.), *Continuing professional development and lifelong learning: Issues, impacts and outcomes* (pp. 161–182). Hauppauge, NY: Nova Science.

Adams, L. (2011). *Learning a new skill is easier said than done.* Retrieved from http://www.gordontraining.com/free-workplace-articles/learning-a-new-skill-is-easier-said-than-done/

Aladağ, M., Yaka, B., & Koç, I. (2014). Opinions of counselor candidates regarding counseling skills training. *Educational Sciences: Theory and Practice, 14,* 870–886.

American Psychological Association. (1947). Committee on Training in Clinical Psychology, Division of Clinical Psychology. Recommended graduate training program in clinical psychology. *American Psychologist, 2,* 539–558.

American Psychological Association. (2010). *Ethical principles of psychologists and code of conduct.* Retrieved from http://www.apa.org/ethics/code/index.aspx?item=4

American Psychological Association. (2015). *Standards and criteria for approval of sponsors of continuing education for psychologists.* Retrieved from https://www.apa.org/ed/sponsor/about/standards/manual.pdf

Andrews, J.J.W., Violato, C., Ansari, A. A., Donnon, T., & Pugliese, G. (2013). Assessing psychologists in practice: Lessons from the health professions using multisource feedback. *Professional Psychology: Research and Practice, 44,* 193–207.

Beddoe, L., & Henrickson, M. (2005). Continuing professional social work education in Aotearoa New Zealand. *Asia Pacific Journal of Social Work and Development, 15,* 75–90.

Beutler, L. E., Crago, M., & Arizendi, T. G. (1986). Research on therapist variables in psychotherapy. In S. L. Garfield & A. E. Bergin (Eds.), *Handbook of psychotherapy and behavior change* (pp. 257–310). New York, NY: Wiley.

Blackmore, C., Tantam, D., & van Deurzen, E. (2008). Evaluation of e-learning outcomes: Experience from an online psychotherapy education programme. *Open Learning, 23,* 185–201.

Bloom, B. S. (2005). Effects of continuing medical education on improving physician clinical care and patient health: A review of systematic reviews. *International Journal of Technology Assessment in Healthcare, 21,* 380–385.

Brodie, J., & Robinson, B. (1991). Distressed/impaired survey: Overview and results. *Minnesota Psychologist, 40,* 7–9.

Brown, R. A., Leichtman, S. R., Blass, T., & Fleisher, E. (1982). Mandated continuing education: Impact on Maryland psychologists. *Professional Psychology, 13,* 404–411.

Butterworth, K., Hayes, B., & Zimmerman, M. (2011). Remote and rural: Do mentors enhance the value of distance learning continuing medical education? *Education for Health: Change in Learning and Practice, 24,* 1–6.

Byrne, D. G., & Davenport, S. C. (2005). Contemporary profiles of clinical and health psychologists in Australia. *Australian Psychologist, 40,* 190–201.

Çalışkan, Y., & Acar, E. (2016). An exploratory analysis of continuing professional development perspectives of Turkish architects according to career stages. *Architectural Engineering and Design Management, 12,* 381–406.

Calvert, S., Kazantzi, N., Merrick, P. L., Orlinsky, D. E., Ronan, K. R., & Staniforth, B. (2007). Professional development of New Zealand social workers who engage in psychotherapy: Perceptions and activities. *Aotearoa New Zealand Social Work Review, 19,* 16–31.

Candy, P. C. (1991). *Self-direction for life-long learning: A comprehensive guide to theory and practice.* San Francisco, CA: Jossey-Bass.

Carpenter, S. K. (2012). Testing enhances the transfer of learning. *Current Directions in Psychological Science, 21,* 279–283.

Cochran, S. B., & Spears, M. (1980). Student self-assessment and instructors' ratings: A comparison. *Journal of the American Dietetic Association, 76,* 253–257.

Daniels, A. S., & Walter, D. A. (2002). Current issues in continuing education for contemporary behavioral health practice. *Administration and Policy in Mental Health, 29,* 359–376.

Davis, D. A., Mazmanian, P. E., Fordis, M., Van Harrison, R., Thorpe, K. E., & Perrier, L. (2006). Accuracy of physician self-assessment compared with observed measures of competence: A systematic review. *Journal of the American Medical Association, 296,* 1094–1102.

Davis, D. A., Thomson, M. A., Oxman, A. D., & Haynes, R. B. (1995). Changing physician performance: A systematic review of the effect of continuing medical education strategies. *Journal of the American Medical Association, 274*, 700–705.

Deci, E. L., Vallerand, R. J., Pelletier, L. G., & Ryan, R. M. (1991). Motivation and education: The self-determination perspective. *Educational Psychologist, 26*, 325–346.

Dolezal, S. E., Welsh, L. M., Pressley, M., & Vincent, M. M. (2003). How nine third-grade teachers motivate student academic engagement. *Elementary School Journal, 103*, 239–267.

Dunning, D., Heath, C., & Suls, J. (2004). Flawed self-assessment: Implications for health, education, and the workplace. *Psychological Science in the Public Interest, 5*, 69–106.

Education Queensland. (2002). *What is higher-order thinking? A guide to productive pedagogies: Classroom reflection manual.* Queensland, Australia: Department of Education.

Epstein, R. M. (1999). Mindful practice. *Journal of the American Medical Association, 282*, 833–839.

Eva, K. W., & Regehr, G. (2013). Effective feedback for maintenance of competence: From data delivery to trusting dialogues. *Canadian Medical Association Journal, 185*, 462–463.

Fagan, T. J., Ax, R. K., Liss, M., Resnick, R. J., & Moody, S. (2007). Professional education and training: How satisfied are we? An exploratory study. *Training and Education in Professional Psychology, 1*, 13–25.

Falchikov, N., & Goldfinch, J. (2000). Student peer assessment in higher education: A meta-analysis comparing peer and teacher marks. *Review of Educational Research, 70*, 287–322.

Fidler, H., Lockyer, J., Toews, J., & Violato, C. (1999). Changing physicians' practices: The effect of individual feedback. *Academic Medicine, 74*, 702–714.

Figley, C. R. (1995). *Compassion fatigue as secondary traumatic stress disorder: An overview.* In C. R. Figley (Ed.), *Compassion fatigue: Coping with secondary traumatic stress disorder in those who treat the traumatized* (pp. 51–81). New York, NY: Brunner/Mazel.

Gao, X., Jackson, T., Chen, H., Liu, Y., Wang, R., Quian, M., & Huang, X. (2010). There's a long way to go: A nationwide survey of professional training for mental health providers in China. *Health Policy, 95*, 74–81.

Good, G. E., Thoreson, R. W., & Shaughnessy, P. (1995). Substance use, confrontation of impaired colleagues, and psychological functioning among counseling psychologists: A national survey. *Counseling Psychologist, 23*, 703–721.

Griscti, O., & Jacono, J. (2005). Effectiveness of continuing education programmes in nursing: Literature review. *Journal of Advanced Nursing, 55*, 449–456.

Guardini, I., Talamini, R., Fiorillo, F., Lirutti, M., & Palese, A. (2008). The effectiveness of continuing education in postoperative pain management: Results from a follow-up study. *Journal of Continuing Education in Nursing, 39*, 281–288.

Hunter, W. S. (1941). On the professional training of psychologists. *Psychological Review, 48*, 498–523.

Institute of Medicine. (2010). *Redesigning continuing education in the health professions.* Washington, DC: National Academies Press.

Jennett, P. A., Laxdal, O. E., Hayton, R. C., Klaassen, D. J., Swanson, R. W., Wilson, T. W., . . . Wickett, R. E. Y. (1988). The effects of continuing medical education on family doctor performance in office practice: A randomized control study. *Medical Education, 22*, 139–145.

Kaslow, N. J., Grus, C. L., Campbell, L. F., Fouad, N. A., Hatcher, R. L., & Rodolfa, E. R. (2009). Competency assessment toolkit for professional psychology. *Training and Education in Professional Psychology, 3*, S27–S45.

Laliotis, D., & Grayson, J. (1985). Psychologist heal thyself: What is available to the impaired psychologist? *American Psychologist, 40*, 84–96.

Lane, J. L., & Gottlieb, P. P. (2004). Improving the interviewing and self-assessment skills of medical students: Is it time to readopt videotaping as an educational tool? *Ambulatory Pediatrics, 4*, 244–248.

Layman, M. J., & McNamara, J. R. (1997). Remediation for ethics violations: Focus on psychotherapists' sexual contact with clients. *Professional Psychology: Research and Practice, 28*, 281–292.

Légaré, F., Freitas, A., Thompson-Leduc, P., Borduas, F., Luconi, F. Boucher, A., . . . Jacques, A. (2015). The majority of accredited continuing professional development activities do not target clinical behavior change. *Academic Medicine, 90*, 197–202.

Mantesso, J., Petrucka, P., & Bassendowski, S. (2008). Continuing professional competence: Peer feedback success from determination of nurse locus of control. *Journal of Continuing Education in Nursing, 39*, 200–205.

Martin, D., Regehr, G., Hodges, B., & McNaughton, N. (1998). Using videotaped benchmarks to improve the self-assessment ability of family practice residents. *Academic Medicine, 73*, 1201–1206.

Mazmanian, P. E., Berens, T. E., Wetzel, A. P., Feldman, M., & Dow, A. W. (2012). Planning for change in psychology: Education, outcomes, and continuing professional development. In G. J. Neimeyer & J. M. Taylor (Eds.), *Continuing education and professional development: Issues, impacts, and outcomes* (pp. 317–341). Hauppauge, NY: Nova Science.

McCauley, J., Jenckes, M. W., & McNutt, L.-A. (2003). The effectiveness of a continuing medical education video on knowledge and attitudes about interpersonal violence. *Journal of Medical Education, 78*, 518–524.

Melnyk, W. T., Allen, M. F., Nutt, R. L., O'Connor, T., Robiner, B., Linder-Crow, J., et al. (2001). *ASPPB guidelines for continuing professional education.* Association of State and Provincial Psychology Boards. Retrieved from https://c.ymcdn.com/sites/asppb.site-ym.com/resource/resmgr/guidelines/asppb_guidelines_for_continu.pdf

Morris, R. (2012). Self-assessment guide and professional development plan: Facilitating individualized continuing professional development. In G. J. Neimeyer, & J. M. Taylor (Eds.), *Continuing education and professional development: Issues, impacts, and outcomes* (pp. 101–133). Hauppauge, NY: Nova Science.

National Board for Certified Counselors. (2016). *Recertify your NCC.* Retrieved from http://www.nbcc.org/Recertification

Neimeyer, G. J., & Taylor, J. M. (2014). Ten trends in lifelong learning and continuing professional development. In W. B. Johnson & N. J. Kaslow (Eds.) *The Oxford handbook of education and training in professional psychology* (pp. 214–236). Oxford, UK: Oxford University Press.

Neimeyer, G. J., Taylor, J. M., & Cox, D. R. (2012). On hope and possibility: Does continuing professional development contribute to ongoing competence? *Professional Psychology: Research and Practice, 41*, 281–287.

Neimeyer, G. J., Taylor, J. M., & Philip, D. (2010). Continuing education in psychology: Patterns of participation and perceived outcomes among mandated and nonmandated psychologists. *Professional Psychology: Research and Practice, 41*, 435–441.

Neimeyer, G. J., Taylor, J. M., & Rozensky, R. (2012). The diminishing durability of knowledge in professional psychology: A Delphi poll of specialties and proficiencies. *Professional Psychology: Research and Practice, 43*, 364–371.

Neimeyer, G. J., Taylor, J. M., Rozensky, R., & Cox, D. (2014). The diminishing durability of knowledge in professional psychology: A second look at specializations. *Professional Psychology: Research and Practice, 45*, 92–98.

Neimeyer, G. J., Taylor, J. M., & Wear, D. M. (2009). Continuing education in psychology: Outcomes, evaluations, and mandates. *Professional Psychology: Research and Practice, 40*, 617–624.

Neimeyer, G. J., Taylor, J. M., & Wear, D. (2010). Continuing education in psychology: Patterns of participation and aspects of selection. *Professional Psychology: Research and Practice, 41*, 281–287.

Neimeyer, G. J., Taylor, J. M., Wear, D., & Linder-Crow, J. (2012). Anticipating the future of CE in psychology: A Delphi poll. In G. J. Neimeyer & J. M. Taylor (Eds.), *Continuing professional development and lifelong learning: Issues, impacts and outcomes* (pp. 377–394). Hauppauge, NY: Nova Science.

Neimeyer, G. J., Taylor, J. M., & Webber, E. (2016). *Continuing education in psychology: A comparison of measured levels of learning resulting from home study methods of continuing education.* Unpublished manuscript. University of Florida, Gainesville, FL.

Newby, G. (2013). Thinking creatively about continuing professional development. In G. Newby, R. Coetzer, & A. Daisley (Eds.), *Practical neuropsychological rehabilitation in acquired brain injury: A guide for working clinicians* (pp. 347–362). London, UK: Karnac Books.

O'Brien, M. A., Freemantle, N., Oxman, A. D., Wolf, F., Davis, D. A., & Herrin, J. (2001). Continuing education meetings and workshops: Effects on professional practice and health care outcomes. *Cochrane Database System Reviews, 2*, CD003030.

O'Donovan, A., Bain, J. D., & Dyck, M. J. (2005). Does clinical psychology education enhance the clinical competence of practitioners? *Professional Psychology: Research and Practice, 36*, 104–111.

Orlinsky, D. E., Botermans, J., & Rønnestad, M. H. (2001). Towards an empirically grounded model of psychotherapy training: Four thousand therapists rated influences on their development. *Australian Psychologist, 36*, 139–148.

Parker, R. W., Alford, C., & Passmore, C. (2004). Can family medicine residents predict their performance on the in-training examination? *Family Medicine, 36*, 705–709.

Piazza-Waggoner, C., Karazsia, B. T., Hommel, K. A., & Modi, A. C. (2015) Considerations for assessing competencies in pediatric psychology. *Clinical Practice in Pediatric Psychology, 3*, 249–254.

Pope, K. S., & Tabachnick, B. G. (1994). Therapists as patients: A national survey of psychologists' experiences, problems, and beliefs. *Professional Psychology: Research and Practice, 25*, 247–258.

Roediger, H. L., & Karpicke, J. D. (2006). Test-enhanced learning: Taking memory tests improves long-term retention. *Psychological Science, 17*, 249–255.

Rupert, P. A., Stevanovic, P., & Hunley, H. A. (2009). Work–family conflict and burnout among practicing psychologists. *Professional Psychology: Research and Practice, 40,* 54–61.

Sharkin, B. S., & Plageman, P. M. (2003). What do psychologists think about mandatory continuing education? A survey of Pennsylvania psychologists. *Professional Psychology: Research and Practice, 34,* 318–323.

Shern, D. (2010, February). *Health care reform, chronic disease and the emerging role for psychologists.* Presentation, Council of Chairs of Training Councils Joint Conference of Training Councils in Psychology: Assuring Competence in the Next Generation of Psychologists. Orlando, FL.

Sholomskas, D. E., Syracuse-Siewert, G., Rounsaville, B. J., Ball, S. A., Nuro, K. F., & Carroll, K. M. (2005). We don't train in vain: A dissemination trial of three strategies of training clinicians in cognitive-behavioral therapy. *Journal of Consulting and Clinical Psychology, 73,* 106–115.

Skovholt, T. M. (2011). Skovholt Practitioner Professional Resiliency and Self-Care Inventory: Burnout prevention and self-care strategies for therapists, counselors, teachers, and health professionals. In T. M. Skovholt & M. Trotter-Mathison (Eds.), *The resilient practitioner: Burnout prevention and self-care strategies for therapists, counselors, teachers, and health professionals.* (2nd ed., pp. xxi–xxiv). New York, NY: Routledge.

Skovholt, T. M., & Starkey, M. T. (2012). The practitioner's intense search for knowing in a sea of ambiguity: Answers from the learning triangle of practice, academic research and personal life. In G. J. Neimeyer & J. M. Taylor (Eds.), *Continuing professional development and lifelong learning: Issues, impacts and outcomes* (pp. 229–247). Hauppauge, NY: Nova Science.

Slotnick, H. B., & Shershneva, M. B. (2002). Use of theory to interpret elements of change. *Journal of Continuing Education in the Health Professions, 22,* 197–204.

Smith, P. L., Moss, S. B., & Burton, S. (2009). Psychologist impairment: What is it, how can it be prevented, and what can be done to address it? *Clinical Psychology: Science and Practice, 16,* 1–5.

Social Workers Registration Board. (2016). *Competence assessment and competence recertification.* Retrieved from http://www.swrb.govt.nz/competence-assessment#RECERTIFICATION

St. Jean, E. (2012). Mentoring as professional development for novice entrepreneurs: Maximizing the learning. *International Journal of Training and Development, 16,* 200–216.

Staniforth, B. L. (2010). *Perspectives on the role of counselling in social work in Aotearoa New Zealand* (Unpublished doctoral dissertation). Massey University, Auckland, NZ.

Stanton, S. (2001). Going the distance: Developing shared web-based learning programmes. *Occupational Therapy International, 8,* 96–106.

Taylor, J. M., Latorre, C., Fouad, N., Santana, M., & Berkey, S. (2016). *Professional competence and personal well-being in graduate school.* Unpublished manuscript. University of Utah, Salt Lake City, UT.

Taylor, J. M., & Neimeyer, G. J. (2015a). The assessment of lifelong learning in psychologists. *Professional Psychology: Research and Practice, 46,* 385–390.

Taylor, J. M., & Neimeyer, G. J. (2015b). Public perceptions of psychologists' professional development activities: The good, the bad, and the ugly. *Professional Psychology: Research and Practice, 46,* 140–146.

Taylor, J. M., & Neimeyer, G. J. (2016). Continuing education and lifelong learning strategies. In J. C. Norcross, G. R. VandenBos, & D. K. Freedheim (Eds.), *APA handbook of clinical psychology* (Vol. 5, pp. 135–152). Washington, DC: APA Books.

Taylor, J. M., Neimeyer, G. J., & Cox, D. (2016). *The impact of stress on professional competence: A nationwide study among board-certified psychologists.* Unpublished manuscript. University of Utah, Salt Lake City, UT.

Taylor, J. M., Neimeyer, G. J., & Wear, D. (2012). Professional competency and personal experience: An exploratory study. In G. J. Neimeyer & J. M. Taylor (Eds.), *Continuing professional development and life-long learning: Issues, impacts and outcomes* (pp. 249–261). Hauppauge, NY: Nova Science.

Topping, K. (1998). Peer assessment between students in colleges and universities. *Review of Educational Research, 68,* 249–276.

Ukens, C. (1995). The tragic truth. *Drug Topics, 139,* 66.

United Way. (2016). "Walk a Mile" in the shoes of a family facing poverty. Retrieved from http://www.uwcm.org/main/walk-a-mile/

VandeCreek, L., Knapp, S., & Brace, K. (1990). Mandatory continuing education for licensed psychologists: Its rationale and current implementation. *Professional Psychology: Research and Practice, 21,* 135–140.

Violato, C., Lockyer, J. M., & Fidler, H. (2008). Assessment of psychiatrists in practice through multisource feedback. *Canadian Journal of Psychiatry, 53,* 525–533.

Vollmer, S., Spada, H., Caspar, F., & Burri, S. (2013). Expertise in clinical psychology: The effects of university training and practical experience as expertise in clinical psychology. *Frontiers in Psychology, 4.* doi:10.3389/fpsyg.2013.00141.

Webb, C., & Horn, J. (2012). Continuing professional development: A regulatory perspective. In G. J. Neimeyer & J. M. Taylor (Eds.), *Continuing professional development and lifelong learning: Issues, impacts and outcomes* (pp. 135–153). Hauppauge, NY: Nova Science.

Webster, T. G. (1971). National priorities for the continuing education of psychologists. *American Psychologist, 26,* 1016–1019.

Wise, E. H. (2008). Competence and scope of practice: Ethics and professional development. *Journal of Clinical Psychology: In Session, 64,* 626–637.

Wise, E. H., Sturm, C. A., Nutt, R. L., Rodolfa, E., Schaffer, J. B., & Webb, C. (2010). Life-long learning for psychologists: Current status and a vision for the future. *Professional Psychology: Research and Practice, 41,* 288–297.

Wood, B. J., Klein, S., Cross, H. J., Lammers, C. J., & Elliott, J. K. (1985). Impaired practitioners: Psychologists' opinions about prevalence, and proposals for intervention. *Professional Psychology: Research and Practice, 16,* 843–850.

Yates, J. (2014). Synchronous online CPD: Empirical support for the value of webinars in career settings. *British Journal of Guidance and Counselling, 42,* 245–260.

Zemansky, M. (2012). A review of concerns in regard to the implementation of the CE mandate in Illinois. In G. J. Neimeyer & J. M. Taylor (Eds.), *Continuing professional development and lifelong learning: Issues, impacts and outcomes* (pp. 179–185). Hauppauge, NY: Nova Science.

12

Advances in Medical Education from Mastery Learning and Deliberate Practice
William C. McGaghie

Note from the Editors   The goal of this edited volume is to explore how the field of mental health can use the science of expertise to improve clinical effectiveness. In this quest, we may benefit by examining similar efforts in other fields. For example, researchers in the field of medicine have spent the past two decades exploring how to use deliberate practice to improve the effectiveness of medical education. One of the leading voices in this movement is William McGaghie, a psychologist at Northwestern University. His research includes exploring new methods of medical training based on deliberate practice and comparing the effectiveness of these new methods with traditional training. We asked Dr. McGaghie to write a chapter for this volume summarizing his research, with the goal of learning from his experiences in medical education.

I begin with a quote drawn from a recent publication about the acquisition of competence in clinical medicine:

> [T]he world famous cardiac surgeon Denton A. Cooley writes in his memoir *100,000 Hearts* (Cooley, 2012) about the countless hours of practice in animal and cadaver laboratories, biomedical engineering laboratories, carpentry shops and focused surgical practice with feedback from different sources he experienced to master and advance his craft. This far exceeds the 10,000-hour rule that Ericsson, Prietula, & Cokeley (2007) ha[s] set as a minimum requirement for the acquisition of expertise in a variety of domains. (McGaghie & Kristopaitis, 2015, p. 223)

Cooley is legendary in the cardiac surgery community. His achievements are matched in different ways by superior performers in other walks of life, such as basketball icon Michael Jordan (1998), virtuoso cellist Yo-Yo Ma (Steinberg, 2015), Nobel laureate psychologist Daniel Kahneman (2011), and IBM chief executive officer Virginia Rometty (Metz, 2011). The common denominator among these diverse, high-achieving professionals is not high IQ or MENSA membership, although all of these persons are bright and thoughtful. What really separates such superior performers from the rest of the public is an intense work ethic

The Cycle of Excellence: Using Deliberate Practice to Improve Supervision and Training,
First Edition. Edited by Tony Rousmaniere, Rodney K. Goodyear, Scott D. Miller, and Bruce E. Wampold.
© 2017 John Wiley & Sons, Ltd. Published 2017 by John Wiley & Sons, Ltd.

that includes untold hours of *deliberate practice*, effortful repetition of professionally relevant tasks with regular feedback and correction toward the goal of constant improvement (Ericsson, 2004, 2015; Ericsson, Krampe, & Tesch-Römer, 1993; Ericsson & Pool, 2016). Michael Jordan (1998), for example, shot at least 500 free throws every day of his storied basketball career. Virtuosity and other signs of very high achievement derive from neither one's genetic endowment nor one's academic pedigree. High achievement has its roots in many years of hard work grounded in deliberate practice.

This chapter uses the critical-realist method to review, synthesize, and report relevant literature (McGaghie, 2015b). The critical-realist approach captures the most compelling studies in a research domain and need not be exhaustive. Roycroft-Malone and colleagues (2012) stated: "A realist review focuses on understanding and unpacking the mechanisms by which an intervention works (or fails to work), thereby providing an explanation, as opposed to a judgment about how it works. . . . [T]he realist approach is particularly suited to the synthesis of evidence about complex implementation interventions" (p. 1).

This chapter has three sections. The first part is a brief history of U.S. medical education and its structure and operation from the early 20th century to the present. Second, the chapter addresses mastery learning (ML) with deliberate practice (DP) in medical education. These are new and rigorous approaches to medical education. Features of ML and DP are defined, and examples are presented to tell how they can unite to produce clinical expertise among physicians. Third, the chapter describes translational outcomes from medical education programs, especially programs grounded in ML, DP, and simulation technology. Translational outcomes go beyond educational results achieved in the classroom or learning laboratory by measuring educational outcomes in terms of improved patient care practices, patient outcomes, and such collateral effects as return on investment, skill retention, and unexpected health system improvements. The chapter concludes with a short coda.

History of U.S. Medical Education

The intellectual origins of traditional clinical medical education have roots in 19th-century thinking about the acquisition of clinical competence expressed by Sir William Osler in an address to the New York Academy of Medicine in 1903. The address, titled "The Hospital as a College," was published later in a collection of Osler's essays titled *Aequanimitas* (Osler, 1932). The essay addressed Osler's earlier experience with European medical education, which he judged superior to the American model. Osler stated: "The radical reform needed is the introduction into this country of the system of clinical clerks" (p. 319). Osler continued: "In what may be called the *natural method of teaching* the student begins with the patient, continues with the patient, and ends his studies with the patient. Teach him how to observe, give him many facts to observe, and the lessons will come out of the facts themselves" (p. 315, emphasis added).

Osler's conception about the *natural method of teaching* was endorsed by his Johns Hopkins surgeon colleague William Halsted, who described "the training of the surgeon" (Halsted, 1904). Osler and Halsted argued that the medical curriculum was embodied in patients—that is, that student exposure to patients and longitudinal experience is sufficient to ensure that physicians in training will become competent doctors. This is a passive clinical medical curriculum based solely on exposure to many patients. Osler and Halsted were visionary in their day. However, they had no idea about such basic educational principles as the utility of structured, graded educational requirements, skills practice, objective evaluation with feedback, accountability, and guided reflection for new physicians to master their craft. The Osler and Halsted clinical curriculum tradition dominated U.S. 20th-century medical education and continued with little variation into the 21st century.

Contemporary medical education is organized and delivered in a manner that is nearly identical to that used in the early 20th century. The customary U.S. medical school curriculum lasts four years. The first two years are occupied by classroom and laboratory instruction and assessment about the sciences that are basic to medical practice, such as gross and microscopic anatomy, physiology, pharmacology, and pathology. The second two years are filled with clinical experiences—clerkships, electives, subinternships—intended to introduce doctors in training to the practical realities of medical care. Rigorous, standardized tests of medical knowledge acquisition known as the United States Medical Licensing Examinations, designed and administered by the National Board of Medical Examiners, shape and channel the learning behavior of medical students in both preclinical and clinical curriculum years.

The early 20th-century model of clinical medical education is expressed in 2017 as undergraduate clinical clerkships, postgraduate residency rotations, and fellowship experiences that are structured by time (weeks or months) and location (clinical site). The clinical education experiences operate in a complex healthcare environment where medical education is often subordinate to patient care and financial incentives. Structural and operational expressions of Osler's natural method of teaching are seen every day at medical schools and in residency and fellowship programs where traditional, time-honored educational practices such as morning report and professor rounds are preserved and sustained.

The key problem with the natural method of teaching—that is, education based on clinical experience alone—is that the educational model does not work very well. Clinical medical education under the Osler tradition is passive. Key learning outcomes among medical students or residents (e.g., clinical skill acquisition, medical record documentation, healthcare team communication) are rarely evaluated with rigor or based on reliable data that permit valid decisions about medical learners and their progress (Holmboe, 2004, 2008). However, traditional educational practices have been maintained by accreditation requirements that, until recently, have preserved the status quo and endorsed educational inertia (Nasca, Philibert, Brigham, & Flynn, 2012).

Scores of medical education research studies published over the past two decades have produced measured outcomes that cast doubt on the educational utility of clinical education based solely on longitudinal clinical experience. Mangione, Nieman, Graceley, and Kaye (1993) and Mangione and Nieman (1997), for example, published studies showing that residents in medicine and family medicine and cardiology fellows perform poorly on objective measures of cardiac auscultation (i.e., listening to and discriminating heart sounds). Training longevity had no effect, because the performance of senior residents did not differ from that of first-year residents. Cardiology fellows performed slightly better (22% correct) than residents (20% correct) on these basic skills. Residents and cardiology fellows in these two studies performed no better than medical students at evaluating heart sounds. Findings from another study (Mangione & Nieman, 1999) on resident proficiency at pulmonary auscultation replicated the poor cardiac auscultation results.

Many other research reports have been published that objectively measure substandard clinical skill acquisition among physicians in training and in practice due to clinical education grounded solely in patient care experience. Three examples are telling.

First, two separate studies performed at the University of Michigan (Lypson, Frohna, Gruppen, & Woolliscroft, 2004) and Northwestern University (Cohen, Barsuk, Moazed et al., 2013) revealed serious skill and knowledge deficits among new postgraduate residents in internal medicine. Measured clinical weaknesses were found in basic proficiency at interpreting critical laboratory values, cross-cultural communication, evidence-based medicine, radiographic image interpretation, aseptic technique, and invasive procedures (e.g., lumbar puncture [LP], intensive care unit skills, cardiac auscultation). Clinical "boot camp" educational experiences were needed at the beginning of residency to prepare the young doctors to care for patients.

Second, research involving 81 beginning residents in internal medicine, emergency medicine, anesthesiology, and general surgery done at Northwestern University in 2013 showed that the residents "could not reliably identify ten basic [electrocardiogram] findings. This is despite graduating almost exclusively from U.S. medical schools and performing at high levels on standardized tests" (Wilcox, Raval, Patel, Didwania, & Wayne, 2014, pp. 197–198).

Third, Barsuk and colleagues (2016) reported an investigation involving 108 experienced attending physicians at 58 U.S. Veterans Affairs Medical Centers from February to December 2014. Ninety percent of these medical centers were training affiliates of civilian academic medical centers. This was a "train the trainer" study where the attending physicians were being prepared to educate residents about how to perform central venous catheter (CVC) insertion to ML standards. All of the attending physicians had been trained earlier, via traditional clinical education, to perform CVC insertion. A rigorous clinical skills pretest is a key feature of the ML "bundle" (McGaghie, Siddall, Mazmanian, & Myers, 2009). Despite an average of over 13 years of clinical experience, only 18% of the attending physicians met or exceeded the minimum passing standard for internal jugular CVC insertion and just 24% of the experienced doctors met or exceeded the minimum passing standard for subclavian CVC insertion on the ML pretest. Barsuk et al. (2016) concluded: "This study demonstrates highly variable simulated CVC insertion performance among a national cohort of experienced attending physicians" (p. 1871).

The educational poverty of reliance on clinical experience alone as a proxy measure of medical skill acquisition is also evident in a study by surgeon Richard Bell and colleagues (Bell et al., 2009). In this investigation, surgery residency program directors graded 300 operative procedures A, B, or C using these criteria:

> A—graduating general surgery residents should be competent to perform the procedure independently; B—graduating residents should be familiar with the procedure, but not necessarily competent to perform it; and C—graduating residents neither need to be familiar with nor competent to perform the procedure. (p. 719)

Records of the operative experience of all U.S. residents (*n* = 1,022) completing general surgery training in June 2005 were reviewed, compiled, and compared with the three procedural criteria.

The study results are sobering and address Osler's natural method of teaching directly. Bell and colleagues (2009) reported:

> One hundred twenty-one of the 300 operations were considered **A** level procedures by a majority of program directors (PDs). Graduating 2005 US residents (n = 1022) performed only 18 of the 121 **A** procedures, an average of more than 10 times during residency; 83 of 121 procedures were performed on average less than 5 times and 31 procedures less than once. For 63 of the 121 procedures, the mode (most commonly reported) experience was 0. In addition, there was significant variation between residents in operative experience for specific procedures. (p. 719)

Bell and colleagues (2009) concluded:

> Methods will have to be developed to allow surgeons to reach a basic level of competence in procedures which they are likely to experience only rarely during residency. Even for more commonly performed procedures, the numbers of repetitions are not very robust, stressing the need to determine objectively whether residents are actually achieving basic competency in these operations. (p. 719)

The story from these and many other studies on clinical medical education is clear, consistent, and compelling. Clinical experience alone is insufficient to guarantee the acquisition of clinical competence among medical learners (Ericsson, 2014; Kyser et al., 2014; Mattar et al., 2013). Osler's natural method of teaching based only on longitudinal clinical experience without curriculum objectives, tight program management, performance expectations, learner practice and supervision, rigorous assessment with feedback, high achievement standards, and clear educational milestones is obsolete and should be restructured and improved.

Mastery Learning with Deliberate Practice

ML with DP is a new framework for training clinical health professionals as individuals and teams. ML is an especially rigorous form of competency-based education (McGaghie, Miller, Sajid, & Telder, 1978) that expects excellence for all. This means that all medical students, residents, or fellows are expected to achieve high learning standards with little or no measured outcome variation. ML programs are not governed by time, unlike most other educational approaches. Instead, in ML, learning time can vary among learners, but learning outcomes are uniform. This is a radical departure from traditional medical education, which has fixed learning times (e.g., days, weeks, semesters) and assumes that learning outcomes are expressed as individual differences distributed on a Gaussian normal curve.

As stated elsewhere (McGaghie, 2015a; McGaghie et al., 2009), ML is an inseparable "bundle" with seven complementary features:

1. Baseline, or diagnostic testing
2. Clear learning objectives, sequenced as units in increasing difficulty
3. Engagement in educational activities (e.g., deliberate skills practice, data interpretation, reading) focused on reaching the objectives

4. A set minimum passing standard (e.g., checklist score) for each educational unit
5. Formative testing to gauge unit completion at a preset minimum passing standard for mastery
6. Advancement to the next educational unit, given measured achievement at or above the mastery standard
7. Continued practice or study on an educational unit until the mastery standard is reached

The goal in ML is to ensure that all learners accomplish all educational outcomes with little or no variation in outcome. The amount of time needed to reach the mastery standard for a unit's educational objectives varies among the learners (McGaghie et al., 2009). Figure 12.1 is an infographic that summarizes key features of ML with deliberate practice in medical education (McGaghie, Barsuk, & Wayne, 2015).

Rigorous measurements that yield reliable data are essential in ML for three reasons. First, reliable data are a source of trustworthy information to give learners feedback about their progress toward mastery goals. Such measurement—that is, assessment *for learning*—qualifies as dynamic testing (Grigorenko & Sternberg, 1998; Sternberg & Grigorenko, 2002) because it is instructive and elicits responses. "[Dynamic] testing involves learning at the time of the test, rather than just static testing of what has been learned before" (Grigorenko & Sternberg, 1998, p. 75). Second, reliable data are needed to make accurate decisions about learner advancement in a mastery curriculum. Third, sound data are needed to advance research, scholarship, and program evaluation. Reliable learner performance data, calculated frequently and rigorously, are a cornerstone of ML education and research programs.

A good example of ML in medical education is available from a study by internist Jeffrey Barsuk and colleagues (Barsuk, Cohen, Caprio et al., 2012) This is a study of first-year internal medicine (IM) residents' acquisition of lumbar puncture (LP) skills in a mastery learning curriculum compared with second-, third-, and fourth-year neurology residents' LP skill acquisition from traditional clinical education. Figure 12.2 shows that IM residents express wide variation in LP skills at baseline testing using an LP simulator. However, after a minimum 3-hour education session featuring deliberate practice and feedback, all IM residents met or exceeded a mastery standard for LP skills. By contrast, only a small number of the traditionally trained neurology residents met the passing standard measured on the LP simulator, even though they had much more LP clinical experience with real patients. The research report concluded: "Few [traditionally trained] neurology residents were competent to perform a simulated LP *despite clinical experience with the procedure* (Basruk, Cohen, Caprio et al., 2012, p. 1327; emphasis added). An editorial that accompanied publication of the LP ML research commented:

> The Barsuk et al. study is clearly a wake-up call for all of us who were trained in the era of "see one, do one, teach one"—the so-called "apprenticeship" model of clinical training. The old training methods are no longer enough to ensure the best education, and thus the best care for patients. (Nathan & Kincaid, 2012, p. 1167)

The efficacy of DP for skill and knowledge acquisition in medical education is well established. As expressed elsewhere, "Deliberate practice is an educational variable associated with delivery of strong and consistent educational treatments as part of the mastery

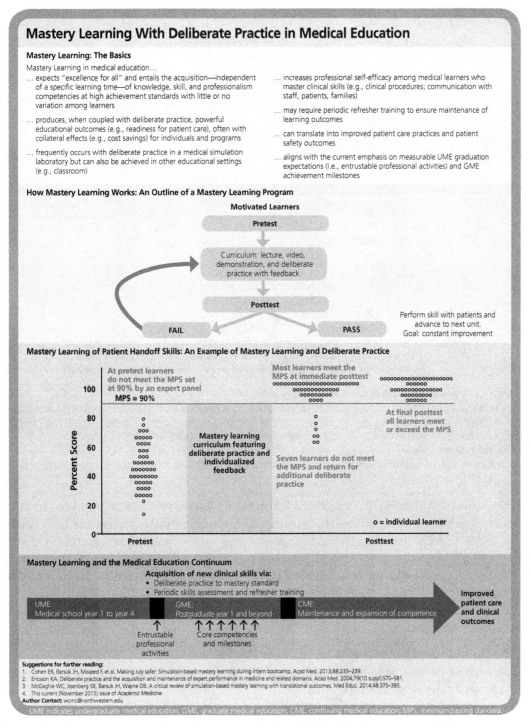

Figure 12.1 Mastery learning with deliberate practice in medical education.
Source: McGaghie et al., 2015. Copyright by the Association of American Medical Colleges. Reprinted with permission.

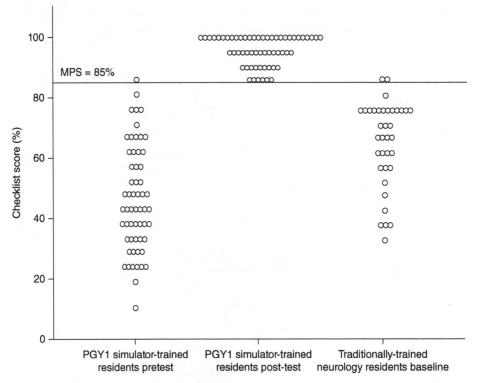

Figure 12.2 Mastery learning of lumbar puncture skills.
Note. Clinical skills examination (checklist) pre- and final posttest performance of 58 first-year simulator-trained internal medicine residents and baseline performance of 36 traditionally trained neurology residents. Three internal medicine residents failed to meet the minimum passing score (MPS) at initial post-testing.
PGY – postgraduate year.
Source: Barsuk, Cohen, Caprio et al. (2012, p. 135). Reprinted with permission of Wolters Kluwer Health.

learning model. Although demanding of learners, deliberate practice is grounded in information processing and behavioral theories of skill acquisition and maintenance" (McGaghie et al., 2009, p. 665). The theoretical foundation and early empirical research on DP were pioneered by psychologist K. Anders Ericsson and his associates (Ericsson, 2004; Ericsson & Charness, 1994; Ericsson et al., 1993; Ericsson, Charness, Feltovich, & Hoffman, 2006; Erics-son & Pool, 2016).

DP has at least 10 components that operate in close partnership with the ML model (McGaghie et al., 2009).

1. Highly motivated learners with good concentration;
2. Engagement with a well-defined learning objective or task; at an
3. Appropriate level of difficulty; with
4. Focused, repetitive practice; that leads to
5. Rigorous, precise measurements; that yield
6. Informative feedback from educational sources (e.g., teachers, standardized patients, simulators); and where

7. Trainees also monitor their learning experiences and correct strategies, errors, and levels of understanding, engage in more DP; and continue with
8. Evaluation to reach a mastery standard; and then
9. Advance to another unit or task; toward the
10. Goal: constant improvement.

DP means that medical learners engage in hard procedural and intellectual work—they concentrate, strive to improve, and even sweat. DP and ML are complementary ideas that, when used together in a medical education curriculum, can produce extraordinary learning results (e.g., Barsuk, Cohen, Vozenilek et al., 2012; Barsuk, McGaghie, Cohen et al., 2009a, 2009b; Malakooti et al., 2015; Reed et al., 2016; Wayne et al., 2006). This new evidence-based educational framework is slowly beginning to replace the apprenticeship, see-one, do-one, teach-one approach to clinical education that has defined knowledge and skill acquisition in medicine for more than a century.

Translational Outcomes from Medical Education

Translational science (TS) is usually defined as biomedical or bioengineering research designed to accelerate movement of results from the laboratory bench to the patient bed-side. The biomedical TS model has recently been extended to medical and health professions education, especially education programs that rely on simulation technology together with ML and DP. To illustrate, Figure 12.3 is a schematic that describes the effects of powerful medical education interventions at three "downstream" measured levels: T1 = knowledge, skills, attitudes, and professionalism measured in a controlled simulation laboratory; T2 = better patient care practices in the clinic or at the bedside; T3 = better patient outcomes in the clinic and the community. Barsuk and Szmuilowicz (2015) amplified the scheme by adding a fourth outcome level: T4 = "extending the measurement endpoint to skill retention, dissemination, and health policy, in which populations or targets other than research subjects [may] benefit from improved health" (p. 117).

Contributions of medical education Interventions to T1, T2, and T3 outcomes.			
Medical education Interventions	**T1**	**T2**	**T3**
Increased or Improved	Knowledge, skill, attitudes, and professionalism	Patient care practices	Patient outcomes
Target	Individuals and teams	Individuals and teams	Individuals and public health
Setting	Simulation lab	Clinic and bedside	Clinic and community

Figure 12.3 Simulation-based medical education as translational science.
Source: McGaghie (2010, p. 1). Reprinted with permission from the American Association for the Advancement of Science.

As McGaghie, Draycott, Dunn, Lopez, and Stefanidis (2011) pointed out:

> A long and rich research legacy shows that under the right conditions, simulation-based medical education (SBME) is a powerful intervention to increase medical learner competence. SBME translational science demonstrates that [short-run] results achieved in the educational laboratory (T1) transfer to improved downstream patient care practices (T2) and improved patient and public health (T3). (p. 542)

A noteworthy example of an SBME TS research program is seen in the work of an interdisciplinary team led by Northwestern University hospitalist physician Jeffrey Barsuk. This research program addressed training internal medicine residents in CVC insertion to ML standards in the medical simulation laboratory, later studying the effects of this training on downstream results. The research program reported that acquisition of CVC insertion skills by medical residents to mastery standards in the simulation laboratory (T1) (Barsuk et al., 2009a) translated to improved patient care practices (T2) (Barsuk, McGaghie, Cohen, O'Leary, & Wayne, 2009b) expressed as fewer needle passes, arterial punctures, and needle adjustments as well as higher success rates and better patient outcomes (T3) (Barsuk, Cohen, Feinglass, McGaghie, & Wayne, 2009) measured by an 85% drop in a medical intensive care unit's catheter-related bloodstream infection rate. These profound clinical results are all directly attributable to the powerful simulation-based mastery learning educational intervention that relies on deliberate practice.

Other examples of downstream (T4) translational outcomes resulting from the SBML educational intervention include CVC skill and knowledge retention over time (Barsuk, Cohen, McGaghie, & Wayne, 2010), unexpected yet welcome collateral effects that document systemic educational improvement among subsequent internal medicine residents, due to rigorous training of prior resident cohorts (Barsuk, Cohen, Feinglass, McGaghie, & Wayne, 2011), the need to raise the ML minimum passing standard due to systemic improvement in trainee quality (Cohen, Barsuk, McGaghie, & Wayne, 2013), and cost-effectiveness expressed as a 7:1 rate of return on financial investment from the SBML program (Cohen et al., 2010). This body of research work shows that powerful medical education interventions grounded in ML with DP not only have proximal impact but also have distal consequences for the professional lives of medical trainees and the welfare of patients they serve.

Translational outcomes in medical education cannot be achieved from single, isolated studies. Instead, TS results in medical education derive from educational and health services research *programs* that are thematic, sustained, and cumulative. Such translational research programs must be designed with thought and care to anticipate and measure downstream results.

The Barsuk team's ability to demonstrate such impressive TS results is a consequence of careful research planning, hard work, and constant attention to the importance of team science. Research groups across the health and human service professions should emulate the thematic, sustained, and cumulative research program carried out by the Barsuk team.

Several recent reviews document the spread and impact of medical education TS research in a variety of medical specialties (Griswold-Theodorson et al., 2015; McGaghie et al., 2011;

McGaghie, Issenberg, Barsuk, & Wayne, 2014; McGaghie, Issenberg, Cohen, Barsuk, & Wayne, 2012; Zendejas, Brydges, Wang, & Cook, 2012; Zendejas et al., 2011). The weight of evidence from these and other studies now clearly shows that powerful medical education interventions improve the skillfulness of doctors who deliver patient care and can improve the health of persons the doctors serve.

Coda

The title of this volume, *The Cycle of Excellence: Using Deliberate Practice in Supervision, Training, and Independent Practice*, is a clear expression of the book's intent to introduce new, evidence-based training models grounded in deliberate practice and perhaps ML to the community of psychotherapy education. Several journal articles that advance this agenda have been published (e.g. Chow, Miller, Seidel, Kane, & Thornton., 2015; Tracey, Wampold, Lichtenberg, & Goodyear, 2014). This chapter will be successful if the ideas and examples it presents from medical education inform educational improvements in other professions including psychotherapy.

Questions from the Editors

Question #1: You make the case that training should strive for mastery learning in which "all medical students, residents, or fellows are expected to achieve high learning standards with little or no measured outcome variation." Expertise, though, implies that some professionals obtain demonstrably better outcomes than others, and so there is inevitable outcome variation.

Answer from Author: There is a difference between (a) achieving very high mastery educational outcomes among medical learners (i.e., students, residents, fellows) with little or no variation, and (b) patient outcomes that are reached, in part, by contributions from medical professionals. These are measurement endpoint issues that need to be distinguished.

In 2010, I published a typology titled "Medical Education Research as Translational Science" to sort out educational and clinical measurement endpoints that result from powerful educational interventions. The typology identifies three cascaded measurement endpoints: (a) T1: educational learning outcomes measured in the classroom or simulation laboratory; (b) T2: patient care practices that are affected by the educational interventions; and (c) T3: patient outcomes that derive from the patient care practices shaped by powerful education. The typology has been amplified by Barsuk and Szmuilowicz (2015) to include a T4 level, which involves skill retention, cost savings, and unexpected collateral effects.

We should also acknowledge that some patient conditions, such as addictions, are refractory despite clinician skillfulness. Clinician educators and outcome evaluators need to be optimistic yet realistic about what rigorous education can deliver.

Question #2: If your goal was to work with independently practicing physicians who were committed to lifelong professional development to become better over their careers, in what ways would you adopt the mastery model you describe in your chapter? Are there any real-life examples to illustrate what that looks like in practice?

Answer from Author: Professional improvement of independently practicing physicians is governed by maintenance of competence (MOC) policies of medical certification boards (e.g., American Board of Internal Medicine, American Board of Pediatrics). Medical MOC policies today usually address attendance at meetings, multiple-choice examinations at fixed intervals, and sometimes practice audits. There are no real-life examples, to my knowledge, of current ML programs that are now used for medical MOC.

Question #3. Your chapter makes a compelling case for using well-developed simulations in training. But simulations are still relatively new in psychotherapy training. What guidelines and advice would you offer those of us who wish to begin designing and using simulations for that training?

Answer from Author: In the short run, simulations for use in psychotherapy training would best involve standardized patients (i.e., persons who are carefully scripted and trained to present patient psychosocial clinical conditions uniformly). Psychotherapists in training could practice their skills with standardized patients, undergo rigorous measurements, receive actionable feedback, and continue with practice until a mastery standard is reached. Nobel laureate psychologist Daniel Kahneman (2011) had it right: "The acquisition of skills requires a regular environment, an adequate opportunity to practice, and rapid and un-equivocal feedback about the correctness of thoughts and actions. When these conditions are fulfilled, skill eventually develops, and the intuitive judgments and choices that quickly come to mind will mostly be accurate" (p. 416).

Question #4: This book is focused on what works to facilitate ongoing professional development. Some individuals have the personal commitment and drive to engage in this practice (i.e., your example of people like Michael Jordan). But widespread implementation of this will require that larger systems and organizations commit resources and implement reward structures to achieve those ends. Are there lessons in what you have described here that might have broader application to the kinds of systems/organizational change that would support broad adoption of what we propose in this book for psychotherapists?

Answer from Author: The American Board of Medical Specialties, an umbrella organization represented by 24 medical specialty boards, has been spearheading MOC efforts for at least a decade. Academic and scholarly advocates of MOC programs featuring rigorous measurement and individual accountability meet stiff resistance from the practitioner community on grounds of cost, time, and other regulatory burdens. Evaluation apprehension is also the gorilla in the room among certified and licensed physicians. Organizational systems need to be designed to incentivize physicians and psychotherapists to regularly boost their skill sets and to use evaluation data as a tool for professional improvement, not as a weapon.

References

Barsuk, J. H., Cohen, E. R., Caprio, T., McGaghie, W. C., Simuni, T., & Wayne, D. B. (2012). Simulation-based education with mastery learning improves residents' lumbar puncture skills. *Neurology, 79,* 132–137.

Barsuk, J. H., Cohen, E. R., Feinglass, J., McGaghie, W. C., & Wayne, D. B. (2009). Use of simulation-based education to reduce catheter-related bloodstream infections. *Archives of Internal Medicine, 169*(15), 1420–1423.

Barsuk, J. H., Cohen, E. R., Feinglass, J., McGaghie, W. C., & Wayne, D. B. (2011). Unexpected collateral effects of simulation-based medical education. *Academic Medicine, 86,* 1513–1517.

Barsuk, J. H., Cohen, E. R., McGaghie, W. C., & Wayne, D. B. (2010). Long-term retention of central venous catheter insertion skills after simulation-based mastery learning. *Academic Medicine, 85*(10, Suppl.), S9–S12.

Barsuk, J. H., Cohen, E. R., Nguyen, D., Mitra, D., O'Hara, K., Okuda, Y., . . . Wayne, D. B. (2016). Attending physician adherence to a 29-component central venous catheter bundle checklist during simulated procedures. *Critical Care Medicine, 44*(10), 1871–1881.

Barsuk, J. H., Cohen, E. R., Vozenilek, J. A., O'Connor, L. M., McGaghie, W. C., & Wayne, D. B. (2012). Simulation-based education with mastery learning improves paracentesis skills. *Journal of Graduate Medical Education, 4*(1), 23–27.

Barsuk, J. H., McGaghie, W. C., Cohen, E. R., Balachandran, J. S., & Wayne, D. B. (2009a). Use of simulation-based mastery learning to improve the quality of central venous catheter placement in a medical intensive care unit. *Journal of Hospital Medicine, 4,* 397–403.

Barsuk, J. H., McGaghie, W. C., Cohen, E. R., O'Leary, K. S., & Wayne, D. B. (2009b). Simulation-based mastery learning reduces complications during central venous catheter insertion in a medical intensive care unit. *Critical Care Medicine, 37*(10), 2697–2701.

Barsuk, J. H., & Szmuilowicz, E. (2015). Evaluating medical procedures: Evaluation and transfer to the bedside. In L. N. Pangaro & W. C. McGaghie (Eds.), *Handbook on medical student evaluation and assessment* (pp. 113–126). North Syracuse, NY: Gegensatz Press.

Bell, R. H., Biester, T. W., Tabuenca, A., Rhodes, R. S., Cofer, J. B., Britt, L. D., & Lewis, F. R., Jr. (2009). Operative experience of residents in US general surgery programs: A gap between expectation and experience. *Annals of Surgery, 249*(5), 719–724.

Chow, D. L., Miller, S. D., Seidel, J. A., Kane R. T., & Thornton, J. A. (2015). The role of deliberate practice in the development of highly effective psychotherapists. *Psychotherapy, 52*(3), 337–345.

Cohen, E. R., Barsuk, J. H., McGaghie, W. C., & Wayne, D. B. (2013). Raising the bar: Reassessing standards for procedural competence. *Teaching and Learning in Medicine, 25*(1), 6–9.

Cohen, E. R., Barsuk, J. H., Moazed, F., Caprio, T., Didwania, A., McGaghie, W. C., & Wayne, D. B. (2013). Making July safer: Mastery learning of clinical skills during intern bootcamp. *Academic Medicine, 88,* 233–239.

Cohen, E. R., Feinglass, J., Barsuk, J. H., Barnard, C., O'Donnell, A., McGaghie, W. C., & Wayne, D. B. (2010). Cost savings from reduced catheter-related bloodstream infection after simulation-based education for residents in a medical intensive care unit. *Simulation in Healthcare, 5,* 98–102.

Cooley, D. A. (2012). *100,000 hearts: A surgeon's memoir.* Austin, TX: Dolph Briscoe Center for American History, University of Texas at Austin.

Ericsson, K. A. (2004). Deliberate practice and the acquisition and maintenance of expert performance in medicine and related domains. *Academic Medicine, 79,* S70–S81.

Ericsson, K. A. (2014). Necessity is the mother of invention: Video recording firsthand perspectives of critical medical procedures to make simulated training more effective. *Academic Medicine, 89,* 17–20.

Ericsson, K. A. (2015). Acquisition and maintenance of medical expertise: A perspective from the expert-performance approach with deliberate practice. *Academic Medicine, 90*(11), 1471–1486.

Ericsson, K. A., & Charness, N. (1994). Expert performance: Its structure and acquisition. *American Psychologist, 49,* 725–747.

Ericsson, K. A., Charness, N., Feltovich, P. J., & Hoffman, R. R. (Eds.) (2006). *The Cambridge handbook of expertise and expert performance.* New York, NY: Cambridge University Press.

Ericsson, K. A., Krampe, R. T., & Tesch-Römer, C. (1993). The role of deliberate practice in the acquisition of expert performance. *Psychological Review, 100,* 363–406.

Ericsson, A., & Pool, R. (2016). *Peak: Secrets from the new science of expertise.* Boston, MA: Houghton Mifflin Harcourt.

Ericsson, K. A., Prietula, M. J., & Cokeley, E. T. (2007). The making of an expert. *Harvard Business Review, 85,* 115–121.

Grigorenko, E. L., & Sternberg, R. J. (1998). Dynamic testing. *Psychological Bulletin, 124,* 75–111.

Griswold-Theodorson, S., Ponnuru, S., Dong, C., Szyld, D., Reed, T., & McGaghie, W. C. (2015). Beyond the simulation laboratory: A realist synthesis of clinical outcomes of simulation-based mastery learning. *Academic Medicine, 90*(11), 1553–1560.

Halsted, W. S. (1904). The training of the surgeon. *Bulletin of the Johns Hopkins Hospital, 15,* 267–275.

Holmboe, E. S. (2004). Faculty and the observation of trainees' clinical skills: Problems and opportunities. *Academic Medicine, 79,* 16–22.

Holmboe, E. S. (2008). Direct observation by faculty. In E. S. Holmboe & R. E. Hawkins (Eds.), *Practical guide to the evaluation of competence* (pp. 119–129). Philadelphia, PA: Mosby Elsevier.

Jordan, M. (1998). *For the love of the game.* New York, NY: Crown.

Kahneman, D. (2011). *Thinking, fast and slow.* New York, NY: Farrar, Straus and Giroux.

Kyser, K. L., Lu, X, Santillan, D., Santillan, M., Caughey, A. B., Wilson, M. C., & Cram, P. (2014). Forceps delivery volumes in teaching and nonteaching hospitals: Are volumes sufficient for physicians to acquire and maintain competence? *Academic Medicine, 89,* 71–76.

Lypson, M. L., Frohna, J. G., Gruppen, L. D., &Woolliscroft, J. O. (2004). Assessing residents' competencies at baseline: Identifying the gaps. *Academic Medicine, 79,* 564–570.

Malakooti, M. R., McBride, M. E., Mobley, B., Goldstein, J. L., Adler, M. D., & McGaghie, W. C. (2015). Mastery of status epilepticus management via simulation-based learning for pediatrics residents. *Journal of Graduate Medical Education, 7,* 181–186.

Mangione, S., & Nieman, L. Z. (1997). Cardiac auscultatory skills of internal medicine and family practice trainees: A comparison of diagnostic proficiency. *Journal of the American Medical Association, 278,* 717–722.

Mangione, S., & Nieman, L. Z. (1999). Pulmonary auscultatory skills during training in internal medicine and family practice. *American Journal of Respiratory and Critical Care Medicine, 159,* 1119–1124.

Mangione, S., Nieman, L. Z., Graceley, E., & Kaye, D. (1993). The teaching and practice of cardiac auscultation during internal medicine and cardiology training. *Annals of Internal Medicine, 119,* 47–54.

Mattar, S. G., Alseidi, A. A., Jones, D. B., Jeyarajah, D. R., Swanstrom, L. L., Aye, R. W., . . . Minter, R. M. (2013). General surgery residency inadequately prepares trainees for fellowship: Results of a survey of fellowship program directors. *Annals of Surgery, 258*(3), 440–449.

McGaghie, W. C. (2010). Medical education research as translational science. *Science Translational Medicine, 2*(19), 19cm8.

McGaghie, W. C. (2015a). Mastery learning: It is time for medical education to join the 21st century. *Academic Medicine, 90*(11), 1438–1441.

McGaghie, W. C. (2015b). Varieties of integrative scholarship. *Academic Medicine, 90*(3), 294–302.

McGaghie, W. C., Barsuk, J. H., & Wayne, D. B. (2015). Mastery learning with deliberate practice in medical education. *Academic Medicine, 90*(11), 1575.

McGaghie, W. C., Draycott, T. J., Dunn, W. F., Lopez, C. M., & Stefanidis, D. (2011). Evaluating the impact of simulation on translational patient outcomes. *Simulation in Healthcare, 6,* 542–547.

McGaghie, W. C., Issenberg, S. B., Barsuk, J. H., & Wayne, D. B. (2014). A critical review of simulation-based mastery learning with translational outcomes. *Medical Education, 48,* 375–385.

McGaghie, W. C., Issenberg, S. B., Cohen, E. R., Barsuk, J. H., & Wayne, D. B. (2012). Translational educational research: A necessity for effective healthcare improvement. *CHEST, 142,* 1097–1103.

McGaghie, W. C., & Kristopaitis, T. (2015). Deliberate practice and mastery learning: Origins of expert medical performance. In J. Cleland & S. J. Durning (Eds.), *Researching medical education* (pp. 219–230). Hoboken, NJ: Wiley.

McGaghie, W. C., Miller, G. E., Sajid, A., & Telder, T. V. (1978). *Competency-based curriculum development in medical education.* Public Health Paper No. 68. Geneva, Switzerland: World Health Organization.

McGaghie, W. C., Siddall, V. J., Mazmanian, P. J., & Myers, J. (2009). Lessons for continuing medical education from simulation research in undergraduate and graduate medical education: Effectiveness of continuing medical education: American College of Chest Physicians evidence-based educational guidelines. *CHEST, 135* (Suppl.), 62S–68S.

Metz, C. (2011, October 25). IBM names Virginia Rometty as first female CEO. *Wired.* Retrieved from http://www.wired.com/2011/10/virginia-rometty/

Nasca, T. J., Philibert, I., Brigham, Y., & Flynn, T. C. (2012). The next GME accreditation system—rationale and benefits. *New England Journal of Medicine, 366,* 1051–1056.

Nathan, B. R., & Kincaid, O. (2012). Does experience doing lumbar punctures result in expertise? A medical maxim bites the dust. *Neurology, 79*, 115–116.

Osler, W. (1932). The hospital as a college. In *Aequanimitas* (pp. 313–324). Philadelphia, PA: Blakiston's.

Reed, T., Pirotte, M., McHugh, M., Oh, L., Lovett, S., Hoyt, A. E., . . .McGaghie, W. C. (2016). Simulation-based mastery learning improves medical student performance and retention of core clinical skills. *Simulation in Healthcare, 11*, 173–180.

Roycroft-Malone, J., McCormack, B., Hutchinson, A. M., DeCorby, K., Bucknall, T. K., Kent, B., . . . Wilson, V. (2012). Realist synthesis: Illustrating the method for implementation research. *Implementation Science, 7*, 33.

Steinberg, M. (2015). Magic cello ride. *Strings, 30*(4), 30–34.

Sternberg, R. J., & Grigorenko, E. L. (2002). *Dynamic testing: The nature and measurement of learning potential.* New York, NY: Cambridge University Press.

Tracey, T.J.G., Wampold, B. E., Lichtenberg, J. W., & Goodyear, R. K. (2014). Expertise in psychotherapy: An elusive goal? *American Psychologist, 69*(3), 218–229.

Wanye, D. B., Butter, J., Siddall, V. J., Fudala, M. J., Wade, L. D., Feinglass, J., & McGaghie, W. C. (2006). Mastery learning of advanced cardiac life support skills using simulation technology and deliberate practice. *Journal of General Internal Medicine, 21*, 251–256.

Wilcox, J. E., Raval, Z., Patel, A. B., Didwania, A., & Wayne, D. B. (2014). Imperfect beginnings: Incoming residents vary in their ability to interpret basic electrocardiogram findings. *Journal of Hospital Medicine, 9*, 197–198.

Zendejas, B., Brydges, R., Wang, A. T., & Cook, D. A. (2012). Patient outcomes in simulation-based medical education: A systematic review. *Journal of General Internal Medicine, 28*, 1078–1089.

Zendejas, B., Cook, D. A., Bingener, J., Huebner, M., Dunn, W. F., Sarr, M. G., & Farley, D. R. (2011). Simulation-based mastery learning improves patient outcomes in laparoscopic inguinal hernia repair: A randomized controlled trial. *Annals of Surgery, 254*, 502–511.

Part IV

Recommendations

13

Improving Psychotherapy Outcomes

Guidelines for Making Psychotherapist Expertise Development Routine and Expected

Tony Rousmaniere, Rodney K. Goodyear, Scott D. Miller, and Bruce E. Wampold

This book offers both a challenge and a roadmap for addressing a fundamental challenge: How can therapists improve and become experts? We began by observing that many domains of human performance have demonstrated continually improved outcomes across time—a fact not true of psychotherapy. We drew from what is known about expertise and continual improvement when constructing a model that will enable individual psychotherapists to improve, which will result in better outcomes for clients. We were fortunate to have some of the field's most thoughtful scholars add specificity to that model. As important as the ideas presented in this volume may be, they do not benefit the field unless they are implemented by not only individual therapists but by supervisors, training programs, regulatory bodies, agency and health system leaders, researchers, and professional associations.

These entities all have critical roles to play in making psychotherapy more effective. Therefore, we end this work by speaking about steps that can be taken to contribute to the mission of improving psychotherapeutic expertise. In suggesting these steps, we draw from both evidence and logic to offer direction.

Training Programs

Trainee Selection

Most therapists are trained in university-based, postgraduate programs. In the United States, admissions decisions to such programs typically are made on the basis of a combination of Graduate Record Examination scores, undergraduate grade point average, the applicant's personal statement, letters of recommendation, and interviews.

Arguably, these sources of information about applicants predict academic success. But there is absolutely no evidence that they predict students' eventual effectiveness as psychotherapists. Many of us believe (or at least at one point in our careers believed) we could interview prospective students and identify those with the requisite interpersonal capacity to

The Cycle of Excellence: Using Deliberate Practice to Improve Supervision and Training,
First Edition. Edited by Tony Rousmaniere, Rodney K. Goodyear, Scott D. Miller, and Bruce E. Wampold.
© 2017 John Wiley & Sons, Ltd. Published 2017 by John Wiley & Sons, Ltd.

become effective therapists. Yet interviews generally are unreliable and poor predictors of performance. This is particularly true of unstructured interviews (Schmidt & Hunter, 1998). Schöttke, Flückiger, Goldberg, Eversmann, and Lange (2015) examined the responses of beginning therapists to a structured interview designed to assess motivation and personal capabilities and strengths (including self-perception, perception of others, communication skills, quality and stability of interpersonal interests, and self-reflection, rated by both cognitive behavioral and psychodynamic experts) and assessed how well they predicted therapy effectiveness later in the students' careers. Despite the exemplary nature of the interview (structure and reliable ratings by experts), the students' responses did not predict their outcomes as therapists. In addition, self-reported social skills of beginning therapists do not predict outcomes with their clients later on in training (Anderson, McClintock, Himawan, Song, & Patterson, 2016).

Fortunately, several studies have identified specific predictors of trainees' future effectiveness. (See Chapter 3.) For example, Schöttke et al. (2015), in the study just discussed that found that interviews did not predict psychotherapy outcomes, identified a means for assessing trainees' potential effectiveness. Applicants were shown a provocative film in a group and asked to discuss the film. The applicants' statements were then coded for motivation and personal strengths, in a similar way to the structured interviews, using items related to interest in patients, experience in and motivation for personal reflection, self-perception, communication, and personal relationships. Importantly, the ratings derived from this interpersonally challenging discussion predicted the therapists' outcomes over the next five years. In another study, Anderson et al. (2016) had trainees in their first weeks in graduate school respond to a video depicting a challenging interpersonal exchange with a patient. Their responses were then coded for verbal fluency, emotional expression, persuasiveness, hopefulness, warmth, empathy, alliance-bond capacity, and problem focus. Expert ratings of the trainees' responses *before* they had received any training predicted their outcomes with patients several years in the future.

Recommendation

These findings lead us to recommend that admissions procedures for psychotherapy training programs use challenge tests involving difficult interpersonal interactions to identify those applicants with the greatest potential to help clients.

Helping Trainees Achieve Competence and Prepare for Expertise Development

Over the past decade, mental health training programs have sharpened their focus on helping trainees attain a broad range of competencies that knowledgeable senior members of the profession have identified as essential (e.g., Falender & Shafranske, 2004; Fouad et al., 2009; Sperry, 2011; Stratton, Reibstein, Lask, Singh, & Asen, 2011; Swank, Lambie & Witta, 2012). Even though these competencies seem not to predict therapist's outcomes with clients, it is our position (see Chapter 4) that mastering them provides an essential foundation for going on to develop expertise. The good news is that many of the learning processes covered in this book as key to developing expertise (assessing baseline functioning, providing feedback, encouraging therapists and trainees continually to stretch beyond their zones of comfort) also are important to developing competence.

Training programs also can play an important role in preparing students for lifelong learning. Trainees should develop the expectation that expertise development is an essential professional responsibility throughout the therapist's career. Training programs can also teach students how to recognize, seek, and use high-quality professional development, which must be more than simply engaging in the sort of knowledge accrual that is sufficient for continuing education (CE) requirements in most jurisdictions. (See Chapter 11.)

Recommendations

In response to these mandates to training programs, we offer several recommendations:

- Trainees should learn at least one model of therapy well. The choice of model does not matter, except that it should be one that is accessible for trainees. Program graduates who have mastered a particular model are better prepared to develop an increasingly unique (and effective) approach to therapy after graduation.
- Supervisors employed by or affiliated with the program should receive training in how to provide supervision that incorporates the major components of the Cycle of Excellence (e.g., deliberate practice, continual performance feedback, simulation-based behavioral rehearsal; see Chapters 2, 3, and 4).
- Trainees should be explicitly taught about both the importance of career-long professional development and effective methods for engaging in it.
- Programs that train mental health professionals should also offer training in supervision. That training should focus not only on competence development (e.g., American Psychological Association, 2015), but on training in the expertise-development model we described in Chapter 4 (or an equivalent approach that emphasizes using deliberate practice for skill acquisition).
- Faculty and supervisors should model their own commitment to becoming more effective as determined by routinely measuring their own outcomes and having individualized professional development plans.
- Routine outcome monitoring (see Chapter 6) should be taught to trainees and used in clinical supervision (e.g., Overington, Fitzpatrick, Hunsley, & Drapeau, 2015). Training programs should monitor the outcomes of trainees and develop appropriate methods for using those data to improve training (e.g., Swift et al., 2015).

Regulatory Boards and Agencies: Overseeing Initial and Ongoing Rights to Practice

Psychotherapy practice is regulated in virtually all national or regional jurisdictions. That regulation concerns who is certified to practice and how psychotherapists then maintain that certification. Although these regulatory bodies typically are governmental entities (or operated under government oversight), some are professional organizations (e.g., the Australian Counseling Association, the Chinese Clinical and Counseling Psychology Registration System and the Korean Counseling Psychology Association; Ju, Han, Lee, & Lee, 2016).

Whatever the source of the authority of these boards and agencies, their purpose is to minimize the likelihood that credentialed therapists will harm those they treat (Beauchamp & Childress, 2009). That is, these therapists should be competent—and the focus of regulatory bodies on competence coincides with that is discussed with trainees worldwide in training programs and postgraduate CE. A good example of that focus is the International Declaration on Core Competences in Professional Psychology, which was released by the International Association of Applied Psychology and the International Union of Psychological Science (2016). Minimizing risk of harm is an essential function, but it presents regulatory bodies with a considerably lower bar than that of assessing actual effectiveness with clients.

Moreover, accurately assessing competencies is challenging (Lichtenberg et al., 2007). Often it is limited to ratings of supervisors that may or may not be valid indicators of ability (Klonoff, 2015). Additionally, when it comes to criteria for assessing therapists, continued right to practice (see Chapter 11), an emphasis on competence fails to address actual effectiveness. Regulatory bodies also are responsible for setting standards for granting the continued right to practice. For that function, they focus only marginally on actual competence. CE typically relies on seminars, lectures, and workshops that are not linked sequentially to one another and focus on imparting knowledge rather than the skills necessary to be an effective therapist.

This is a missed opportunity. Currently, external incentives for therapists to engage in serious skill development disappear once they obtain formal approval to practice. If the field is committed to increasing overall expertise, it will be insufficient to count on therapists' intrinsic motivation to engage in the hard and sustained work necessary for measurable professional development. Regulatory boards and agencies are in a position to provide helpful support and encouragement. In some countries (e.g., England, Australia, and New Zealand), various professional disciplines require ongoing supervision. Although this is a step in the right direction, a necessary next step would be that this supervision focus on continued skill development and that the outcomes of that work be documented.

Recommendations

We recommend that the governmental agencies and professional associations that regulate the practice of psychotherapy adopt requirements that:

- Require as a condition of maintaining their credentials to practice that therapists engage in supervision intended to increase their effectiveness as measured by client outcomes. This supervision must include observation of the therapist's actual work, via video or live observation, and monitoring outcomes.
- Require that those who provide that supervision themselves be credentialed for that work and that these credentials be based on assessed competence in providing the conditions that will increase therapist expertise (i.e., major components of the Cycle of Excellence, such as deliberate practice, continual performance feedback, simulation-based behavioral rehearsal; see Chapters 2, 3, and 4).
- Offer CE units to therapists who make documented efforts to develop and use a personalized professional development plan (e.g., individual consultation on challenging cases).
- Require that therapists applying to renew their credentials provide data on their effectiveness with clients.

Supervisors and Consultants

Deliberate practice and the Cycle of Excellence require effective performance feedback delivered by a coach or supervisor (Ericsson, 2006). Performance feedback poses a challenge for mental health, as practitioners currently receive insufficient training in how to provide effective supervision. Perhaps as a result, data suggest that supervision—as currently practiced—does not have a reliable impact on client outcome. (See Chapter 4.) Becoming a supervisor commonly requires little formal training or role induction beyond attending 5 to 10 hours of lecture-style learning. Rather, since the days of Freud, it has been assumed that experience as a clinician is sufficient to make one an effective supervisor. This assumption stands in contrast to many other fields, which define the role of a coach as clearly distinct from that of a performer and do not assume that great performers are automatically effective coaches. Furthermore, there currently are insufficient efforts to track supervisors' performance, and the current lists of supervisor competencies lack a focus on client outcomes (Goodyear, 2015).

Recommendations

On the basis of these findings, we recommend that:

- Selection criteria for supervisors should emphasize key components of deliberate practice, such as flexibility, responsiveness to feedback, and interpersonal skills.
- Supervisor competency criteria should be enhanced with a focus on skill acquisition and client outcome.
- Clinical supervision training programs should be developed to teach all this to new supervisors.
- Methods for supervisors to both track their performance as supervisors (including impact on client outcome) and get feedback on their supervision should be developed and empirically tested.

Administrators of Clinics, Agencies, and Mental Health Systems

Lifelong skill development requires motivation, financial resources, energy, and time. Administrators have an important role in helping therapists engage in this hard work. For example, administrators at Calgary Counselling Centre have integrated the Cycle of Excellence and deliberate practice into their therapists' routine work process (see Chapter 10), and the Child Outcomes Research Consortium in the United Kingdom has implemented procedures to help therapists collect and use outcome data (see Chapter 7).

Recommendations

We recommend that administrators:

- Create a culture of effort toward continual improvement, as exists in many other professional fields, such as athletics, music, aviation, and the military.
- Require the use of routine outcome measurement data for both therapists and supervisors.

- Require ongoing clinical supervision of therapists (by someone who is not an administrative supervisor).
- Create space in the work schedule to allow for both supervision and deliberate practice.
- Provide funding for therapists to pursue continual skill development.

Professional Associations

Professional associations have an important role in maintaining the professional culture that guides how therapists are trained and work. As it currently stands, most professional associations endorse the importance of lifelong learning. But few provide meaningful guidelines or incentives for effective skill development. There is a great opportunity for professional associations to take additional steps to support therapists in this regard.

Recommendations
We recommend that professional associations:

- Develop guidelines for therapists to assess their own effectiveness using both quantitative and qualitative methods. (See Chapters 5 and 6.)
- Develop awards for demonstrably effective therapy (based on client outcome), similarly to how awards currently are given for research, academic achievement, and other major domains of professional work.
- Develop similar awards for demonstrably effective lifelong skill development.
- Issue grants to researchers and agencies to encourage development of new methods for supportive lifelong skill development.
- Emphasize skill development tracks at professional conferences and in publications.
- Promote a culture of clinical peer review to support therapists in showing their work to consultants, supervisors, and peers.

Research

Most of the field's current clinical supervision and training practices are in wide use because they have been handed down via tradition rather than intentionally adopted on the basis of the research evidence (e.g., Ellis & Ladany, 1997). As a result, the pedagogy has mixed and unreliable impact on actual clinical effectiveness (e.g., Owen, Wampold, Rousmaniere, Kopta, & Miller, 2016; Watkins, 2011). Likewise, the field has limited access to valid and reliable methods to assess the effectiveness of clinical work. There is considerable potential for research to benefit both of these areas.

Recommendations
We recommend that researchers:

- When engaging in implementation research, reemphasize the ultimate goal of improving the effectiveness of actual therapists in the field and rely solely on client outcome as a measure of goal attainment.

- Develop more methods for assessing client outcome, including both quantitative and qualitative methods. (See Chapters 5 and 6.)
- Identify effective methods of training used by other fields and consider whether they may be of use for mental health.

Practicing Psychotherapists

The focus of this book has been on improving the effectiveness of psychotherapists. This shared responsibility falls to training programs, on regulatory boards and agencies, and on supervisors and consultants. But a considerable responsibility falls on the individual therapists.

Meaningful skill acquisition is hard work that requires persistence, openness to critical feedback, and continuous effort despite delayed gratification (Ericsson, 2006). Taken together, these qualities have been called grit (Duckworth, Peterson, Matthews, & Kelly, 2007). Grit has not been traditionally emphasized as an important character component for therapists.

Recommendations
We recommend that therapists:

- Seek supervisors and consultants who (a) are focused on skill development and (b) can assess clinical skill and design learning experiences to improve skills.
- When seeking employment, consider the support potential employers give to lifelong skill development (e.g., funding, time in the schedule).
- When in private practice, create environmental supports that will enable regular and ongoing expertise development.
- Engage in continual assessment of their own effectiveness via external sources (e.g., ROM data, qualitative data, peer review).
- Find like-minded peers who themselves are committed to ongoing skill development.

References

American Psychological Association. (2015). Guidelines for clinical supervision in health service psychology. *American Psychologist, 70*, 33–46.

Anderson, T., McClintock, A. S., Himawan, L., Song, X., & Patterson, C. L. (2016). A prospective study of therapist facilitative interpersonal skills as a predictor of treatment outcome. *Journal of Consulting and Clinical Psychology, 84*(1), 57–66. doi:10.1037/ccp0000060

Association of State and Provincial Psychology Boards. (2010). *Model Act for Licensure and Registration of Psychologists*. Retrieved from https://c.ymcdn.com/sites/asppb.site-ym.com/resource/resmgr/guidelines/final_approved_mlra_november.pdf

Beauchamp, T. L., & Childress, J. F. (2009). *Principles of biomedical ethics*. New York, NY: Oxford University Press.

Duckworth, A. L., Peterson, C., Matthews, M. D., & Kelly, D. R. (2007). Grit: Perseverance and passion for long-term goals. *Journal of Personality and Social Psychology, 92*(6), 1087–1101. doi:10.1037/0022-3514.92.6.1087

Ellis, M. V., & Ladany, N. (1997). Inferences concerning supervisees and clients in clinical supervision: An integrative review. In C. E. Watkins (Ed.), *Handbook of psychotherapy supervision* (pp. 447–507). New York, NY: Wiley.

Ericsson, K. A. (2006). The influence of experience and deliberate practice on the development of superior expert performance. In K. A. Ericsson, N. Charness, P. J. Feltovich, & R. R. Hoffman (Eds.), *The Cambridge handbook of expertise and expert performance* (pp. 683–703). Cambridge, UK: Cambridge University Press.

Falender, C. A., & Shafranske, E. P. (2004). *Clinical supervision: A competency-based approach.* Washington, DC: American Psychological Association.

Fouad, N. A., Grus, C. L., Hatcher, R. L., Kaslow, N. J., Hutchings, P. S., Madson, M. B., . . . Crossman, R. E. (2009). Competency benchmarks: A model for understanding and measuring competence in professional psychology across training levels. *Training and Education in Professional Psychology, 3*(4, Suppl.), S5–S26. doi:10.1037/a0015832

Goodyear, R. (2015). Using accountability mechanisms more intentionally: A framework and its implications for training professional psychologists. *American Psychologist, 70*(8), 736–743. doi: 10.1037/a0039828

International Association of Applied Psychology/International Union of Psychological Science. (2016). *International declaration on core competences in professional psychology.* Retrieved from https://goo.gl/xZ2bI1

Ju, Y. A., Han, Y. J., Lee, H., & Lee, D. G. (2016). Counselling psychology in South Korea. *Counselling Psychology Quarterly, 29*(2), 184–194.

Klonoff, E. A. (2015). Assessing competencies: "What have you done for me lately?" *Clinical Psychology: Science and Practice, 22*(4), 404–409.

Lichtenberg, J. W., Portnoy, S. M., Bebeau, M. J., Leigh, I. W., Nelson, P. D., Rubin, N. J., . . . Kaslow, N. J. (2007). Challenges to the assessment of competence and competencies. *Professional Psychology: Research and Practice, 38*(5), 474–478.

Overington, L., Fitzpatrick, M., Hunsley, J., & Drapeau, M. (2015). Trainees' experiences using progress monitoring measures. *Training and Education in Professional Psychology, 9*(3), 202–209. doi:10.1037/tep0000088

Owen, J., Wampold, B. E., Rousmaniere, T. G., Kopta, M., & Miller, S. (2016). As good as it gets? Therapy outcomes of trainees overtime. *Journal of Counseling Psychology, 63*, 12–19.

Schmidt, F. L., & Hunter, J. E. (1998). The validity and utility of selection methods in personnel psychology: Practical and theoretical implications of 85 years of research findings. *Psychological Bulletin, 124*(2), 262–274. doi:10.1037/0033-2909.124.2.262

Schöttke, H., Flückiger, C., Goldberg, S. B., Eversmann, J., & Lange, J. (2015). Predicting psychotherapy outcome based on therapist interpersonal skills: A five-year longitudinal study of a therapist assessment protocol. *Psychotherapy Research.* doi:10.1080/10503307.201 5.1125546

Sperry, L. (2011). *Core competencies in counseling and psychotherapy: Becoming a highly competent and effective therapist.* New York, NY: Routledge.

Stratton, P., Reibstein, J., Lask, J., Singh, R., & Asen, E. (2011). Competences and occupational standards for systemic family and couples therapy. *Journal of Family Therapy, 33*(2), 123–143.

Swank, J. M., Lambie, G. W., & Witta, E. L. (2012). An exploratory investigation of the Counseling Competencies Scale: A measure of counseling skills, dispositions, and behaviors. *Counselor Education and Supervision, 51*(3), 189–206.

Swift, J. K., Callahan, J. L., Rousmaniere, T. G., Whipple, J. L., Dexter, K., & Wrape, E. R. (2015). Using client outcome monitoring as a tool for supervision. *Psychotherapy, 52,* 180–184.

Watkins, C. E. (2011). Does psychotherapy supervision contribute to patient outcomes? Considering thirty years of research. *Clinical Supervisor, 30,* 235–256. doi:10.1080/07325223.2011.619417

Webb, C. A., DeRubeis, R. J., & Barber, J. P. (2010). Therapist adherence/competence and treatment outcome: A meta-analytic review. *Journal of Consulting and Clinical Psychology, 78*(2), 200–211.

Index

Page numbers in *italic* indicate figures.

10,000 hour concept 9, 249

Printed in the USA
CPSIA information can be obtained
at www.ICGtesting.com
JSHW051805010224
56280JS00007B/173

9 781119 165569